D0915648

The Secret Police in Lenin's Russia

Lennard D. Gerson

The Secret Police in Lenin's Russia

Temple University Press, Philadelphia

Temple University Press, Philadelphia 19122
© 1976 by Temple University. All rights reserved
Published 1976
Printed in the United States of America

International Standard Book Number: 0-87722-085-9
Library of Congress Catalog Card Number: 75-44707

For
Kurt London

As a republic rests on virtue, a monarchy on honor, so a despotic government rests on fear.

Montesquieu, *The Spirit of the Laws,*
Book III, Chapter IX

Contents

Illustrations

Following page 88:

Dzerzhinsky Square and the Lubianka
Prison photograph of Dzerzhinsky, 1914
Dzerzhinsky and members of the VCheka Collegium, 1919
Dzerzhinsky in 1919
Martyn Latsis
Dzerzhinsky in 1925

Following page 192:

Latsis and members of the All-Ukrainian Cheka, 1919
Dzerzhinsky and members of the Collegium of the GPU, 1922
Dzerzhinsky and Joseph Stalin, 1924
Dzerzhinsky in his coffin, 1926
Chekist leaders at Dzerzhinsky's grave, 1926
Tenth anniversary celebration of the VCheka/GPU/OGPU, 1927

Preface

Steadfast and unflinching in his greatcoat, the forty-foot statue of Felix Dzerzhinsky, first chief of the Soviet secret police, dominates the Moscow square that bears his name. Located in an old section of the city a short distance from the Kremlin, Dzerzhinsky Square has witnessed many important events in Russian history. As early as 1612 bitter fighting occurred in the vicinity between Polish invaders and native Russian forces. Mass meetings were held in the square in October 1905, the year of the first Russian revolution. The square was also the scene of fighting in October 1917, and the point from which revolutionary detachments launched their attack on the Kremlin. At the head of the square is a seven-story building erected at the end of the last century, its first two floors faced with gray-black granite. For more than fifty years this imposing edifice, known to the world as the Lubianka, has been the nerve center of the omnipresent Soviet secret police, and today there is hardly a facet of Soviet life that is untouched by its ramified apparatus of repression and control.

The subject of this book is the formative period of this vital tool of Communist rule. It was under Lenin's guidance and direction that the salient features of the secret police—its organization and powers, its elaborate system of societal controls, and its functional position in the Soviet governmental structure—were crystallized. After Lenin's death, the secret police was gradually transformed into an instrument of Stalin's personal dictatorship.

But it was Lenin, the founder of the Soviet state, not Stalin, who entrenched the power of the secret police and created the institutional foundations for rule by terror.

My purpose has not been to survey the antecedents of the Soviet secret police or to explore the complex role the apparatus has played in Russian history since Lenin's death. A good case can be made that the early Soviet secret police borrowed many of the techniques employed by the Tsarist Okhrana. The fact remains, however, that the basically defensive security forces created by the Tsars to counter the threat posed by the revolutionary movement were not the equivalent, either in scope or powers, of the offensive apparatus of repression established by Lenin and perfected with such devastating consequences by Stalin.

Official secret police publications and directives, the writings of secret police spokesmen, the Soviet press, the early decrees of the Soviet government, and recently published (albeit carefully selected) documents from the Soviet archives provided the raw materials for this portrait of an institution long recognized as central to the Soviet political system. Of course, without direct access to Soviet archives there remain many intriguing aspects of secret police history that cannot be dealt with adequately. The ambitions and rivalries of the top echelons of the secret police are not evident on the basis of available information. Even such a crucial question as Stalin's role in the development of the early secret police is still shrouded in mystery. Nevertheless, enough tested information does exist to make possible this attempt at a reasonably complete and objective study of the contribution made by the secret police to the consolidation of Bolshevik power in Lenin's Russia.

For the most part I have adhered to the Library of Congress system of transliteration. Exceptions to this usage in the text will be found in the spelling of Russian proper names and in the elimination of diacritical marks. Dates are given according to the calendar in use in Russia at the time (Old Style before February 1918 and New Style thereafter).

I would like to express my gratitude to the Earhart Foundation of Ann Arbor, Michigan, for a research and travel grant that made it possible for me to consult many of the hitherto unpublished documents utilized in this study. I am also grateful to the staffs of the major repositories where much of the research for this book was done: the Library of Congress, the National Archives, the New York Public Library, the Archive of Russian and East European History and Culture of Columbia University, the Hoover Institution Archives at Stanford University, the Public Record Office in London, and the Lenin Library in Moscow. I am greatly indebted to the pioneering research of Robert M. Slusser, Simon Wolin, and Ernest V. Hollis, Jr., and to Lothar Metzl, who first sparked my interest in Dzerzhinsky and the secret police. Special thanks are due Constantin Kallaur, who was always willing to help me with a difficult translation. I also wish to thank Michael Lazna for his sound editorial advice and Robert Block, Anthony Brescia, and Emil Vigilante, all good friends and colleagues, who read parts of the manuscript and offered valuable comments and suggestions. I cannot express in words all that I owe my wife, Roberta. Without her loving encouragement and support this book could not have been written.

The Secret Police
in Lenin's Russia

1

From the Butyrki to the Lubianka

The Soviet secret police was created less than a month and a half after the October Revolution of 1917. Throughout the years of civil war that followed, it stood as the ultimate guardian of the Bolshevik regime. The contribution that the secret police made to the consolidation of Bolshevik rule during this tumultuous period of internal strife and external danger was second only to that of the Red Army, a fighting force with which it was often favorably compared.[1] According to a leading Bolshevik official, "not one government measure would have been implemented nor one decree fulfilled" during the formative years of the Soviet state without this "razor-sharp" apparatus of coercion and repression.[2] As its chief spokesmen noted, the VCheka was not a court: it did not judge the foes of the regime; it destroyed them.* Appropriately, for their insignia the masters of the Lubianka chose the shield and the sword, fitting symbols of their mission to protect the Bolshevik regime from all opposition and to strike down without mercy any who dared challenge its monopoly of power.

*"VCheka" is an acronym derived from the first letters of the Russian rendering of the All-Russian Extraordinary Commission *(Vserossiiskaia chrezvychainaia komissiia),* the official title of the secret police from 1917 to 1922. The designation "VCheka" is customarily used to distinguish the central All-Russian Extraordinary Commission in Moscow from the many provincial and district Extraordinary Commissions, or Chekas, scattered throughout the country. Since Lenin's day, secret police agents have called themselves Chekists.

3

Lenin's Theory of Terror

When Lenin began to order the employment of repressive measures on a wide scale in Soviet Russia, he did not act in defiance of his convictions. Violence and terror had been fundamental methods of his program long before 1917. Throughout his career as an underground revolutionary, he had subscribed to the view that communism could not be achieved without bloodshed. Although Lenin did repudiate the conspiratorial terror of an earlier generation of Russian revolutionaries who stalked the Tsars and their entourage, he was never opposed to political killing as such. He only insisted that to be effective it had to be well organized and extensively applied. As early as 1901 he had written: "In principle we have never rejected, and cannot reject, terror. Terror is one of the forms of military action that may be perfectly suitable and even essential at a definite juncture in the battle, given a definite state of the troops and the existence of definite conditions."[3] And again, in his 1905 pamphlet *Two Tactics of Social Democracy in the Democratic Revolution,* Lenin explained that after the revolution the new form of proletarian rule

> will be precisely a dictatorship, i.e., it must inevitably rely on military force, on the arming of the masses, on an insurrection, and not on institutions of one kind or another established in a "lawful" or "peaceful" way. . . . Without a dictatorship it is impossible to break down [the resistance of the landlords and bourgeoisie] and repel counterrevolutionary attempts.[4]

In *Lessons of the Commune,* written in 1908, Lenin said that the victory of the proletarian revolution required "armed struggle and civil war." It was because the revolutionary workers of Paris had failed to grasp this fundamental truth that the Commune of 1871 was drowned in blood. The "excessive magnanimity" of the Communards was a grave error; instead of using halfway measures, the Parisian workers should have "exterminated" their enemies en masse.[5]

The Bolshevik leader fully accepted Marx's definition of the state as an instrument of class rule. According to Lenin, the state "consists of special bodies of armed men having prisons, etc., at their disposal."[6] While recognizing that methods of coercion can change and will generally correspond to the technical level of a particular epoch, Lenin held that the ruling class always requires an "apparatus of violence" to maintain its power. The victorious regime of the revolutionary proletariat would be no exception to this rule.

State and Revolution, which Lenin wrote during August and September 1917, incorporated these and other propositions into a more complete theory of the proletarian state. Considered one of his most important works, this treatise put great stress on the Marxist concept of the "dictatorship of the proletariat," which Lenin once succinctly defined as "rule won and maintained by the use of violence by the proletariat against the bourgeoisie, rule that is unrestricted by any laws."[7] The proletarian dictatorship was to control and direct the postrevolutionary state "for the entire historical period which separates capitalism from classless society, from communism."[8] The transition from capitalism to communism Lenin foresaw as "inevitably . . . a period of an unprecedentedly violent class struggle in unprecedentedly acute forms."[9] Not the least important reason for this was that the transition had to be undertaken "with human nature as it is now, with human nature that cannot do without subordination, control, overseers and bookkeepers."[10] Like other historical forms of class rule, the dictatorship of the proletariat was an outgrowth of the need "to forcibly suppress the resistance of the class that is losing its sway." In another sense, however, the proletarian dictatorship would be unique in history. While the dictatorship of the former ruling class was intended to suppress the vast proletarian majority of the population, the dictatorship of the proletariat would have only to crush the resistance of the vanquished exploiters of other people's labor, "an insignificant minority of the population, the landowners and capitalists."[11]

The ultimate goal of the Communists, Lenin insisted, was the complete abolition of the state and of "all organized and systematic violence, all use of violence against people in general."[12] But this goal would be achieved only under full communism. The state would then be unnecessary because in a classless communist society "there is nobody to be suppressed—'nobody' in the sense of a class, of a systematic struggle against a definite section of the population."[13] In the meantime, under the proletarian dictatorship, a bitter class struggle would be unavoidable. The resistance of the former ruling class would have to be crushed; for only "when the capitalists have disappeared, when there are no classes, . . . only then [does] it become possible to speak of freedom."[14]

Lenin was optimistic that the suppression of the former exploiting classes would be "comparatively so easy, simple and natural a task that it will entail far less bloodshed than the suppression of the risings of slaves, serfs or wage-laborers, and it will cost mankind far less."[15] In *State and Revolution* he declared that "the exploiters are unable to suppress the people without a highly complex machine for performing this task, but the people can suppress the exploiters even with a very simple 'machine,' almost without a 'machine,' without a special apparatus, by the simple organization of the armed people."[16] Two months after the Bolshevik seizure of power and still in the flush of easy victory Lenin said in the same vein: "There might be a handful of men in Russia today fighting against Soviet power, but such eccentrics are few, and they will disappear in a matter of weeks."[17]

Events were soon to shatter this naive notion. The foes of Soviet power were innumerable, and the All-Russian Extraordinary Commission, the "simple machine" created to deal with them, developed into one of this century's most sanguinary instruments of state-organized violence. Lenin's secret police was established and grew to awesome proportions because, as one writer put it, "people who insisted on acting like class enemies proved to be vastly more numerous than [Lenin's] pre-revolutionary theory had been capable of forecasting."[18]

The initial resistance to Bolshevik rule came from those segments of Russian society that had lost positions of privilege and status and had good reason to think that their lives were endangered by the advent of the new revolutionary regime. Lenin, in turn, was fully prepared to employ the most severe and ruthless measures against them. In April 1918 he wrote:

> The bourgeoisie in our country has been conquered, but it has not yet been uprooted, not yet destroyed, and not even utterly broken. That is why we are faced with a new and higher form of struggle against the bourgeoisie, the transition from the very simple task of further expropriating the capitalists to the much more complicated and difficult task

of creating the conditions in which it will be impossible for the bourgeoisie to exist, or for a new bourgeoisie to arise.[19]

Yet it was not only the embittered resistance of the capitalists and landlords—that "insignificant minority of the population"—that threatened to topple the Soviet regime. No less dangerous was the growing opposition and resistance of the toiling masses in whose name the Bolsheviks had seized power in the first place.

The transformation of the dictatorship of the proletariat into the unabashed dictatorship of the minority Bolshevik Party, which was well under way by the spring of 1918, together with the adoption of such drastic and unpopular economic measures as the introduction of iron discipline in the factories and the forced requisition of grain in the villages, not only eroded the Bolsheviks' proletarian base of support, but turned large segments of Russia's peasant majority against them as well.[20] The ensuing wave of strikes, peasant uprisings, and mutinies that swept across the Soviet heartland posed a threat to the Bolsheviks' precarious control of power as menacing as the armies of Kolchak, Denikin, and Wrangel.

The growing animosity of the masses was an important consideration in the creation of the secret police. One of its founders wrote:

> The need for this organ [the secret police] was felt more acutely because the Soviet government had no apparatus for the spiritual re-education of the people. . . . The masses of the people were still imbued with the old spirit . . . and not infrequently joined with their class enemies against the Soviets. Hence the acute necessity for an apparatus of coercion and purification.[21]

Reinforced by the conviction that they were not acting for their personal advantage but as representatives of a class destined to inherit the world, the Bolsheviks moved from the theoretical acceptance of force as an indispensable weapon in the struggle against a handful of landlords and capitalists to the use of violence and terror against anyone, regardless of class origin or social status, who obstructed the path to the victory of the proletarian dictatorship.

As a political realist par excellence, Lenin was quick to grasp the urgency of creating a reliable organ to defend Bolshevik rule against its many adversaries and to harness the vital human and material resources of the "internal front"—the territory nominally under Soviet control—without which his regime could not survive. It is in this context that the early Soviet secret police achieves its historical significance. For without heavy reliance on internal force and violence, as embodied in the All-Russian Extraordinary Commission and its successor organs, the Bolsheviks might never have weathered the ordeal of their first years in power. When, shortly after the Bolshevik seizure of power, Lenin decided to create an institution capable of defending Soviet power on the internal front, he entrusted the task to a man who was in many ways like himself—resolute, tireless, and incorruptible—Felix Edmundovich Dzerzhinsky.

Felix Dzerzhinsky: The Proletarian Jacobin

A leading official of the early Soviet secret police once wrote: "The organization of the Cheka and its work is so closely connected with the name of Comrade Dzerzhinsky that it is impossible to speak about them separately. He established the Cheka, he organized it, he shaped it."[22] In the history of the Soviet state Dzerzhinsky's role was auxiliary to those of Lenin and Stalin. But in the history of the Soviet secret police Dzerzhinsky's contribution and example were of the greatest importance because he was its architect and master builder.

Felix Edmundovich Dzerzhinsky was born on September 11, 1877, in the Oshmiansk district of Russian-occupied Poland. His father, Edmund-Rufin, came from the Polish gentry and was a well-educated man for his time, having graduated from the University of St. Petersburg. For several years Edmund-Rufin Dzerzhinsky taught physics and mathematics at the Taganrog gymnasium in the south of Russia. But suffering from tuberculosis, he returned to the family estate in 1875. A small pension and the income derived from renting part of their land to local peasants provided the family with a very modest standard of living.

As was generally the rule among the Polish gentry, Felix was raised in the spirit of strict Catholicism and Polish patriotism. What were later to become his most notable traits—the intensity of his political convictions and the absolute devotion to his cause—were already apparent in the youngster's religious zeal, which was not at all contemplative. His stormy, passionate temper would force his less devout brothers to join him in prayer. Many years later, when he was the chairman of the All-Russian Extraordinary Commission, Dzerzhinsky told a friend: "Once when I went home on vacation, my oldest brother asked me how I could prove to myself that there was a god, and I answered: 'God is in the heart.' And I added: 'If I ever come to the conclusion that there is no god, I would put a bullet in my head.' "[23]

The Dzerzhinsky children grew up in an unhappy land, still suffering the aftermath of the unsuccessful Polish uprising of 1863. The insurrection had been led by Polish nationalists bent on restoring the independence of a proud nation carved up over the years between its more powerful neighbors, Russia, Prussia, and Austria. Its leaders never succeeded in creating a well-trained, disciplined army, nor did they win the active support of the large, poor, and generally indifferent peasant population. The uprising was doomed from the start and was ruthlessly suppressed by the Tsarist government, which turned the country into a virtual barracks. Under the administration of Governor-General Muraviev, who soon acquired the nickname "The Hangman," the Russians tried to obliterate all manifestations of Polish nationalism. Roman Catholicism, the dominant religion of Poland, suffered systematic persecution; many monasteries were closed and their land and property transferred to the ownership of the Russian Orthodox Church. The civil government of Poland, deprived of every trace of independence, was reorganized on the model of other parts of the Russian Empire. To guard against the recurrence of an armed uprising, 300,000 Russian troops were stationed in the country. The height of St. Petersburg's Russification policy was reached in the 1880s when the Polish language was prohibited in all official institutions and schools.

From his parents, who had early cultivated in their children a love of their native land in its struggle against the Russian overlords, Felix heard stories about "Hangman" Muraviev and the history of the oppression imposed upon Poland by the Tsars. And like many other Polish youths Dzerzhinsky dreamed of revenge. In his childhood fantasies he imagined himself the possessor of a magic cap that would make him invisible and give him the power, as he said, "to slay all the Russians."[24]

It was in this repressive political and cultural milieu that Felix Dzerzhinsky in 1887 entered the Vilna gymnasium, where the curriculum was dedicated to the thorough Russification of its students. At the outset Dzerzhinsky was not a very successful student; he had to repeat his first year of studies because of his poor performance in Russian. One of his classmates remembered the young Dzerzhinsky "as lively as quicksilver, and almost epileptically nervous. . . . An irrepressible lad, Felix was constantly dashing through the corridors like a hurricane, noisy, mischievous, impertinent."[25] Dzerzhinsky's Soviet biographers make no mention of significant occurrences in the young student's life until 1894, when his name suddenly appeared in the minutes of a faculty meeting as a student who was "dissatisfied" with the existing order and the German instructor demanded his expulsion.

It happened that during this, his seventeenth year, Dzerzhinsky abandoned his previously unshakable religious faith—the result of his contact with a Marxist study circle organized by the Lithuanian Social-Democratic Party in Vilna. Before the school year was over, Dzerzhinsky had found a substitute for religion in the theoretical and polemical texts of Marx and Engels. Having become a convinced socialist, Dzerzhinsky sought every opportunity to persuade and convert his classmates, incurring the great displeasure of his teachers. His difficulties at school seem only to have buttressed his resolve to follow the path of a rebel. Together with a small group of other young converts to socialism, Dzerzhinsky swore an oath "to fight against evil to the last breath."[26]

In the fall of 1895, while still a gymnasium student, Dzerzhinsky joined the Lithuanian Social Democratic Party. His first task was to establish links with the local working class. These early efforts to cultivate the class consciousness of the Vilna proletariat were not always welcome. On one occasion a group of "unclassconscious" workers from Goldstein's tanning factory caught up with the uninvited young Marxist agitator in their midst and beat him so severely that a doctor was required to stitch his head wounds.[27]

Of his early underground work in the socialist movement Dzerzhinsky never spoke a word in the family circle. He was especially careful to hide his dangerous activities from his mother, whose health was declining. But after her death in January 1896, Dzerzhinsky quit the gymnasium to devote himself exclusively to his new calling. "I left school of my own accord," he later wrote, "holding that I should practice what I believed in, and that it was necessary to be among the masses and to learn from them."²⁸ Felix Dzerzhinsky, at the age of nineteen, thus embarked on his career as a professional revolutionary.

He quickly earned a reputation as a capable agitator and organizer but was obliged to leave Vilna after a few months when his activities came under police surveillance. His new assignment was to establish a Social Democratic organization in the small industrial town of Kovno. There his revolutionary career involved printing and distributing a clandestine newspaper and trying to organize local factory workers. He might have accomplished more had not one of the "advanced" workers he trusted betrayed him to the police for ten roubles in July 1897. Dzerzhinsky spent the next year in the Kovno prison but did not lose heart. "Prison is terrible," he wrote to his sister, "only for those who have a weak spirit."²⁹ Months passed before the prosecution summarized the evidence against Dzerzhinsky: "Describing himself as a socialist, Dzerzhinsky began to propagandize among the workers and others the notion that if the workers in the cities would rise up, the peasantry would join with them, and it would then be easy to deal with the government and set up a republic as in the United States."³⁰ In consideration of the prisoner's youth, the court was lenient. Instead of prison, the twenty-year-old revolutionary was sentenced to three years in exile under police observation. In May 1898, Dzerzhinsky began the journey to his new residence, the town of Nolinsk in the Siberian province of Viatka. To support himself he worked in a tobacco factory and dreamed of the day when "I shall be free and they will pay for everything."³¹

Not even Siberian exile, however, could dampen Dzerzhinsky's proselytizing spirit. His ceaseless efforts "to influence a number of people who were formerly quite reliable" were noted in police records and earned him a reputation as "highly unreliable politically." Soon the local authorities ordered Dzerzhinsky removed from Nolinsk "to such a point in the province where there would be less possibility to spread his influence over those around him."[32] He was removed to the village of Kaigorodsk, several hundred miles farther north. From this desolate place Dzerzhinsky managed to escape in August 1899, after serving a little over a year of his sentence.

Dzerzhinsky's subsequent years as a revolutionary gave him ample opportunity to demonstrate his fearless and unsparing dedication. Never one for factional disputes or idle theoretical speculation in the safety of self-imposed European exile, he thrived on the demands of active conspiratorial and underground organizational work in the enemy camp: "I must either be entirely in the fire with work that is suitable to me or otherwise I will be carried to the cemetery," he once wrote to some of his comrades. Nor did the ever present danger of arrest deter him: "If I should be arrested," he added in the same letter, "then my example will give you strength to demand the same sacrifice from others."[33]

"The Tsarist government turned its eyes on Felix Dzerzhinsky when he was only twenty years old," wrote a Soviet author, "and from that time on it tried not only to keep him in sight but also to keep him in the grip of its paws."[34] Of his two decades in the revolutionary underground, from 1897 to 1917, Dzerzhinsky spent eleven years in the Tsar's prisons and places of exile. He was arrested six times: in 1897, 1900, 1905, 1906, 1908, and 1912. Thrice he was sentenced to Siberian exile and thrice he escaped, once after serving just seven days of a life sentence. Dzerzhinsky's health never completely recovered from the physical hardship of the years in Tsarist jails. But most difficult for him to bear was the forced immobility and isolation from action. There were moments of despair when Dzerzhinsky wondered if he could remain firm. After being sentenced to prison for the fifth time, he wrote:

> When I begin to think about the long days I shall have to live in prison, day after day, hour after hour, I experience a feeling of horror and from the depths of my soul the words break out: I cannot endure it! Still I will find the strength, as others will, just as many more have endured much worse torment and suffering. At times I think that I cannot understand how it is possible to hold out, but I recognize that it can

be done and I become conscious of a proud desire to do so. . . .
Should I fail to muster the strength, death will come and rid me of the
feeling of helplessness and resolve everything. So I am resigned.[35]

Dzerzhinsky was able to endure his tormenting prison existence because, as he once said: "The song of life is in my heart. And he who hears this song in his heart will never, regardless of what suffering he must endure, curse his life and will not wish to change it to another peaceful, normal one."[36]

Dzerzhinsky's determination and the aspirations that helped sustain him are nowhere better revealed than in his prison diary and in the letters he wrote to friends and relatives during his long years of confinement. On New Year's Eve, 1908, he wrote:

This is the last day of 1908—the fifth time that I will have met the New Year in prison (1898, 1901, 1902, 1907); the first time was eleven years ago. In prison I came to manhood in the torments of loneliness, of longing for the world and for life. But never for a moment have I doubted the righteousness of our cause.[37]

Dzerzhinsky's cause was socialism. Its realization was the supreme aim of his life, and neither the path he followed to arrive at that end nor the quality of the good to be obtained from it was ever open to question.

Dzerzhinsky was not, however, an abstract or doctrinaire Marxist. One will find little in his writings about economic determinism or the laws of the dialectic. Dzerzhinsky was above all a practical man, a natural organizer, and his commitment to socialism was "emotional rather than doctrinal."[38] He believed that socialism had to be more than "merely a scientific preview of the future." It had to be a "torch kindling in the hearts of the people indomitable faith and energy" and capable of leading mankind out of the "present hellish life with its wolfish exploitation, oppression and violence" into a new world "based on harmony, a full life embracing society as a whole."[39] Dzerzhinsky viewed the world outside his prisons as a struggle between good and evil. He detested the social and economic order that condemned millions to a life of injustice, oppression, and fratricidal strife, and consecrated himself to creating a world cleansed of filth and a humanity surrounded with love. In this great struggle he vowed: "For me the end . . . can only be the grave."[40]

As Dzerzhinsky disregarded his own sufferings and sacrifices, so did he disregard those of others. There was a strong streak of pitilessness in this crusader against injustice who could write: "The hunger and sufferings of the masses of the people, the weeping of children and the despair of their mothers are the sacrifices which the people must make in order to overcome the enemy and to triumph."[41] The foe was not only a social evil that had condemned countless innocent people "to a pitiful and inhuman existence"; it was a personal enemy as well. And Dzerzhinsky lacked neither the ability nor the willingness to take any measures, without scruple, hesitation, or remorse, that would bring about its destruction. Like the founder of Bolshevism, Dzerzhinsky believed that "life is such that it rules out sentiment, and woe to the man who lacks the strength to overcome his feelings."[42]

Dzerzhinsky's sympathy for the downtrodden never caused him to overestimate the ability of the working class to determine its own destiny. Although he often ate with workers and shared their homes, he never idealized them and was always conscious of their shortcomings. They were often weak and vacillating, while he and his fellow revolutionaries had many times demonstrated their strength and steadfastness in the face of adversity. His lifelong conviction that the toiling masses would have to be led to socialism by "a small but ideologically strong handful of people uniting the masses around their banner" drew him naturally to the side of Lenin and the Bolsheviks.[43]

Felix Dzerzhinsky was arrested for the sixth and final time in Warsaw in September 1912. He was not to experience freedom again until after the collapse of Tsarism in 1917. This was Dzerzhinsky's longest and most trying period of incarceration, and he spent much of it in solitary confinement. After almost four years in prison he wrote to one of his brothers:

> You ask, have I changed? I don't know. My youth has passed. Life has left me with many furrows and not only on my brow. Apart from the alien torment I have no regrets whatever. . . . I have lived in order to fulfill my mission and to be myself. . . . I am powerless and useless. But my brain counsels me not to give in. I must carry on to the end. It cannot be otherwise. I have no qualms. And although I do not know what fate has in store for me, in my mind I am always tracing the

contours of the future with which the struggle will be crowned. I am, as you see, an optimist.[44]

Dzerzhinsky served the last part of his sentence in the Moscow Central Transit Prison—popularly known as the Butyrki—which was reserved for the Tsar's most implacable political foes. Fortunately for Dzerzhinsky, the prison authorities found him unfit for heavy manual labor and assigned him to work as a tailor's apprentice. Though still in leg irons, Dzerzhinsky's existence was not unbearable. In the last letter he would ever write from behind prison bars, he mused: "At the moment I am dozing, like a bear in his winter den; all that remains is the thought that spring will come and I will cease to suck my paw and all the strength that still remains in my body and soul will manifest itself. Live I will."[45]

The Origins of the All-Russian Extraordinary Commission

The abdication of Tsar Nicholas II early in March 1917 ended the three-hundred-year-old Romanov dynasty. But already during the last week of February, the Tsarist authorities had lost all effective control in the capital city of Petrograd. The whole hierarchy of state officialdom that had governed Imperial Russia was quickly swept away in a tide of riots, mutinies, resignations, and hasty flights.[46] News of the momentous events spread rapidly to other parts of the Russian Empire. In Moscow, thousands of exultant people poured into the streets to demonstrate their support of the revolutionary city of Petrograd. Soon the Kremlin, the post office and telegraph station, the major bridges, and other strategic points were seized, with very little bloodshed, by the revolutionary throngs. It was inevitable that the Butyrki—itself one of the most hated symbols of the Tsarist autocracy—should become a target of the revolutionary ardor of the Muscovites. A large crowd gathered at the prison gates to demand the immediate release of all political prisoners. When the demand was not promptly met, the gates were stormed. In minutes hundreds of political prisoners were released from their cells and led to the streets. Among them was Prisoner 217, emaciated in his shabby prison robe, his weakened legs barely able to carry his weight as he limped along. It was nine o'clock in the evening of March 1, 1917, when Dzerzhinsky's last imprisonment came to an end.[47]

In the days that followed, Dzerzhinsky rushed from one meeting of workers and soldiers to another, agitating for the cessation of fighting at the front and the achievement of world peace through socialism. This sudden hectic activity, after so many years of forced isolation and privation, overcame Dzerzhinsky's weakened constitution, and he fell ill during the latter part of March. But after a week's rest in the country he plunged back into Bolshevik propaganda and organizational work in Moscow and Petrograd with his characteristic fervor. By June, he had again worn himself out and had to sacrifice six weeks of precious time recuperating in Orenburg Province.

Meanwhile, under Lenin's ceaseless prodding, the Bolsheviks began to mobilize their forces for a final confrontation with the Provisional Government. The Bolsheviks chose the Smolny Institute near the center of Petrograd as their headquarters. Since 1764, the Smolny had served as a finishing school for young ladies of the nobility, but it became known historically as the building in which Lenin, Trotsky, and other leading Bolsheviks orchestrated the final preparations for their seizure of power.

In a letter of September 1917 addressed to the Central Committee of the Bolshevik Party, Lenin raised the question of organizing a staff headquarters to direct the seizure of power and

> distribute . . . forces, move the reliable regiments to the most important points, surround the Alexandrinsky Theatre, occupy the Peter and Paul Fortress, arrest the General Staff and the government, and move against the officer cadets and the Savage Division those detachments which would rather die than allow the enemy to approach the strategic points of the city.[48]

The Military-Revolutionary Committee, established by the Bolshevik-dominated Petrograd Soviet on October 12, 1917, was just what Lenin had in mind—a body that could serve the Bolsheviks as the "legal staff" of the insurrection. But it was also the direct institutional predecessor of the Soviet secret police, which was created in part to continue on a more permanent basis the punitive and security functions of this strictly provisional entity.

At the time of the Bolshevik seizure of power, there were fourteen Left Socialist Revolutionaries, four Anarchists, and forty-eight Bolsheviks working in the Military-Revolutionary Committee. The most prominent Bolshevik members were Dzerzhinsky, Sverdlov, Antonov-Ovseenko, Uritsky, Skrypnik, Latsis, Unshlikht, Stalin, and Blagonravov. The Bolshevik majority was in firm control of the various departments of the Military-Revolutionary Committee, although its official president was the youthful Left Socialist Revolutionary, Pavel Evgenievich Lazimir. Exactly when Dzerzhinsky began to exercise a position of leadership within the Military-Revolutionary Committee cannot be determined from the available evidence. An early indication of his presence is found in a directive issued by the Committee in mid-October, signed jointly by Lazimir, Antonov-Ovseenko, and Dzerzhinsky, which forbade the factory committee of a Petrograd cartridge manufacturer to distribute ammunition without the Military-Revolutionary Committee's authorization.[49]

The final preparations for the seizure of power were made at a meeting of the Bolshevik Central Committee on October 24, 1917. Each member of the Central Committee was given a specific assignment in guiding the uprising scheduled to begin later that day. Dzerzhinsky was to organize and direct the seizure of the central post office and telegraph station. These two strategic targets were taken a few hours later without a shot being fired. By the morning of October 25, all major government buildings (with the exception of the Winter Palace) were in the hands of the insurgents. The Military-Revolutionary Committee, from its cramped headquarters on the third floor of the Smolny Institute, announced at ten o'clock that all state power had been transferred to it as an agency of the Petrograd Soviet. It went into action immediately to consolidate the precarious grip on power of the preceding twenty-four hours. Commissars were dispatched to all corners of Petrograd, taking over city police functions, threatening recalcitrant workers and government officials with trials before revolutionary courts, issuing appeals to railroad workers to keep the trains moving and to the Cossacks stationed nearby not to attack the city.

As soon as the Bolsheviks took control of the government, the Military-Revolutionary Committee, originally conceived as an instrument of insurrection, assumed another vital task. It was made responsible for defending the new revolutionary order against the various manifestations of counterrevolution and general anarchy that prevailed in Petrograd during those stormy days—a situation Lenin described to his intimates as "a mess, not a dictatorship."[50] The Military-Revolutionary Committee's duties included "the defense of the revolutionary order," "the struggle against counterrevolution," and "the defense of the strongholds of the Soviet of Workers' and Soldiers' Deputies and the Council of People's Commissars."[51] In one of its first proclamations the Committee warned the citizens of Petrograd that it would not tolerate violations of revolutionary order: "Theft, brigandage, assaults and attempted pogroms will be mercilessly punished."[52]

The Smolny Institute, which housed the Bolshevik Central Committee, the Petrograd Soviet, and numerous other organizations, trade unions, and editorial offices, was the real nerve center of the new government, and its security also fell to the Military-Revolutionary Committee. The defense of the Smolny Institute was a task to which Dzerzhinsky devoted his personal attention. Food and fuel had to be provided for the many inhabitants (including the persons arrested by the new regime, who seemed on occasion to outnumber the resident Communists) and the premises guarded all around. Under Dzerzhinsky's direction the Smolny was rapidly converted into an armed fortress with artillery and machine guns at the front portico and a thousand sentries and Red Guards stationed at the entrances and patrolling the grounds. The numerous visitors' passes bearing his signature are only one indication of Dzerzhinsky's role in protecting this citadel of the revolution. So strict, in fact, was security at the Smolny Institute that one day even Leon Trotsky, the president of the Petrograd Soviet, was temporarily refused entry when he could not produce his pass for inspection at the front gate.[53]

The safety of the regime did not rest exclusively with the Military-Revolutionary Committee. Vladimir Bonch-Bruevich, one of Lenin's close associates, was entrusted with a staff of 150 to carry out a struggle against drunken riots in Petrograd. Workers and soldiers had been looting the wine cellars of the Winter Palace and other places, getting drunk, brawling, and creating anarchy and disorder. An announcement that appeared in *Izvestiia* on December 6 indicated that Bonch-Bruevich's Extraordinary Commission for the Defense of Petrograd was authorized to use terroristic methods to keep order in the city. The inhabitants of the city were warned that "attempts to break into wine-cellars, warehouses, factories, stalls, shops, private apartments, and so on, will be broken up by machine-gun fire without any kind of warning."[54] The streets were patrolled by armored cars to make good this threat.

The newly formed People's Commissariat of Internal Affairs also had security responsibilities. Although its main task was to establish Bolshevik power in the localities, the direction of the militia, the supervision of prisons, and the maintenance of an apparatus of surveillance also came within its scope. Several Bolshevik members of the Military-Revolutionary Committee, including Dzerzhinsky, were appointed to important posts in the Commissariat of Internal Affairs, perhaps in recognition of the overlapping functions of these two agencies. But Felix Dzerzhinsky seldom attended the meetings of the Commissariat's directors. He had already decided that the task of preserving Bolshevik hegemony depended primarily on the weakening of the regime's political opponents; and to this end he preferred to devote most of his time to his duties in the Military-Revolutionary Committee, where he specialized in the struggle against counter-revolution and banditry in Petrograd.

Traces of Dzerzhinsky's labors during the first weeks of Bolshevik rule are visible in a number of orders and decrees he signed as a leading member of the Military-Revolutionary Committee. Late in October, he issued an order calling for the arrest of members of the former "Tsentroflot" who were unwilling to help in the work of preserving the revolution.[55] This was followed by an order addressed to the Commandant of the Peter and Paul Fortress to distribute weapons and ammunition to the officers and crew of the Second Baltic Fleet.[56] Dzerzhinsky also took part in the reorganization of the Petrograd militia, signing a decree calling for the dismissal of all militiamen not loyal to the new regime and ordering the establishment of a commission to reorganize the defense of the city.[57] Nor was he moved by the appeals of some prominent Moscow industrialists for the release of the ministers of the Provisional Government who had been arrested during the Bolshevik seizure of power. Dzerzhinsky responded to their plea by pointing out that the arrest of the ministers had not been an act of vengeance, but rather had been dictated by their anti-Bolshevik sentiments. This, he said, "proved how dangerous it would be to give them freedom. Therefore, the Military-Revolutionary Committee is not able to free the ministers."[58]

Still groping for an effective means of dealing with their internal foes, the Council of People's Commissars met on December 6 to consider the latest threat to Bolshevik rule, which had come in the form of a spreading strike of government officials. Since the first days of the revolution, the Bolsheviks had had to contend with the passive resistance of large numbers of government workers who refused to serve the Soviet regime. The actions of these Tsarist officials, accustomed as they were, in the opinion of one Bolshevik official, "to servile obedience to their masters," had placed them squarely in the enemy camp. Encouraged and financed by the Petrograd bourgeoisie, who considered a strike of state employees a sure way to bring about the speedy collapse of Soviet rule, the bureaucrats were in a position to disrupt a host of vital government services. "The majority of them," according to the same writer, "did not come to work. Only the lowest employees, like the couriers, office cleaners, chauffeurs, and furnace-men remained at their places, and not even all of them."[59] In November, the striking officials formed the Union of Employees of Government Institutions and threatened to bring the entire Soviet state apparatus to a halt. The Council of People's Commissars defined their action as "sabotage" and decided "to instruct Comrade Dzerzhinsky to establish a special commission for ascertaining the possibility of a struggle with such strikers by means of the most energetic revolutionary measures [and] for ascertaining methods of suppressing the malicious sabotage."[60] Dzerzhinsky was to present his plans at the next day's session of the Council of People's Commissars.

In the intervening hours Lenin addressed a note to Dzerzhinsky setting forth his own views on the proper way to handle sabotage and counterrevolution. Lenin's note was composed of two parts: a preamble indicting the bourgeoisie for attempting to undermine the revolution, and a list of specific measures to deal with counterrevolutionaries and saboteurs. The preamble is frequently quoted in Soviet sources to prove that Lenin directed Dzerzhinsky to establish the All-Russian Extraordinary Commission. Yet the list of measures that followed Lenin's denunciation of the bourgeoisie made no mention of any such organization. Rather, Lenin envisaged an administrative procedure for dealing with "persons belonging to the wealthy classes (i.e., having incomes of five hundred roubles or more per month . . .)" encompassing fines and imprisonment. At no point did Lenin mention the creation of a special agency to impose the punishments.[61]

Felix Dzerzhinsky presented his report to the Council of People's Commissars on the evening of December 7. He is said to have addressed the leaders of the revolution in these words:

> Long conversations are not necessary here. Our revolution is in clear danger. We have been too complacent in looking at what is going on around us. The opposition is organizing its strength. Counterrevolutionaries are active in the countryside, in some places winning over our own forces. Now the enemy is here, in Petrograd, at our very hearts. We have incontrovertible evidence of this. We must send to this front—the most dangerous and the most treacherous front of all—resolute, steadfast and devoted comrades for the defense of the conquests of the revolution. I propose, I demand the organization of revolutionary violence against the counterrevolutionaries. And we must not act tomorrow but today, immediately.[62]

The Bolshevik leaders hardly needed to be reminded of how unsure their control of power was as the winter of 1917–18 descended on Petrograd. Not only did the fledgling government face the passive but nonetheless damaging resistance of the bureaucracy, but there was also the ever present danger of uprisings on the part of anti-Bolshevik political parties and groups, not to mention the breakdown of revolutionary discipline among the citizenry at large. Dzerzhinsky's own list of "enemies of the people" against whom immediate action had to be taken included:

> 1. Those who, having disguised themselves as friends of the people, have penetrated the ranks of the revolutionary organs for provocative or mercenary reasons and who . . . by their criminal deeds discredit Soviet power.

2. Those who forge and use counterfeit commissions, orders and licenses, etc. of revolutionary organs.

3. Perpetrators and disseminators of deliberate and false slanders against Soviet power, and the authors and distributors of slanderous and anonymous leaflets and newspapers, etc.

4. Organizers of plots, pogroms, and drunken brawls, etc.

5. Marauders, speculators, merchants. . . .[63]

The creation of a special organ of "revolutionary violence" was all the more imperative now that the Military-Revolutionary Committee, with its important internal security functions, was no longer the center of the Bolshevik universe. When Dzerzhinsky made his report to the Council of People's Commissars, the once powerful Military-Revolutionary Committee (which had never been intended to be more than a provisional body) was just a few days away from complete dissolution. Most of its functions had already been transferred to the newly established People's Commissariats.[64] The Soviet secret police was established at this particular juncture in part to fill this impending operational and administrative void which, if it remained unfilled, could only pose a grave threat to the continued existence of the Bolshevik regime. As Dzerzhinsky once said, the organization of the secret police "coincided with the dissolution of the Petrograd [Military-Revolutionary] Committee, i.e., it was created at the moment when no agency was available to take responsibility for the struggle against counterrevolution, sabotage, and speculation."[65]

There was, however, another important and purely political consideration behind the decision to create the All-Russian Extraordinary Commission at this point. Under considerable pressure from their socialist rivals, the Bolsheviks were just then nearing the completion of negotiations with the Left Socialist Revolutionaries for the formation of a coalition government. With the prospect of representatives of another political party entering the highest government circles, the creation of a security and punitive apparatus unquestionably loyal to the Bolshevik Party took on additional urgency. A high-ranking secret police official later remarked that while it might have been possible to entrust the Commissariat of Internal Affairs with the task of combating the spread of counterrevolution in Petrograd and the provinces, there lingered in the minds of the Bolshevik leaders the danger that the Left Socialist Revolutionaries, no matter what, would demand a place for themselves in this commissariat (which in fact took place), the Collegium of which had meanwhile been made up exclusively of Bolsheviks. If the Left Socialist Revolutionaries entered the People's Commissariat of Internal Affairs, what kind of struggle with counterrevolution would there be? Therefore, the thoughts of the leadership began to work in a different direction—the necessity of creating a special extraordinary organ of struggle with counterrevolution, not a commissariat, but a commission, from which the Left Socialist Revolutionaries could be excluded, and, if let in, then not on the basis of a demand on their part, but on the basis of business-like considerations. These thoughts are what gave rise to the organization of the VCheka.[66]

This revealing statement, published at a time when it was still possible to speak with relative candor on even such a sensitive subject as the Soviet secret police, reminds us of the calculated political motivation behind the organizational form given to the All-Russian Extraordinary Commission in December 1917.

And so it was that, having heard Dzerzhinsky's report on the organization and staffing of a commission to fight sabotage, the Council of People's Commissars—in its hastily drafted Protocol No. 21—decreed that the All-Russian Extraordinary Commission for the Struggle with Counterrevolution and Sabotage should be established. The tasks of the Commission were "to investigate and liquidate all counterrevolutionary and sabotage attempts and activities throughout Russia, from whatever place they originate; to turn over for trial by the revolutionary tribunal all saboteurs and counterrevolutionaries and to work out means of struggle against them; to carry out only an initial investigation, insofar as this is necessary for the suppression of these acts." The Commission was to "concentrate its attention upon the press, sabotage, etc., of the Right Socialist Revolutionaries, saboteurs, and strikers." The Council of People's Commissars also defined the punitive measures that could be applied by the VCheka: "confiscation, house arrest, deprivation of ration cards, publication of lists of enemies of the people, etc."[67] It is significant that the VCheka was explicitly conceived as an investigative organ and was denied the right to impose severe punishment by administrative action. The mild sanctions it was originally authorized to inflict on violators of the revolutionary order were a far cry from the executions and prison and concentration camp sentences that were soon to become accepted methods of disposing of class enemies.

As for the selection of Dzerzhinsky as chairman of the All-Russian Extraordinary Commission, a recent Soviet work assures us that this was "of course, not accidental." Dzerzhinsky's experience as a leading participant in the Military-Revolutionary Committee's campaign to safeguard the new Soviet state "testified to the fact that the defense of the conquests of the October Revolution would be in safe hands."[68] The tasks entrusted to the Extraordinary Commission gave Dzerzhinsky an opportunity to apply his organizational talents to an area in which he had already begun to distinguish himself—the life-and-death struggle of the Bolshevik regime against its internal foes. Surely Lenin also recognized and appreciated the value of Dzerzhinsky's boundless zeal and partisanship, his propulsive energy that both impressed and frightened his colleagues, and his overwhelming ambition to conquer and triumph on behalf of Bolshevism. In the person of Felix Edmundovich Dzerzhinsky, Lenin found the ideal proletarian Jacobin to entrust with the sword of the revolution.

At the same time Dzerzhinsky faced little competition, if any, for the job. While Dzerzhinsky showed by word and deed that he was capable of giving himself fully to the rigorous demands of his new assignment, other prominent Bolsheviks shunned the idea of service in the Extraordinary Commission and considerable difficulty was encountered in recruiting its staff. In the minds of many otherwise dedicated Communists, the memory of imprisonment and exile at the hands of the Tsarist authorities was still fresh, and these men showed little enthusiasm for participating in that new round of searches, arrests, and interrogations that it was the duty of the VCheka to carry out. Perhaps it was this attitude that explains the sudden departure of several members of the original VCheka Collegium to other posts within just a few hours of their appointment. No such reservations or doubts troubled Dzerzhinsky's mind. He understood that "revolutions cannot be made in silk gloves." And his long, hard years of deprivation in prison had only intensified his hatred for the representatives of the old regime, the capitalists, merchants, landowners, and their allies, anyone, in fact, who opposed the policies of the Bolshevik regime.

The VCheka's First Steps

Dzerzhinsky wasted no time in organizing his forces. Although the protocol of the Council of People's Commissars of December 7 stated that the Extraordinary Commission would be constructed the following day, Dzerzhinsky called the first meeting of the VCheka Collegium that same night. At this meeting it was decided to create three departments in the VCheka: for information, for organization, and one to specialize in the struggle against counterrevolution and sabotage. The original VCheka Collegium included Dzerzhinsky as chairman, and Peters, Ksenofontov, Averin, Ordzhonikidze, Peterson, Evseev, Trifonov, Zhedilev, and Vasilevsky as members.[69] The influence of the defunct Military-Revolutionary Committee was clearly evident in the fact that six of the ten men in the VCheka Collegium had previously served on its staff.

The beginnings of the institution that was soon to become a pillar of the Soviet state were modest enough. When the VCheka Collegium moved from the Smolny Institute to its own headquarters in the home of the former mayor of Petrograd at 2 Gorokhovaia Street, the office was in Dzerzhinsky's briefcase, and the entire budget (initially one thousand roubles and then ten thousand) was kept in the desk drawer of the acting treasurer, Yakov Peters.[70] The whole staff of the VCheka at first numbered only twenty-three people, including the secretaries and couriers. And since these Cheka agents, a group composed mainly of Red Guards, soldiers, and sailors, had no prior experience or training in their new work, Dzerzhinsky and other members of the VCheka Collegium frequently accompanied them on searches and arrests, "by their own example showing the Chekists how and what to do."[71]

The first statement announcing the creation of the VCheka appeared in *Izvestiia* on December 10, 1917. The citizens of Petrograd were advised:

> By decision of the Council of People's Commissars of December 7, the All-Russian Extraordinary Commission for the Struggle with

Counterrevolution and Sabotage attached to the Council of People's Commissars has been formed.

The Commission is located at No. 2 Gorokhovaia Street. Receiving hours: 12 till 5 o'clock.[72]

A few days later, on December 15, *Izvestiia* carried another VCheka announcement, this one directed to the local soviets, notifying them of its existence and asking that "all evidence and data about organizations and persons whose activity is directed against the revolution and popular authority" be forwarded to it. In addition the soviets were asked to set about the organization of local Chekas: "The resistance of the enemies of the revolution will be more rapidly and easily subdued by common efforts," the announcement said.[73]

No doubt confirming Bolshevik suspicions, it was less than a week before the Left Socialist Revolutionaries in the person of Issac Steinberg, the twenty-nine-year-old Commissar of Justice in the newly formed coalition government, began to challenge the powers of the VCheka and what already appeared to some to be its uninhibited practices in making arrests without regard for existing procedural arrangements. Steinberg's determined but ultimately futile attempts to curb the powers of the VCheka only served to further crystallize its privileged position in, and value to, the Bolshevik-dominated government. In the course of the dispute, which raged for several weeks in the Council of People's Commissars, the basic responsibilities of the VCheka, together with its status vis-à-vis other government institutions, were worked out in greater detail. And always the Extraordinary Commission, with strong support from Lenin, successfully resisted efforts to curb its expanding powers.

Steinberg wrote in his memoirs: "As Commissar of Justice, it became my lot to fight against Dzerzhinsky from the very start on this question of priority: law and justice versus security of the revolutionary regime."[74] It was evident from the outset that the Bolshevik majority in the Council of People's Commissars gave their priority to the VCheka's role as the loyal guardian of the revolutionary order and that "whatever actions the Cheka considered necessary to defend the dictatorship, including arrest, imprisonment and execution, would be approved by the Party leadership, notwithstanding any formal or legal limitations on its powers."[75]

On December 15, Steinberg signed a resolution demanding that "the delivery of arrested persons to the buildings of the Smolny Institute . . . without a special order [from the Commissar of Justice] shall cease," and that prisoners being detained under VCheka auspices be transferred to jails under the jurisdiction of the Commissar of Justice.[76] This directive, which in effect denied any special powers to the VCheka, was ignored, and a few days later Dzerzhinsky ordered the arrest of members of the Union for the Defense of the Constituent Assembly, an organization with anti-Bolshevik leanings. At this point Steinberg decided to act on his own initiative. Early on December 19, he gave orders that the arrested members of the Union for the Defense of the Constituent Assembly be freed. The issue had now been joined: by whom (and how) could decisions of the VCheka be reversed?

The Council of People's Commissars met the same day to resolve this question. The young Commissar of Justice was sharply reprimanded for his intervention in the fate of prisoners who had been detained on Dzerzhinsky's orders. The resolution of the meeting, passed over the signatures of Lenin and Stalin, stated:

> The Council of People's Commissars declares that any changes whatsoever in the decisions of Dzerzhinsky's Commission, as well as of other commissions appointed by the Soviets, shall be permitted only by means of appeals of those decisions to the Council of People's Commissars, and in no case by the personal order of the Commissar of Justice.[77]

The resolution added that Steinberg's actions were "illegal" both in form and substance since they violated the rights of Dzerzhinsky's organization as well as earlier decisions of the Council of People's Commissars approving the detention of the prisoners. The result of this episode was to strengthen the position of the VCheka as an administrative organ of the Council of People's Commissars, independent of other government agencies, in operations directed against political opponents.

Undaunted by this setback, Steinberg returned to the Council of People's Commissars with a draft proposal outlining the relationship he thought should prevail between the Commissariat of

Justice and all other investigative agencies, including the VCheka. In essence, Steinberg proposed that the activities of the VCheka proceed under the supervision and control of the Commissariat of Justice. Steinberg wanted to see the VCheka subject to the same procedural rules that applied to any other investigative agency of the Soviet government. Steinberg hit another very sensitive nerve when he asked that "arrests and proceedings against members of the Constituent Assembly and other persons, whose detention has a notably political meaning, occur only with the consent of the People's Commissariat of Justice."[78]

As might be expected, Lenin vigorously objected to all those points in Steinberg's draft that required the subordination of the VCheka to the Commissariat of Justice. The most salient parts of the final resolution, as it was drafted and edited by Lenin and approved by the Council of People's Commissars, stated:

> 1. "The All-Russian Commission" attached to the Council of People's Commissars is established for the purpose of a merciless struggle against counterrevolution, sabotage, and speculation.
> 2. The results of its work are to be turned over to the Investigating Commission attached to the Revolutionary Tribunal or [the VCheka] discontinues the case. . . .
> 6. Concerning arrests having a significant political meaning, the Commission is to *inform* [my emphasis] the People's Commissariat of Justice and the People's Commissariat of Internal Affairs. . . .
> 8. Conflicts appearing between the VCheka and the Commissariats of Justice and Internal Affairs and the Presidium of the Petrograd Soviet are to be ultimately resolved by the Council of People's Commissars, but without the suspension of the usual activities of the Commission.[79]

This last point was suggested by Stalin, who was already showing a keen interest in matters dealing with the secret police. Its significance was that, even in the event of future interdepartmental conflicts, the operations of the VCheka would not be interrupted, and no other governmental agency would have a veto power over the measures employed by it.

In this manner was the place of the VCheka in the dictatorship of the proletariat gradually clarified. It was acknowledged to be an administrative and political organ in the fight against counterrevolution, functioning under the direct control of the highest echelons of the Bolshevik Party. This control "was a guarantee," in the words of a recent Soviet study, "that the enormous power granted to the VCheka would not be used except in the interests of the revolution."[80] From the Bolshevik point of view Steinberg's interference threatened to obstruct the operations of the VCheka, a specifically Bolshevik instrument of power. At no time, of course, did any of his proposals to subordinate the VCheka to the Commissariat of Justice have the least chance of Bolshevik approval.[81]

The adamant refusal of Lenin and Dzerzhinsky to surrender control over the VCheka led Steinberg and the Left Socialist Revolutionaries to the conclusion that a new approach was necessary. Unable to achieve the desired degree of control over the VCheka from outside, the Left Socialist Revolutionaries, on January 7, 1918, brought the question of assigning some of their own colleagues to the VCheka before the Council of People's Commissars. As Steinberg explained this move: "The party of the Left Socialist Revolutionaries was hostile to the entire machinery and 'spirit' of the Cheka. They nevertheless considered it necessary to have their representatives on the Cheka Council so as to exercise their control."[82]

Dzerzhinsky came out strongly against this idea, declaring the "unacceptability of any system of reinforcing . . . the Commission by means of the selection of new members by the party of Left Socialist Revolutionaries."[83] In this instance, however, Dzerzhinsky had to yield ground. Since the coalition with the Left Socialist Revolutionaries was still in effect, the proposal was a legitimate one that could not be rejected out of hand. It was agreed to permit a few Left Socialist Revolutionaries to serve on the VCheka Collegium with the understanding that each candidate had to be approved by the Council of People's Commissars.[84] Not until the abortive uprising of the Left Socialist Revolutionaries in July 1918 was the VCheka purged of its noncommunist elements and returned to its earlier pristine status as an all-Bolshevik organ. But even the presence of the Left Socialist Revolutionaries, though annoying at times, had no real effect on the general direction of the Commission's work since Dzerzhinsky and his Bolshevik colleagues retained a majority on the VCheka Collegium.

The creation of the VCheka, it will be recalled, was connected with a discussion in the Council of People's Commissars of means to deal with strikes on the part of government employees. The "founding decree" of December 7, 1917, had called upon the VCheka to give special attention to eradicating the strike movement. According to a leading secret police spokesman, there was "only one way to get rid of this sore—burn it out with a red hot iron. And this is what the Extraordinary Commission [did]."[85] Within two weeks the VCheka was ready to move against the Union of Employees of Government Institutions, which was behind the strike in Petrograd. Evidence gathered by the Chekists led them to an apartment at 46 Liteiny Street that was used by the strike leaders as a meeting place. On December 22, Dzerzhinsky ordered a search of the apartment. In the raid that followed, thirty or so persons were arrested and many documents relating to the activities and plans of the Union were seized. Among those arrested was an official of the Ministry of Internal Affairs, A. M. Kondratev, who was suspected by the VCheka to be a chief organizer of the strike and the chairman of the Union of Employees of Government Institutions.

Dzerzhinsky is said to have personally examined all the evidence collected by his men and interrogated many of the arrested. This and the painstaking piecing together of scraps of paper hastily torn up but not completely destroyed during the raid enabled the Chekists to determine the identity of the most active members of the Union. On the basis of all the evidence thus assembled, Dzerzhinsky compiled a list of more than one hundred persons who had to be arrested for the final destruction of the strike organization.

The final results of the VCheka's investigation indicated that the Union of Employees of Government Institutions was preparing a nationwide strike and that it was closely connected with anti-Bolshevik groups and with representatives of the banking and industrial interests who were providing the funds to the strikers. According to one observer, "It was the realization of the strike fund contributors that the Bolsheviks were firmly in power, followed by their refusal to pay strike benefits, which finally broke the strike."[86] Those arrested by the VCheka, after giving a promise not to participate in future acts of sabotage, were released. Even Kondratev, the chairman of the Union, was released unharmed after two months in prison.[87]

In handling this first major case, the VCheka acted with considerable restraint. Only in ordering the arrest and detention without trial of those suspected of leading the strike movement did Dzerzhinsky's commission exceed the formal limitations on its powers. This early in its existence its organization and resources were still meager and it lacked the authority to pass and carry out its own sentences. But not for long. Soon "the need for swift and decisive measures to suppress saboteurs and plotters forced the revolution to renounce the strict delimitation of functions" contained in Protocol No. 21.[88]

On February 26, 1918, the VCheka took an ominous step. Without publicity, it executed an extortionist, who used the name Prince Eboli, and his female accomplice, Britt. The executions were carried out by a special decree of the Collegium of the VCheka. Prince Eboli and his companion thereby had the dubious distinction of being the first persons shot without trial by the Soviet secret police.[89] Prince Eboli's fate was sealed by Dzerzhinsky himself, who demanded the death penalty on the grounds that the culprit had conducted his criminal activities under the guise of a Chekist. "It was impossible," wrote one of Dzerzhinsky's associates in relating this episode, "to permit the name of the VCheka to be compromised. Its name had to be kept clean." When the Commissar of Justice protested this flagrant abuse of VCheka authority, Lenin refused to discuss the matter. In shooting Prince Eboli and Britt, the VCheka had clearly exceeded its original mandate, which had limited its power to the conduct of preliminary investigations. But Lenin "understood that Comrade Dzerzhinsky was right. You cannot go against life. Thus, life itself legalized the right of the VCheka to deal out direct reprisals . . . the right to execute."[90] Lenin and Dzerzhinsky, both resolute men, realized that revolution and internal crisis impose their own methods, and they were not slow to grasp them.

It was subsequently claimed by a VCheka spokesman that only twenty-two "bandits and speculators" were executed by the secret police during its first six months of operation. This figure was offered as evidence of the generosity and forbearance of the Chekists in the face of numerous counterrevolutionary assaults.

Only after months of anti-Bolshevik plots, espionage, and assassinations did the leaders of the revolution finally decide to let the axe fall on their political opponents.[91] In fact, however, any leniency on the part of the VCheka during these formative months was due less to the revolutionary idealism of Dzerzhinsky and his Bolshevik acolytes than to the stubborn refusal of the Left Socialist Revolutionaries to approve the uninhibited use of the death penalty. For this we have the word of the leading historian of the VCheka, who wrote that when it came to shooting "they [the Left Socialist Revolutionaries] always voted against, and for a death sentence a unanimous decision was necessary."[92] Not until the expulsion of the Left Socialist Revolutionaries from the VCheka in July 1918 was this last internal restraint on the use of the death penalty removed.

Meanwhile, the military situation confronting Lenin's government continued to deteriorate. The German advance into Russian territory, which had begun on February 18, showed no signs of slowing down. Fearing the possibility of a German occupation of Petrograd itself, Lenin proposed that the Soviet government move to Moscow. This suggestion generated heated debate in Party circles. Many seemed to believe that abandoning Petrograd and the Smolny—the symbols of the revolution—would weaken Bolshevik morale. To these critics Lenin retorted: "Why do you prattle about the symbolic importance of Smolny? The Smolny is what it is because we are in it. When we are in the Kremlin, all your symbolism will move to the Kremlin."[93] Finally, the opposition to the move was defeated, and the plans for the transfer were worked out in great secrecy. Lenin and his party left the Smolny at 9:30 in the evening of March 10 to board the train at the small station of Tsvetochnaia Square. The VCheka organized the security measures along the route, and the Bolshevik leader's train arrived safely in Moscow on the evening of March 11.

While Lenin and his family settled temporarily in the Hotel National, Dzerzhinsky chose as his headquarters the premises of the former Rossiia Insurance Company, located just a few minutes' walk from the Kremlin. With its many rooms, side entrances, cellars, and courtyard, the building was ideally suited for use as a prison. The address—2 Bolshaia Lubianka—was soon to become the most dreaded in all Russia. (Before the revolution, this part of Moscow had been the home of some of Russia's largest insurance companies, and the gallows humor of the day noted that in a sense the new occupants were still engaged in the business of "life insurance".) The facade of the VCheka's residence, which was considerably enlarged during the Stalin era, gave no hint of what went on inside. The Lubianka was not surrounded by barbed wire or machine-gun emplacements. Sentries stood guard at the main entrance, but this was not unusual since sentries were also posted at many Soviet institutions. Inside, however, the Lubianka was an armed camp. A half-dozen heavily armed Chekists immediately embraced anyone who stepped over the threshold, and along the corridors were innumerable guards and checkpoints. A contingent of Cheka troops was also on duty to defend the headquarters of the secret police in an emergency. Located in the courtyard of VCheka headquarters was another, smaller building, previously a tenement, which was surrounded by high neighboring buildings and thus hidden from street view. This building was converted into the "inner prison" of the VCheka and was the last known address of many an enemy of the people.[94]

Day and night, for months on end, Dzerzhinsky was at his desk in the Lubianka, signing arrest orders and death warrants, studying evidence, disregarding all personal suffering, intent only on safeguarding the conquests of the revolutionary proletariat. The chairman of the VCheka departed from 2 Bolshaia Lubianka Street only to attend meetings at the Kremlin and to participate occasionally in searches and arrests with his fellow Chekists. Dzerzhinsky's small and sparsely furnished office overlooked the courtyard of the Lubianka; it was considered too risky to have his window face the street. A desk, some chairs, and a small book-case were the most conspicuous furnishings. One side of the office was partitioned off with a screen; behind it was a steel frame bed with an army blanket thrown over it. After working sixteen to eighteen hours a day, Dzerzhinsky often slept in his office. (Later, when his family arrived in Moscow, the Dzerzhinskys moved into a small apartment in the Kremlin.) At five and six in the morning, when the Chekists returned to the Lubianka to file their reports on the searches and arrests of the previous night, Dzerzhinsky was often waiting to learn the results of the operations, look over evidence, and give further instructions.

From these unpretentious surroundings, Felix Edmundovich

Dzerzhinsky orchestrated the seemingly endless struggle against the various foes of Soviet power. Letters written during his first few months in Moscow reveal his absorption in the grisly task the revolution had assigned him, which he pursued without any trace of sentiment:

> *May 27, 1918:* I am in the very thick of the struggle, leading the life of a soldier for whom there is no rest because it is necessary to save the house. . . . The work and the struggle are hellish. But in this fight my heart remains just exactly as it was in the past.
>
> My purpose compels me to be merciless and I am firmly resolved to pursue it to the end. . . .
>
> The ring of enemies is steadily closing in on us, approaching nearer to the heart. . . . Each day compels us to resort to ever more resolute measures. . . . Having been appointed to a post in the front line, I am determined to fight and to look with open eyes at all the danger of the threatening situation, and I too must be merciless.
>
> *August 22[?], 1918:* Like a soldier, I am constantly in battle, and it may be that this will be the last one.
>
> *August 29, 1918:* We are soldiers at our fighting posts. I live for that which confronts me because this demands the utmost attention and vigilance in order to secure victory. My will is for victory and despite everything, despite the fact that a smile rarely breaks on my face, I am sure of the victory of the mission and the movement for which and in which I live and work. . . .
>
> We are witnessing the dance of life or death, a moment of truly bloody struggle, of titanic effort.[95]

And a strange figure of fate Dzerzhinsky was. His sudden rise to prominence coincided with the moment when the country was at a historic turning point. The old order was refusing to go quietly to its grave, and the birth of the new was proving far more difficult and painful than originally expected. In this life-and-death struggle Dzerzhinsky emerged as the avenging angel of the Bolshevik dispensation. For his sword he forged the deadly weapon of terrorism and resolved to smite with it anyone whose actions threatened the survival of the revolutionary order that was coming into being. He performed his task so well that he soon became the most feared man in Russia. And this was a fear sensed not only by the masses who were directly or indirectly affected by his vast power, but by many leading Bolsheviks as well. Many of Dzerzhinsky's colleagues, notwithstanding their respect for his energy and talents, regarded him with loathing. Thus, Karl Radek, a well-known Bolshevik luminary, had this to say about one of his contacts with Dzerzhinsky:

> Last week, accompanied by Dzerzhinsky (this will seem strange to you, but I can't help it, duty is duty) I traveled south and witnessed for myself how our Felix acts. Yes, he is a real broom. At each station we passed, everybody was quivering and trembling, from the station-master down to the last pointsman. Do you know that in the course of our two days' journey Dzerzhinsky arrested about three hundred railway officials, of which over one-half will forever be struck from the lists of the citizens of our socialist mother country! I suppose there is no other way out. During the years of civil war this band of robbers has become so arrogant that they look upon the railways and transport merely as a source of income for themselves, and one cannot travel one inch without a bribe. A slight disinfection is always useful. And although I don't care much for Dzerzhinsky, I must admit that it would have been impossible to find a better disinfector.[96]

When the VCheka moved to Moscow, Dzerzhinsky was forty years old. Over the years his disposition and outlook had not changed. He remained as always aloof and puritanical, yearning only to be consumed by the cause to which he had devoted his life. In appearance he was tall, slender, and slightly stoop-shoul-dered; like a soldier in the front lines of the struggle against the internal enemy, he dressed usually in a military uniform of high boots, riding breeches, and field jacket. A small mustache and goatee, high cheek bones, and long, thin aristocratic nose were conspicuous facial features. People were drawn most of all to his unusual eyes—watery and limpid, with drooping eyelids—which seemed to be almost without expression. Dzerzhinsky's gaze could be strange and unsettling, fixing upon some object or person and remaining frozen for a long time, creating the impression that, as one writer put it, he was "looking but not seeing or that he saw too much."[97]

Dzerzhinsky's total conviction of the righteousness of his cause combined with his life long self-denial made him implacable toward those dehumanized objects, labeled collectively "class enemies," who dared to obstruct the path to salvation under socialism. A contemporary once said after meeting Dzerzhinsky:

> One feels he can neither understand nor forgive moral weaknesses in others, since he himself possesses that fanatical devotion which has made it possible for him to travel the hard, bitter road where his ideals lead. . . . Such a man can sign away life with an unruffled firmness that would break one of a warmer temperament. He needs only to be convinced that his course is righteous; nothing else matters.[98]

In renouncing any personal advantage in the bloody struggle he waged, Dzerzhinsky could kill with a clear conscience, for he was acting as an agent of history. Dzerzhinsky conceded: "For many there is no name more terrifying than mine." But he insisted at the same time that the "sole determinant" of his actions remained his "striving for justice." In the historic battle under way between the "most unfortunate and the most downtrodden people" and "the world of the rich and wealthy," he could not remain neutral.[99] Every measure, no matter how deplorable it might at first appear, became admissible since the goal was no less than the eradication of all evil and the construction of a new type of society in which man's exploitation by man would be unknown.

Shortly after its arrival in Moscow, the VCheka cordially solicited the cooperation and assistance of the city's populace:

> The All-Russian Extraordinary Commission will appreciate each item of information on the whereabouts of thugs, unlawful occupants, illegal distillers of spirits, speculators, saboteurs, and counterrevolutionaries. . . . It is necessary to inform promptly the All-Russian Extraordinary Commission of each irregular, illegal, or criminal action on the part of anyone, without distinction as to status or occupation, it henceforth being known that all such denunciations, written or oral, will be met with sincere gratitude.

Proclaiming the determination to weed out of all Soviet institutions the "undesirable elements" that had infiltrated them in the "guise of sympathizers and confederates," the announcement ordered that all lethal weapons be registered with the Commission; that explosives and explosive mechanisms in private hands be turned over immediately; and that thieves, murderers, illegal occupants, and the like either leave Moscow within twenty-four hours or else expect to be "promptly shot" at the scene of any future offense.[100]

Unfortunately, however, the Muscovites, in the words of a leading Chekist, "in general did not welcome the VCheka."[101] Two early incidents caused the VCheka to acquire an unwholesome reputation at its new home base. Not long after the VCheka moved to Moscow, a shootout occurred in a teahouse when some Chekists came under attack from a "gang of drunken hooligan bandits." One Chekist was killed, and seven captured assailants were executed the same night. On another occasion a group of Chekists attending a circus performance took offense at unflattering remarks about the Soviet government made by Bim-Bom the clown and decided to arrest him on the spot. The crowd was greatly amused by the scene and thought it was part of the act—until the clown tried to flee and the Chekists opened fire, causing a panic.

Meanwhile, the Moscow press continued to issue the appeals and requests of the VCheka. On April 7, 1918, all local soviets were asked to send to the VCheka's Bureau for Combating Abuses of the Press "all regular numbers of periodicals, brochures, leaflets, etc., published in the provinces."[102] And on April 10, the VCheka informed all "interested persons" that relatives and friends of persons being held by the VCheka were causing a nuisance in their attempts, admittedly to be expected under the circumstances, to gain the release of prisoners or the reduction of their sentences. By force of "bourgeois habit" some people were said to be turning to various lawyers for help, paying them large sums of money for their professional intervention. But the VCheka advised the public that "lawyers do not enjoy any advantage in the Commission and, quite the contrary, only worsen the status of the case." All "interested persons" were invited to present themselves personally at the VCheka's Information Bureau, where they would be provided with "quick and plain answers" to their queries.[103]

2

The Chekas Work Better Every Day

For the first three months of its existence, the All-Russian Extraordinary Commission was ''all Russian'' in name only since its operations were confined to Petrograd, the first capital of the Soviet Republic. And even when Felix Dzerzhinsky moved the Commission's headquarters to Moscow early in March 1918, the entire staff numbered only about 120.[1] Yet within less than five years, the VCheka expanded its operations into virtually every area of Soviet life that had any bearing on the security of the Bolshevik regime, and the chairman of the VCheka commanded a far-flung organization consisting of many thousands of well-armed men.

One indication of the spectacular growth of the Soviet secret police may be found in its budget, which increased more than 2000 percent in the eighteen-month period from July 1918 to December 1919 as more and more state funds were allocated to the rapidly expanding VCheka apparatus. During the second half of 1918, the total budget of the VCheka came to about 53 million roubles, most of which was earmarked for the maintenance of the proliferating network of provincial and district Chekas. In the period from January to June 1919, the budget increased to more than 348 million roubles, again most of the funds going to support the local Chekas. During the second half of 1919, the VCheka budget soared to more than 2.2 billion roubles with the largest portion designated for the upkeep of the Internal Security Troops of the VCheka, an armed force that had already become an indis-

38

pensable weapon in the struggle for Bolshevik supremacy on the internal front.[2]

The Provincial and District Chekas

Ten days after the VCheka arrived in Moscow, Dzerzhinsky launched a drive to establish a secret police presence in localities under Bolshevik control. In a decree published in *Izvestiia* on March 22, 1918, the chairman of the VCheka called upon all soviets to organize Extraordinary Commissions in their areas of jurisdiction immediately. "From now on," Dzerzhinsky's order stated, "the right to conduct all arrests, searches, requisitions, confiscations, etc., connected with [such crimes as counterrevolution, speculation, and malfeasance] belongs exclusively to the Extraordinary Commissions . . . ."[3] During the spring and summer local Cheka organs began to appear all over the Soviet landscape. By the end of August, the fragile revolutionary order was already being defended by 40 provincial and 365 district Extraordinary Commissions.[4]

A brief statement on the back page of *Izvestiia* at the end of April announced the VCheka's intention of calling a conference of provinicial and district Chekas to "elaborate overall plans and methods of struggle" against counterrevolution and to coordinate the activities of the emerging network of local Chekas.[5] It was subsequently reported that under the guidance of the VCheka leadership this convocation of Chekists would work out the details of secret police organization and lines of authority and control from "the all-Russian to the village level." Appropriate measures for the struggle against speculation and banditry were to be discussed together with plans for purging the Soviet state apparatus of "undesirable elements." The organization of an intelligence service and armed Cheka detachments, as well as other aspects of internal procedure, finance, and communications, was also mentioned in the agenda. Each Extraordinary Commission was asked to send two representatives to the conference, making certain that they came only from the ranks of the Bolshevik Party or the Left Socialist Revolutionaries with whom the Bolsheviks were still sharing power.[6]

Sixty-six delegates representing forty-three Extraordinary

Commissions, as well as representatives of the VCheka high command, took part in the first All-Russian Conference of Extraordinary Commissions, which met from June 11 to June 14, 1918. The published synopsis and resolutions of the meeting constitute a valuable source of information on the early development of the Soviet secret police. Several delegates spoke at length on the various dangers confronting Soviet Russia. Thousands of armed counterrevolutionaries were said to be roaming the interior of the country, spreading chaos and destruction in their attempts to overthrow the Soviet government. The anti-Soviet agitation conducted by the clergy, the village kulaks, the local bourgeoisie, and spokesmen for such rival political parties as the Mensheviks and the Right Socialist Revolutionaries proved that these groups too had joined the enemy camp. These threats to Soviet security, as formidable as they were, had thus far been contained, and the Chekists expressed satisfaction that revolutionary order had been maintained in the provinces, thereby guaranteeing "a normal progress of state life" in the young Soviet Republic.[7]

The published resolutions of the first All-Russian Conference of Extraordinary Commissions showed the Chekists in unanimous agreement on "the necessity of organizing Chekas in all the territories of Soviet Russia which would take upon themselves the whole burden of working for the defense of the revolutionary order and the merciless struggle against counterrevolution, speculation, and abuses of office." The Chekists warned both the open and covert enemies of the October Revolution that they would show neither mercy nor vacillation in dealing with the opponents of Soviet power "regardless of what flag they take refuge under." At the same time, spokesmen for the VCheka and its local organs admitted that certain deficiencies in the secret police apparatus were hindering the discharge of their vital duties. The lack of "specialized, disciplined troops for Soviet defense in general and a trustworthy railroad guard dedicated to Soviet power in particular" were said to be permitting all kinds of speculation to go unpunished. The Chekists were further handicapped by the absence of a "special, reliable border defense and control," which made possible the easy shipment of large quantities of essential goods over the Soviet frontiers. Only the creation of specialized Cheka departments to combat speculation and a network of reliable Cheka railroad defense units offered hope of putting an end to "that criminal speculation which the bourgeoisie and its agents are supporting in the cities and in the localities."

The conference also resolved to organize "an apparatus that would mercilessly eliminate the evil of official malfeasance," a form of crime especially prevalent among the bourgeoisie who, in the absence of trained officials of working-class origin, were using their government posts to undermine the Soviet authorities. Finally, the Chekists took the position that a successful struggle against the enemies of Soviet power would be impossible "without constant communication and the participation of the broad revolutionary working masses and their organizations." To this end, the conference pledged to maintain close contact between the Chekas and all Party and state organs through frequent reports on secret police activities.[8]

Not all aspects of the conference's work were published in the Soviet press. More precise instructions regarding the duties, prerogatives, and organization of the emerging network of local Chekas were contained in a top secret *(sovershenno sekretno)* directive adopted by the conference entitled "Regulation on the Local Extraordinary Commissions."[9] The provisions of this rare document, which eventually found its way to the Hoover Institution Archives at Stanford University, merit attention because the principles embodied in them guided the Soviet secret police throughout its formative years. The regulation began by stipulating that each regional, provincial, and district soviet executive committee select "a group of persons devoted to the cause of the revolution and Soviet power" to form the administrative nucleus of a Cheka in their respective areas of jurisdiction. The regulation described the local Chekas as "organs of administrative power" and charged them with a number of tasks, including:

> *(a)* the conduct of a merciless struggle against counterrevolution and speculation by all means available to the Commissions; *(b)* the surveillance of the local bourgeoisie and all counterrevolutionary activities carried on by its members; *(c)* the provision of information to local and central authorities concerning disorders and abuses and the taking of measures to suppress them; *(d)* the conduct of investigations into state crimes; *(e)* the surveillance of persons crossing the frontiers;

(f) the surveillance of foreign intelligence agents; *(g)* the apprehension of persons hiding from the authorities; *(h)* the preservation of order in the absence of the militia and the rendering of assistance to the latter as needed to restore revolutionary order; *(i)* the strict implementation of the orders and decrees of the Soviet government.

To enable the Chekists to discharge their various duties effectively, the regulation bestowed broad powers upon them. Provincial secret police organs were given the right to (1) propose the declaration of martial law on a province-wide scale; (2) issue ordinances on questions of revolutionary order applicable to the given province; (3) subject criminals to arrest by administrative action and assess fines by general procedures; and (4) search the premises of and arrest anyone "suspected of counterrevolutionary activities" or of doing anything "directed against Soviet authority." (No formal authorization to impose the death penalty was granted the secret police until September 1918.)

The regulation also provided for a functional division of labor within the provincial Chekas, the secret police organs that then and later constituted the chief territorial units of the VCheka system. Every provincial Cheka was to be composed of four departments, each with its own area of competence. The departments for combating counterrevolution were to conduct "a general and merciless struggle against all manifestations of counterrevolution, conspiratorial organizations, and pogroms of Black Hundreds groups" and were "everywhere [to] constitute the vigilant guardians of Soviet revolutionary order and tranquillity, carrying on this work selflessly and honestly." The departments for combating speculation were to "combat all manifestations of speculation and banditry," supervise arrivals and departures of cargo, and conduct surveillance of "bourgeois agents" who might have infiltrated Soviet supply, distribution, and other economic agencies. The departments for combating abuses of office were responsible for investigating criminal malfeasance committed by state officials and taking appropriate measures against such persons. Finally, the liaison departments were "responsible for maintaining close contact with subordinate Chekas and with the VCheka," as well as performing certain duties of internal management and inspection.[10]

District soviet executive committees were instructed by the

regulation to select from the ranks of "experienced and trustworthy comrades" a number of commissars to serve as the staff of a Cheka "in every small town." The representatives of the Lubianka at the district and village levels were made responsible for

> supervising the revolutionary order in their areas; preventing counter-revolutionary agitation; maintaining a vigilant watch over the local bourgeoisie; implementing surveillance of suspected counterrevolutionary elements including kulaks, speculators, and other enemies of the Soviet authorities; and taking measures to suppress such elements.

No area under Bolshevik control escaped the organizing influence of the secret police. The Chekas were among the first agencies of Soviet power to be established in newly conquered territory and among the last to be evacuated when the enemy approached. Creating the nucleus of a Cheka in those localities where one had not yet been established was the principal task of a special cadre of roving Cheka "instructors." A rare secret police document, which originated in the All-Ukrainian Cheka sometime in 1919, required that every provincial Cheka maintain a well-trained staff of instructors whose responsibilities and duties were defined as follows:

> 1. Instructors must have a knowledge of all laws of the Worker-Peasant Government and must keep a careful watch for any new decrees and orders emanating from either the central or local Soviet authorities.
> 2. Upon setting out on a mission, the instructor must take with him a list of his mission's objectives, his mandate, and materials necessary for the organization of a Cheka . . . .
> 4. In areas where a Cheka does not yet exist, [the instructor] proceeds to organize one in cooperation with the local soviet executive committee. In areas where Chekas exist but where their actions are at cross purposes with the Soviet authorities, the instructor shall be responsible for the reorganization and proper direction of Cheka work.
> 5. If the local Soviet authorities are not acting in accordance with the Constitution of the Ukrainian Soviet Socialist Republic, and if they are sabotaging or holding back the planned work of the Cheka, the instructor must gather the most precise evidence and facts concerning the illegal acts of the local Soviet authorities and present them in writing to [his superiors] . . . .

7. In places where Soviet power has not been established except for the presence of a Revolutionary Committee, the instructor must get in touch with the Revolutionary Committee and organize a soviet and a Cheka.[11]

The creation of new Chekas was hardly a complicated or difficult task since all that was required at the outset was an administrative staff of five trustworthy "comrades" who would select from among themselves a chairman and a secretary. A recruitment drive to build up a larger staff of operatives was the next step, but this would be the job of the new Cheka itself, not of the instructor. Having laid the groundwork, he would have already moved on to his next destination.

Recently published documents from the Ukrainian State Archive of the October Revolution provide a glimpse into the organizational work of several Cheka instructors who traveled the countryside at this time. Thus one M. N. Pataskaev, an instructor attached to the Kursk Provincial Cheka, reported that he arrived at the junction of Koronevo on November 27, 1918. Finding "absolutely no authority there whatsoever," he called an urgent meeting of local officials, who agreed to "the immediate organization of strong power" in the form of a Revolutionary Soviet and a Cheka.[12] Another report, this one filed by Instructor Andreenko of the All-Ukrainian Cheka, indicated that a Cheka was first established in the town of Starobel on January 19, 1919, consisting of "three members and three cooperating Communists." By February 1, the Cheka of Starobel had already taken ninety-three representatives of the old regime into custody and had started to register the property of the local bourgeoisie. Only the lack of detailed instructions from the center was said to be impeding the further work of this energetic small-town Cheka.[13] The most complete of these published reports from the Ukrainian archives was written in February 1919 by a pair of Cheka instructors recently returned from the town of Pavlograd in Ekaterinoslav Province. They wrote:

> We arrived at our destination, the town of Pavlograd, on January 30, and set about organizing the Cheka jointly with members of the Cheka Collegium, which had been chosen by the local soviet executive committee and the Communist Party organization. In our work we at no time exceeded the limits of the instructions given to us by the Instruc-

tion Department. From among the members of the Cheka Collegium we selected the heads of the departments, the secretary of the Commission, and a commandant, all of whom were acquainted with the work of the Cheka . . . . We approved two investigators to handle the cases of arrested persons and selected some office workers. The Commission's counterintelligence agents and commissars are all members of the Communist Party. At the meeting of the Cheka Collegium it was decided to register immediately all local officers and weapons and launch the most decisive struggle against speculation.

The instructors closed their report on this optimistic note: "We hope that in the future the deeds of the [Extraordinary] Commission will justify its appellation."[14]

That the instructors of the provincial Chekas of the Ukraine had their counterparts working out of VCheka headquarters in Moscow is confirmed by an article in an issue of the *VCheka Weekly*. Here it was reported that a VCheka instructor had recently rendered valuable assistance to the Chekists of Riazan Province. Early in September 1918, a conference of representatives from Riazan's district Chekas heard this VCheka instructor discuss the most urgent problems confronting the secret police in the localities. The instructor is also said to have provided badly needed advice to "the representatives of several weakly organized Chekas" and participated in the investigation and purge of a local regiment found to be harboring "counterrevolutionary elements."[15]

The provincial, district, and village Chekas that soon dotted the country probably did more to estrange the peasant population than any other government agency. Since they were far removed in actuality from close supervision by the Lubianka, there was little to prevent the sundry nonentities who gained employment in the local Chekas from using their virtually unlimited powers to settle personal grudges or satisfy a lust for revenge. Others gratified their sadistic appetites by beating and torturing defenseless peasants. "In some villages," it was reported, "the Cheka locked masses of peasants in cold warehouses, stripped them, and beat them with gun butts. Local officials said: 'They told us in the center: better to oversalt than not to salt enough.' "[16] Moreover, as the principal enforcement arm of Soviet power in the countryside, the Extraordinary Commissions worked closely with the Commissariat of Food Supply in carrying out the forced requisition of peasant grain and livestock that Lenin had made the cornerstone of his agrarian policy. Armed food detachments, often led by or composed of Chekists, provoked widespread enmity in the villages as they went about seizing bread with bayonets. Bloody clashes between Chekists and enraged peasants who rose up in revolt were almost daily occurrences, and the casualties on both sides ran into the thousands.

It was therefore a matter of the greatest interest when, on January 24, 1919, the Soviet government announced a major reorganization of the network of local Chekas. It was decreed that within a period of twenty days "all district Extraordinary Commissions shall be abolished." The stated objective of this decision was to organize the struggle against counterrevolution, speculation, and malfeasance on a "more planned basis." (It was expected that "active workers" from the district Chekas would be offered employment by their comrades at the provincial level.)[17] The chairman of the VCheka subsequently explained that the reorganization was prompted by improved conditions on the internal front. The threatening situation that originally made it necessary to create Cheka organs with emergency powers at the district level had been overcome. The struggle was no longer against large groups of former officers, Tsarist officials, and bourgeoisie but rather against subversion from within. It was appropriate, Dzerzhinsky said, that the VCheka now terminate its period of expansion and indeed contract, dissolving nonvital organs like the district Chekas.[18]

A leading VCheka spokesman was quick to point out that the abolition of the district Chekas "by no means signifies a slackening of repressive measures against the counterrevolutionaries." Quite the contrary, even more was now expected of the provincial secret police organs:

> Yes, the district Chekas have been abolished, but the Civil War continues. The laws of civil war must therefore remain in force. District soviet executive committees must see to it that this idea is grasped not only by our own comrades, but by our enemies as well. And provincial Chekas must have their tentacles in the localities. The work of provincial Chekas is increased manifold with the abolition of their subordinate organs.[19]

This much heralded secret police reorganization therefore did not have quite the results one might have expected from the unequivocal provisions of the government's decree. In some sixty districts where the threat of counterrevolution seemed greatest the Chekas were not abolished at all but continued to function as before. District Chekas also reappeared throughout the Civil War to suppress various uprisings and other disorders.[20]

The Urban Chekas

The secret police organs in the countryside had their counterparts in the cities under Bolshevik control. By the end of the Civil War, every urban center in Soviet Russia could boast of its own resident Cheka apparatus. The Petrograd Extraordinary Commission, established in March 1918 to fill the vacuum left by the evacuation of the VCheka to Moscow, was the first such big-city Cheka. Under the leadership of its first chairman, Moisei Uritsky, the Petrograd Cheka quickly established a formidable reputation as guardian of the revolutionary order. There was hardly an aspect of the city's life that escaped its scrutiny. Thus on August 3, 1918, Uritsky signed a decree which warned the proprietors of the city's restaurants, cabarets, dance halls, and other entertainment establishments that they would be subject to arrest, a fine of up to 100,000 roubles and three years in prison for failure to close their premises by 11 P.M. Customers, too, who refused to leave their favorite haunts at least five minutes before closing might also find themselves under arrest.[21]

By the end of the Civil War, the sprawling headquarters of the Petrograd Cheka on Gorokhovaia Street were reported to house a staff of almost a thousand. Bolstering this staff, a Cheka battalion of seven hundred infantrymen and seventy cavalrymen stood ready at a moment's notice to carry out special orders or cope with any serious disturbances that might arise in the city. One of the largest sections of the Petrograd Cheka was the Secret-Operational Department. This department, which employed more than 120 persons, was responsible for the conduct of search and arrest operations and the registration of Cheka prisoners. Between January 1, 1920, and May 1, 1921, over 21,000 persons were arrested and registered by the agents and staff of this busy department.[22]

An Extraordinary Commission was established in the historic city of Kiev, a major Ukrainian trade center overlooking the Dnieper River, in February 1919 immediately after Red Army troops had occupied the city. According to the testimony of one of its officials, however, the initial phase of this particular Cheka's operations, was chaotic and unproductive. Neither the chairman of the Kiev Cheka, a drunk by the name of Volkov, nor his secretary, Kovalev, possessed the character or ability to run the Cheka effectively. The ensuing confusion in every Cheka department was compounded by the constant state of alarm in which these steadfast guardians of the revolutionary order were compelled to live. Twice their headquarters on Podvalnaia Street were assaulted by angry mobs, and troops from the local garrison had to be called in to rescue the besieged Chekists.

The searches and arrests conducted by the Chekists during this period amounted to undisguised plunder. Gold, diamonds, and liquor were the favored objects of Cheka agents sent out to search the premises of the local bourgeoisie. And so haphazard were Cheka record-keeping procedures that none of the goods confiscated during the first months of operations could later be accounted for. Extortion and bribery were also rampant; even the chairman of the Cheka was rumored to have enriched himself by 100,000 roubles in dealings with a local landlord.

Prisoners were held in a shed next to Cheka headquarters. The prisoners' fates were decided in a most arbitrary manner without benefit of even a perfunctory investigation of the charges against them. The loss of prisoners' dossiers was commonplace, and many files consisted of nothing more than the name of the arrested and the charges against him. Those finally sentenced to death were shot by personnel of the Commandant's Office during predawn hours; a small placard on each body testified to the crime for which the condemned had been executed.

The sudden and unexpected arrival early in April of a special inspection group brought this undisciplined and disorganized period of Cheka operations in Kiev to an abrupt end. A complete change in leadership was accompanied by the demotion, discharge, or arrest of many former employees. The next step was to find new quarters for the Cheka. In view of the ready availability of so many imposing and commodious private residences abandoned by, or confiscated from, the bourgeoisie, it seemed unreasonable for the Cheka to remain in its cramped and strategically disadvantageous location on Podvalnaia Street. The Chekists settled on a spacious residence on Ekaterinskaia Street and surrounded their new headquarters with nine sentry posts and a machine-gun emplacement to guard the main entrance. The cellar was turned into a storehouse, while part of the first floor was converted into a jail with six cells of varying size capable of holding more than a hundred prisoners. One cell was reserved for delinquent Chekists, Communists, and Soviet officials; another was set aside for female prisoners; the condemned spent their final hours in Room 5. The first floor also contained a restaurant and recreation facility for the Chekists, many of whom resided in a second-floor dormitory.

"If the first period of Cheka work bore the character of a cottage industry," to quote the analogy used by our Chekist informant, "then in the second period it assumed a production line character." Mass arrests of class enemies and a merciless struggle against criminals followed in the wake of a rapid increase in the number of Cheka personnel. From a total of 40 employees during the first phase of operations, the staff swelled to almost 300. (The Kiev Cheka also had at its disposal an armed detachment of 450 infantry and 60 cavalry.) The initial results of Cheka work in Kiev may be summarized briefly: more than 600 cases were processed by one or another of the Cheka's departments; an additional 350 cases were transferred to other institutions; and 148 persons were executed. Not until the end of August 1919, when General Denikin's troops were pounding on the city's gates, were the Kiev Chekists ordered to evacuate their headquarters on Ekaterinskaia Street. A steamer carried them up the Dnieper River to safety behind the new Red lines.[23]

The creation of a vast network of Chekas throughout Bolshevik-held territory soon required the VCheka to concentrate more of its attention on the administration of the secret police network as a whole. To free itself for this task, a decision was made late in 1918 to create the Moscow Extraordinary Commission.[24] The exploits of the Moscow Cheka, which was responsible for safeguarding revolutionary order in the vital nerve center of the Soviet Republic, are particularly well documented and may serve as a case study of secret police activity at the city level.

Due to the unreliability of the existing police and judicial agencies, the Moscow Chekists were initially obliged to devote much of their energy to a struggle against an infestation of armed robbers and other criminal types. As one contemporary put it: "Not only were the ordinary citizens exposed to the danger of being robbed on the streets or in their homes, but even responsible Soviet workers were not safe."[25] This human debris was gradually cleaned out, together with the corrupt top echelons of the city's Criminal Investigation Department, who were alleged to have shared in the bandits' booty. The initial preoccupation of the Moscow Chekists with common crime was reflected in official secret police figures. Almost 47 percent of the cases handled between December 1, 1918, and August 1, 1919, involved armed robberies and other felonies; 338 persons were executed for banditry during the first two years of Cheka operations.[26]

The most serious internal obstacle confronting the Moscow Cheka in the proper discharge of its duties during the first few months of its operations was the lack of sufficient personnel, in both quantity and quality. Yet even in the face of this severe handicap, the Moscow Chekists are said to have performed stupendous feats of labor and endurance. The Speculation Department, for example, composed at first of only seven "responsible workers," is credited with having uncovered more than sixty major cases of speculation between May and August 1919. In just one month, the Chekists of the Speculation Department confiscated nearly two million roubles in cash, not to mention large quantities of food and manufactured goods as well as substantial amounts of gold and silver. During the first half of 1919, the Investigation Department, with a staff of only twelve, managed to process no fewer than eight thousand cases, or about three cases a day for each Cheka investigator. In commenting upon these achievements, a spokesman for the Moscow Cheka hastened to add:

> If one bears in mind that only in rare instances were fewer than five persons brought in for interrogation in connection with each case, the usual number being ten to fifteen, with many cases requiring the interrogation of up to one hundred persons, it becomes clear why an inves-

tigator often had to work thirty to forty hours without rest, why only a few were able to endure such punishing labor for any length of time, and why the interrogation of various counterrevolutionaries, saboteurs, and speculators did not always take place immediately after arrest.

Under these circumstances, allowances had to be made, according to the same writer, for the errors and "irritability" sometimes associated with the work and personal comportment of the Moscow Chekists. After all, considering how overworked they were, nothing less than superhuman effort was required of these steadfast defenders of the revolutionary order.[27]

The Moscow Cheka was so understaffed, it was claimed, simply because "there were no new people, and the best ones had to be sent to the front lines (thirty in August 1919 alone)." The public was reassured, however, that the leaders of the Moscow Cheka were "straining every nerve" in their efforts to eliminate the evils of "subjectivity, one-sidedness, and prejudicial actions" on the part of Cheka commissars and investigators. A campaign had been launched to recruit "a more intelligent and educated cadre of workers, especially for assignment to the Investigation Department." As for the "worst elements" at work in the Moscow Cheka, these rascals were thrown out by means of a "constant purge of the personnel."[28]

It was only toward the end of 1919 that the Moscow Cheka, having put its own house in order and having rid the streets of the most dangerous criminal elements, was able to assume its true role as a weapon of the proletarian dictatorship. At long last the Moscow Chekists could concentrate on those types of crime that were intended to be the chief objects of their attention. The new direction taken by the Moscow Cheka was evidenced by the manifold increase in the number of cases of counterrevolutionary activity uncovered by its agents: from 429 during the first third of 1919 to 1,139 between May and July, and 2,896 from August 1 to December 31, 1919. Altogether, the Moscow Cheka uncovered fifty-nine "counterrevolutionary organizations" and arrested more than five thousand persons for political crimes during the period from December 1, 1918, to November 1, 1920. Among these prisoners were former Tsarist officials and policemen, more than 900 members of various opposition political parties ranging from monarchists to anarchists, 305 hostages, 565 persons accused of anti-Soviet agitation, and 2,622 persons loosely charged with "counterrevolutionary activity." The number of cases involving speculation also increased dramatically through 1919 and 1920. Speculators were arrested in droves—more than 26,000—by Cheka agents who combed the commercial and trading centers of the city.[29]

The Moscow Chekists devoted special attention to the Sukharevka market, a picturesque and bustling open-air emporium situated just a short distance from the Commissariat of Foreign Affairs. Throughout the years of civil war the Sukharevka was a thriving center of illicit trade and speculation. Here, in the midst of universal scarcity, there was hardly any commodity that money could not buy. Street vendors did a brisk trade in such hard-to-find items as fresh fruit and vegetables, clothes, shoes, blankets, kitchen utensils, furniture, books, soap, cigarettes, and even gramophones and records. Some of the people who did business at the Sukharevka were professional speculators, but there were others—such as former members of the nobility—who in desperation put their last possessions up for sale in order to buy bread or fuel.

To curb the illegal trade that flourished in the shadow of the Kremlin, a special Sukharevka subdepartment was set up in the Moscow Cheka, and its agents made frequent raids on the marketplace. Sometimes these raids were directed against a particular class of illegal traders, while at other times they seemed aimed at apprehending deserters or persons without proper identification papers. According to one habitué of the Sukharevka, it was always possible to tell when a Cheka raid was about to commence:

Warned by a mysterious system of wireless telegraphy, sellers and buyers alike began to grow restless, wares were gathered up in bundles, portable stands were dismounted, their owners scuttling down side streets and vanishing mysteriously into open doorways. Then a panicky movement of the crowd began, the more timid simply taking to their heels and running. Those who were unlucky enough not to make a quick getaway soon found all exits blocked by militiamen, who examined all documents and looked into all packages. Those who were caught with illegal merchandise or who were unprovided with proper documents were herded en masse, surrounded by a cordon of militiamen, and marched off to the Cheka.[30]

Booty seized from the traders and their customers was piled on carts and removed to Cheka headquarters. But within half an hour buyers and sellers would reassemble and business would return to normal as if nothing unusual had happened.

A total of 42,878 persons was arrested for various offenses by the Moscow Cheka during its first two years of operation. Speculation and malfeasance together accounted for 80 percent of all Moscow Cheka cases during this period, while political crimes accounted for a modest 13 percent, and other kinds of criminal activity such as armed robbery, illegal possession of weapons, counterfeiting, and graft another 7 percent. The more than 13,000 searches conducted by the Moscow Cheka yielded millions of roubles' worth of money, manufactured goods, and produce. The Chekists also sentenced 25,008 persons to prison terms, transferred the cases of 10,700 to other administrative or judicial institutions, placed 5,214 in concentration camps, sent 1,649 to forced labor, and executed 578 persons.[31]

Administering the vast secret police empire, which soon extended from the frozen shores of the White Sea to the Caucasus and from the Dnieper River to the Urals and beyond, was the VCheka itself. The bureaucratic structure of the VCheka was never a subject for public discussion, and only carefully selected aspects of it were ever revealed. The following sketch of the VCheka's internal organization was published in 1921:

> All administrative work, maintaining liaison with the provinces, managing Cheka personnel, inspection, control, and instruction, is carried out by the Administrative-Organizational Directorate.
>
> All work involved in the struggle against counterrevolution and similar crimes and the proper direction of this struggle among the civilian and military population is the task of the Secret-Operational Directorate.
>
> The registration of all counterrevolutionaries and suspected persons and the keeping of records on the work of all the Chekas is carried on by the same Directorate.
>
> The Transport Department . . . is responsible for work in the transport field, i.e., for combating counterrevolution, sabotage, and similar crimes on the railways and water routes.

The struggle against espionage and counterrevolution in the army and fleet, formerly the responsibility of the Special Department, is now one of the functions of the Secret-Operational Directorate.

All struggle against speculation and crimes committed by officials in economic agencies is the task of the Economic Directorate.[32]

Recent Soviet studies of the VCheka have identified other major departments including the Foreign Department, the Information Department, the Finance Department, the Investigation Department, and the Prison Department.[33] By the end of the Civil War, several thousand people were employed in the VCheka's numerous departments and subdepartments that together occupied about twenty buildings clustered around Lubianka Square.

Important decisions were made by the VCheka Collegium composed of the chairman and the heads of the various departments. In a letter to his deputy, I. K. Ksenofontov, dated July 23, 1920, Dzerzhinsky, who was about to leave Moscow for the Polish front, explained the principles that were to guide the work of the VCheka Collegium in his absence (and that, it may be assumed, were in effect when he himself was present):

> Collective leadership is in general held to a minimum. The full responsibility for the work of a department is borne by its chief, who serves on the Collegium. The Deputy Chairman is responsible for the work of all the departments. When it is necessary to reach a decision regarding a particular department, the Deputy Chairman consults with the head of that department and gives the necessary instructions. When it is necessary to issue orders affecting all departments or solve new organizational questions, the Deputy Chairman summons all department heads and Collegium members for a conference and the orders are issued in the name of the Collegium. For implementing a decision through the legislative organs, drafts are discussed at a meeting . . . of interested Collegium members . . . and supported before the Council of Defense, the Central Executive Committee, and the Council of People's Commissars by . . . that member of the Collegium who is most interested in the implementation of the decree, if the Deputy Chairman finds this necessary.[34]

As we have seen, the secret police chain of command, like that of the Bolshevik Party itself, resembled a military hierarchy, with each Cheka organ subordinate to the next higher one. According to provisions of the previously mentioned "Regulation on the

Local Extraordinary Commissions,'' provincial Chekas not only had the right to oversee the work of district Chekas within their areas of jurisdiction, but were also empowered to arrest and bring to trial any employee of a district Cheka accused of malfeasance. Likewise, the Cheka commissars working at the village and town levels took their orders from and reported to the district Chekas. The VCheka, of course, exercised "overall guidance and direction" of the entire apparatus. The orders and instructions issued by VCheka headquarters in Moscow were binding on all lower-level Chekas and could not be overruled or modified in any way by them or any other agency of the Soviet government.[35]

"Warm Hearts, Cool Heads, and Clean Hands"

The VCheka's struggle against the enemies of Soviet power was a crucial battlefront of the Civil War, and participation in its campaign to defend the revolutionary proletariat's conquests was considered the duty of all honorable Communists. Lenin himself once said "a good Communist is . . . a good Chekist."[36] Yet, as the leading Chekists admitted, many revolutionaries failed to appreciate the Lubianka's vital mission and viewed service in the VCheka as humiliating and degrading. Spokesmen for the VCheka, in turn, had nothing but contempt for those comrades who, as one of them put it, "expect others to do all the dirty work necessary for establishing the new Communist order which they can then enter with unstained hands and clean starched collars."[37]

Dzerzhinsky and his aides worked feverishly to uncover and smash the plots that were daily hatched by the Bolshevik's internal foes, but they fully realized that their best endeavors would not be successful unless the proliferating secret police apparatus could be staffed with sufficient numbers of politically reliable cadres. Faced with what seems to have been a widespread reluctance to volunteer for service in the secret police, the VCheka chiefs had to appeal for reinforcements to the supreme organs of state power. In late April 1918, the chairman of the VCheka addressed an urgent message to the Soviet government requesting an infusion of proven comrades for work in his organization. The VCheka, Dzerzhinsky pointed out, had assumed the difficult task of struggling against all the internal enemies of the revolution. Up until this moment and to the limits of their strength, the Chekists had "firmly and unflinchingly" discharged their duties. But now, "owing to internal and external conditions," Dzerzhinsky added, "there stands before us the prospect of a colossal increase in [VCheka] work both in volume and in intensity." It was entirely possible that "the very existence of the Soviet Republic would depend on the measures taken by the VCheka." Therefore, Dzerzhinsky concluded:

> We ask, comrades, that you size up the situation intelligently . . . and respond to us with brotherly support by sending new workers to our Commission.
>
> We realize that you are not rich in workers either, but we are still confident that the present situation gives us the right to expect that, even at the expense of some of your strength, you will not refuse to aid us by providing the essential reinforcements from among the most ideologically responsible comrades for the strenuous but necessary work of defending the new order of our workers' revolution.[38]

The Central Committee of the Bolshevik Party responded favorably to his appeal and resolved to "reinforce the Commission with new comrades."[39] One of the new comrades was Martyn Ivanovich Latsis (1888–1938), a Latvian-born farm laborer's son with many years of experience in the revolutionary underground. Latsis was to earn a reputation as one of Dzerzhinsky's right-hand men, serving as a member of the Collegium of the VCheka and as chairman of the All-Ukrainian Cheka. He also acquired a measure of literary renown as the most prolific chronicler of VCheka exploits during the Civil War.

After two full years of relentless struggle on the internal front, the VCheka was still plagued by a shortage of reliable manpower. On December 24, 1919, the Bolshevik Central Committee was obliged to issue an appeal, addressed to all provincial and district Party committees, urging that "the most tested and firm Communists" be sent to work in the Extraordinary Commissions. Declaring that the task of the Chekas was to "sweep out with an iron broom all signs of treason, sabotage, malfeasance, and speculation," the Central Committee reminded the local Party organizations that "positive results" could be achieved "only when all responsible posts [in the Chekas] are occupied by Communists—

fully conscious, unyielding fighters for the power of the workers and peasants." Unfortunately, many important positions continued to be filled by "non-Party People." Work in the secret police, it seemed, imposed special hardships on Communist Chekists. All too often they found themselves isolated from the general life of the Communist Party. The pressure of work made it difficult for many Communist Chekists to discharge such basic obligations as attendance at Party meetings. The local Party committees, in their eagerness to correct this regrettable byproduct of service in the Chekas, were only making matters worse by their ill-considered practice of recalling Communist Chekists and assigning them to less demanding duties. This could no longer be tolerated since it only further depleted the already scarce supply of necessary personnel. The Central Committee sought to correct the situation by increasing the number of Communists working in the Chekas and by making it more difficult to remove them:

> In the first place the greatest number of steadfast, fully responsible comrades must immediately be sent to work in all Cheka departments in order to assure that responsible posts are filled by Communists.
> In the second place, during subsequent Party mobilizations in no case should commissars, intelligence agents, investigators or members of Cheka collegiums be mobilized . . . without the consent of the respective Cheka collegium and without replacing those mobilized [for other duties] with equally qualified workers.[40]

Dzerzhinsky's appeals for reinforcements were echoed by Cheka and Party officials in outlying areas. From Nikolaev Province came word that "the counterrevolutionary forces are well organized" but the provincial Cheka "has no people."[41] The general picture was no different in the Melitopol district of Ekaterinoslav Province, where the local Party committee heard a report from Cheka officials in April 1919, on the insufficient number of Communist workers in their organization. The decision of the Party committee was to "assign good workers from the Party to the Cheka."[42] And in June 1920, the Central Committee of the Ukrainian Communist Party announced that uprisings in the rear of the Red Army and acts of espionage and provocation masterminded by the "Polish bourgeoisie" had created a dangerous situation that required an immediate response from the Cheka. The success of the Cheka's struggle against counterrevolution depended, in turn, upon an awareness that participation in this struggle was the "most important obligation imposed by membership in the Party." The Ukrainian Party chiefs added:

> While the responbility for the success of the struggle against counter-revolution belongs in a formal sense to the Cheka, in point of fact the responsibility rests with our Party. This is why all provincial Party organizations must, on the one hand, establish closer ties with the Chekas, and, on the other hand, assign workers to them, especially in those departments which conduct intelligence operations.[43]

Although the secret police, with its avowedly terroristic mission, was not a likely candidate for designation as the most beloved of all Soviet institutions, one still wonders what caused so many otherwise steadfast Communists, whose courage and dedication to the cause were beyond question, to shun service in the organization called upon to defend the very existence of the Soviet government and the ruling Communist Party. The prominent Chekist Yakov Peters expressed a point of view undoubtedly shared by other denizens of the Lubianka when he wrote that some Communists had failed to grasp the fundamental difference between the VCheka and its predecessor, the despised Tsarist Okhrana:

> The deeds of the Tsarist secret agents who had fought against the proletariat, searched them, sent them to Siberia, imprisoned them, and sent them to the gallows—all this remained fresh in the memory of every Communist. And here a new power was being organized, the power of the workers and peasants, and once again there were searches, arrests, and violence.
>
> To many there was no clear difference between the repressions of the past and present . . . . Many did not understand that the October days did not solve the question of the class struggle, that this struggle had only begun, that the enemy was not asleep, but only in hiding, gaining strength; that therefore there was no time for sentimental dreaming—the enemy had to be finished off. They did not understand that the situation was extremely grave—the country devastated and hungry—and that the proletariat and workers as a whole would not immediately understand the revolution completely. All these factors inclined many to be so sentimental that they only reluctantly entered the service of the VCheka and only reluctantly took part in searches, arrests, and the conduct of investigations. A long period of struggle and

defeat was needed before every revolutionary clearly recognized that
revolution is not made in silk gloves, that where there is war there are
casualties.[44]

Peters thus ascribed the low esteem in which the VCheka was
held to the squeamishness of his fellow revolutionaries who stubbornly refused to accept the necessity of such an organ in the
armamentarium of the proletarian dictatorship.

A factor not mentioned by Peters was the deep-rooted preju-
dice shared by Russians of the better sort against employment in
the police, an institution that had long had a reputation as one of
the most corrupt and vilest of all branches of government service.
Then, too, the Chekists themselves bore a heavy responsibility
for the wall of revulsion and fear that quickly came to surround
the Lubianka and its local outposts. Dzerzhinsky wanted his
Chekists to be above all loyal servants of the Communist Party
and "not specialists in arrest."[45] But such sentiments did little
to dispel the VCheka's well-earned reputation for ruthless repression, a reputation deliberately cultivated by the publication
of lethal warnings to the public and seemingly endless lists of arrested and executed. How hypnotized some Chekists were by the
virtually unlimited power bestowed upon them may be judged by
a speech that Gregory Zinoviev, the head of the Petrograd Communist Party organization, delivered to a conference of local
Chekists in 1918. Zinoviev pointed to the "internal life" of the
local Chekas "and noted with Communist straightforwardness
the undesirable phenomenon of controversies concerning what is
higher in state work. He gave as an example one Cheka in which
the question arose as to whether or not it could, in case of need,
arrest the Council of People's Commissars. . . . Such a Cheka
forgets the principle of internal discipline upon which the Communist Party is based."[46]

Moreover, deliberate efforts were made from the outset to
isolate the Chekists from the rest of the population. In the more
secure Soviet strongholds like Moscow and Petrograd, the
Chekists lived in their own compounds where they had special
restaurants, shops, and recreational facilities. In outlying areas it
was customary for Chekist contingents—well aware of the hatred
they engendered among the local population and the fate that
would doubtless await them in the event of a successful anti-

Bolshevik takeover—to sequester themselves behind barbed wire and machine guns where they carried on like the fighting monks of an embattled order.

The striking number of non-Russians in the ranks of the VCheka made its isolation from the rest of society even more pronounced. Foreigners and nonethnic Russians, in particular Poles, Latvians, and Jews, constituted a significant percentage of those employed by the secret police in the frontal zones and at the center. Not only was the chairman of the VCheka a non-Russian, but so were many of his closest collaborators—Latsis, Peters, Menzhinsky, and Unshlikht, to name just a few. Indeed, the Moscow Cheka employed so many Latvians during the Civil War that it came to be known as "the Lettish colony" and a publication of the Left Socialist Revolutionary Party observed: "Letts flock to the Extraordinary Commission of Moscow as folk emigrate to America, and for the same reason—to make their fortune."[47] It was no wonder, therefore, that many native Russians came to view the secret police as an alien occupying force.

In many parts of Bolshevik-occupied Russia, according to a well-informed secret police defector, foreigners were generally the only people who could be trusted. In the absence of documentary proof that the recruitment of non-Russians for service in the secret police was part of a deliberate policy, this statement may explain why they were so conspicuous in its ranks.[48] Cheka recruitment patterns in the Ukraine offer a good illustration of the preference for staffing the secret police with nonethnic Russians. In the Ukraine the Bolsheviks faced a basically hostile population whose loyalties belonged for the most part either to the White Guards or to the various Ukrainian nationalist groups that appeared on the scene during the turbulent years of internal strife. One major exception were the Jews. A long history of persecution and discrimination had driven many Jews, especially among the educated class, into the revolutionary movement. Jews were not only conspicuous in the general Soviet administration of the Ukraine but in the Ukrainian Cheka apparatus as well. About 70 percent of the Kiev Chekists, including its chairman, secretary, commandant, and the chiefs of several departments, were said to have been Jews.[49] (A defector who fled the Soviet Union after

World War II and who was familiar with government operations in Belorussia, an area with a large Jewish population, reported that as late as the 1940s many of the top generals of the secret police were still Jewish.)[50] The Jewish Chekists were not foreigners in the same sense as the Poles, Letts, and Chinese whose contributions to Bolshevik victory on the internal front have been chronicled in Soviet writings on the period, but their traditional exclusion from the mainstream of Ukrainian life caused them to be viewed as aliens nevertheless.

The favored recruitment of foreigners and nonethnic Russians not only contributed to the social isolation of the secret police, but also helped assure that the severity of its repressive measures would not be mitigated by feelings of sympathy or pity. There was no better way to guarantee that the Chekists would not be diverted from the strict discharge of their duties by feelings of compassion for those whom they were called upon to arrest, interrogate, and not infrequently execute than to ensure that the jailers and executioners shared as little as possible in the way of family or community ties with their victims.[51]

Sometimes Dzerzhinsky was able to make special use of his fellow non-Russian Chekists. Recently published documents from the Soviet archives offer a case in point. In July 1920, Red Army troops turned back the invading Polish army of General Pilsudsky, and the Soviet government, in a burst of revolutionary enthusiasm, ordered an advance into the enemy's territory in an attempt to spread the world revolution beyond Russia's frontiers with bayonets. The Bolsheviks even set up what they hoped would become Poland's postrevolutionary Communist government. It was composed of several Polish-born Communists who had already demonstrated their talents in Russia's own revolution and civil war. Among them was Felix Dzerzhinsky, who was appointed a member of the Provisional Revolutionary Committee of Poland on July 30, 1920.[52] One of Dzerzhinsky's special tasks, for which his experience highly qualified him, was to rid the territory occupied by the Red Army of spies and saboteurs. To assist him in this important work Dzerzhinsky called upon the services of his fellow Polish Chekists. With the approval of the Central Committee of the Communist Party, all Poles working in Cheka organs were placed under Dzerzhinsky's command. On August 1, 1920,

Dzerzhinsky issued the following order: "All Polish Chekists in Moscow must be sent to . . . Minsk for distribution to Medved [Chief of the Special Department of the Western Front, a VCheka organ responsible for security in the Red Army] and us."[53] Dzerzhinsky believed that the invasion of Poland was "a turning point" that would "decide the destiny of the world."[54] He and his comrades in the Provisional Revolutionary Committee of Poland came to within thirty miles of Warsaw before the Red Army was defeated. Toward the end of August the Soviet offensive was turned back, and there was nothing Dzerzhinsky or his Polish Chekists could do about it. By August 25, Dzerzhinsky was back in Minsk, and he never returned to his native land.

The secret police was adept at terrorizing people, but this alienated it still more from the anonymous mass of Russian workers and peasants whose interests it was supposedly defending. Its almost unlimited power, its reputation for ruthlessness, its self-imposed separation from the general population, and the presence of large numbers of foreigners and nonethnic Russians in its ranks all contributed to the low esteem in which the VCheka and its local organs were held by Communists and non-Communists alike.

The reputation of the secret police was further tarnished by its employment of many people whose morals and scruples left much to be desired. When Latsis declared that a primary condition for the success of the Cheka's mission was that its members be Communists above political and personal suspicion, "of steadfast character, unswerving will, unbiased view . . . , and of good reputation," he was setting forth conditions as he would have liked to see them rather than conditions as they were.[55] For it was conceded that by a kind of natural selection the VCheka and its local branches attracted men and women whose personalities were marked by suspicion, embitterment, and a strong dose of sadism. Thus, Akhmetov, an official of the Kharkov Provincial Cheka, stated in December 1919 that a lack of trustworthy Party workers had made it possible for "unsatisfactory elements" to find a home in the Cheka with a resulting increase in the frequency of "undesirable occurrences." To make matters even worse, the older and more reliable members of the Cheka, considering that their obligation to the proletarian cause had been met, were asking to be relieved of their duties. Akhmetov urged that the local Party organization launch a thorough purge of the Kharkov Provincial Cheka in order to rid it of this blight.[56] A few months later, the chairman of the Ekaterinoslav Provincial Cheka reported that many "criminal elements" had penetrated the Chekas in his region. Their "improper actions," he said, "often caused unfavorable criticism to be brought to the door of the Cheka."[57]

Comrade Deich of the Saratov Cheka was one such unsavory character whose exploits were given wide publicity in the pages of *Pravda*. Deich was said to be a former member of the Bund, an organization of Jewish socialists, who had lived for a time in America. He returned to Russia after the revolution, joined the Bolshevik Party, and quickly found employment in the Saratov Cheka. He was described as an imposing and colorful figure who liked to prance around town on a white stallion wearing a wide-brimmed Mexican sombrero that he had brought from America and sporting three revolvers and a hand grenade at his belt. "He strikes terror into the bourgeoisie," wrote *Pravda's* correspondent, "and is an unprecedented success with the ladies. He shoots people with his own hand, firing two revolvers at once." Comrade Deich boasted, "I have found a way to kill two birds with one stone." Eventually removed from his post in the Extraordinary Commission for "extraordinary cruelty," Deich became chief of the Saratov militia. His first order was that all militiamen wear sombreros (and indeed ten thousand were sent for). Convinced that what was most lacking in the wartorn country was a sufficient number of joyous celebrations, Deich held parades in Saratov at every opportunity. The marching militia, with their sombreros adorned with red ribbons, and Comrade Deich astride his white steed with his revolvers and hand grenades were truly a sight to behold. "Anyone who has not seen Comrade Deich's parades," remarked a local resident, "has not seen anything really grand."[58]

Dzerzhinsky was aware that the hasty recruitment of large numbers of secret police personnel, often without even a perfunctory review of their fitness, made it possible for many unstable and unwholesome individuals to find a home for themselves in the Chekas. But he made use of them anyway because he knew that such types made willing Chekists. Tales abound of the cruelties perpetrated by such notorious Cheka torturers and executioners as the Letts, Maga and Ryba of Moscow, Artabekov of Ekaterinodar, Kalichenko of Odessa, and Shulman of Tiflis. There were, in addition, hundreds of small-town Cheka potentates, and they yielded nothing in bestiality to the big-city executioners.[59] It was the incorruptibility of men like Dzerzhinsky that provided the VCheka with its institutional strength and integrity. Unfortunately for the reputation of the secret police, however, there were few men with Dzerzhinsky's brand of ruthless idealism but many Chekas. The expanding secret police apparatus required more and more henchmen—that vast corps of informers, interrogators, and executioners—who could be trusted to carry out any order without question or remorse, men, as one contemporary put it, "strong in muscle and quick on the trigger."[60]

It was also widely recognized that a post in the VCheka apparatus could be highly profitable. Not only did Chekists receive extra allotments of food and clothing, but confiscated goods often ended up in their possession as well. Thus, a high-ranking Ukrainian official noted that one of the most serious defects in the local Cheka apparatus was the great number of persons who entered its ranks, not to fight for Soviet power as "honorable revolutionaries," but rather "exclusively from mercenary motives."[61] Realizing that this kind of predatory behavior only further alienated the populace, secret police officials issued orders to curb the plundering. In April 1919, Martyn Latsis reported to Lenin that one of the first steps he took upon being appointed chief of the All-Ukrainian Cheka was to forbid his men from taking "possession during arrests of anything besides material evidence. But our Russian man reasons: did I not deserve those pants and shoes which until now were worn by the bourgeoisie? They were earned by my labor. This means I can take them for my own. There is no harm in that." It was this kind of reasoning, Latsis said, that had led to the "frequent infractions" he and other leading Chekists in the Ukraine were trying to eliminate.[62] And as the following VCheka order dated September 5, 1918, indicates, it was not only rank-and-rifle Chekists who were prone to violate the norms of revolutionary legality:

A mass of information is being brought to us that many members of the Chekas, including chairmen and treasurers, are taking for themselves a considerable amount of money that belongs to the Commissions.

Considering such a situation to be abnormal and intolerable, we therefore order all Commissions and Cheka commissars, without exception, to obtain (either by confiscating or requisitioning from the bourgeoisie) steel safes for the storage of money belonging to the [Soviet] Republic and assigned to the Commissions for spending.

Those guilty of noncompliance with this order were promised a trial before a revolutionary tribunal.[63]

The situation was apparently not as serious in Moscow and Petrograd, where the supervision of VCheka and Communist Party officials was able to prevent excessive abuses. But the farther the Chekas were from the scrutiny of the central leadership, the fewer the controls and the more dishonorable the Chekists were likely to become. In a moment of candor Latsis wrote that work in the Extraordinary Commissions, conducted "in an atmosphere of physical coercion, attracts corrupt and outright criminal elements who, profiting from their positions as Cheka agents, blackmail and extort, filling their own pockets." Even the most moral and scrupulous persons could be affected by prolonged exposure to the physical and psychological strains of Chekist life: "However honest a man is, however pure his heart, work in the Cheka, which is carried on with almost unlimited rights and under conditions greatly affecting the nervous system, begins to tell. Few escape the effect of the conditions under which they work." It was for this reason that Latsis laid down as a cardinal rule of Cheka procedure that employees be afforded frequent rests and opportunities to work in less strenuous fields.[64]

While the Chekist high command had a clear understanding of its mission, the same could not always be said of many provincial and district-level Cheka commissars who had not yet become habituated to the self-discipline and unconditional obedience that was expected of them by their superiors in the Lubianka. Evidence that malfeasance, misfeasance, and nonfeasance were reaching epidemic proportions throughout the secret police apparatus led, in the summer of 1918, to the establishment of the

Liaison Department of the VCheka to "regulate, instruct, and direct" the work of the network of provincial Chekas. Although the "absolute subordination of lower [Cheka] organs to higher" ones was the organizational principle applicable to all secret police agencies, the officials of the VCheka's liaison department quickly discovered that "separatism and distinctive local methods of struggle and forms of punishment" existed in many provincial Chekas.[65]

Something was clearly amiss, for instance, in the Nizhegorod Cheka. Its liaison department, with a skeletal staff of three, was hardly in a position to discharge its important supervisory duties. At the same time, the economic department, which was entrusted with keeping Cheka accounts and handling confiscated and requisitioned goods, had reached elephantine proportions with sixty employees. This lopsided and completely unacceptable division of labor strongly suggested that some of the employees were using their positions to line their own pockets, and, from the point of view of their reliability, were proper candidates for a firing squad or a prison cell.[66]

On August 30, 1918, in a circular to all provincial and district Chekas, the chief of the VCheka's liaison department noted the disturbing fact that "despite the instructions worked out and adopted by the [first] All-Russian Conference of Extraordinary Commissions and circulated among all Chekas, many provincial Commissions are completely ignoring these decisions and consider them not binding on themselves." Secret police organs in some towns were not even using the prescribed appellation. (The Chekists of Perm named their organization the committee for the Struggle Against Counterrevolution while their counterparts in Saratov called themselves the Extraordinary Staff.) In other localities Chekists had established "all-powerful departments" not envisaged by the VCheka leadership. Such disregard of orders was considered by the Lubianka as a "completely intolerable" form of "disorganization." All local Chekas were admonished to be "strictly guided" in the future by VCheka directives.[67]

The persistent and all too frequent signs of a dilatory and sometimes even defiant attitude on the part of the Chekists in the provinces—some of whom conducted themselves in such a man-

ner as to suggest that they were answerable to no one—
demonstrated the urgent need for other devices to assure compliance with superior decisions. One of the supplementary
methods adopted by the VCheka for the coordination of activities
and the dissemination of information was to call periodic
conferences of representatives from local Chekas. Between 1918
and 1920, four all-Russian conferences of Extraordinary Commissions are known to have taken place in Moscow. They provided a convenient forum for the airing of local problems and the
transmission of important instructions. (Lenin himself delivered a
lengthy speech to the Fourth Conference of Provincial Extraordinary Commissions in February 1920.) Similar convocations of
Chekists were held from time to time at the regional and provincial levels.[68]

Naturally, the VCheka chiefs were empowered to take
whatever measures they deemed necessary to eliminate malfeasance or any other defects that appeared in the local secret
police organs. According to the "Regulation on the Local Extraordinary Commissions" the VCheka had "the right to conduct
emergency inspections of provincial Chekas and take appropriate
measures to eliminate abuses and derelictions of duty."[69] On occasion Dzerzhinsky dispatched his own hand-picked emissaries
to fortify the local Extraordinary Commissions and strike fear
into the hearts of their errant commissars. Such was the task of
the prominent Chekist Mikhail Kedrov, whose armored train
roamed far across the Soviet heartland in the summer of 1919.
The peripatetic journey of the "Kedrov Commission" was
prompted by the full-scale offensive that General Denikin had
launched against the Bolsheviks in May of that year. Denikin's
troops swept through forty-eight provinces of southern and
central Russia and confronted the Bolsheviks with what Lenin
frankly described as their "most critical moment." As a plenipotentiary of the VCheka, Kedrov was given special powers "to
intensify the activities of the fighting agencies of the Vcheka in
the front area, and to reorganize them in the sense of adapting
them to the needs of the front." Kedrov's train passed through
the provinces of Voronezh, Kursk, Orel, Tambov, and Smolensk,
"everywhere infusing a fresh spirit into that 'land of Nod' which
is to be observed in all Soviet institutions as well as the Chekas."

According to Kedrov, the main task of his mission was "to conduct a purge of the departments of the Chekas of hangers-on not only of a counterrevolutionary but also of a criminal character." Kedrov and his entourage turned up evidence of serious abuses in several provincial Chekas. The Kursk Provincial Cheka was particularly infested with undesirable elements, and a thorough purge was required to eliminate them. "Many representatives of the Chekas," Kedrov said, "were turned over to the courts and several were shot." Nor did the plenipotentiary of the VCheka show mercy to cowardly deserters or those who inflicted wounds upon themselves in order to avoid military service, a number of whom were also shot along the route of his train. By the time the Kedrov Commission completed its journey, hundreds of suspicious persons had been arrested and dozens executed.[70]

The undeniable presence of "alien elements" in the VCheka apparatus did not prevent leading Communist Party officials from bestowing lavish public praise on the secret police at every opportunity. In Lenin's opinion, the VCheka was "magnificently organized" and its cadres indispensable for the preservation of revolutionary order.[71] Gregory Zinoviev, the Bolshevik proconsul in Petrograd, declared that the Cheka was "the pride and joy of the Communist Party," and Latsis, who never tired of extolling the virtues of the secret police, boasted that the Cheka was "the best that Soviet institutions can evolve."[72] The chairman of the VCheka was also fond of reiterating his belief that Chekists had to be men with "cool heads, warm hearts, and clean hands." In a speech to his colleagues on the fifth anniversary of the founding of the VCheka, Dzerzhinsky said: "Those of you who have become hardened, those of you whose hearts cannot relate sensitively and attentively to the sufferings of prisoners, should leave this organization. Here, more than anyplace else, one must have a heart that is kind and sensitive to the suffering of others."[73]

Faced, nevertheless, with the realization that many of his subordinates were murderers, thieves, and swindlers, Dzerzhinsky sometimes saw no solution but to shoot the worst offenders. There were many Chekists who, in Gorky's words, made "their way into power like foxes, used it like wolves, and when caught, perished like dogs."[74] Such was the fate, for instance, of Chudin, a member of the Collegium of the Petrograd Extraordinary Commission. According to the newspaper account, at some unspecified time in 1919 Chudin had "established an intimate connection" with Nina Svobodina-Sidorova, the mistress of an arrested speculator. The woman pleaded with Chudin to intervene on behalf of her lover and attain his release. Although Chudin did not accept the 25,000-rouble bribe that was offered to him, he also did not arrest Nina Svobodina-Sidorova or report the matter to the Cheka, but rather continued his "criminal connection" with her. For this and other related transgressions of Cheka morality, a six-man investigating commission headed by Dzerzhinsky sentenced Chudin to be shot. Nina Svobodina-Sidorova and her hapless lover were also shot for their involvement in attempted bribery.[75]

Chudin's fate demonstrated that Dzerzhinsky could be as harsh toward delinquent members of his own organization as he was toward certified class enemies. Yet not all violators of the VCheka code of conduct suffered the same penalty. We have evidence that on at least two occasions even the most brazen acts of theft and extortion—when committed by particularly valuable agents—failed to ignite the wrath of the chairman of the VCheka, but, quite the contrary, found him testifying in court on behalf of the accused. The story of the Chekist Berezin is such a case. Berezin began his career with the secret police as an agent of the Petrograd Cheka. As early as January 1918 this cheerful representative of the Workers' and Peasants' Government had been brought to trial for the murder of a prisoner whom he was interrogating. The trial was interrupted by the evacuation of the court to Moscow, and a verdict was never reached because the files in the case mysteriously disappeared. In March 1918, Berezin was working for the VCheka in Moscow, specializing in the arrest of speculators. He made his headquarters in the back room of the Vienna Restaurant. From morning to night, according to witnesses, informers and other shady characters filled his office to denounce speculators and partake of the food and liquor that was always in abundant supply.

What brought Berezin to the attention of the judicial authorities for the second time was the unexplained disappearance of two hundred bottles of rum and brandy that he had confiscated. The Moscow Revolutionary Tribunal requested Berezin to appear for a hearing, but he refused. It was only by force that he was finally brought to court. The decision of the tribunal was to detain Berezin in jail pending the completion of its investigation, but not even prison could hold him for long. A few days later it was discovered that not only was Berezin inexplicably at liberty, but he had also resummed his work in the VCheka. A third arrest followed, and new details came to the surface.

Dzerzhinsky himself appeared as a character witness for Berezin. The chairman of the VCheka was willing to admit that Berezin had a very short temper as well as a fondness for "cheap effects"—things like gold rings, chains, and watches. Moreover, it turned out that Dzerzhinsky had been responsible for Berezin's sudden and unexpected release from prison. It seemed that while in custody Berezin claimed to have overheard some "White Guard inmates" discuss a planned attack on Lenin's life, and he dutifully passed this information on to his jailers. Rumors of this kind were common in those days, and Berezin's information proved to be false. Dzerzhinsky nevertheless considered this episode sufficient proof of Berezin's reliability and ordered his release. The Moscow Revolutionary Tribunal meanwhile decided to continue its investigation of Berezin's alleged past and present criminal deeds. Unfortunately, we cannot know the final outcome of the inquiry since no further mention of the case ever appeared in the Soviet press.[76]

The Berezin case, with its revelations of wrong-doing among lower-level Cheka operatives, was soon overshadowed by the more spectacular trial of Uspenskaia, a twenty-two-year-old VCheka secret informer, and F. M. Kosyrev, a member of the Control-Inspection Board of the VCheka. This trial, which was conducted before the Supreme Revolutionary Tribunal, disclosed the presence of corruption in the highest ranks of the secret police apparatus. The young woman Uspenskaia was said by the prosecutor to be a typical representative of the formerly privileged class of society who, lacking moral stamina and unable to adjust to the new order of things, had turned to a life of crime under the guise of a Chekist to maintain her "material situation." After all, the prosecutor asked, why should a clever and unprincipled young woman like Uspenskaia accept employment at 500 roubles a month in the Commissariat of Trade or some other government office when she could get her hands on thousands of roubles in one day by the pitiless extortion of relatives of VCheka prisoners? Uspenskaia admitted that she first offered her services to the VCheka as a secret informer only from greed. Paid for on a "piecework" basis, her job was to locate the whereabouts of hidden caches of speculative goods. The understanding was that she would share half of all the proceeds from any confiscated goods with one Viktorov, another VCheka functionary also under arrest.

Soon Uspenskaia decided to supplement her income by means of extortion. Her first victim was the sister of an arrested merchant. The distraught woman agreed to pay Uspenskaia 5,000 roubles upon learning that she was in a position to "arrange things" for her brother. On another occasion, Uspenskaia approached a woman named Meshcherskaia, the wife of an industrialist held by the VCheka, and offered to gain his release for 17,000 roubles. This undertaking could not be consummated, however, without the active involvement of several members of the VCheka's Control-Inspection Board, which had been set up in the fall of 1918 to examine complaints and abuses connected with the work of all departments and persons working in the VCheka. (The Control-Inspection Board was authorized to eliminate any irregularities it uncovered by reversing the decisions of all VCheka organs with the exception of the VCheka Collegium itself.) As it turned out, four of the five members of this important body had questionable pasts, and one—F. M. Kosyrev—was a convicted murderer. During the trial it was brought out that Kosyrev had been sentenced to ten years at hard labor in 1908 for murder and robbery, a sentence he avoided by escaping to Siberia. Again in 1915, Kosyrev was arrested, tried, and convicted on another charge of robbery only to be freed after the revolution by posing as a political prisoner. Kosyrev ended up in Moscow where his non-Party status did not prevent him from gaining employment in the VCheka, working at first as an investigator. His feats in this capacity attracted the favorable attention of Dzerzhinsky himself, who, having great confidence in Kosyrev, personally appointed him a member of the Control-Inspection Board on September 15, 1918.

When Kosyrev and several of his cohorts on the Control-Inspection Board became involved in the Meshcherskaia affair, the price for the release of the imprisoned man jumped to 600,000 roubles (250,000 in advance, with the balance due upon his return to freedom). This ambitious extortion plan, concealed "behind the mask of socialism," was finally brought to light by the lawyer Yakulov. Dzerzhinsky, it seems, had given his personal promise that Yakulov would be protected if anyone "interested in the case" tried to have him arrested in order to prevent more disclosures. Yakulov was soon arrested nonetheless, allegedly for taking a large bribe himself. It was later admitted in court that Yakulov's sudden arrest was in fact a "misunderstanding" caused by misinformation supplied to the VCheka by "interested parties" anxious to silence the lawyer.

Undoubtedly the most sensational aspect of the proceeding was the appearance made by Dzerzhinsky on behalf of the accused. The chairman of the VCheka denied any knowledge of Kosyrev's criminal past and praised him as an "experienced and conscientious investigator." Dzerzhinsky hoped that Kosyrev would not "fall victim to the political passions which have recently flared up around the VCheka" (see Chapter 6). The Supreme Revolutionary Tribunal was not moved by Dzerzhinsky's appeal but agreed with the demand of the prosecutor that the VCheka had to be purged of those who "disgraced the revolution." Kosyrev was accordingly sentenced to death and Uspenskaia to five years in prison.[77]

The Soviet secret police had been established to uncover counterrevolutionaries, spies, saboteurs, and other enemies of the people, and, despite widespread bribery and corruption, uncover them it did—over 128,000 in central Russia alone during the first two years of its operations. (It was readily admitted that not all of those arrested were actually guilty of crimes against the revolutionary order; over 54,000 were said to have been released after a preliminary investigation.)[78] Still, the mere act of taking so many tens of thousands of people into custody depended upon the proper functioning of a fairly complex internal machinery for the detection, arrest, interrogation, and punishment of suspected counterrevolutionaries. The creation of this machinery was one of the major preoccupations of the VCheka leadership. A first-hand description of how this internal machinery worked in an important Cheka center, from the time a suspect was arrested until the final determination of his fate, was contained in the testimony of Mikhail Ivanovich Bolerosov, an official of the Kiev Cheka. It is clear from Bolerosov's testimony that a prescribed procedure did exist for the daily routine of search, arrest, interrogation, and punishment but that it left ample opportunity for Chekist misconduct.

Any Cheka operative could on his own initiative arrest a suspected enemy of Soviet power at any time or place without special authorization. However, most search and arrest operations of any magnitude were set in motion only after the Cheka's staff of intelligence agents and secret informers had provided the necessary incriminating information. A search or arrest order was then filled out, signed by the Cheka's top officials, either the chairman, the deputy chairman, or the heads of the various departments, and stamped with the Cheka's round seal. The actual conduct of a search or arrest was the responsibility of the secret-operational department and its staff of Cheka commissars, who were often accompanied on their missions by Cheka troops. According to regulations, a search or arrest had to be conducted in the presence of a representative of the house committee or a neighbor who was expected to serve as a witness. The Cheka commissar in charge had to complete a brief report (in triplicate) right at the scene and have the witnesses sign it. Prisoners and all material evidence were then taken under guard to Cheka headquarters.

As we have seen, an almost total lack of accounting procedures in the handling of confiscated goods made it possible for enterprising Chekists to enrich themselves with almost no risk whatsoever. Small packages habitually disappeared without a trace; the employees of the Kiev Cheka customarily turned over to the state treasury only the least valuable bank notes while keeping the more valuable coins; wine and food went straight to the Cheka commune.

Meanwhile, the fate of a prisoner rested in the hands of the Cheka investigator assigned to his case. It was the investigator's task not only to ascertain the guilt or innocence of the accused but also to "indicate, propose, recommend, and sometimes even insist upon a particular form of punishment." It was normal procedure for an investigator to interrogate his prisoner before reaching a conclusion, frequently resorting to torture and beatings in the process. But an interrogation was not mandatory. Decisions were sometimes reached on the basis of the investigator's own "intuition" without any face-to-face contact at all. The Cheka's juridical department met twice a week to review the work of the investigators. The staff of the department was not authorized to inflict punishment on the accused, but it could reach one of several preliminary verdicts. It could decide to close the case and release the prisoner for lack of evidence, to transfer the case to a revolutionary tribunal, or to forward the case to the Cheka collegium for final sentencing, often with a recommendation that the death penalty be applied. (At this point in the processing of a case the more unscrupulous Chekists found great opportunities for extortion. It usually took several days before all clerical work could be completed in the cases of persons ordered released by the juridical department. Chekists informed of these decisions sometimes took advantage of the ensuing delay to approach the relatives of the prisoners and offer to have them freed for a substantial sum.)

At its meetings the all-powerful Cheka collegium not only decided the ultimate fate of prisoners but also dealt with all kinds of routine administrative, organizational, and financial questions. These sessions, which were usually accompanied by food, drink, and friendly banter, were closed to all except the Cheka's top echelons. After having heard the reports and recommendations of his staff, the chairman of the Cheka would ask if anybody else had any questions. If there were none, the chairman would call for a vote to fix sentences for the accused. If a majority decision was not reached on the first ballot, another vote would be taken. Death sentences were commonplace and were promptly implemented by the staff of the commandant's office. The condemned learned of their fate usually about 1 A.M., the time when executions were normally carried out. They were called out of their cells "with things," that is, with all their meager possessions, and escorted to a shed, where they were ordered to undress. Death came quickly from a shot in the back of the head at point-blank range.[79]

A confidential report prepared early in 1920 by an independent government commission sent to investigate the "political physiognomy" of the All-Ukrainian Cheka, next to the VCheka the largest in the country, confirms that the internal mechanism for the orderly conduct of Cheka business was plagued by serious defects. The commission began its report with a review of the organization of the All-Ukrainian Cheka. Martyn Latsis, at the time the chairman of the Cheka, was said to be the "sole responsible person"; other Chekists occupying important positions took their orders from him and were answerable only to him. This concentration of power in the hands of one man was judged to be harmful to the functioning of the Cheka. Not only did the chairman and his closest aides make important decisions without consulting anyone, but they also manifested a contemptuous attitude toward the rank-and-file Chekists. This was said to be having a demoralizing effect "as a result of which a lack of unity is noticeable in the work of the Cheka as well as a kind of animosity among the comrade Communists." Moreover, it was impossible for the chairman alone to direct all aspects of secret police operations. The predictable result, in the opinion of the commission, was that a disturbing degree of "chaos" had come to characterize the internal life of the Cheka:

> Employees in a majority of cases do not understand their duties and exceed their authority; scandalous practices occur during searches with things being taken away which should not be confiscated; arrested persons are beaten. Insults and threats of execution are directed at prisoners, etc. A lack of conscious discipline is in evidence both outside the walls of the Cheka as well as inside.

There was also evidence of great waste in the Cheka's financial management. Thus, for some reason, only eleven horses were available to the Chekists for transportation, and an enormous amount of money was spent daily on cab fares. In just the preceding ten days, for example, the operational department was said to have spent 18,000 roubles on cabs. Altogether, hundreds of thousands of roubles were dispersed by one or another Cheka department with only the most rudimentary accounting or supervision.

Even worse, "innocent citizens, workers, and even Communists" often ended up in the cells of the Cheka. It was common practice for prisoners to be held several days (and sometimes several weeks) at Cheka headquarters before being questioned and without an accusation being brought against them. An inspection of local prisons revealed that the majority of prisoners docketed to the All-Ukrainian Cheka also waited weeks before they found out what crime they were charged with. And not uncommonly, when they were finally brought before a Chekist interrogator, prisoners were beaten with ramrods and whips. Moreover, the commission added, "one seldom finds capitalists, bourgeoisie, and other such enemies of the Workers' Republic among the prisoners; but quite often one finds workers, Communists, and purely proletarian types."

A serious lack of coordination in Cheka clerical work was another source of confusion. There were prisoners whose files ended up in more than one department and who thereby became the subjects of two simultaneous investigations, with one department ordering their acquittal and the other finding them guilty of being counterrevolutionaries. In fact, persons were held by the Cheka without any material evidence at all. These and numerous other defects in the operations of the All-Ukrainian Cheka were said to be the result of a generally "defective organization," and to put things right the commission recommended a thorough plan of reorganization. Without a complete overhaul, the commission concluded, it would not be possible for the Cheka to accomplish the important tasks assigned by the revolutionary proletariat. Whether the commission's reorganization plan was accepted or implemented by the All-Ukrainian Cheka is not known.[80]

Surveying the vast terror machine that had evolved under the Lubianka's guidance and direction, the Chekist Peters noted with obvious pride on the second anniversary of the founding of the Soviet secret police: "The VCheka has established an enormous apparatus. All of Russia is covered with its network of provincial Chekas . . . and the entire apparatus works better every day."[81] True, there had been an initial period of administrative groping and uncertainty during which the VCheka sought to create suitable "organizational forms and methods of struggle." It was no wonder that mistakes had been made and that some scoundrels had managed to penetrate the apparatus. But despite the defects that annoyed its leaders, the nightmare years of domestic strife had given the VCheka ample opportunity to prove its value to the defense of the revolutionary order. In the hands of the VCheka's nationwide staff of agents and commissars, who were said by Latsis to number 31,000 in 1921, rested "the lives of the citizens of the Soviet Republic, the defense of Soviet power and the ruling Communist Party." The Chekists were everywhere because, as Latsis said, there was no aspect of Soviet life that was immune from the ruinous work of the counterrevolutionaries. The deadly enemies of the working class were to be found "in factories and plants, in Soviet institutions, in the armed forces, in the villages, and in the cities."[82] And wherever the danger of counterrevolution lurked, the punishing fist of the proletarian dictatorship had to be ready to strike it down.

3

In Defense of the Revolution

"There is no sphere of our life," boasted the Chekist Moroz, "where the Cheka does not have its eagle eye."[1] In a similar vein Martyn Latsis explained that "the sphere of the Extraordinary Commission's work is determined by the activity of the counterrevolutionary elements. And since there is no sphere of life that the counterrevolutionaries have not penetrated and that does not show evidence of their destructive work, the Extraordinary Commission must often intervene positively in all areas of life—in food supply, transportation, the Red Army and Navy, the militia, schools, foreign consulates, industry, distribution, and so on."[2] To safeguard the internal front against the constant threat of sabotage and counterrevolution, the VCheka created a number of specialized, or "functional," components that were even more vital to the defense of Soviet power than the network of provincial and district Chekas. By the end of the Civil War, there was hardly any significant or strategic aspect of Soviet life that escaped the surveillance of the secret police or was immune from its harsh methods of repression. The following pages examine the major functional components of the VCheka apparatus in the light of the contributions they made to Bolshevik victory on the internal front.

The Armed Forces of the VCheka

An especially urgent requirement of the newly established Bolshevik regime was to deploy an unquestionably loyal armed force to relieve the Red Army of the duty of quelling the many peasant revolts and other local disorders that flared up throughout the Soviet heartland between 1918 and 1921. Neither the Red Army, whose commanders complained that the discipline, training, and equipment of their troops suffered from such punitive campaigns, nor the local militia, whose rank and file tended to sympathize with the insurgents and often gave them support, could be relied upon to carry out these onerous but vital pacification duties. It was the VCheka that took up the challenge of putting into the field an armed force capable of crushing large-scale domestic unrest.

From the first days of the All-Russian Extraordinary Commission, Felix Dzerzhinsky showed a preference for staffing the secret police apparatus with politically reliable cadres drawn from the ranks of the military. One of Dzerzhinsky's first moves as chairman of the VCheka was to request Red Guard headquarters to provide his organization with "five to ten comrades . . . fully conscious of their mission as revolutionaries, and accessible to neither bribery nor corruption by the influence of gold" to staff a subdepartment to combat sabotage among bank officials.[3]

The first armed detachment of the VCheka was created in December 1917; it was composed of fifty Petrograd workers, who volunteered for service, and sixty soldiers from a bicycle battalion of the former Tsarist army. Later, on January 14, 1918, the Council of People's Commissars instructed Dzerzhinsky to organize a detachment of fighters from the ranks of politically reliable sailors to combat speculation. This detachment, we are told, "soon became involved in more than just the roundup of speculators and searches of illegal storehouses of food and manufactured goods." It also distinguished itself in operations aimed at destroying such counterrevolutionary organizations as the Black Dot and the White Cross.[4]

In the early spring of 1918, at the same time that steps were being taken to expand the network of secret police agencies in the provinces, efforts were also being made to consolidate the armed units at the disposal of the VCheka. On March 31, all the various VCheka armed detachments were unified into a single Fighting Detachment of the VCheka. By the end of April, the Fighting

Detachment included within its ranks 750 infantrymen (6 companies), 50 calvarymen, 60 machine gunners, 80 bicyclists *(samokatchiki),* and 3 armored vehicles.[5] The first major operation in which the detachment took part was the surprise attack on the Anarchist strongholds in Moscow on the night of April 11–12, 1918. Twelve Chekists were killed in this predawn battle, which involved the use of artillery and machine guns on both sides.

When the first All-Russian Conference of Extraordinary Commissions met in mid-June 1918, only a few local Chekas possessed their own armed detachments. Nevertheless, in another move toward greater centralization of control, the Conference endorsed a decision to unify all existing Cheka armed forces in the provinces and at the center into a new Special Corps of VCheka Troops *(Osobyi korpus voisk VChK)* to defend Soviet power from its internal enemies. A resolution on the Special Corps stated that it

> must be composed of well-disciplined and militarily competent people. It is to be composed exclusively of proletarian elements on the recommendation of professional unions, Party collectives, and factory organizations.
>
> . . . There must be iron revolutionary discipline and strictest centralization [of control] in the Corps.[6]

At first, the Special Corps of VCheka Troops was composed of volunteers. Those entering the ranks gave a written pledge to observe the strictest revolutionary discipline and to suppress without mercy any encroachments upon Soviet power. By the end of July, the Special Corps had already grown to thirty-five battalions, which were distributed as the situation demanded to the most important industrial centers and to regions where concentrated anti-Bolshevik strength posed the most serious threats.

A more detailed picture of the growing network of Special Corps of VCheka Troops is to be found in the "Regulation on the Formation of the Corps," published by the VCheka in September 1918.[7] The Corps, it was stated, "is under the complete direction of the All-Russian Extraordinary Commission in its struggle against counterrevolution, speculation, and abuses of office." The chief of staff of the Corps, who was appointed by the

VCheka, had responsibility for organizing, training, and directing the Corps, but orders relating to the movement of troops had to be countersigned by the chairman of the VCheka. In addition, "orders of the Staff to liquidate this or the other counterrevolutionary uprising must be signed by the Chairman of the VCheka, the head of the Liaison Department, and the Secretary."

The rank-and-file personnel of the Corps was to be recruited from "the workers and poorest peasants on the recommendation of [organizations of] the Communist Party (Bolsheviks), trade unions, factory committees, committees of the village poor, and also on the recommendation of two members of the Communist Party." Men from the ages of nineteen to thirty-six were eligible for service in the Special Corps; their pay was to be the same as that of Red Army soldiers. Upon entering the Corps, a new recruit pledged to serve at least six months, to follow all orders without exception, to observe the strictest revolutionary discipline, not to steal or rob, and "to be always of good cheer, steadfast and unflinching in the defense of Soviet power." The commanding officers of individual units of the Special Corps of VCheka Troops were to be nominated by the provincial Chekas and confirmed by the Staff of the Corps and the VCheka.

The "Regulation on the Formation of the Corps" also stipulated that the armed forces of the VCheka consist of "completely mobile fighting units" numbering 750 men each, exclusive of housekeeping and noncombatant personnel. In turn, each fighting unit (or "detached battalion") was to be composed of three regiments of infantry, one detachment of calvary, one machine-gun detachment, one artillery section, and one communications unit. The Corps also had in its arsenal "the necessary number of armored units."

VCheka Order No. 72, signed by Felix Dzerzhinsky in mid-September 1918, sheds some light on one of the many armed Cheka units then operating in the countryside.[8] Dzerzhinsky's order singled out for special praise the detachment of the Tambov Provincial Cheka, which was formed from a local Red Army regiment and numbered about a thousand men, "almost all of them members of the Party." The fighting Chekists of Tambov were said to have participated in "big operations in the suppression of all kinds of counterrevolutionary uprisings," not only in Tambov

Province but in neighboring provinces as well. Indeed, hardly a day passed when these steadfast defenders of the proletarian revolution were not called out to assist the Tambov Cheka or some other Soviet institution in the struggle against counterrevolution. Their heavy responsibilities in defense of Soviet power did not prevent the Cheka troops from pursuing a wide range of "Party and cultural-educational activity" during their spare moments. The detachment had its own Party collective, a school, a team of agitators, and a "good library."

General guidance and supervision of the detachment was the responsibility of the Tambov Provincial Cheka, and its leading officials were said to have found the detachment an excellent recruiting ground for "many good intelligence operatives [and] commissars." Pasinkov, the commander of the Tambov Cheka detachment, was a former postman and noncommissioned officer in World War I. From the first day of the revolution, according to the chairman of the VCheka, Pasinkov had "actively fought on the side of the Communist Party" and had recently devoted all his energy to creating the Tambov Cheka detachment.

Despite its noteworthy achievements, certain deficiencies in the detachment's day-to-day operations had to be corrected. Its links with the staff of the VCheka Corps in Moscow were "very bad," with the result that several orders from the center had not been immediately carried out. Moreover, an inexplicable delay on the part of the Tambov Chekists in requesting uniforms and other supplies had created unnecessary hardships for the troops. These shortcomings notwithstanding, Dzerzhinsky was clearly pleased with the overall performance of the Tambov Cheka detachment, and he ordered that it be reinforced by a platoon of light artillery, an armored detachment, three trucks, three motorcycles, an automobile, and a band. As for Commander Pasinkov, he was to remain at his post and "reform" all detachments connected to the district Chekas in his area along lines laid down by the center. For his unstinting efforts on behalf of the Tambov Cheka, Dzerzhinsky offered Commander Pasinkov his "comradely thanks."

VCheka troops were often called upon to turn their machine guns and artillery against angry and rebellious peasants. Entire villages rose up against the forced requisition of grain that Lenin instituted in the spring of 1918. It was then that the Soviet government banned the private sale of grain and announced that henceforth all surpluses above that required by the peasants to maintain their families and cattle and meet their sowing needs would become the property of the Workers' and Peasants' Government. (Lenin later admitted: "We actually took from the peasant all his surpluses and sometimes even a part of his necessaries to meet the requirements of the army and sustain the workers." The Mensheviks and Socialist Revolutionaries blamed the Bolsheviks for the suffering this caused, but Lenin thought "we deserve credit for it.")[9] The state's grain monopoly was enforced by thousands of armed detachments, which were sent into villages to seize with bayonets the supplies needed to feed the half-starved workers and Red Army men upon whose loyalty the fate of the Bolshevik regime depended. Lenin's crusade against the villages enabled the Soviet government to supply its defenders with their meager rations, but the price was high. Wave after wave of peasant revolts swept across the country engulfing entire districts and provinces from the black soil region of central Russia to western Siberia. VCheka troops were the Soviet government's first line of defense against these uprisings. According to Martyn Latsis, VCheka troops suppressed 344 peasant uprisings in just twenty provinces of the Soviet Republic during 1918 and the first seven months of 1919.[10]

The Soviet authorities customarily attributed the uprisings to the machinations of the kulaks, the small minority of rich peasants, and their counterrevolutionary allies, the priests, former landlords, and representatives of anti-Bolshevik political parties. To admit that Bolshevik policy in the rural areas was driving ordinary Russian peasants to take up arms against their own government was out of the question. But the fact remained that poor peasants, middle peasants, and the numerically insignificant kulaks rose up as one to repel the rapacious food-requisitioning detachments and Cheka units sent out from the cities and provincial centers to plunder their villages. Latsis could only explain this phenomenon by insisting that the cunning and treacherous kulaks "compelled" the poor peasants to join them by "promises, slander, and threats."[11]

One of the many otherwise indistinguishable "kulak uprisings" included in Latsis's figures ("one is very much like the other," he wrote) broke out in November 1918 and quickly engulfed the provinces of Smolensk, Kaluga, and Tula. Troops from the provincial Cheka of Kaluga were dispatched to crush the peasant insurgents. After the capture of the strategic town of Medyn, Felix Dzerzhinsky telegraphed further instructions to the commander of the Cheka troops on the scene. The uprising, he said, was to be put down within three days "with a firm hand [and] without any wavering." At the same time, the commander was to bear in mind that "we don't need unnecessary blood spilled. Punish the leaders and kulaks, but don't harm the people who have been fooled or intimidated by them. We will hold you strictly responsible for this."[12]

Not long after this revolt was suppressed, the Collegium of the VCheka issued an order dealing with the proper conduct of armed Cheka operations in the countryside.[13] The order noted that measures taken by the Chekas against "kulaks" and "White Guards" in the villages, if they were not to worsen the situation, had to be carried out in a manner that would not cause unnecessary suffering or sow bitterness among the village poor. The Chekists were to explain to the poor peasants that the criminal designs of the kulaks and their counterrevolutionary accomplices would, if successful, only bring about the return of the landlords and the capitalists. Repression alone, in the opinion of the VCheka, was not sufficient; it had to be combined with "political-explanatory work" among the peasant masses. Only a judicious balance of repression and propaganda could guarantee the support of the village poor in the future—a sure sign that up to this point such support had been generally lacking.

The VCheka leadership's concern for avoiding the needless estrangement of poor peasants was probably genuine enough, since this segment of the rural population was believed to be a natural ally of the Bolshevik cause. But, as the Chekists admitted more than once, it was not always possible to make a distinction between kulaks and poor peasants. The poor peasants were the majority in the villages, and they bore the brunt of the repressions. An article published in the *VCheka Weekly,* entitled "A Few Words on Preventing White Guard and Kulak Uprisings in the Countryside," noted the "dismal fact" that after the suppression of counterrevolutionary uprisings in the villages it was the poor peasants who were punished most severely, the kulaks and instigators usually managing to escape. To nip these uprisings in the bud, local Chekas were urged to imitate the example of the Perm Regional Cheka, which had recently taken seventy-eight hostages from the local bourgeoisie and opposition political parties. The Chekists of Perm intended to shoot these hostages at the first sign of any "kulak uprising."[14] How the execution of still more innocent victims was to alleviate the underlying causes of peasant unrest was not explained.

While the Cheka troops were busy crushing peasant insurgents, several other government agencies continued to maintain their own special military forces. For instance, the People's Commissariat of Food Supply also employed troops to assist in the collection of grain, while the main directorates of petroleum, sugar, and textiles had their own armed units to guard enterprises and storehouses. As vital as these and other armed forces were during the early part of the Civil War, lack of a unified command limited their contribution to the preservation of revolutionary order on the internal front. To remedy this situation, the Council of Workers' and Peasants' Defense decreed that as of June 1, 1919, all auxiliary special forces under the jurisdiction of various government agencies and departments be combined into a single force under the direction of the People's Commissariat of Internal Affairs. The Special Corps of VCheka Troops was also to become a part of this new and enlarged military force, to be known as the Internal Security Troops *(Voisk vnutrennei okhrany).*[15] Overall direction and control of the Internal Security Troops *(VOKhR)* did not stray far from the hands of the leading Chekist because the People's Commissar of Internal Affairs at this time was Felix Dzerzhinsky.

An order issued early in 1920 by the Military Council of the Internal Security Troops, its highest policy-making body, gave a clear picture of the basic tasks assigned to the VOKhR forces. The defense of the revolutionary order was declared its paramount duty and to facilitate the discharge of this heavy responsibility all VOKhR troops were relieved of ordinary guard and garrison work. More specifically, the Internal Security Troops were to conduct an armed struggle against counterrevolution everywhere on the internal front; guard Soviet transport, factories, and customs houses; carry out the orders of the VCheka and the Commissariat of Food Supply; and wage an energetic campaign against desertion.[16] An order dated March 17, 1920, added far-ranging judicial powers to the Internal Security Troops. It authorized that the cases of persons arrested in front-line areas in connection with such anti-Soviet activities as armed robbery and banditry be turned over to the newly established revolutionary tribunals of the Internal Security Troops. This measure, according to a recent Soviet work, was of great significance in the struggle against crime because it "reinforced and brought together the operational activities of the Internal Security Troops and rapid judicial repression."[17] In other words, the Internal Security Troops became the judge, jury, and executioner of persons arrested for violating the revolutionary order in front-line areas.

By mid-1920, a brigade of Internal Security Troops, consisting of from four to six infantry battalions and one or two cavalry squadrons, was deployed in every province under Soviet control. Very close relations existed between the Internal Security Troops and the local Chekas. The commander of each brigade of Internal Security Troops served simultaneously as a member of the collegium of the provincial Cheka in his area of operations. One battalion of Internal Security Troops was placed under the exclusive control of each provincial Cheka and could not be sent into action without its consent.[18]

The 125,000 VOKhR troops in the field were, in Dzerzhinsky's words, trained in the spirit of "iron, proletarian-conscious discipline." This made it possible for them to be "sent to the most dangerous spots at a moment's notice. According to regulations," Dzerzhinsky added, "a third of our VOKhR troops must always be at the front."[19] Units of the elite Internal Security Troops were indeed deployed at critical moments to buttress the Red Army at the front lines and to protect its rear. In September 1919, when General Denikin's forces were scoring one victory after another on the southern front around Orel and Tula, fourteen battalions of Internal Security Troops were dispatched to the combat zone, and Dzerzhinsky approved the formation in Moscow of two more regiments to help maintain revolutionary order in the capital itself.[20]

On April 26, 1920, the day after Polish forces invaded the western Ukraine, confronting the Soviet government with another serious military challenge, the Politburo of the Communist Party ordered Dzerzhinsky to proceed immediately to the battle zone, where he was to take all necessary steps to maintain revolutionary order in the rear of the Red Army. On May 5, accompanied by 1,400 VOKhR troops, Dzerzhinsky set out for Kharkov. Within a week of his arrival in the Ukraine, he reported to Moscow on what appeared to him the most glaring deficiencies of Soviet administration in that wartorn region:

> The general defect of the apparatus of power is quite simply its complete absence. Drafts and plans and good intentions are in abundance, but in most of the central organs only idling is in full swing. . . .
> . . . It is immediately necessary to strengthen the central organs of the [Ukrainian Cheka]. Otherwise it will be impossible to lead either the organizational or the combat activities of the local Chekas. The necessity for this is dictated by the fact that the Polish offensive has turned the entire Ukraine into a boiling cauldron. Uprisings are breaking out all over. . . . Therefore it is necessary to have a unified leadership of all the local Chekas. This in turn requires an apparatus that up until this time has not existed.[21]

In a letter to the deputy chairman of the VCheka, I. K. Ksenofontov, Dzerzhinsky wrote at about the same time: "I am fascinated by the thought of staying here—not for a tour—but for a more extended period of time. Remaining here with the support of the Central Committee of the Party, I should in the course of two or three months be able to strengthen the Cheka."[22] The Central Committee moved quickly to grant Dzerzhinsky's wish, and on May 29, it added another title to what was already an imposing list of responsible and demanding posts, Chief of the Rear of the Southwestern Front. (Dzerzhinsky was already chairman of the VCheka, People's Commissar of Internal Affairs, and chairman of the Main Committee for Universal Labor Conscription.)

When Dzerzhinsky arrived at Cheka headquarters in Kharkov he immediately took command of the 10,727 VOKhR troops then on duty on the southwestern front. Throughout this period of foreign invasion and military crisis, the VOKhR troops formed the indispensable enforcement arm of Soviet power in the rear of the Red Army. Dzerzhinsky rallied all VOKhR units and Chekas in the Ukraine to battle with these words:

> The task of the Red Army is to defend the socialist Fatherland. Our task is to defend the army from anything that might weaken or slow down its thrust, that might cause it harm and result in unnecessary casualties.
>
> Comrades! Every counterrevolutionary organizing plots in the rear to divert the front-line effort is a traitor and a murderer and must be destroyed immediately—not tomorrow but today, immediately.
>
> . . . You, comrades, as the defenders of the Revolution, must be everywhere: in the towns and villages, at crowded meetings, and in deserted out-of-the-way places. Our brothers at the front must know that in the rear you are demonstrating the same selflessness, vigilance, and decisiveness as the Red Army in this final battle that has been thrust upon us by the Polish landowners. You must prevent kulak uprisings, destroy spies, counterrevolutionaries, and speculators. The internal front is like the external front. Any negligence, sluggishness, or indecisiveness is criminal.
>
> Comrades! You are the guardians of the Revolution. There is and cannot be a more responsible and honorable role for a revolutionary than this. . . .
>
> Everyone to their places! Everyone for the unity of the revolutionary front and the revolutionary rear![23]

In addition to waging a relentless struggle against the many marauding bandit gangs that roamed the area, the VOKhR troops in the rear of the southwestern front guarded strategic bridges, railroad lines, telegraph and postal communications, factories, storehouses, and military depots; they also took part in food-requisitioning detachments and suppressed numerous counterrevolutionary uprisings and espionage organizations. It was not long, however, before Dzerzhinsky came to realize how inadequately manned and equipped the VOKhR forces under his command were. For instance, to protect the nearly 7,000 miles of vital railroad supplying the front lines, an estimated 15,750 men were needed; yet Dzerzhinsky had only 5,700 VOKhR troops to spare for this most important assignment. The troops were also very deficient in barbed wire, machine guns, and calvary. To make matters worse, the ranks of VOKhR troops in the rear were being depleted by military commanders who drew upon them for combat duty.[24]

Dzerzhinsky Square and the Lubianka (photograph by Roberta Gerson, 1972)

Prison photograph of Dzerzhinsky, 1914

Dzerzhinsky *(center)* and members of the VCheka Collegium, 1919

Dzerzhinsky in 1919

Dzerzhinsky in 1925

Martyn Latsis (no date)

Dzerzhinsky dashed off requests to the authorities in the Ukraine and Moscow to help remedy this grave situation. On June 19, he sent the following telegram to his comrade-in-arms Joseph Stalin, at the time a member of the War Council of the Southwestern Front:

> VOKhR units, which carry out almost all work connected with the struggle against banditry, are extremely poorly equipped: thus, there is only one machine gun for five hundred men. Meanwhile, it is no secret that army units possess machine guns above any norms and that for lack of a sufficient number of machine gunners these weapons constitute a useless burden. Therefore, I request that a catagorical order be issued to the commanders of the 12th, 13th, and 14th armies . . . to put fifty machine guns from each army at the disposal of the Directorate of the Rear of the Front, the commanders to be allowed ten days to fulfill this order.[25]

Dzerzhinsky's request for more arms was quickly approved, but this did not resolve the even more critical shortage of manpower.

To strengthen his forces, Dzerzhinsky first shifted units of VOKhR troops from the central provinces of Russia to the Ukraine. Immediately upon his arrival in Kharkov, he called for a battalion of the Moscow Cheka, and on June 10, an additional ten VOKhR battalions were dispatched to the Ukraine. A few weeks later the Ukrainian Council of People's Commissars requested the Kremlin to authorize the transfer of another 107 VOKhR battalions to the Ukraine together with one cavalry division and six artillery batteries. A decision was adopted at the same time prohibiting the use of VOKhR troops for purposes not connected with the military defense of the rear.[26]

The VOKhR reinforcements sent to the Ukraine made possible a more energetic campaign to rid the rear of the southwestern front of the many marauding bands which roamed the area. The bands of Molchanov, Volk, Nikitenko, Orlov, Kovalenko, and Artamanov, to name just a few, were composed chiefly of peasants, deserters from both the Red and White armies, criminals, and plain adventurers, and were reliably reported to number about 38,000 in 1920.[27] Their attacks on villages and Soviet institutions, vital lines of transportation and communication, warehouses and supply depots, and Red Army units themselves posed a serious threat to the human and material resources of the rear.

Dzerzhinsky ordered the VOKhR units under his command to take the offensive and pursue the bands until they were completely wiped out. This strategy of attack and pursuit demanded the creation of mobile and easily maneuverable VOKhR units. In a telegram to the chief of staff of the Internal Security Troops, Dzerzhinsky called for the dispatch of still more Cheka cavalry units to the Ukraine. Without them, he said, "the struggle with the bands will be too protracted and the enemy will elude us." Two hundred cavalrymen were immediately dispatched from each VOKhR sector to Dzerzhinsky's headquarters in Kharkov.[28] For reconnaissance and keeping track of the movement of the bands, two airplanes and an armored train were also placed at the disposal of the VOKhR troops. As a result of Dzerzhinsky's tireless work, in the words of one of his Soviet biographers, "the wave of banditry in the Ukraine gradually died down. A large number of bandits were killed in battle while others, sensing the hopelessness of their situation, gave themselves up; only a small number of the most brutal bands continued for a short time to terrorize the population in front-line areas."[29]

Still another consolidation of all forces having important internal security functions occurred on September 1, 1920, with the formation of the Internal Service Troops (*Voisk vnutrennei sluzhbi*), or VNUS. The railroad security troops, the water militia, and various other auxiliary forces that had escaped earlier moves toward unification under a single command were combined with the VOKhR troops to form this military force for deployment on the internal front.[30] As Commissar of Internal Affairs, Dzerzhinsky remained in charge of the Internal Service Troops.

The history of the Internal Service Troops as a distinct entity was a short one. With the successful conclusion of the Civil War, the Soviet government early in 1921 undertook a reorganization and reduction of its armed forces, and by mid-year according to Western intelligence, the seventeen divisions and fourteen detached brigades of VNUS troops had been completely disbanded.[31] Yet the need for a loyal and reliable armed force to carry on in the tradition of the VOKhR and VNUS units of the Civil War years was as great as ever. Tens of thousands of armed bandits and peasant insurgents continued to spread havoc in the central provinces of the RSFSR and in the border regions. Perhaps because the Soviet government still did not wish to rely on the regular armed forces to preserve order on the internal front, the VCheka was again ordered to step into the breach.

The Troops of the VCheka *(Voisk VCheka)*, established by a decree of January 19, 1921, were made responsible for guarding Soviet borders, railroad stations, docks, and harbors as well as for the continued struggle against uprisings and banditry. By the summer of 1921, over 137,000 VCheka troops were on duty throughout the length and breadth of the Soviet Republic, their actual distribution reflecting the Kremlin's security requirements on the still volatile internal front.[32]

The Special Department of the VCheka

From the February Revolution of 1917 to the signing of the Treaty of Brest-Litovsk in March 1918, the dissolution of the Imperial Russian Army proceeded swiftly. Widespread desertion was compounded by poor morale and discipline among those soldiers who remained in the ranks. It was upon this weak foundation that the Bolsheviks were compelled to build a fighting force capable of opposing the armies of Kolchak and Denikin. To plug the serious leadership gap that resulted from a shortage of militarily trained Bolsheviks, Leon Trotsky, Commissar of War, began early in 1918 to recruit former Tsarist officers for service in the nascent Red Army. As Latsis pointed out, however: "It was not written on the foreheads of any of them whether they would serve honorably or betray us."[33] To ensure the loyalty of these officers, who numbered more than 48,000 by the middle of 1920, and of the rank and file generally, a complex system of controls was established. It was composed of two parallel hierarchies that operated (as they still do today) side by side with the professional military command. One consisted of the political commissars, who were assigned to every level of the armed forces. Their job was to direct Party work, conduct propaganda among the hundreds of thousands of peasant recruits, and verify the political reliability of the officer corps. The other was composed of the Cheka organs known as special departments *(osobye otdeli)*.

The special departments performed the same functions in the Red Army as did the territorial organs of the VCheka throughout the Soviet Republic. They were responsible for combating espionage and counterrevolution in the armed forces and in front-line and adjoining areas. These Cheka organs, which viewed every officer and soldier as a potential traitor, also maintained a constant vigil over the state of political morale in the Army and were empowered to root out anyone suspected of harboring anti-Soviet leanings. In addition, the special departments were charged with collecting intelligence, looking after the personal security of political commissars and other top military officials, and helping to maintain discipline by punishing desertion and other forms of insubordination.

Originally designated as front-line *(frontovye)* Chekas, they first appeared in July 1918, when the ubiquitous Chekist, Martyn Latsis, was appointed by Lenin to head the Extraordinary Commission on the eastern front.[34] The front-line Chekas were established, according to Latsis, because of a pressing need to unify the work of all Chekas located in the front zones and to purge the rear "of all counterrevolutionary elements." This in turn "required the application of special measures not provided for in the general statute on the Chekas."[35] Created at first on an *ad hoc* basis as the situation demanded, the early front-line Chekas were usually dissolved as soon as fighting on a front had ceased. It was not long, however, before they began to appear on all fronts and in all armies, and to guide their work the Military Department of the VCheka was established under the direction of the veteran Bolshevik, Mikhail Sergeevich Kedrov (1878–1941).[36]

At the outset there was considerable difficulty in determining the relationship that was to prevail between the front-line Chekas and the territorial network of secret police agencies that was then emerging. A VCheka official reported in the fall of 1918 that, on the basis of observations he made during an inspection trip to Kazan and Simbirsk, "the situation of all Chekas that have formed in front areas with respect to their mutual relations and organization is extremely uncertain and confused."[37] It seemed that the front-line Chekas, which were continually shifted from one battle zone to another, were not only independent of the territorial system of provincial and district Chekas but were also prone to disrupt regular Cheka work by trying to take over all secret police activity once they moved into an area. Friction arose, for example, over the question of which organ—the provincial Cheka or the front-line Cheka—was to direct the activities of the district Chekas located in the front area. The result of this intradepartmental bickering was that in certain localities the relation between the two rival Chekas was one of complete chaos. Indeed, in some places secret police operations had come to a virtual standstill in the absence of leadership from the provincial center and a mutually acceptable chain of command. In large part the disharmony was said to stem from the fact that the front-line Chekas received their funds from the Political Department of the Red Army Staff and therefore considered themselves subordinate to the military command. This, of course, made it very difficult for the front-line Chekas "to carry out that energetic work against all kinds of counterrevolutionary phenomena and abuses in the [military] staffs that is so necessary."

Following the publication of this and other evidence of growing dissatisfaction about the lack of VCheka control over the proliferating network of front-line Chekas, the second All-Russian Conference of Extraordinary Commissions meeting in late November 1918 proposed to dissolve the front-line Chekas and create in their place a new system of front and army Chekas "subordinate in their activities to the VCheka and the Military Department."[38]

The major obstacle to the speedy implementation of this proposal was the presence of a rival and parallel counterespionage organization in the Red Army, directly under the control of the Commissar of War. The Department of Military Control *(Voenkontrol)* had been established in May 1918, and, according to a highly critical Soviet work, it was

> an unwieldy and clumsy apparatus. But its major flaw was that the majority of its workers were not inspired by any political faith. On Trotsky's orders, the Department of Military Control was composed of so-called experienced people. This meant, for the most part, former officers who hated Soviet power. A preposterous situation developed: the weapon for combating espionage in the army fell into the hands of opponents of Soviet power.[39]

As long as the Department of Military Control existed, the VCheka's role as guardian of revolutionary virtue in the Red

Army would surely be limited. But it was only a matter of time before the industrious Chekists began to uncover evidence of dangerous counterrevolutionary plots taking place right under the nose (if not with the actual connivance) of the Department of Military Control.

On the eastern front, for instance, Military Control was headed by a man named Faierman, who, with his staff, it has been said, "not only did not fight against White Guard espionage, but, on the contrary, worked for the Whites. When Kazan and Simbirsk fell, the majority of Military Control officials went over to the side of the enemy." On the southern front, also, the Military Control apparatus sheltered many traitors and spies. "It was not accidental," according to the same Soviet writer, "that all Communist intelligence operatives sent to the Ukraine in the summer [of 1918] through the southern front were immediately arrested and shot by German counterintelligence." Had it not been for the "stubborn opposition" of Trotsky, who did everything possible to impede the work of the front-line Chekas, the Department of Military Control might have been exposed more quickly for what it really was—"a nest of espionage and counterrevolution in the Red Army.⁴⁰

Finally, in late 1918, after the VCheka had executed twenty "White Guard spies and wreckers" discovered in the Vologodsk section of Military Control, Lenin appointed Dzerzhinsky to head a commission to investigate the entire Military Control apparatus. Not unexpectedly, Dzerzhinsky recommended the complete abolition of Military Control and the transfer of its functions to the VCheka, a suggestion endorsed by the Central Committee of the Bolshevik Party on December 19, 1918. This decision called for the dismantlement of both the Department of Military Control and the Military Department of the VCheka and the transfer of their overlapping counterespionage and security functions to a new organ: the Special Department of the VCheka.⁴¹

It was not until February 21, 1919, however, that the decree "On the Special Departments Attached to the All-Russian Extraordinary Commission" was published.⁴² That more than two months passed before an official decree on the Special Department and its local organs was issued may be taken as a sign of the difficulties encountered in drafting an enactment acceptable to the Commissar of War, who would hardly have been pleased by the prospect of a permanent and unchecked VCheka presence in the Red Army. The decree bearing the signatures of the chairman of the VCheka and the Commissar of War that finally emerged was a compromise to preserve the integrity of both institutions, but the crucial provisions dealing with the locus of authority over the special departments were decidedly favorable to the military command. The decree entrusted the Special Department of the VCheka in general terms with the conduct of "the struggle against counterrevolution and espionage in the army and navy," while simultaneously placing it "directly under the control of the Revolutionary War Council of the Republic," all of whose orders it was to carry out. (The Revolutionary War Council of the Republic was established in September 1918 to direct the war effort; its chairman was Leon Trotsky.) The law also provided for two types of special departments: those attached to the provincial Chekas, and those attached to the various fronts and armies, replacing the front-line Chekas of the preceding period. Both were to be "directly subordinate to the Special Department of the VCheka," which was authorized to "lead the work of the local Special Departments and control their activity." At the same time, however, the front and army special departments were required to fulfill all the tasks assigned them by the Revolutionary War Council of the Republic, while the special departments attached to the provincial Chekas were put at the disposal of the local military commissariats.

To discharge properly their numerous responsibilities, which also included the conduct of espionage—the Special Department of the VCheka was to "organize and lead the work of agents abroad and in areas [of Russia] occupied by foreign powers and White Guard forces"—the special departments were given the right "to conduct investigations and all activities connected with them, such as searches, seizures, and arrests." Finally, the objection of the VCheka leadership, noted earlier, to having the secret police organs in the Red Army financed by the Army Staff—one of the most important objects of Cheka surveillance—was also resolved; the law provided that "funds for the maintenance of all special departments shall be made by means of standard procedures adopted by the All-Russian Extraordinary Commission."

Within a few months, the VCheka's grip on the special departments in the fronts and armies was weakened still further, most likely as a result of continued pressure from the Commissar of War, by the provisions of a supplementary decree published on May 17, 1919.[43] The law of February 21 had stated that the front and army special departments were "directly subordinate" to the Special Department of the VCheka, but this enactment gave the VCheka only "general direction over the work of the special departments of fronts and armies," which henceforth were to be "directly subordinate to one of the members of the appropriate Revolutionary War Council" (that is, to a representative of the directing military body of the given front or army). That the front and army special departments were effectively controlled by the Red Army command was confirmed by no less an authority than Martyn Latsis, who wrote in 1921 that the special departments preserved a large measure of independence from the VCheka and carried out "all orders" of the Revolutionary War Council, "like front-line troops."[44]

Although the VCheka was denied exclusive control over the secret police network in the Red Army, the Chekist official Moroz could still declare that its contribution to the Bolshevik cause was of inestimable value. Writing at one of the darkest moments of the Civil War, when General Denikin's forces were advancing rapidly toward Moscow, Moroz said that the Red Army now required the greatest attention since the counterrevolutionaries were concentrating their efforts on it. "Combating espionage, combating treason, combating deliberate sabotage in the Army—this is the chief work of the Cheka in [the most recent] period," he wrote.[45]

The special departments that appeared in all front-line zones, armies, military districts, divisions, and regiments are said to have destroyed "several hundred large counterrevolutionary organizations" operating in the Red Army and in the rear during the Civil War.[46] One of these anti-Bolshevik organizations called itself the Volunteer Army of the Moscow Region. Composed of former Tsarist officers, the organization managed to assemble an impressive underground arsenal of weapons, including armored cars and artillery, with which it planned to seize power in Moscow. The coup was to take place in mid-September 1919 and was to coincide with General Denikin's advance toward the capital of the Soviet Republic. At the most opportune moment, the leaders of the Volunteer Army of the Moscow Region had intended to storm the Kremlin, send combat units to seize the railroad stations, dispatch demolitions specialists to destroy communications between Moscow and the front, and arrest the leaders of the Soviet government. By paralyzing Moscow at the critical moment, the plotters hoped to ensure a decisive White victory. But the Special Department of the VCheka got wind of the plot and struck first. More than one thousand members of the Volunteer Army of the Moscow Region ended up in the dungeons of the Lubianka.[47]

To uncover plots and conspiracies against Soviet power more easily, the Special Department of the VCheka encouraged the public to come forward with confidential denunciations of suspected enemy agents working in military staffs and institutions. On February 21, 1920 (the first anniversary of the decree establishing the Special Department), the Information Section of the Special Department of the VCheka appealed to "all comrade workers, Red Army men, Communists, and all citizens":

> Come to . . . aid in the struggle against the enemies of the Soviet Republic and, not standing on ceremony as to form or composition, send information on all noted episodes where it is possible to suspect espionage, sabotage, treason, and all other actions of the secret enemies of the Republic that are aimed at undermining the strength of the Red Army.

Any such information, it was added, could be delivered either in person or by mail to the Information Section of the Special Department at 2 Bolshaia Lubianka.[48]

In carrying out their counterespionage and general security duties, the special departments exercised strict control over the movements of Soviet citizens in front-line areas. A decree of July 29, 1919, for example, provided that permits for travel into or out of frontal zones for all except certain categories of Soviet officials required the permission of the Special Department of the VCheka.[49] And on November 11, 1919, Dzerzhinsky warned that persons found in front-line zones or on railway transport headed for the front or suspected of trying to leave the country illegally would be prosecuted for military espionage and punished by "not less than confinement in a concentration camp at forced labor for the duration of the Civil War."[50]

There is evidence that once the Red Army occupied territory previously held by the enemy the special departments pacified it by eliminating known or suspected supporters of the anti-Bolshevik cause. "Responsible work fell to the lot of the special departments," wrote a high ranking VCheka official, "in purging the rear areas, especially in the Crimea after the liquidation of the Wrangel front; the rest of the counterrevolutionaries left behind by the White Guards in the Crimea were basted with red-hot iron."[51] Another secret police official, a veteran of the Georgian Cheka, recalled what happened when the Red Army entered Baku in 1920:

> The occupation of the city and then all of Azerbaijan took place almost without a shot being fired. The entry of the Red Army was totally unexpected not only by the population, but by several members of the government of the Azerbaijan Republic.
>
> Thousands of officers, all kinds of officials and representatives of the prosperous class were taken by surprise. The Cheka and the Special Department were fierce in their dealings with them. Hundreds of the arrested prisoners were taken without trial or investigation to the island of Nagren, located not far from Baku, where the Chekists shot them in batches.

It was a long time before the residents of Baku could forget the horror and bloodshed of the "week of strangling the bourgeoisie."[52]

After the Civil War, the Special Department of the VCheka continued to play an important role in the struggle against anti-Soviet uprisings in central Russia, the Ukraine, the Caucasus, and Siberia. For its varied contributions to strengthening the fighting ability of the Red Army and its heroic struggle against all kinds of internal and external foes, the Revolutionary War Council of the Republic, on December 20, 1922, awarded the Special Department the coveted Order of the Red Banner.[53]

In addition to the many important assignments specifically entrusted to Cheka troops and the Special Department, the Soviet secret police as a whole made valuable contributions to the Bolshevik war effort. The following examples of defense-related

Chekist operations during the Civil War have been gleaned from published Soviet sources:

To overcome one of those rare threats that could not be blamed on the perfidy of the bourgeoisie, the Council of Workers' and Peasants' Defense, on February 15, 1919, ordered the chairman of the VCheka to arrest members of soviet executive committees in those localities where the clearing of snowdrifts from railroad tracks was not proceeding satisfactorily. Local Chekas were also instructed to take hostages from among the peasants, who were actually performing the labor, and shoot them if the snowdrifts were not removed in short order.[54]

On June 25, 1919, Felix Dzerzhinsky ordered provincial Chekas to confiscate a variety of weapons from the general public. All persons possessing firearms, explosives, ammunition, bayonets, and binoculars without permission of the proper authorities were to turn them in to the local Chekas within two weeks or face severe punishment. After the expiration of this two-week period, the Chekists were further instructed to launch a search for illegal arms proceeding "house by house, village by village, and street by street." Not a single bullet or bayonet was to remain in the hands of any suspected enemy of Soviet power.[55]

On September 24, 1919, the Council of Workers' and Peasants' Defense issued a decree aimed at increasing the supply of overcoats for the Red Army and suppressing the speculative trade in these badly needed items of clothing. The VCheka was instructed to requisition "all overcoats made of grey and protective cloth" from the civilian population and from employees of Soviet institutions. More detailed instructions issued a few days later exempted poor workers and peasants who did not have any other warm clothing.[56]

In June 1920 the Moscow Cheka reported uncovering a "counterrevolutionary organization" in the provisioning organs of the Red Army. According to the newspaper account, "a criminal gang consisting of officials of the 2nd Main Military Warehouse . . . systematically plundered textiles from various warehouses which were destined to be turned into uniforms for the Red Army and supplied them to the speculative market." The Collegium of the Moscow Cheka sentenced five of the culprits to death and three others to long terms of imprisonment and hard labor.[57]

Faced with a severe fuel shortage, the Council of Labor and Defense, on February 11, 1921, ordered the VCheka and its local organs to render full assistance to the fuel agencies of the Soviet government and take "all decisive measures to suppress the embezzlement of fuel and wage a struggle against red tape in the fulfillment of fuel orders." Representatives of the VCheka were also called upon to serve on a special commission to combat the fuel crisis.[58]

The VCheka also took a very dim view of desertion and waged a relentless campaign against it. Said Latsis: "We shoot traitors. And a deserter is a traitor. To save his own skin, he dooms tens and hundreds of Red Army men at the front to death. Therefore, the Cheka has shot malicious deserters." Desertion reached flood proportions in the provinces of Tambov, Smolensk, Orlov, Novgorod, Tula, and Kazan, and to combat it the VCheka conducted "mass roundups in the cities and in the forests" with "brilliant results." In Riazan Province alone, according to Latsis's figures, 54,697 deserters were apprehended and sent back to the front in the period up to September 18, 1919; in Tver Province between September 28 and October 12, 1919, the total was 5,430; and in Moscow Province from September 16 to September 23, 1919, a more modest 3,329. Only the claim that a mere 102 soldiers were shot for desertion in 1918 and the first six months of 1919 (39 in 1918 and 63 in 1919) in twenty provinces of central Russia seems improbable in view of the scope of the problem and the sanguinary tone of Latsis's own statements.[59]

The Border Chekas

Before the revolution the remote, quiet town of Orsha on the Dnieper River could hardly be distinguished from many similar district crossroads in the province of Mogilev. But in the spring of 1918 the muddy streets of Orsha suddenly came to life with bustling activity. Almost overnight, the little town was transformed into a supply center for such scarce and disparate items as soap, knitted goods, chemicals, textiles, and saccharin, which were transported to cities such as Minsk, Smolensk, Moscow, and

Petrograd, where they were sold at very high prices. This remarkable metamorphosis was the result of Orsha's strategic location on the demarcation line established by the Treaty of Brest-Litovsk between Soviet-occupied and German-occupied Russian territory. With its convenient border location, Orsha quickly became a mecca for smugglers and speculators who poured into the town. Poles, Latvians, Armenians, and Russians from both sides of the poorly guarded border engaged in what one VCheka official characterized as an "orgy" of smuggling and speculation.[60]

It was to cope with this and similar occurrences of widespread disorder along the Soviet border that the Council of People's Commissars, on May 28, 1918, established the Main Administration for Border Security *(Glavnoe upravlenie pogranichnoi okhrany)*, under the jurisdiction of the People's Commissariat of Finance. Its duties included the prevention of smuggling and the unauthorized passage of goods and persons over the land and sea frontiers, the protection of border settlements from attacks by bandits, and the supervision of maritime activities (such as fishing rights and the observance of international rules of navigation) within a twelve-mile maritime customs zone.[61]

The idea of establishing a separate network of border Chekas also originated, according to a VCheka source, in May 1918, when "evidence of outrages perpetrated in all the demarcation zones" came to light. The Chekists attributed the smuggling, pillage, and general disorder in the border zones to "the social and economic decomposition of the corpse of the bourgeoisie," which had infected the demoralized army troops straddling the entire demarcation line with Germany. As a first step toward restoring order, the military units would have to be moved inland at least twenty miles. In addition, it was essential that a strong border security force composed of trustworthy cadres with firm class convictions be created immediately to combat "all manifestations of evil in border life."[62]

In mid-June, the first All-Russian Conference of Extraordinary Commissions declared that "the lack of a special and reliable border guard is conducive to the removal of essential goods over the border, which only further undermines the economic life of the country." Only the creation of "a unified apparatus of struggle" in the "trustworthy hands of the Extraordinary Commission" could put an end to this and other forms of "criminal speculation, which the bourgeoisie and its agents are encouraging in the centers and in the localities."[63] In July and August, border Chekas *(Pogranichnye chrezvychainye komissii)* were first set up at major traffic-control points along the demarcation line established by the Treaty of Brest-Litovsk.[64]

The border Chekas prided themselves on having engaged in an unremitting struggle against counterrevolution, speculation, and smuggling. Probably typical of their operations at this time was a report submitted by the Zhelobovsk Border Cheka covering the period from August 3 to September 9, 1918. The majority of people arrested during this five-week period (the exact number was not published) were smugglers and persons trying to cross the demarcation line without authorization. Persons taken into custody for these offenses were usually released after the confiscation of any illicit goods they were carrying and the imposition of fines up to five hundred roubles. Border violators who aggravated their offense by trying to bribe Cheka commissars, in addition to being fined, might also be transferred to the provincial Cheka or to the revolutionary tribunal, where more severe punishment awaited them. Some culprits were also detained under guard by the Zhelobovsk Border Cheka for a week of "social labor," chopping wood and carrying water for passing trains.[65]

The evacuation of the German-occupied western regions of Russia in the fall of 1918 added hundreds of thousands of square miles to the Soviet Republic and caused the VCheka to entrust the border Chekas with a new and important assignment. Instructions issued by the VCheka in September 1918 indicated that the majority of poor people in territory previously occupied by the Germans were expected to welcome the arrival of Soviet power as their liberator from the dual tyranny of German imperialism and Russian "bourgeois bandits." But there were other elements of the population whose privileged positions would be threatened by the advent of Soviet rule. These bourgeois "beasts of prey" were already, according to evidence received by the VCheka, well organized and in possession of substantial supplies of weapons. The task confronting the border Chekas, the "foremost vanguard" of Soviet power, was to move in on the heels of the departing Germans and "quickly, decisively, and methodically" liquidate these counterrevolutionary elements. To help the border Chekas "purify" newly acquired territory, local Soviet authorities were ordered to place at their disposal all necessary personnel and forces. In addition, a cadre of propagandists was to be assigned to the border Chekas "to explain to the poorest part of the population the need on their part to render the broadest active support to Soviet power and its fighting organs, the Extraordinary Commissions, in order to prevent the White Guards from forming another Krasnovite front." From the border Chekists themselves, the VCheka demanded nothing less than "complete decisiveness and vigilance." For "on our will, on our ability," the instructions concluded, "depends the most successful fulfillment of the task assigned to the VCheka."[66]

Whatever hopes and plans the VCheka leadership had for its nascent network of border Chekas seem to have been set aside, at least temporarily, by the end of 1918. This is evident from provisions of the secret "Instructions to the Extraordinary Commissions in the Localities," issued by the VCheka on December 1, 1918. Although the surveillance and registration of persons crossing the Soviet borders was included among the duties assigned to provincial secret police agencies, the directive made no mention of a border department in the VCheka, and the local border Chekas themselves were described merely as appendages of the liaison departments of provincial and regional Chekas located in the border zones.[67]

A conspicuous silence in official Soviet and VCheka sources on the activities and organizational development of the border Chekas between the latter part of 1918 and the summer of 1920, that is, during the most critical period of the Civil War, is the best indication that the VCheka and its local agencies were relegated to a peripheral role at best in the field of border security. During this troubled time of foreign intervention and bitter fighting on all fronts, when at one point the Soviet Republic held sway over a territory no larger than that of the fifteenth-century princes of Muscovy, and even leading Bolsheviks were doubtful of their regime's chances of survival, what borders the Soviet Republic possessed consisted for the most part of shifting perimeters marked by the fighting fronts. It was logical under these circumstances that the Soviet government should increasingly turn to the Red Army as the first line of border defense.[68]

It was not until the summer of 1920, after the defeat of Kolchak and Denikin, that the VCheka began to reassert its own claims to a pre-eminent position in the field of border security. On July 17, 1920, V. R. Menzhinsky, the chairman of the Special Department of the VCheka, issued an order calling upon his department to establish "border organs" along those frontiers where the Soviet Republic was at peace, to "maintain political control over the passage of persons bound to and from the RSFSR and also to see to the defense of these same frontiers."[69] A few months later, on November 24, 1920, the Council of Labor and Defense resolved that "the security of all borders of the RSFSR shall be the responsibility of the Special Department of the VCheka for Border Security" *(Osobyi otdel VChK po okhrane granits)*. The newly created Special Department for Border Security was specifically charged with preventing the movement of "politico-military" and "economic contraband" across the Soviet borders. This assignment was to be accomplished by means of a network of posts set up at appropriate points along the Soviet border. The military force necessary to ensure the security of the borders was at first provided by the Internal Service Troops situated in the border zones and after January 19, 1921, by units of the Troops of the VCheka.[70] By the summer of 1921, according to U.S. military intelligence estimates, over 90,000 VCheka troops were already deployed on border guard duty from the Finnish frontier to Siberia.[71]

The VCheka jealously guarded its hegemony on the Soviet frontiers against all bureaucratic intrusions. Thus, in June 1921, the VCheka issued a stern rebuke to the Commissariat of Food Supply for trying to create a parallel border network of its own for the apprehension of smugglers. The VCheka bluntly pointed out that the struggle against smuggling, as well as all other aspects of defending the borders of the Soviet Republic, was the exclusive domain of the Special Department for Border Security. "If at the present time," the VCheka's letter stated, "it is still possible to transport contraband goods across the border at a few points without hindrance, it is only because the military units defending the border are not yet up to strength." The VCheka considered the antismuggling detachments organized by the Commissariat of Food Supply "superfluous and ineffective," not to mention the source of unnecessary "incidents" with the Special Department for Border Security. "If the People's Commissariat of Food Supply has armed units at its disposal which it proposes to put to work on the borders," the VCheka concluded, "it might be desirable to transfer them to the Troops of the VCheka where they could be used for the immediate defense of the borders instead of for organizing a second line of defense."[72]

With the final expulsion of General Wrangel's forces from the Crimea in late 1920, the Russian Civil War was finally brought to a victorious conclusion. But for the Chekists on duty along the Soviet Republic's many thousands of miles of frontier, the struggle against counterrevolution, banditry, and smuggling continued unabated. Between July 1, 1921, and June 30, 1922, for example, almost 14,000 smugglers were captured on the Soviet borders.[73] Even more menacing, however, were the hundreds of guerrilla detachments, anti-Communist insurgent bands, and ordinary marauding bandit gangs that obstructed the consolidation of Bolshevik control in the border zones. In the immediate post–Civil War period, the Special Department for Border Security and the Troops of the VCheka were involved in operations against these diverse armed foes along the entire length of the Soviet Republic. In Karelia they fought the "White Finns"; in the Ukraine, the bandit gangs of Tiutiunik, Bulak-Balakovich, and Petlura; in the mountainous Caucasus, the local separatist "counterrevolutionary groups"; in Turkestan, the rebellious Basmachi; and on the distant Mongolian frontier, the troops of Baron Ungren and the robber bands of Foma Timofeev.[74]

The Transport Chekas

In 1917 the Bolsheviks inherited a railway network that was not only inadequate for normal peacetime use but had also been severely disrupted by several years of war-inflicted damage and neglect. The devastation on the railways was compounded after the October Revolution by what Lenin described as a "struggle between the element of petit-bourgeois laxity and proletarian organization." The "best part of the proletarian elements" rallied to the Soviets and were fighting for discipline; but the "administrative elements," whose loyalty belonged to the old regime, provided in Lenin's opinion "a host of saboteurs and bribe-takers." At the same time there were many "waverers" and "weak characters" among the ordinary workers who could not resist the "temptation of profiteering, bribery, and personal gain obtained by spoiling the whole apparatus."[75] By the fall of 1918, the situation had so deteriorated that a VCheka spokesman could declare Soviet transport to be suffering from an "epidemic" of large-scale speculation, counterrevolutionary agitation, and malfeasance, all of which were flourishing on the railroads as nowhere else.[76]

This railway network, for all its deficiencies, was nevertheless of critical importance to the Kremlin. The Bolsheviks were almost totally dependent upon it for the transport of food, fuel, and other necessities to the hungry cities and of military equipment and troops to the front-line areas. Guarding these vital arteries of the young Soviet Republic and suppressing any manifestations of bribery, speculation, and counterrevolution was a task ideally suited to the VCheka, which, with characteristic energy and dispatch, soon came to dominate the railroad-security field.

Special Cheka units for service on the railways were first mentioned in the secret "Regulation on Local Extraordinary Commissions" of June 11, 1918, a product of the first All-Russian Conference of Extraordinary Commissions. According to this document, "the struggle on the railways" was to be one of the responsibilities of the liaison departments of provincial Chekas. The regulation called for the posting of Cheka units and commissars to railroad stations, large and small alike, where they would take all necessary measures to establish and maintain revolutionary order.[77]

In the meantime, however, the Council of People's Commissars had already established the Extraordinary Commission for Safeguarding the Railroads, under the jurisdiction of the People's Commissariat of Ways of Communication. The Commission was made responsible for "the planned provision of the population with the most vital food supplies," and for combating speculation, unauthorized transportation of cargo, and ticketless travel on the railways.[78] It was only a matter of days before the

VCheka picked up the scent of corruption in this rival security agency. On June 19, 1918, *Izvestiia* reported that the VCheka had recently been engaged in an "energetic inspection" of its main competitor for supremacy in railroad security. According to the newspaper account, it all came about quite by accident. The VCheka arrested a minor railroad official who confessed that one of his superiors in the Extraordinary Commission for Safeguarding the Railroads had been engaged in speculation and malfeasance. Other arrests followed and soon led to the chief of the Commission, Krupanov, who was discovered to have sold six hundred rifles from government warehouses to the White Guards.[79]

The Extraordinary Commission for Safeguarding the Railroads met its swift and inglorious end on July 27, 1918, when it was abolished by the Council of People's Commissars. By the same decree, the VCheka was ordered to create a railroad security force of its own to fill the gap.[80] A few weeks later, the Chekist Peters announced that the Railroad Department of the VCheka would henceforth "regulate the struggle against counterrevolution, speculation, and sabotage on the entire railroad network"; at the same time local railroad departments would be established in every provincial Cheka. Cheka units were to be assigned to all large railroad stations and intersections, while individual Cheka commissars were to carry on the struggle at smaller stations.[81] Although they had gained much of the control they desired in the transport field, the hegemonic appetite of the Chekists was still not completely satisfied. As the VCheka official Fomin put it: "Parallel with the task of creating a powerful network of Cheka organs to safeguard means of communication, it is necessary to remove all other organs which unfortunately continue to conduct their uncoordinated work in the same area. The fewer departments that are involved in the transport apparatus, the more successful will be the results."[82] The following four examples will give some idea of the valuable services rendered by the transport Chekas to the Bolshevik war effort:

Prompted by what was described as a "catastrophic fuel situation," the Council of Workers' and Peasants' Defense decreed on November 12, 1919, that the Transport Department of the VCheka (established late in 1918) take a series of measures to increase fuel supplies and control their expenditure. In addition to giving full assistance to the fuel agencies of the Soviet government, local transport Chekas were ordered to determine fuel supplies in the vicinity of the railroad lines and report their whereabouts to the Chief Fuel Directorate; supervise the "correct expenditure of all kinds of fuel by the railways"; and "combat the unnecessary powering of locomotives at high temperatures."[83]

VCheka Order No. 203, dated November 21, 1919, ordered provincial transport Chekas to join in an all-out struggle against a widespread epidemic of typhus. The Chekas were instructed to pay particular attention to the cleanliness of railroad stations, see to the disinfection of troop trains, prevent travel by private individuals in troop trains, assure the quarantine of troops returning from the eastern front, provide hospitals and infirmaries with such essential items as food, medicine, and linen and bathhouses and laundries with fuel and soap. The additional manpower required to carry out these vital tasks was to be provided by Red Army deserters formed into penal battalions and by passengers found in railroad stations and peasants from nearby villages who were subject to mobilization for emergency service.[84]

Decrees issued on February 20, 1920, authorized local transport Chekas to take all necessary measures to prevent Soviet officials and all other persons from requisitioning or stealing supplies of salt and ice stored at railroad stations which were used to keep shipments of food from spoiling; and to combat the spoilage of food transported in refrigeration cars by making certain that no passengers traveled in these cars, that only perishable items such as meat, fish, and butter were loaded on to them, and by guarding against the damage or theft of refrigeration equipment. Persons guilty of violating these orders were to be arrested and punished "according to the laws of military-revolutionary times."[85]

At the end of the Civil War the Soviet government found itself faced with the illegal and disorderly movement of large numbers of refugees to Moscow and the western provinces of the Soviet Republic. This human traffic, which caused considerable damage to railroad property and threatened to become a source of epidemics, had to be stopped. On June 1, 1921, the Council of Labor and Defense ordered the VCheka and all its local organs, "especially the Transport Department of the VCheka," to prevent the illegal movement of refugees by arresting them as well as those guilty of giving them permission to travel on the railroads and by seizing the rolling stock that had been illegally placed at their disposal.[86]

The zeal with which the Chekists first set about purging the railroads of undesirable elements quickly led to a disruption of service and a rare rebuke from the top Party leadership. On August 9, 1918, the VCheka was directed to release and restore to their occupational rights all arrested railwaymen "who were dismissed and arrested without any basis, and against whom there are no accusations of armed attack upon Soviet authorities, participation in . . . White Guard revolts, or other serious crimes." Henceforth, railwaymen were to be dismissed and arrested only pursuant to court order or by the local Chekas with the approval of railroad trade union organizations; on their own authority the Chekists could only order provisional suspensions from work.[87]

Nevertheless the VCheka's transport responsibilities continued to grow. The second All-Russian Conference of Extraordinary Commissions, held in late November 1918, resolved:

> For the purpose of regulating the struggle with counterrevolution, speculation, and criminality in general on the railroads, water routes, highways, and in the post and telegraph department, a special Transport Department shall be formed in the VCheka composed of railroad, water-route, highway, and post and telegraph subdepartments.

Local transport departments directly subordinate to the Transport Department of the VCheka were to be established as part of each provincial and regional Cheka. The Chekists assigned to duty on the transport front were to wage a "direct struggle" against counterrevolution, sabotage, and speculation as well as control cargo and passengers and help maintain general order on the right-of-way without interfering in the "internal administrative-technical life" of the railroads.[88]

Continued friction and jurisdictional disputes between the VCheka and other Soviet agencies involved in transport matters, the Commissariat of Ways of Communication in particular, prompted the Council of Workers' and Peasants' Defense to issue a decree on March 2, 1919, providing that a representative of the Commissariat of Ways of Communication "enter the Transport Department of the VCheka for regular liaison and work." Henceforth, all complaints about the activities of the transport Chekas were to go directly to this official. Finally, as long as martial law on the railroads continued, local transport Chekas were authorized to shoot persons found guilty of bribery, theft of freight and railway material, and malfeasance.[89]

In what appears to have been another attempt to curb their punitive powers over the technical management of the railroad system, the Transport Department of the VCheka and its local agencies were reorganized by a decree of January 16, 1920. The transport Chekas were no longer to have a free hand in dealing with "service offenses" committed by railroad workers and employees. Arrests for such acts could henceforth be carried out only with "the agreement in each case" of the appropriate railroad officials or members of the Collegium of the People's Commissariat of Ways of Communication. Moreover, the VCheka had to obtain the agreement of the latter before appointing either the chairman of the central Transport Department or the heads of local transport Chekas. Although the basic task of the transport Chekas—to "combat malicious sabotage and speculation on the railroads"—was unchanged, the Transport Department of the VCheka and its local agencies were in addition instructed by this degree to "fulfill the assignments of responsible persons in the railway administration in all cases when the latter shall request the Transport Department of the VCheka and its organs for assistance in gathering information, conducting searches, suppressions, and arrests." Finally, the local transport Chekas were to keep the People's Commissariat of Ways of Communication informed of transport conditions in their areas of jurisdiction.[90]

The inference that the Transport Department was relegated, at least temporarily, to the status of a service organization vis-à-vis the railroad administration was confirmed by Latsis. In a publication of 1921 he noted that for an unspecified time "certain features of the transitional period and the opinions of the leaders" created a situation in which the Transport Department (like the Special Department) "preserved . . . a very large measure of independence from the VCheka." By the end of the Civil War, however, the situation had apparently changed, for Latsis pointed out that the Transport Department had once again become "an integral part of the VCheka system."[91]

The VCheka's control over the Soviet transport system was further enhanced by the appointment, in April 1921, of Felix Dzerzhinsky as People's Commissar of Ways of Communication, a post he held until early 1924 while simultaneously serving as Commissar of Internal Affairs and chairman of the VCheka and its successor agencies, the GPU and the OGPU. In this new capacity Dzerzhinsky was able to bring the resources of the secret police and his own considerable administrative and organizational talents directly to bear on the reconstruction of the Soviet transport system. Assisted by his Lubianka colleague Fomin, head of the VCheka's Transport Department, Dzerzhinsky immediately launched a fierce campaign against corruption and mismanagement in what he described as "the most sensitive area of our economic organism—the railroads." Bribery and speculation had become entrenched in the Soviet transport system. For a bribe, which greedy hands were always ready to accept, one could buy and sell almost anything on the railroads. Criminal speculators, Dzerzhinsky said, had covered all of Russia "with their spider's web" and were diverting essential supplies from the Soviet Republic's needy citizens. In his capacity as chairman of the VCheka and Commissar of Ways of Communication, Dzerzhinsky warned the railroad workers that the transport Chekas would no longer tolerate this disgrace and promised to eradicate bribe-taking on the railroads once and for all. "Wherever these scoundrels are to be found, whether in offices behind fancy desks or in sentry boxes, they will be rooted out and turned over to the revolutionary tribunal, whose punishing hammer will fall with all of its shattering force upon them since no mercy will be shown these deadly enemies of our rebirth."[92] In addition to purging the railroads of criminals, Dzerzhinsky also determined to reduce drastically the size of the transportation system's bloated bureaucracy. Thousands of superfluous officials, both at the center and in the localities, were smothering the railroads in red tape and paper work. By the end of 1921, more than 500,000 persons had been cut from the payroll.[93] Such were among Dzerzhinsky's first major accomplishments as commissar of the Soviet Republic's transport system.

The VCheka and the Soviet Economy

The Russian economy was in a shambles even before the Civil War got under way in 1918, and the subsequent bloodshed left Russian agriculture and industry in a state of almost complete ruin. Long habituation to poverty and deprivation helped many to survive, but millions of others died of starvation and disease during the long, terrible years of internal strife. Life was particularly difficult in the large cities, which were in constant danger of being cut off from essential supplies of food and fuel. The urban population responded to the crisis of perpetual scarcity by moving en masse back to the villages; between 1917 and 1919, for example, the population of Petrograd declined from 2,300,000 to 700,000. Yet it was on the cities that the fate of Lenin's regime depended, for that was where the Bolsheviks' popular support was concentrated. If the urban workers were not fed, clothed and kept warm, the revolution would be doomed.

The scarcity of the most essential necessities of life drove many city dwellers to extralegal means to sustain themselves. Black-market dealings and direct barter with the peasants for food and fuel became everyday occurrences. Most of those who resorted to the black market did so just to keep alive, but unscrupulous individuals saw an opportunity to profit from the widespread misery. They bought up scarce goods and sold them later at exorbitant prices. Regardless of motivation, however, the Soviet authorities viewed such entrepreneurial activities with alarm and entrusted the VCheka and its local agencies with the responsibility for suppressing it.

As explained by Latsis, the economic situation that prevailed during the Civil War required the government to maintain the tightest possible control over the distribution of all essential supplies in order to meet the basic requirements of all Soviet citizens equitably. Thus, the government sought to control the purchase and distribution of such basic provisions as bread, butter, meat, sugar, salt, and tea by establishing fixed prices for them. Naturally, this policy did not please those persons who had a surplus of such goods and wished to sell them on the side for a profit. And, unfortunately, because the demand for food, fuel, and clothing was so great, there were plenty of "empty stomachs" that could readily be induced to pay almost any price for these staples.

The speculator, said Latsis, was "a clever fellow" capable of devising all kinds of ingenious methods of conveying his illicit goods. Alcohol, for example, might be carried in specially made tin containers tied around the abdomen and thighs. Tobacco might be transported instead of wadding in quilted clothing, and diamonds carried in boiled eggs. While some speculators made trips into the countryside to buy goods directly from the peasants, others who worked in Soviet food warehouses obtained them by fraudulent means. To carry out their "dirty dealings" speculators were not above bribing railway employees, militiamen, and other government employees. Yet speculation was more than a corrupting influence. Its pernicious effects were felt by the starving workers in the cities as well as by the Red Army, which had to contend with a chronic shortage of bread and clothing. The VCheka accordingly waged a stubborn struggle against speculation and considered execution a suitable punishment for those engaged in it.[94]

One indication of the importance attached to the suppression of speculation was that the earliest addition made to the organizational structure of the VCheka was the Department to Combat Speculation, created on December 11, 1917.[95] During the formative Petrograd period, the VCheka's Department to Combat Speculation did not achieve any spectacular results, its major accomplishment being a case that resulted in the imposition of a fine of one million roubles. The alleged reasons for the relative inactivity of the department during this time were lack of experience in coping with speculation, the problem of establishing a sound organizational basis for the department's work, and the overall preoccupation of the VCheka with counterrevolution and sabotage. Organizational and personnel problems hounded the Department to Combat Speculation even after the VCheka moved to Moscow, where the problem of speculation was "ten times greater than in Petrograd." These difficulties were eventually overcome, and the department "declared a merciless struggle against all Moscow speculators."[96]

During March 1918, its first month of operation in Moscow, the Department to Combat Speculation carried out only 21 searches and arrested a mere 77 persons. The department's increased efficiency was evident by June of that year, when 269 searches were conducted, 517 persons arrested, and almost two million roubles in fines collected. The department itself, without the consent or approval of the courts or the revolutionary tribunal, is said to have determined the punishment to be applied in "a colossal number of cases," because in the opinion of its staff the judicial machinery of the Soviet state was "too indulgent" in its treatment of speculators—"these worst enemies of the revolution."[97]

Side by side with its parent institution, the Moscow Cheka was also extremely active in the campaign against speculation. Between December 1, 1918, and November 1, 1920, the Moscow Cheka arrested 26,692 persons for speculation. A byproduct of these arrests and the searches and confiscations that accompanied them was the seizure of an enormous amount and variety of money and goods. Millions of roubles' worth of paper money, interest-bearing securities, gold and silver coins, photographic equipment, clothing, shoes, leather, medicine, wine, sugar, tobacco, tea, coffee, fish, flour, bread, meat, pocket watches, typewriters, bicycles, binoculars, and perfume were among the items confiscated by the Moscow Cheka.

The Moscow Chekists adopted a variety of methods in their never-ending struggle to bring speculation under control. Surprise raids on the city's marketplaces, for example, would be conducted from time to time and all persons found in possession of excessive quantities of scarce or rationed goods were arrested and held for further questioning. These raids, we are told, at first produced good results; but after a time the professional speculators learned to avoid the public marketplaces and conducted their business in secluded alleyways and private apartments. A new approach became necessary, and the Chekists found it in the form of the mass search. Usually conducted in the predawn hours, these searches encompassed whole neighborhoods. Entire blocks of the city would be cordoned off, and all houses and apartments within the designated area thoroughly searched. Nocturnal operations of this sort caught many speculators off guard and led to the discovery of numerous hidden caches of food and manufactured goods. Unfortunately, however, the mass searches proved to be counterproductive in the long run because they aroused the anger and resentment of the law-abiding citizens, who were, to put it mildly, greatly inconvenienced by the Chekists' intrusions. In due course, mass searches were abandoned except in cases where there was good reason to suspect that a given area would yield a particularly rich harvest of speculators.

Finally, large numbers of speculators were apprehended by individual agents of the Moscow Cheka who patrolled the city's markets and public gathering places—the teahouses, inns, and alleyways—which speculators and their customers were known to frequent. The more adroit and clever Chekists pretended to be potential customers themselves in order to gain access to the secret hiding places and apartments of their prey. On a good day a successful Chekist-provocateur could hope to take up to 150 speculators and illegal traders into custody by this means.[98]

The struggle against speculation was carried on by other Chekas all over Soviet-held territory. From June 20 to September 1, 1918, the Department to Combat Speculation of the Ivanovo-Voznesensk Provincial Cheka reported the confiscation of more than 100,000 roubles' worth of goods and the imposition of fines totaling 203,550 roubles.[99] The Department to Combat Speculation of the Ural Regional Cheka was not neglecting its duties either in the summer of 1918. From May 1 to August 31, this department handled 430 cases of speculation, arrested 265 persons, confiscated 3,651,300 roubles' worth of goods, and imposed fines totaling 135,027 roubles.[100] The Chekas in the Ukraine, besides their routine pursuit of speculators and officials suspected of malfeasance, applied a variety of "measures of struggle" against the bourgeoisie as a class. Mass searches and confiscations conducted throughout 1919 and 1920 in such cities as Kharkov, Kiev, and Odessa yielded tens of millions of roubles' worth of goods desperately needed by the Soviet Republic.[101]

Speculation in the eyes of the VCheka was inseparably linked with official malfeasance. There was abundant evidence that many Soviet employees, whose loyalty to the new regime was suspect to begin with, were actively engaged in the systematic plunder of government warehouses and supply depots. Tempted by bribes and the prospect of a share in the profits that came from the black-market sale of government-owned goods, Soviet workers provided speculators with such useful items as forged ration cards and fraudulent orders for the distribution of food and other scarce supplies. To deal with this kind of economic crime, the VCheka began to establish close surveillance over the personnel of Soviet economic and trade agencies.

In the fall of 1919, three new entities were added to the VCheka machinery. On October 1, 1919, the VCheka announced the creation of an Economic Administration *(Ekonomicheskoe upravlenia)* to combat "abuses and sabotage in institutions administering the national economy and the supply of goods to the population of the Republic." The VCheka requested all citizens and institutions to inform the newly established Economic Administration of the VCheka about "all instances of malfeasance and sabotage known to them in the institutions of the Supreme Council of the National Economy, the People's Commissariat of Supply, the People's Commissariat of Agriculture, and the Unified Unloading Agency," this information to be delivered to the complaint desk at 12 Bolshaia Lubianka.[102]

The Special Revolutionary Tribunal of the VCheka, a punitive organ in no way related to any existing judicial body, was created on October 21 to handle cases dealing with large-scale speculation, bribery, forgery, and embezzlement. Consisting of three members appointed by the Collegium of the VCheka, the Special Tribunal was to be guided in its deliberations "exclusively by the interests of the revolution" and was not bound by "any forms of legal procedure." Its decisions were final and could not be appealed.[103] Addressing the first session of the Special Revolutionary Tribunal of the VCheka, Dzerzhinsky said:

> For the final triumph of Soviet power we need not only victory on the external front but also mastery over the entire economic apparatus of the country—production, distribution, and transport. And in this area the class struggle is especially acute. Not only must we have recourse to the help of the old apparatus, but all kinds of specialists, self-seekers, and people dedicated to the bourgeoisie are hanging on to us hoping to weaken Soviet power by using all means for this purpose— our own mistakes, weakness, hunger, and cold.

While welcoming former capitalists and members of the bourgeoisie who sincerely wished to serve the Soviets,

Dzerzhinsky warned that the Special Revolutionary Tribunal would destroy all those who attempted to "return to the past."[104]

Finally, the Council of People's Commissars also authorized the creation of the Special Interdepartmental Commission *(Osobaia mezhduvedomstvennaia komissiia)* of the VCheka. Composed of representatives of the VCheka, the Supreme Council of the National Economy, the People's Commissariat of Supply, and several other economic agencies, the Special Interdepartmental Commission was to investigate and combat "all sources of speculation and abuses of office connected with it." In the provinces, interdepartmental commissions, created in each provincial Cheka, were made responsible for scrutinizing the entire economic apparatus within their areas of jurisdiction, executing the orders of the central Interdepartmental Commission in Moscow, and developing effective measures for the struggle against malfeasance, speculation, and the embezzlement of state property.[105]

In an interview published in the Soviet press late in 1920, the chief of the Interdepartmental Commission made it clear that in recent months his department had gone far beyond the mere apprehension of speculators and miscreant officials and was both supervising and intervening in the day-to-day operations of Soviet economic agencies. "Instead of struggling with concrete transgressions of the law," he said, "attention has been turned to the study of the fundamental defects of our economic structure by means of which speculation develops." The enormous amount of detailed information gathered by the Interdepartmental Commission and its local branches enabled the Soviet government to issue several decrees that struck at the heart of the speculative market. Thus, in an attempt to prevent the unauthorized removal of goods from Soviet warehouses, a decree was promulgated imposing strict rules on the management of these facilities; another law was aimed at "putting an end to the development of privately owned capitalist enterprises under the guise of domestic cooperatives" by regulating domestic industry.

The head of the Interdepartmental Commission added that since "the necessity for a competent organ which, parallel with the positive work of our central economic institutions, would expose their shortcomings and defects" had "become clear to everyone," the staff of his department was being enlarged and the "fighting apparatus" of the VCheka reorganized "in a new way." A statistical section was to be created in the Lubianka for assessing economic data from all over the country, and vital economic agencies were to be subjected to thorough investigations aimed at eliminating such defects as "red tape, bureaucratism, and lack of precise inventory controls." In general, the VCheka could henceforth be expected to take action conducive to "the development and growth of the economic institutions of the Republic by means of appropriate supervision, and, when necessary, by bringing pressure to bear on one or another aspects of their work."[106]

The importance of the VCheka's role in the Soviet economy was underscored by Lenin himself. In a speech to the fourth All-Russian Conference of Extraordinary Commissions on February 6, 1920, the Bolshevik leader noted that the military triumphs of the past several months had required

> resort to measures of coercion in the face of all lamentations, regrets, and complaints. Both before and after the October Revolution we held the view that the birth of a new order was impossible without revolutionary coercion, that all the regrets and complaints that we hear from non-Party petit-bourgeois intellectuals are simply reactionary.
>
> History has shown that without revolutionary coercion victory cannot be achieved.

This, then, had been the great contribution of the VCheka during the first two years of Soviet rule. As the chief instrument of domestic coercion, the secret police had fought valiantly against both the "avowed enemies of the workers and peasants" as well as the "wavering and unstable elements among the masses themselves." But now that the acute phase of the struggle against counterrevolution seemed to be passing, the VCheka and its local organs were faced with new and more complex challenges. Without weakening the apparatus for the suppression of the former exploiting class, the VCheka "must realize and make allowances for the transition from war to peace, little by little changing tactics and changing the character of repression."

The Soviet government, Lenin pointed out, was still faced with serious problems on the home front. Food and fuel were in short supply, and the transport system was threatened with a complete stoppage. Hence, the work of the Chekas had to be "aimed at helping the country to extricate itself from this critical plight, which without exaggeration can be said to verge on catastrophe." The manpower needed to clear the railroad tracks of snow and provide fuel for the trains and food for the cities depended, Lenin said, on "raising the social consciousness of the masses and appealing to them directly." Considerable difficulty, however, had been encountered in convincing the worker and peasant population to give themselves wholeheartedly to these tasks. The peasants, whom Lenin characterized as "very unwilling and unfriendly," refused to accept Soviet promises of future compensation in exchange for their labor and grain. It was clear that "still greater discipline" was required of the workers and peasants if starvation was to be averted and industry put back on its feet. Here was a task made to order for the VCheka:

> The use of revolutionary coercion turns this discipline into something real and definite, showing that the class-conscious working class has set itself a definite practical task, which we shall see through to its conclusion. Just as in the period of our most difficult struggle . . . we achieved the maximum exertion of the people's energy, and we won; so today, too, we must set ourselves the same aim and achieve it at all costs by the same methods. . . .
> . . . The agencies of the Cheka must become an instrument for carrying out the centralized will of the proletariat, an instrument of discipline such as we succeeded in creating in the Red Army.

There was no reason, Lenin believed, why the Chekists could not achieve results on the economic front comparable to "those we achieved in the armed struggle."[107]

Expressing the will of the Bolshevik leadership, the chairman of the VCheka called upon his comrades in the provinces to develop new approaches to their work. The time had come to put aside the "weapon of terror," which "the proletariat uses . . . only when it would be defenseless without it." At the moment, the nation's shattered economy presented a danger "a hundred times greater" than any that had been faced during the darkest days of General Denikin's advance. But this was a threat that could not be repulsed with terror:

Instead of the weapon of terror, the weapon of arrests and searches,
. . . we must reorganize the secret-operational department; it is
essential that we try to find methods which will permit us to dispense
with mass searches and terror, all the while conducting surveillance
and nipping the intrigues and conspiracies of our enemies in the bud.

From now on, the secret-operational departments were to turn all
their attention "to the economy, to food supply, to distribution,
to transport, and other institutions" as well as to speculation, that
remnant of the capitalist past which had taken hold of Soviet economic life.[108]

For a firsthand description of how the VCheka made its
presence felt in the economic administration of the Soviet Republic, we may turn to the memoirs of Simon Liberman, for
several years a non-Communist *spets* (specialist) employed by
the Soviets to help manage the vital timber industry. Liberman, a
Menshevik with "a capitalist past," recalled that he and his entire
department were viewed by the Chekists with undisguised distrust. Summoned in the fall of 1919 to appear before a three-man
VCheka committee set up to maintain a close watch over his and
other economic agencies, Liberman was warned that he would be
a candidate for a firing squad if within the next three months the
railroads should come to a halt for lack of fuel. To oversee the
day-to-day performance of Liberman's office, the VCheka
assigned its own agents to work side by side with him. Liberman
wrote: "Soon I was surrounded by persons who, I did not doubt,
reported to the Cheka all my conversations, telephone calls, the
contents of my correspondence, instructions to my subordinates,
and everything else. There was a ceaseless watch over all my
movements." It was not long before the oppressive atmosphere
of fear produced by the VCheka's representatives became
unbearable and threatened to disrupt Liberman's work. Only
after an unusual private "heart-to-heart talk" with the dreaded
chief of the VCheka was Liberman able to convince Dzerzhinsky
that his department would function more effectively without the
openly hostile attention of the secret police.[109]

By its very nature, the VCheka was particularly well suited for
overseeing the system of compulsory mass labor introduced by
the Soviet government early in 1919. Soviet labor conscription affected millions of urban and rural workers, but, while industrial

workers were for the most part merely frozen in their current jobs, the rural population

> was uprooted and torn away from its normal way of life and work and was forced to carry out tasks of a particularly onerous character. . . . The peasant—and his horse—were called upon to perform all sorts of "socially necessary" work: cutting timber, sawing firewood and bringing it to town, hauling requisitioned grain to railroads and other shipping points, driving state and Party officials from place to place, clearing roads and railroads of snow, repairing roads, loading and unloading freight cars, cultivating the fields and harvesting the crops of the families of Red Army soldiers, sweeping streets, doing janitor work in railroad stations, and similar work.[110]

On February 3, 1920, the Soviet government promulgated a decree that made virtually the entire population (with some qualifications as to age, health, and the like) liable to temporary or permanent service in whatever positions or forms of labor the state mandated. The application of compulsory labor on such a broad scale required a well-organized and ramified apparatus for planning and coordinating the manpower requirements of the Soviet Republic. This apparatus was established by the same decree in the form of the Chief Committee on Compulsory Labor *(Glavkomtrud)*.[111] Its first chairman was Felix Dzerzhinsky. One writer has suggested that Dzerzhinsky was chosen for this job "in the expectation that the reputation he had gained as Chairman of the dreaded Extraordinary Commission . . . would frighten people into taking the new Compulsory Labor Committee seriously."[112] A "Regulation on the Compulsory Involvement of Persons Not Occupied in Socially Useful Labor," signed by Dzerzhinsky on April 7, 1920, indicated that the secret police played an important part in the administration of the compulsory labor system. The VCheka and its local agencies were required by this regulation to mobilize various categories of persons, including those living on unearned income, merchants guilty of violating trade regulations, and willful work evaders, for mandatory service under the direction of *Glavkomtrud*.[113]

The exact number of workers and peasants who were mobilized throughout the Soviet Republic during the Civil War for compulsory labor is not available. But the magnitude of the operation is suggested by some figures released by *Glavkomtrud* for the first six months of 1920 and covering thirty-six provinces in which labor drafts were used for the procurement of firewood. According to these figures, 5,824,182 rural workers and 4,161,859 horses were mobilized for firewood and cartage duty.[114] This and other published evidence demonstrates that the VCheka made a major contribution to the economic and manpower needs of Lenin's Russia.[115]

The Chekists and the Bezprizornye

Mercilessness in the persecution of class enemies was not Felix Dzerzhinsky's only conspicuous trait. His Soviet biographers never fail to remind us that the dreaded chairman of the VCheka was also a man imbued with a deep love of mankind. Children in particular were his lifelong passion. Dzerzhinsky's fondness for children, especially the underprivileged, can be traced back to his years of imprisonment and exile. From his cell in Warsaw's Siedlce Prison, Dzerzhinsky wrote to his sister on October 8, 1901: "The tragedy of life is the suffering of children. I have seen children, puny, weak, and with the eyes and speech of aged people. And what a terrible sight this is! Poverty, no family warmth, motherless, brought up solely on the street, in the beerhouse—these are the things that martyrize the children."[116] And from Geneva he wrote in 1902:

> I don't know why it is that I love children more than anyone else. In their company my bad mood immediately disappears. I have never been able to love a woman in the way I love children, and I doubt if I could love my *own* children better than those of others. At times when I am despondent I dream that I have taken charge of a child abandoned on a doorstep, that I devote myself wholly to him and we are both happy. I live for him, feel him near me, feel that he loves me with that child love in which there is nothing false, I feel the warmth of his love and I passionately want to have him near me. But this is only a dream. . . . Often, very often, it seems to me, that not even a mother loves children as ardently as I do.[117]

The young revolutionary said that he loved children because they were the future and had not yet been corrupted by the evil around them. There was nothing false, he believed, in their pure young hearts.

Twenty years later, the ravages of revolution, internal war, and famine left their indelible mark on another generation of Russian children, millions of whom were left homeless, hungry, and adrift. In 1921, it was estimated that there were already four million orphans and homeless children (or *bezprizornye*, which in translation is "roofless ones") in the Soviet Republic, and the famine that swept large parts of the country in subsequent years swelled their numbers still more.

The *bezprizornye* were for years Soviet Russia's most pathetic apparition and one of its most serious social problems. Covered with scraps of sheepskin or cloth, their feet swathed in rags and stuffed into broken and discarded boots filched from the trash, the *bezprizornye* roamed the countryside in a never-ending search for food and warmth. Traveling in unruly and larcenous packs, these pitiful legacies of war and domestic strife inspired panic and fear wherever they went. In the cities, they prowled the streets by day begging and stealing, and at night they were the undisputed masters of the sewers and urinals. Natural selection and starvation eliminated many of these young vagabonds while countless others turned to a life of crime.[118]

The chairman of the VCheka, himself responsible for making orphans of thousands of children, worried about the unfortunate waifs. Early in 1921, he approached the Commissar of Education, Anatoly Lunacharsky, and in his characteristically impassioned manner proposed to put the secret police to work in the cause of saving the children. Said Dzerzhinsky: "I want to devote some of my energy and that of the VCheka to the struggle against homeless children." This decision, he added, was based on two considerations:

> In the first place, we are faced here with a terrible calamity. The fruits of the revolution are not for us but for the children. But in the meantime how many of them have been crippled by the struggle and poverty! We must immediately rush to their aid just as we would to save drowning children. The Commissariat of Education cannot cope with this task alone. The support of the entire Soviet public is required. We must create a broad-based commission as part of the Central Executive Committee with, of course, the closest cooperation of the Commissariat of Education and all other departments and organizations that can be useful in this matter. . . . I would want to head

this organization myself and include the VCheka in its work. A second consideration prompts this: I think our apparatus is one of the most efficient. Its branches are everywhere. Its opinion is taken into consideration. People are rather afraid of it. And even in such a matter as saving and providing for the welfare of children you encounter negligence and greed. We have made the transition to peaceful construction and I wonder: why not use our fighting apparatus for a struggle against a misfortune such as that confronting us in the homeless children?[119]

Thus, on January 27, 1921, the Commission to Improve the Life of Children *(Komissiia po uluchsheniiu zhiznii detei)* was established as part of the Presidium of the Central Executive Committee with Felix Dzerzhinsky at its head—yet another demonstration of the truth of Latsis's assertion that no area of Soviet life was immune from the influence of the VCheka. The seven members of the children's commission, which was charged with coordinating and controlling the work of all government agencies with responsibilities in the area of child welfare, included representatives of the commissariats of health, education, and food, the Workers' and Peasants' Inspection, and the VCheka (Dzerzhinsky's deputy was V. S. Kornev, the chief of staff of the VCheka Troops). Local branches of the children's commission were established in the provinces, where, in the majority of cases, the chairmen of the provincial Chekas occupied their leading positions. The first meeting of the children's commission took place, appropriately enough, in the Lubianka.[120]

In a circular letter addressed to the local Chekas, Dzerzhinsky announced the creation of the commission and called upon the Chekists under his command to do their utmost to support its work. "The Chekas," he wrote, "as organs of the dictatorship of the proletariat cannot remain on the sidelines but must help the Soviet authorities as much as they can in their work of protecting and caring for children." Dzerzhinsky added that the Chekas could achieve worthwhile results in this area not by paralleling or interfering with the work of other Soviet agencies but rather by rendering them full support and working in close contact and agreement with them. More specifically, Dzerzhinsky ordered the local Chekas to provide Soviet agencies concerned with the welfare of children, as well as the VCheka, with thorough and objective reports regarding the numbers, whereabouts, and condition of homeless children in their areas of jurisdiction, to aid local Soviet agencies in providing for the material needs of the *bezprizornye,* and to keep a watchful eye out for all instances of theft and malfeasance connected with the management of children's affairs. "The care of children," Dzerzhinsky concluded, "is the best means of destroying counterrevolution. Having met the challenge of providing material security and well-being for children, Soviet power will win supporters and defenders in every worker's and peasant's family and wide support in the struggle against counterrevolution."[121]

During 1921–22, the children's commission, with the help of the local Chekas, evacuated 150,000 children from the famine-stricken provinces of Russia and distributed rations and clothing to another nearly five million needy children. The Chekas also supervised the distribution of food and manufactured goods designated by the Soviet government for the use of children's homes and institutions. Nor were the Chekists found wanting when it came to making personal sacrifices on behalf of the *bezprizornye.* A number of children's homes are said to have been established with money contributed by the Chekists from their own salaries.[122] There were occasions, however, when the Chekas failed to respond to the urgent needs of Russia's homeless and sick children, and Dzerzhinsky himself had to call them to account. Thus, when the chairman of the VCheka discovered that the special department of the Tambov Cheka had just moved into a reconditioned residence while facilities for a local children's hospital were still lacking he telegraphed the chairman of the Tambov Provincial Cheka on April 14, 1921:

Immediately take steps to render complete assistance to the provincial representative of the Commission to Improve the Life of Children. The reconditioned house occupied by the special department to be transferred to the children's hospital together with the kitchen garden. Improving the material well-being of children is one of the important problems of the Republic and the provincial Cheka must help in every way possible and not become a hindrance.[123]

The readers of *Izvestiia,* accustomed for years to lethal warnings and to announcements of plots uncovered and counterrevolutionaries executed over Dzerzhinsky's signature, found an entirely different tone in his appeal "to all the workers of the USSR" published on March 31, 1923.[124] In his capacity as chairman of the Commission to Improve the Life of Children, Dzerzhinsky called upon his countrymen to make an all-out effort to save the millions of Russian children "who have neither shelter nor care." Dzerzhinsky began his appeal by declaring:

> Our young workers' republic has emerged victorious from a bitter and bloody struggle against its sworn enemies—internal and foreign counterrevolution. With new strength, which is unknown to the dying bourgeois world, the pulse of the workers' public life has begun to beat, looms have begun to work, machines to make themselves heard, and the plow has started moving more tranquilly and freely, breaking fertile soil.
>
> But this great victory of the workers was costly. As a result of the titanic struggle, deep wounds have remained in our country, which can only be healed by great efforts of the workers and peasants of Soviet Russia. One of these wounds is the material well-being of the children of the country, which is far from adequate.

It was a depressing picture of child neglect that Dzerzhinsky drew. Undernourished, exposed to epidemic diseases that literally mowed them down, driven to crime and prostitution to survive, the growing generation of Russian children was threatened "with the most serious consequences [that] compel us to sound the alarm." Dzerzhinsky appealed not only to the workers and peasants of the Soviet Republic to come to the aid of children but to foreign workers and organizations as well. "Don't stand on ceremony with regard to either the form or amount of assistance," Dzerzhinsky said. "Remember that only through the overall united efforts of the vast worker-peasant masses will we be able to emerge with honor from the struggle on this serious front of child-neglect."

Dzerzhinsky was particularly concerned with the fate of the many *bezprizornye* who had turned to a life of crime. (It was reported that in Moscow alone in 1922 more than 4,600 serious crimes had been committed by children, and incomplete statistics from 1924 indicated that 118 murders had been committed by children, 42 of them by children under eleven years of age. Overall, 50,000 juvenile delinquents were registered between

1921 and 1924.)[125] Dzerzhinsky's motto for dealing with these youthful offenders was: "Labor is the best teacher of children and teenagers."[126] At the initiative of Dzerzhinsky and some of his colleagues in the Lubianka, an unusual experiment was begun under secret police auspices to salvage some of the worst juvenile delinquents and transform them into productive Soviet citizens. The Chekists wanted to prove that a change of environment could transform the worst criminals while they were still young and malleable. In 1925, the first OGPU labor commune was created at Bolsheva in the suburbs of Moscow. All the inmates of Dzerzhinsky's "baby farm," as it was called in Cheka circles, had prison records for theft, robbery, or murder. The OGPU's labor commune for the *bezprizornye* was a unique penal institution. There were no guards or bars and the children were free to leave at any time. The only outside control consisted of a superintendent and a staff of teachers. The youngsters made and enforced their own rules of conduct, and the only conditions they had to accept were that they learn to read and write, learn a trade, and manage the commune on a self-sufficient basis. An American journalist who was permitted to visit the commune a short time after it opened reported:

> In the colony, we found the boys, about 150 of them, in fine trim. They were a self-governing body organized in teams. One team ran a shoe factory, another a machine shop, a third specialized in carpentry. They cooked their own meals, cleaned their rooms, made up their beds, played in an orchestra, sang in a choir, played football and even baseball. Boys showing aptitude for higher education were prepared for entrance examinations to high schools or to the military academy.[127]

One of the few diversions Dzerzhinsky allowed himself was frequent drives out to the Bolsheva labor commune to visit his wards. He once confided to Kursky, the Commissar of Justice: "These dirty faces are my best friends. Among them I can find rest. How much talent would have been lost had we not picked them up!"[128] By 1928, there were thirty-five OGPU labor communes for the *bezprizornye* in the USSR, and they have been credited with rescuing thousands of juveniles from a life of criminality.

Humanitarian concerns were not, however, the only considerations behind the keen interest shown by Dzerzhinsky and his fellow Chekists in the *bezprizornye.* According to the testimony of defectors from the Soviet secret police, during the 1920s the OGPU recruited substantial numbers of cadres from among the alumni of these institutions. The graduates of the labor communes and children's homes had the background and qualities made to order for service in the secret police. Hardened in their struggle for survival and isolated from the rest of society, which they tended to view with suspicion and animosity, they were in a sense foreigners in their own land. Without family or community ties, the *bezprizornye,* like the Poles, Letts, Chinese, and other foreigners who were recruited for service in the VCheka during the Civil War period, could be trusted to carry out their orders without pity or remorse.[129]

Since Lenin's day, Soviet writers have been understandably prone to emphasize the defensive character of the VCheka and the extreme circumstances that compelled the Bolshevik leaders to create it in the first place. Threatened from within—by a hostile bureaucracy, the economically debilitating activities of hordes of speculators, the counterrevolutionary designs of the Tsarist officer corps and the bourgeoisie, and the opposition of their socialist rivals—and from without—by the German occupation forces poised within striking distance of the capital city of Petrograd—the Bolsheviks had to resort to decisive measures to preserve their tenuous grip on power. And just as the Red Army was established to combat the open enemies of Soviet power on the military fronts, so the VCheka was brought into being to fight the internal enemy in the rear. Between these two fighting forces there existed, in Latsis's words, "only a division of labor."[130] The initial decision to create the VCheka may indeed have been prompted in large part by real fears of attack or subversion, but the subsequent development of the secret police cannot be ascribed to the same considerations.

In his study of the early Soviet secret police, Ernest V. Hollis, Jr., correctly pointed out that "as time went on the main continuing contribution of the VCheka system lay in its ability to apply the lash of fear to a generally weary and negatively disposed domestic population in order to galvanize it to greater efforts."[131] Recalcitrant or dishonest government officials, reluctant or disobedient Red Army troops, uncooperative or rebellious peasants, discontented or striking factory workers, in addition to speculators, outright criminals, and counterrevolutionaries, all felt the crushing blows of the fist of the proletarian dictatorship. Without a powerful and ramified apparatus of coercion capable, in Latsis's words, of "forcing action with the deadly weapon of terrorism," it is doubtful that the Soviet regime could have survived the crucible of civil war.[132]

4

Enemies of the People

In the latter part of 1918, the inhabitants of the former Russian Empire, only recently liberated from the autocratic rule of the Tsar, began to experience a new and unprecedented wave of political arrests and executions. By the time it subsided some three years later, the Bolshevik reign of terror had claimed far more victims than had all the Tsarist state security forces in the previous century. Together with other Soviet leaders, Dzerzhinsky in his public statements characterized the Red Terror of 1918–21 as "nothing but the expression of the inflexible will power of the poorest peasants and proletariat to crush all attempts at uprisings against us."[1] Far from it. Rather than being a spontaneous expression of the pent-up hostility of the toiling masses toward their former oppressors, the Red Terror was a deliberate and carefully calculated instrument of Bolshevik domestic policy. Conditions indicated to the insecure Bolshevik leaders that terror operations on a wide scale were required if they were to retain their precarious grip on power. The purpose of the Red Terror, which was implemented with the utmost ruthlessness by the VCheka and its network of local organs, was not only to suppress open counterrevolutionary assaults on the part of the bourgeoisie. It was also intended to help preserve Bolshevik rule against the mounting disaffection and resistance of multitudes of people with impeccable proletarian credentials.

The Year 1918

Every Friday was "Party day" in Moscow. Members of the Council of People's Commissars and other high-ranking Bolshevik Party and state officials fanned out over the city to address mass meetings of workers and soldiers in offices and public places. On Friday, August 30, 1918, Lenin was scheduled to appear at an assembly of factory workers at the former Mikhelson plant. News of the assassination a few hours earlier of Moisei Uritsky, chairman of the Petrograd Cheka, did not deter Lenin from keeping his engagement. Later that evening he concluded a fiery speech to a crowd of about a thousand workers with the words: "For us there is one alternative: Victory or Death." Before the applause had ended, Lenin was making his way to the automobile waiting to take him back to the Kremlin. Suddenly, just as he was about to reach the curb, a woman bystander forced her way through the crowd that had surrounded the Bolshevik leader, pulled out a revolver, and fired three times. Hit in the shoulder and chest, Lenin fell to the ground.[2] These shots ushered in a sanguinary period in Soviet history known ever since as the Red Terror.

Although Fanny Kaplan, Lenin's would-be assassin, was a dissident socialist who had spent time in a Tsarist jail for underground revolutionary activity, the Soviet leaders seized upon the episode as an excuse and basis for launching their own reign of terror.[3] Pitiless mass murder became the order of the day as the Soviet government exhorted its officials, from the capital to the most remote village crossroad, to take to the sword and cut down all class enemies. Typical of the homicidal appeals issued in the wake of the Lenin assassination attempt was a proclamation signed by Yakov Peters, deputy chairman of the VCheka:

> The counterrevolution is raising its head. The enraged bourgeoisie, aided by capitalist flunkeys, is trying to snatch from our ranks the leaders who fight for the worker-peasant cause. The criminal hand of a member of the Socialist Revolutionary Party, instigated by the English and French, has dared to fire on the leader of the working class. The bullet was directed not only against Comrade Lenin but also against the working class as a whole.
>
> At this crucial moment it is your duty to tighten your ranks and crush the counterrevolutionary beast with a mighty effort.

The criminal adventure of Socialist Revolutionaries, White Guards, and other pseudo socialists forces us to reply to the criminal designs of the enemies of the working class with mass terror. The avenging hand of the working class is engaged in breaking the chains of slavery, and woe to him who stands in the way of the working class and dares to place obstacles before the socialist revolution.

Peters's edict threatened immediate execution to anyone caught possessing arms without authorization and banishment to concentration camps for those agitating against the Soviet government. Persons taking part in counterrevolutionary plots were warned that they too would be "crushed by the heavy hammer of the revolutionary proletariat."[4]

At about the same time, the Bolshevik Commissar of Internal Affairs, Petrovsky, addressed to all local soviets a peremptory order:

The least opposition, the least movement among the White Guards, should be met with wholesale executions. Local provincial executive committees should take the initiative and set the example.

Chekas and militia should make special efforts to locate and arrest all those living under assumed names and to shoot without formality everyone mixed up in White Guard activities. . . .

The rear of our army must be finally and thoroughly cleared of any White Guards and all dirty plotters against the power of the working class and the poorest peasantry. Show no wavering or indecisiveness in carrying out mass terror.[5]

And on September 5, 1918, the campaign of state-sanctioned homicide was given the formal blessing of law, when the Council of People's Commissars issued the famous "Decree on the Red Terror," which stated:

The Council of People's Commissars, having heard the report of the Chairman of the All-Russian Extraordinary Commission . . . on its activities, finds that in the present situation the safeguarding of the rear by means of terror is of primary importance; that to improve the work of the All-Russian Extraordinary Commission . . . and give it a more planned character, it is necessary to reinforce it with a greater number of responsible Party comrades; that it is necessary to secure the Soviet Republic from its class enemies by means of isolating them in concentration camps; that all persons involved in White Guard organizations, plots, and uprisings shall be subject to execution; that it is necessary to publish the names of all who are executed together with the reasons for taking this measure against them.[6]

This law brought to an end a period of actual though still unofficial terror. In the months that had passed since the execution of Prince Eboli, the VCheka and its local organs continued to impose the death penalty on class enemies without benefit of published authorization. After the attempt on Lenin's life, however, massive state terror displaced the individual terror of the preceding months, and the secret police was endowed with virtually unlimited powers of life and death over the entire citizenry. A deliberate decision had been made by the highest Bolshevik leadership to liquidate part of the population in order to control the rest through fear and intimidation. The logic of the plan was succinctly stated by Leon Trotsky: "A victorious war, generally speaking, destroys only an insignificant part of the conquered army, intimidating the remainder and breaking their will. The revolution works in the same way: it kills individuals and intimidates thousands."[7]

The claim traditionally advanced by Soviet writers that the Red Terror was inaugurated only after the attempt on Lenin's life as an extreme measure of self-defense seems arbitrary at best. Lenin himself began to lay the foundations for his regime's terror campaign almost from the day in October 1917 when he appeared before the Petrograd Soviet to proclaim the birth of the Workers' and Peasants' Government. Thus, upon hearing that capital punishment for soldiers had been repealed without his knowledge on the day of the Bolshevik seizure of power, Lenin said: "Nonsense. How can you make a revolution without firing squads? Do you think you will be able to deal with all your enemies by laying down your arms? What other means of repression do you have? Imprisonment? No one attaches any importance to this during a civil war when each side hopes to win."[8] Lenin constantly admonished his wavering colleagues to stiffen their spines. Leon Trotsky, in his biographical sketch of Lenin, recalled: "Any signs of sentimentality, of easygoing cordiality, of softness—and there was a great surplus of all this—angered him not intrinsically, but because he saw in them a sign that even the elite of the working class was not fully aware of the extraordinary difficulties which could be accomplished only by means of quite extraordinary energy."[9] Lenin did not miss an opportunity, whether at the closed-door sessions of the Council of People's Commissars or in pronouncements intended for public consumption, to stress the necessity of terroristic measures. "Where is our dictatorship?" Lenin would ask rhetorically. "Well, show it to me! We have a mess, not a dictatorship. If we are incapable of shooting a White Guard saboteur, then what sort of a great revolution is this? Just look what those bourgeois wretches are writing in their newspapers! Where is the dictatorship? Nothing but prattle and mess."[10]

In an essay entitled "How to Organize the Competition," written early in December 1917, Lenin called for a purge of the Russian land "of all vermin, of fleas—the rogues, of bugs—the rich, and so on and so forth." And who was included in these categories of vermin and bugs? Naturally, such class enemies as the "idle rich," "priests," "scribes," "bureaucrats," "slovenly and hysterical intellectuals," and all the rest of "the spawn of capitalism." Lenin wanted a "war to the death" against "these survivals of accursed capitalist society, these dregs of humanity, these hopelessly decayed and atrophied limbs, this contagion, this plague, this ulcer that socialism has inherited from capitalism." But the vermin and parasites Lenin wanted to sweep from the face of the earth sometimes also took the form of ordinary working-class people. Workers, for example, who shirked their duty, like the compositors in the Party's Petrograd printing shops, were vermin to be imprisoned. Indeed, vermin could be found in every village, town, and factory in the country, and "thousands of practical forms and methods" would have to be adopted to rid Russia of them. One out of ten idlers might be shot as an example for others; some could be put to cleaning latrines; still others might be jailed. The possibilities for dealing with the vermin were limitless.[11]

Typical also of Lenin's attitude toward violence and terror was his report to the Third All-Russian Congress of Soviets in January 1918 in which he said: "We must not depict socialism as if socialists will bring it to us on a plate all nicely dressed. That will never happen. Not a single problem of the class struggle has ever been solved in history except by violence. When violence is exercised by the working people, by the mass of exploited against the exploiters—then we are for it!"[12] And in June 1918, when V. Volodarsky, a Petrograd official in charge of propaganda and agitation, was assassinated, Lenin complained in a note to Zinoviev that local Communist authorities were restraining the workers of Petrograd from carrying out their wish to "revenge the death of their favorite by mass terror." Lenin found this unacceptable and added:

> I protest most emphatically!
> We are discrediting ourselves: we threaten mass terror in resolutions of the Soviet of Deputies, yet when it comes to action we obstruct the revolutionary initiative of the masses, a quite correct one. This is im-pos-sible!
> The terrorists will think us old women. This is wartime above all. We must encourage the energy and mass character of the terror against the counterrevolutionaries, and particularly in Petrograd, the example of which is decisive.[13]

Nor was the VCheka unprepared for the Red Terror. Numerous pronouncements made during the early months of Bolshevik rule left no doubt of the VCheka's intentions. As early as February 1918, the VCheka informed the public that "until now the Commission has been generous in the struggle against enemies of the people, but at the present time when inspired by the treacherous assault of the German counterrevolutionaries the hydra of counterrevolution becomes more brazen with each passing day, when the worldwide bourgeoisie attempts to strangle the vanguard of the revolutionary international—the Russian proletariat—the All-Russian Extraordinary Commission . . . sees no other way to combat counterrevolutionaries, spies, speculators, criminals, hooligans, saboteurs, and other parasites than by mercilessly destroying them at the scene of the crime."[14]

In an interview published in June 1918 the chairman of the VCheka announced:

> We stand for organized terror—this should be frankly admitted. Terror is an absolute necessity during times of revolution.
> Our aim is to fight against the enemies of Soviet power and of the new order of life. Among such enemies are our political opponents as well as bandits, swindlers, speculators, and other criminals who undermine the foundations of socialist power. In dealing with such

persons we show no mercy. We terrorize the enemies of Soviet power in order to suppress crime at its roots.[15]

And in August *Izvestiia* published Latsis's disquisition on "the law of civil war," which observed that such accepted rules of warfare as the inviolability of peace delegations and the taking of prisoners did not apply to the struggle in Russia:

This is the law of civil war—kill all who are wounded in the battle against you. . . . It is necessary not only to destroy the active forces of the opponent, but to demonstrate that anyone who raises the sword against the existing regime will perish by the sword. This is the meaning of civil war.

In a civil war, the enemy is not tried in a court.

It is a life-and-death struggle. If you do not kill, you shall be killed. Therefore, kill that you may not be killed.[16]

During the early days of the Terror it was believed that wide publicity of the sanguinary deeds of the VCheka and its local organs would more effectively intimidate the citizenry. As Latsis wrote: "The Extraordinary Commissions always tried to do their work in such a way that only the mention of the Commissions would destroy any desire to sabotage, extort, and plot."[17] To strike fear into the people and to demonstrate the absolute futility of opposition to the Bolshevik regime, the VCheka and the government press began to publish regular announcements of executions carried out in defense of the revolutionary order. So it was that as the first wave of slaughter submerged the cities, towns, and villages under Bolshevik control, word was received that five hundred hostages had been shot in Petrograd in revenge for the assassination of Uritsky, chairman of the local Cheka, and the attack on Lenin; at the same time it was also announced that "the criminal attempt" on the life of the leader of the Workers' and Peasants' Government had exhausted "the patience of the revolutionary proletariat of Nizhny-Novgorod" and that the local Cheka had shot forty-one persons "from the enemy camp."[18] The first number of the *VCheka Weekly,* which was published for "the instruction and ideal guidance" of provincial and district Chekas, issued the following call to battle:

It is time—before it is too late—to introduce in deeds, not words, the most merciless, properly organized mass terror. In bringing death to thousands of white-handed people, . . . we shall save the socialist revolution.

. . . We have drawn the sword and will not sheath it as long as one single foe remains.

Tremble, ye foes of the workers' and peasants' Russia! Our hand will not tremble. Just wait. Your turn is coming.[19]

There was never any mention that a single prisoner or hostage executed in response to such calls for bloodshed had played any role—direct or indirect—in the shooting incident at the Mikhelson plant.

At least initially the Chekists were encouraged to select for summary execution persons who belonged to the formerly privileged and propertied classes—factory owners, big land-owners, merchants, priests, Tsarist officials, army officers. These might be expected to form the nucleus of organized opposition to the Bolshevik dictatorship, and rendering them harmless was given top priority. The victory of the toiling masses, so it was argued, could not be achieved without inflicting terrible losses on the hostile classes. "Its sturdiest, bravest, most intelligent sons must be cut down. The best of its life-blood must be drained."[20] As Latsis put it: "We are not warring against individual bourgeois. We are out to destroy the bourgeoisie as a class." This objective was to guide all Chekists in the conduct of their interrogations:

Whenever a bourgeois is under examination the first step should be, not to endeavor to discover material proof that the accused has opposed the Soviet government verbally or actually, but to put to the accused these three questions: "To what class does the accused belong?" "What is his origin?" "Describe his upbringing, education, and profession." Solely in accordance with the answers to these three questions should his fate be decided. For this is what "Red Terror" means, and what it implies.[21]

As the months and years of Red Terror passed, however, the secret police began to claim ever more victims from the ranks of the toiling masses themselves until finally, by the end of the Civil War period, the Soviet authorities had to admit that their prisons and concentration camps were overflowing not with the bourgeoisie but with ordinary workers and peasants. And what was true of the prisons and concentration camps was, we may presume, true also of the countless unmarked graves filled by Cheka executioners.

More than 47,000 persons were officially reported to have been arrested by the Soviet secret police in 1918. The approach that was supposedly to guide Chekists in handling their prisoners had been outlined by Dzerzhinsky and his colleague Zaks months before the Red Terror was launched. Early in June 1918, in response to charges that the VCheka was not abiding by such "normal state procedures" as trials, personal guarantees, and investigations, Dzerzhinsky stated that the "character and task" of his organization had not been properly understood by "the public and the press." The VCheka, he pointed out, had "nothing in common" with the juridical institutions of the Soviet state. It was VCheka practice to "judge quickly":

> In the majority of cases only a day or a few days pass between the apprehension of the criminal and his sentence. But this, however, does not mean that our sentences are not well founded. Of course, we can make mistakes, but up to this time no mistake has been made. Our records prove this. In almost all cases the criminals, trapped by the evidence, confess their crimes. And what sort of argument has greater weight than the accused's own confession?

Zaks, a member of the VCheka Collegium, was quick to respond to charges that the secret police used torture to obtain these confessions:

> All rumors and stories about the supposed use of coercion in the course of interrogations are absolutely false. We ourselves are carrying on a struggle with those elements in our ranks who show themselves unworthy of membership in our Commission.[22]

In actuality, Cheka practices in 1918 and later years bore little resemblance to the declarations of Dzerzhinsky and Zaks. Not only did the Chekists commonly hold prisoners under arrest for weeks and months before formally charging them with a crime, but torture (or "physical methods of persuasion") was already in widespread, though not universal, use in Cheka offices around the country. In their relentless pursuit of class enemies the Chekists were hindered by only the most rudimentary procedural requirements. The closest approximation to a formula of criminal procedure binding upon Cheka commissars consisted of a few provisions contained in a secret document entitled "The Structure of the Departments of Extraordinary Commissions" that was issued by the VCheka in August 1918.[23] These provisions merely required that orders for searches and arrests be signed by the appropriate Cheka official, that the orders contain precise addresses and accurate identification of those to be arrested, and that careful records be kept of all items confiscated during an operation. Aside from these minimal requirements (supplemented in December 1918 by a law requiring the Chekas to notify within two days those institutions directly affected by the arrest of responsible workers and specialists) "there was never any question," as one writer put it, "but that [the] Chekas could arrest anyone, anywhere, in the absence of any legally incumbent formalities, at any time of the day or night, on any basis of suspicion whatsoever."[24]

Since many of the prisoners of the Chekas were arrested solely on the basis of their class origins, political affiliations, or prerevolutionary occupations, their involvement in the Red Terror was, in a sense, impersonal; but the effect on their lives in terms of misery and suffering was not. The suffering was painful, and often ended with an agonizing death. The harrowing experiences of some Cheka victims were described in a report compiled by an official commission of inquiry appointed by General Denikin after his forces had obtained control of much of south Russia. Based on the testimony of witnesses and survivors, the report conveys a vivid impression of how the Decree on the Red Terror was translated into reality in the city of Tsaritsyn, an important river port on the Volga (later renamed Stalingrad and known today as Volgagrad).[25] The Extraordinary Commission of Tsaritsyn was established at the end of May 1918. For their headquarters the Tsaritsyn Chekists requisitioned the Galdobin house, a large two-story brick residence overlooking the Volga. The Chekists used the upper floor for their offices and living quarters, but two rooms were set aside for the interrogation of prisoners. On the ground floor several rooms were partitioned and turned into makeshift cells. One cell was reserved for those who had been condemned to death, while the remaining cells were used for general confinement. With the balconies and entrances barricaded by well-oiled machine guns and the premises guarded all around by heavily armed detachments of Letts and Chinese, the Tsaritsyn Chekists set out to rid the city of White Guards and other enemies of the people.

The local newspapers and the official press organ of the Tsaritsyn Cheka published the names of hundreds of persons arrested for counterrevolutionary activity, participation in anti-Soviet plots, concealment of arms, and speculation. But many others were arrested without any apparent reason or on the flimsiest foundations. A waiter found himself under arrest for having asked ten roubles for a watermelon, the price set by the owner of the hotel. The guest turned out to be a Chekist, who considered the price too high and vented his displeasure on the unfortunate employee. On another occasion a Cheka commissar arrested a sailor who had tried to buy a few roubles' worth of tobacco from a street vendor on the grounds that the transaction had been speculative. The Chekist took his man to headquarters but was immediately sent out on another mission and could not complete his report. Meanwhile, the sailor was "temporarily" put into one of the common cells. There he remained for two months until his case was finally straightened out. In general, a citizen was a prime candidate for a cell if the Chekists, in their frequent mass searches and roundups, found shoulder straps or military decorations in his possession, for these were taken as proof of White Guard sympathies. It was easy to be arrested by the Tsaritsyn Cheka, but release was arduous. "The majority of prisoners," according to the report, "were held under guard for months, not only without announcement of any kind of charge, but also without being interrogated, not even knowing precisely of what they were suspected and by whose denunciation they had been arrested."

In the Galdobin house the overcrowding of cells caused much suffering. A cell measuring ten by twenty-three feet might contain up to forty persons. At one point in November 1918, a cell of only slightly larger dimensions held 133 prisoners. During the day, sitting or standing, the prisoners could manage, but at night there was not enough room for everyone to lie down on the floor and many had to stand against the walls. All day long an endless line stood in front of the prison's sole lavatory, while at night the inmates had to manage with a single night pail in each cell; but as these were of totally inadequate size and could not be taken out and emptied before a certain hour, they often overflowed before morning. The prison officials seemed purposely to encourage filth as a means of tormenting the prisoners. They were denied any opportunity to clean their cells, bathe, or wash their clothing so that not only was the air foul and stifling from the stink of excrement and unwashed bodies, but lice and other parasites swarmed over everything and everybody. Appeals or complaints to the Commandant of the Cheka, a man by the name of Trotskin who quickly distinguished himself by his cruelty, were met with abuse and derision. When one of the prisoners dared approach him with a request for a transfer to another cell, Trotskin seized the man by the collar, dragged him out to the lavatory, and forced his head into a pail of excrement.

The daily food ration in the Galdobin house consisted of three-quarters of a pound of bread. Conditions were even worse in the other places of confinement maintained by the Tsaritsyn Cheka. The former Emerkhanov house (renamed The House of Preliminary Detention No. 1) and two barges moored in front of the Galdobin residence were reserved for the clergy, intelligentsia, and officers arrested as hostages. Here the basic ration was reduced to one-eighth of a pound of bread a day. Those prisoners who received no food parcels from outside endured slow starvation and were driven in desperation to extracting scraps from the night pail.

An indignant letter published in the pages of the *VCheka Weekly* in October 1918 bearing the signatures of the chairman and secretary of the Nolinsk Cheka in Viatka Province, together with the editorial comment that accompanied it, is an early indication that the use of torture was tacitly approved by the VCheka leadership. In their letter the Chekists of Nolinsk expressed a sense of dismay over the excessively lenient treatment received by the British diplomat Bruce Lockhart, who was arrested by the VCheka a few weeks before in connection with a counterrevolutionary plot only to be released unharmed a short time later. The Chekists of Nolinsk wrote:

We say bluntly . . . the VCheka has still not rid itself of petit-bourgeois ideology, the damned inheritance of the prerevolutionary past.

Tell us, why didn't you subject him, this same Lockhart, to the most refined tortures in order to extract evidence and addresses, which such a goose must have had in abundance? With such information you could have easily uncovered a whole series of counterrevolutionary organizations, perhaps even destroying the possibility of financing them in the future, which is undoubtedly tantamount to destroying them. Tell us, why was it that instead of subjecting him to tortures the very description of which would have filled counterrevolutionaries with cold terror, you instead allowed him to "leave" the VCheka in great confusion? . . .

Enough of sentimentalizing. . . .

A dangerous scoundrel was caught. Get out of him what you can and send him to the next world.

The editorial staff of the *VCheka Weekly* saw no reason to chastize the Nolinsk Chekists for extolling the use of "refined torture." Instead, the VCheka merely stated for the record: "Not objecting in principle, we only wish to point out to the comrades who sent this letter and reproached us for sentimentality that it is not at all in our interest to 'send to the next world scoundrelly intriguers' representing 'foreign people.' "[26]

Nobody could accuse the Tsaritsyn Cheka of excessive sentimentality when it came to extirpating the class enemy. The Cheka interrogators of Tsaritsyn, according to the findings of the Denikin Commission, were for the most part brutal and sadistic men. They usually conducted their interrogations late at night. Prisoners would be awakened by a torrent of abuse and taken to the second floor, where the Chekists' offices were located. "Examinations were often accompanied by cruel beatings and torture," according to the report of the Denikin Commission. One day a local resident came to the headquarters of the Tsaritsyn Cheka to seek a meeting with his son who was imprisoned there. He was shown to the waiting room adjacent to the study of the chairman of the Cheka. The door of the study was ajar, and the visitor thus came to witness a ghastly scene. Cherviakov, the chairman of the Cheka, his assistant Ivanov, and the Commandant, Trotskin, together with three other heavily armed men, were "examining" four prisoners (three men and one woman). At first all was quiet. Suddenly Cherviakov yelled: "You are counterrevolutionaries! Confess!" With that, the

Chekists pounced on the prisoners and began to beat them with their revolver butts. The screams and cries of the prisoners were interrupted by Cherviakov, who warned them: "Not a sound, or a bullet stops it." The prisoners lay on the floor, blood streaming from their faces, but the "examination" continued accompanied by more cries and groans. Presently, Cherviakov became aware of the visitor in the other room and hastily ordered the area cleared, thus ending the examination for the time being.

A lawyer, newly arrived in one of the cells of the Tsaritsyn Cheka, tried to get some information from his cellmates about the way inquiries were conducted and how accusations were formulated. A Cossack officer who had been interrogated the previous evening volunteered an answer. The officer rose slowly and painfully from the floor and with a neighbor's help tore off the bloody shirt stuck to his back. "This is how they examine here," he said. The officer had first been placed, barefoot, on a red-hot frying pan; this torture was abandoned and he was beaten with a whip with metallic ends until his back, from the neck to the pelvis, was one mass of torn, dangling flesh. (On the following day the officer was removed from the cell and shot.)[27]

E. V. Dumbadze, an ex-Chekist from the Caucasus, described in his memoirs a method of intimidation ("often practiced in Cheka organs") he used in order to extract confessions from particularly stubborn prisoners:

> I sat the arrested person down facing me, drew my revolver and, aiming it into his eyes, I fired, purposely missing him. As soon as the smoke cleared, as if amazed to note that the arrested man was "alive," I summoned a soldier and shouted at him:
> "Why did you give me a faulty revolver? Give me the mauser!"

This was usually sufficient to produce the desired "confession." To this description of his favorite method of interrogation, Dumbadze added: "I have often chanced to read about all kinds of tortures as evidenced by persons who were under investigation. . . . But, except for the indicated means of intimidation, in reality a method of moral cruelty, I personally know of no others."[28]

But, of course, there were others. The Chekists by no means limited themselves to such conventional and unimaginative tortures as floggings, beatings, burnings, and fake executions. The following two examples indicate the range of their ingenuity. In the confinement torture, prisoners still uncertain of their own fates would be confined with the dead bodies of earlier victims. The confinement was usually in the same room or cellar where executions normally took place. In some cases prisoners were put into coffins with the corpses of those who had been shot the day before.[29] Our second example, the rat torture, was a specialty of the Kiev Cheka and caused unimaginable suffering. The prisoner was tied to a stake and one end of a hollow tube a few inches in diameter was attached to his midsection. A live rat was inserted into the tube at the other end, which was then sealed with wire mesh. The tube was then held over a flame, and the rat, in its mad frenzy, tried to escape the heat by gnawing its way through the prisoner's body.[30]

By late September, Lenin had sufficiently recovered from his wounds to return to his writing with "The Character of our Newspapers," a call for "war" against those elements of the working class who persisted in behaving like the "custodians of capitalist traditions" (that is, workers who refused to work for nothing and went on strike).[31] Lenin wanted Soviet newspapers to give less attention to well-known and worn-out political themes "like the foul treachery of the Mensheviks" and the "struggle between the two camps [of the] insurrectionary proletariat and the handful of capitalist slaveowners," and more space to economic matters. By economics Lenin did not mean "general discussions, learned reviews, intellectual plans, and similar piffle," but rather economics stressing "the actual organization of the new life." More specifically, Lenin wanted to know why the newspapers had not done more to expose those workers whose lagging class-consciousness qualified them for membership in the enemy camp. In another article, published on November 20, Lenin was even more blunt: "It would be ridiculous and foolish to refrain from employing terror against and suppressing the landowners and capitalists and their henchmen, who are selling Russia to the foreign imperialist 'Allies.' "[32] Lenin's words show that the attempt upon his life had only reaffirmed his commitment to terror as an indispensable weapon of Bolshevik rule. For over a year now his terroristic propaganda had fanned the flames of inhumanity and licentiousness, and with predictable results.

The savage, bloody nightmare of Red Terror unleashed by the Lenin assassination attempt claimed, according to Latsis's admittedly incomplete statistics, more than 6,300 victims by the end of 1918. The chief historian of the VCheka classified these executions as punishments for the following crimes: espionage, 56; revolts, 2,431; participation in counterrevolutionary organizations, 1,637; inciting to revolt, 396; speculation, 39; banditry, 402; desertion, 39; malfeasance, 157; miscellaneous [*sic*], 1,173.[33]

Did the directors of the terror actually believe that all those subjected to arrest and execution posed a real threat to the revolutionary order? The answer appears to be that they did not. The psychological and deterrent effect of mass arrests and arbitrary imprisonment and execution on those still at liberty seems to have been uppermost in the minds of the VCheka high command. As Latsis pointed out in another of his writings, a prime consideration in determining the ultimate fate of a prisoner was the impact his execution would have on other actual or potential opponents of the Workers' and Peasants' Government. "For the most part," Latsis wrote, "the supreme measure of punishment was applied for the purpose of influencing the counterrevolutionary element, for the purpose of producing the necessary effect, intimidation."[34]

The Year 1919

A turning point for the beleaguered Bolsheviks occurred in 1919. Major battles were fought on all fronts of the Civil War—in the north, south, east, and west—and, on one front after another the Red Army broke the backs of its divided and poorly coordinated enemies. In January, advancing in the west and south, the Red Army captured Riga, capital of Latvia, and Kharkov and Kiev, two of the largest cities in the Ukraine. In April, Bolshevik forces reached Odessa and the Crimea, while also halting General Kolchak's western advance to the Volga. To be sure, 1919 was not a year of steady and uninterrupted military successes; some serious reversals also occurred. In the spring, General Denikin launched his own counteroffensive in the south; between May and October, his troops recaptured Kharkov, Kiev, Odessa, and Tsaritsyn, and at one point came to within 250 miles of Moscow. In the north, General Yudenich's drive on Petrograd approached the city's gates before his troops were turned back in bitter fighting. Yet, by the end of 1919, these dangers had been repulsed and there could be no doubt that the tide of battle had shifted decisively to the side of the Bolsheviks.

Meanwhile, the "punishing sword of the revolution" was not rusting in its scabbard. The victories of 1919 not only afforded the VCheka a much enlarged field for its own operations, but created new challenges and priorities as well. On February 17, 1919, Felix Dzerzhinsky told a meeting of the Central Executive Committee, somewhat prematurely as it turned out, that the chief internal foes of the Workers' and Peasants' Government—the former officers, bourgeoisie, Tsarist officialdom, and all their hangers-on—had been dispersed:

> Some fled to the other side, some we destroyed, and some, giving up any hope of quick victory, have resigned themselves to economic necessity and have met us half way. . . . Now our enemies' system of fighting against us has changed. They are trying to worm their way into our Soviet institutions in order to sabotage us from within and await the moment when our external enemies are ready to strike again.
> Then, having taken control of the organs and apparatus of power, they will use it against us.

There were dangerous enemies, Dzerzhinsky added, "in almost all of our institutions." But the VCheka could not apply its old methods and simply smash these Soviet institutions. Instead, the VCheka and its local organs would have to change their methods of struggle drastically. In general, a more rational and carefully planned approach to dealing with enemies of the people had to be devised.

Dzerzhinsky proposed, for example, that more use be made of concentration camps and forced labor. This was a form of punishment ideally suited to the current manpower needs of the Soviet government:

> In addition to court sentences, it is essential to retain administrative punishment, namely concentration camps. At the present time we are far from utilizing the labor of prisoners on public projects, and so I propose to retain these concentration camps for the use of the labor of arrested persons—for the gentry who are living without working, for those who are unable to work without a certain degree of compulsion. Consider also our Soviet institutions. Here too we must apply a form

of punishment for careless attitudes toward work, for delay, for negligence, and so forth. By this means we can even tighten up our own workers.[35]

On the same day the Central Executive Committee dutifully passed a decree that stated in part: "The All-Russian Extraordinary Commission is granted the right to sentence to a concentration camp."[36]

Concentration camps and forced labor made their appearance in the Soviet Republic more or less simultaneously during the early months of Bolshevik rule and have remained permanent features of the Soviet system. Forced labor was first mentioned in a decree of January 1918 that stipulated: "Work details are to be formed from among the prisoners able to work, for the carrying out of tasks necessary for the state, tasks no more strenuous than those of unskilled workers."[37] Lenin thought that concentration camps were well suited for the incarceration of proven or suspected counterrevolutionaries. In August 1918, he sent the following order to the chairman of the Penza Province Executive Committee in connection with an uprising that had broken out in that region a few days earlier: "Essential to organize a reinforced guard of selected and reliable people to carry out a campaign of ruthless mass terror against the kulaks, priests, and whiteguards; suspects to be shut up in a detention camp outside the city."[38] The Decree on the Red Terror, promulgated by the Council of People's Commissars on September 5, 1918, had also pointed to the necessity of safeguarding the Soviet Republic "from class enemies by means of isolating them in concentration camps."[39]

The improvised forced labor camp set up by the Kamyshinsk Cheka in the late summer of 1918 was typical of the early experiments utilizing the labor of suspected class enemies. According to one of its officials, "the Cheka has registered all the big bourgeois, and at the moment they are being kept on a barge; during the day they work in the town." When suddenly the imprisoned bourgeois fell mysteriously ill, the Cheka agreed to call in a highly recommended physician from Saratov, who immediately prescribed more and better food for the prisoners and release from their work duties in the town. The Chekists soon became suspicious of the doctor and began investigating his background. The doctor turned out to be an impostor. "Now he too is on the barge," the Chekist official noted with obvious satisfaction.[40] In setting up its own makeshift forced-labor camp, the district Cheka of Kamyshinsk was imitating the example of the Chekas of Moscow, Petrograd, and other Soviet centers that had already, according to an authoritative Soviet source, established forced-labor facilities.[41]

More detailed provisions regarding forced-labor camps did not appear until the spring of 1919, when two important decrees were issued by the Soviet government. According to a decree of April 11, 1919, forced-labor camps were henceforth to be placed under the jurisdiction of the administrative sections of the provincial soviets.[42] The provincial Chekas continued to be responsible for the initial organization and supervision of the camps, but were ordered to transfer them to the soviets "upon notification from the central government." Persons subject to confinement in the forced-labor camps were to include "individuals and categories of individuals concerning whom there is a decision by the administrative departments [of provincial soviets], the Chekas, the revolutionary tribunals, the people's courts, and other Soviet institutions granted this power by decrees and orders." The entire nationwide network of forced-labor camps was in turn to be administered by the newly created Central Administration for Forced Labor attached to the People's Commissariat of Internal Affairs, the agency with overall responsibility for guiding and directing the work of the local soviets. A supplementary decree of May 12, 1919, in addition to spelling out in considerable detail the regulations that were to guide the administration of forced-labor camps, reaffirmed the role of the secret police in their initial organization. The decree called upon provincial Chekas to establish "forced-labor camps with a capacity of not less than 300 prisoners . . . in every provincial center."[43]

The VCheka's continued important role in the expanding forced-labor camp network was assured not only by provisions of these and other decrees, but also by the fact that the Central Committee of the Communist Party had just recently appointed Dzerzhinsky People's Commissar of Internal Affairs. Dzerzhinsky's new post greatly enhanced his power and that of the secret police in all areas of Soviet internal security. According to a recent Soviet biography of the Cheka leader, his appointment as Commissar of Internal Affairs "had great political significance. This measure ensured unified leadership and coordination of the activities of all organs responsible for the struggle against counterrevolution and crime and the maintenance of social order."[44]

By the end of the Civil War there were tens of thousands of prisoners in Soviet forced-labor camps. The People's Commissariat of Internal Affairs reported in 1922 that it had 132 forced-labor camps under its jurisdiction, excluding those in the Ukraine and the Kirghiz Autonomous Republic where they were run by the local "organs of justice." These camps were scattered over forty-two provinces of central and northern Russia and Siberia and were said to hold approximately 60,000 prisoners, about 30 percent of them charged with counterrevolutionary activity. One of the largest camps, the Petchora River Penal Settlement, was located some four hundred miles northeast of Arkhangelsk and had a population of about five thousand. Despite the appalling conditions and the high death rates in the camps, the population was maintained at a fairly constant level by a continuous stream of fresh arrivals.[45]

The provisions of a top-secret document issued by the All-Ukrainian Cheka may serve as another example of how the more rational, planned approach to combating Bolshevism's internal foes called for by Felix Dzerzhinsky early in 1919 was carried into effect in a major theater of secret police operations. The document, entitled "Instructions to the Juridical Department," was intended to guide the work of local Cheka investigators *(sledovateli).*[46] (A staff of investigators was attached to each district and provincial Cheka. The investigators were responsible for examining all information and evidence collected during search-and-arrest operations and for interrogating the prisoners. Indeed, the ultimate fate of every occupant of a Cheka cell rested in their hands. For the conclusions and recommendations of the Cheka investigator usually formed the basis for the brief deliberations of the Cheka collegiums whose final verdict determined whether a prisoner lived or died.)[47]

The instructions began by pointing out that it was not the business of the Chekas to conduct trials of apprehended criminals; this was properly the job of the courts. "Our task," it was stated, "is to *influence morally* [my emphasis] the suspect and thereby prevent the repetition of the crime." Evidence of guilt was not required before "moral influence" could be brought to bear upon "exploiters of other people's labor or counterrevolutionaries." It was sufficient merely "to determine such a person's social status and political physiognomy in order to subject him to administrative measures [that is, imprisonment and/or execution] as a class enemy of the proletariat and communism."

Cheka investigations, the instructions continued, could fall into any of three distinct categories, each guided by special objectives and procedures: cases of disclosed crimes; cases of suspected crimes; and cases for secret investigation. In cases of "disclosed crimes" *(raskrytie prestupleniia)* the Cheka investigator was to bear in mind that it was more important to incriminate other as yet unidentified participants in the crime than prove the guilt or innocence of the accused in an impartial manner. According to the instructions:

> One should never interrogate the accused, or confront him with material evidence convicting him of guilt at the beginning of the interrogation. It is important to ascertain first other participants in the case and the possibility of other yet undisclosed crimes. Only after this has been done should an accusation be produced on the basis of material evidence. After the final interrogation of the accused, the investigator must formulate his opinion or indictment and read it to the accused and have the latter sign the document.

If, on the basis of the evidence, the Cheka investigator had reason to believe that other persons whose guilt had still to be determined might be involved in the case, he could request the secret department of the Cheka to take "preventive measures" against these new additional suspects. Acting without the knowledge or consent of the courts, the secret department was authorized to arrest and imprison additional suspects for indefinite periods.

Cases of persons who were only suspected of having committed a crime had to be handled "with extreme caution." "Formal investigations" and "repressive measures" were to be avoided. In dealing with suspected violators of the revolutionary order, the Chekists were urged to do nothing that would cause the suspect to believe he was under investigation. Only after the interrogation of witnesses and the careful gathering of all incriminating evidence was the suspect to be arrested and charged with a crime. Cheka investigators were ordered to work in close contact with their colleagues in the secret department, who could provide valuable assistance in cases of suspected criminals. The instructions noted laconically: "What cannot be achieved through official channels can be accomplished through secret ones." Regarding cases that fell under the intriguing heading of "secret investigations," the instructions noted only that they were in the exclusive domain of the secret department and that Cheka investigators had the right to request the results of these investigations (whatever their subjects may have been) in written form.[48]

In the spring of 1919, the Soviet government faced a sudden turn for the worse on the external front. The Bolsheviks' armed opponents began to advance on all sides—General Kolchak from the east, General Denikin from the south, and General Yudenich from the northwest. At the same time that Lenin called upon the Bolshevik Party and the Red Army to exert the utmost effort to regain the Volga, the Urals, and Siberia, Felix Dzerzhinsky summoned his Chekists to maximum vigilance and severity in defending the internal front. Announcements of executions and strong warnings to the public appeared once more in the Soviet press, as the VCheka reverted to the most drastic measures to purge the Soviet rear of all enemies and traitors. In mid-March, Cheka troops from Moscow, Smolensk, and Kaluga joined forces with local authorities to suppress a counterrevolutionary uprising in Briansk involving five thousand soldiers of the 34th and 35th regiments.[49] On March 18, the chairman of the VCheka informed the public that a series of recent "disorders" had demonstrated the willingness of the Bolsheviks' erstwhile allies, the Left Socialist Revolutionaries and the Mensheviks, to make common cause with the White Guards. Representatives of these dissident socialist parties were damaging the fighting ability of the Red Army and undermining the industrial, transport, and supply work of the Soviet government. From now on, Dzerzhinsky said, the VCheka would "make no distinction between White Guards of the Krasnov stripe and White Guards from the Menshevik and Socialist Revolutionary parties. The punishing hand of the Chekas will fall with equal weight upon the heads of one and the other.

Left Socialist Revolutionaries and Mensheviks arrested by us will be considered hostages, and their fate will depend upon the behavior of both parties."[50]

Its vast practical experience had convinced the VCheka that taking hostages was a measure of self-defense that could be used to both thwart the hostile plans of the counterrevolutionaries and save the lives of Soviet comrades who had fallen into the hands of the enemy. As early as November 6, 1918, the Soviet government had decreed that "the necessity of keeping hostages under arrest . . . can be established, in each individual case, only by the VCheka. No other organization has the right to take hostages and hold them under arrest."[51] For the guidance of local Cheka officials, Dzerzhinsky defined a hostage as "a member of a group or organization who is fighting against us." It was important that the Chekists not seize just anyone but rather take their hostages only after carefully weighing their likely value to the enemy. A hostage, Dzerzhinsky added, must be someone highly prized by the other side, someone the White Guards would be glad not to have killed, and someone who might be exchanged for Soviet prisoners. "The enemy will not plead for some country schoolteacher or other, a forester, a miller or small shopkeeper, much less for a Jew," Dzerzhinsky said.

> Whom do they value? They value high state officials, big landowners, manufacturers, prominent workers, scholars, relatives of persons known to be on their side, etc.
> It is from these circles that hostages must be taken. But since the value of a hostage and the expediency of taking him into custody is not always easy to establish in the localities, the center should always be consulted. Henceforth, hostages cannot be taken without the permission of the Presidium of the VCheka. Your task is to make a list of all persons who have value as hostages and send this list to us.[52]

By the middle of 1919, there were more than 13,000 hostages in the dungeons of the VCheka and its local organs. Their number included both prominent representatives of the former privileged classes and members of opposition political parties.[53]

The fate of many Cheka hostages held in southern Russia was sealed in the course of General Denikin's advance toward Moscow in the spring and summer of 1919. Denikin's offensive forced the Bolsheviks to evacuate one stronghold after another, and customarily these hasty retreats were preceded by a flurry of sanguinary activity around Cheka headquarters. By the time that Kharkov, the largest city of the eastern Ukraine, fell to the Volunteer Army it was already too late for scores of Cheka prisoners. More than a hundred had already been "sent to the next world" by Saenko, the Commandant of the Kharkov Cheka and one of the most notorious of all Cheka executioners to leave his mark on the bloody history of the Russian Civil War.[54]

By the time of his appointment as commandant of the Kharkov Cheka early in 1919, this former carpenter and soldier had already earned a reputation as a scourge of the local bourgeoisie. Witnesses described him as small of stature and usually armed to the teeth, with machine-gun belts crisscrossing his chest and a revolver and sword strapped to his waist. As it turned out, the local authorities chose well when they made Saenko the chief executioner of the Kharkov Cheka. This Chekist plenipotentiary, who was once overheard to say "I have shot eighty-five men today—how easy and pleasant it is to live," had ample opportunity to indulge his passion for torture and murder before the Bolsheviks evacuated the city.

For his assistants Saenko chose two workers, Bondarenko and Ostapenko, and a sailor by the name of "Edward," none of whom had anything to learn from Saenko about heartless brutality. Saenko's next step was to requisition four large houses on Tchaikovsky Street. Three were turned into lodgings and offices for Cheka personnel and a barracks for the Cheka's armed detachment, while the fourth was converted into a prison. By May, the prison was overflowing with class enemies—mainly former officers, landowners, merchants, lawyers, professors, priests, and police officers. These people were raked in by the hundreds; specific accusations were rarely formulated against them. Many were frankly told that they were being held as hostages and would be shot on the approach of the Volunteer Army.

Nightly executions began to take place on the prison grounds at the beginning of June. By then the prisoners' strength and will to resist had been broken by months of exhausting work, mental anguish, and lack of food and sleep. On the night of June 22, with the artillery of the Volunteer Army pounding in the distance,

Saenko and some of his assistants appeared in the prison office and announced that they had constituted themselves a "commission for unloading the prison." They hastily perused the prisoners' files while guards dug a burial pit in the prison yard. After two or three hours the "commission" had reviewed the records of more than 350 prisoners and sentenced 79 to be shot forthwith. The condemned were escorted in groups of eight to ten under guard to the yard, where Saenko greeted them with coarse jokes that raised peals of laughter from the Chekists standing about. The victims were made to undress, approach the pit, and kneel at its edge. Saenko and his fellow executioners then took turns methodically shooting each prisoner in the back of the head. The shooting continued for over three hours, interrupted only by short intervals of silence as the executioners reloaded and a new batch of condemned were brought from their cells. For those left behind in the prison and still uncertain whether they might not be called out next, the night seemed eternal. This slaughter was the last at the Tchaikovsky Street prison. The next day the remaining hostages were led out of their cells and marched off to the railway station. Some were released at the station by Saenko, while the rest were loaded into cars and transported to other prisons behind the Red Army lines.

The Volunteer Army entered Kharkov on June 25, and two days later the graves on Tchaikovsky Street were opened. A total of 114 bodies was found. Medical examination of the remains ascertained that 106 persons had been killed by rifle and revolver shots at point blank range; in the majority of cases the bullet had been fired into the victim's head. Five victims had been hacked to death, two had been bayoneted, and one had been buried alive with a nonmortal wound in the jaw. The five put to death by the sword had been dealt such strong blows across the neck that the cervical vertebrae had been cut through, and the heads were attached to the bodies only by a thin strip of skin. A dozen of the slain had also been subjected to the most ghastly tortures before being shot. Some had been flogged or scalded with a boiling liquid; others had suffered broken ribs, arms, legs, and fractured skulls. So well had Saenko and his comrades done their work that only twenty-four of the bodies could be positively identified.[55]

Meanwhile, in the face of General Denikin's continued advance toward Moscow, the Soviet government on June 20 authorized the VCheka and all provincial Chekas in areas under martial law to impose "summary justice (up to shooting)" on persons engaged in a variety of criminal acts including:

1. Belonging to counterrevolutionary organizations and participating in anti-Soviet plots.
2. Treason, espionage, and the harboring of traitors and spies.
3. Concealment of weapons for counterrevolutionary purposes.
4. Counterfeiting and the forgery of documents for counterrevolutionary purposes.
5. Setting off explosions or starting fires for counterrevolutionary purposes.
6. Deliberately destroying or damaging railroad equipment, bridges and other structures, telegraph and telephone communications, military warehouses, and food supplies.
7. Banditry (participation or complicity in murdering and plundering gangs or the harboring of such gangs).
8. Armed robbery.
9. Breaking into Soviet warehouses for the purpose of illegal plunder.
10. Illegal trade in cocaine.[56]

The next day the chairman of the VCheka issued Order No. 174, which called upon all provincial Chekas to implement the provisions of this decree with the utmost vigor and determination. Dzerzhinsky told his co-workers in the provinces that

with the issuance of this decree the Chekas are made responsible for tasks more difficult than ever before—the purge of the Soviet Republic of all enemies of worker-peasant Russia. . . . The Chekas, in this difficult time, must display the maximum energy, the maximum effort, in order to secure the rear of our army. All Chekas must become armed camps, ready at any time to frustrate the plans of the White Guard plotters. All overt and covert enemies of Soviet Russia must be registered by the Chekas, and upon the slightest attempt at damaging the revolution, must be punished with a stern hand. With the issuance of this decree, the Chekas are given broad powers, and much is required of them. The Chekas have been made responsible for the tranquillity of the revolutionary order in the rear. Everyone to his post in the defense of the revolution—this is the slogan of the day for the Cheka.[57]

In mid-July, the chairman of the VCheka appealed to all honorable Soviet citizens with any information at all about the existence of White Guard organizations to present themselves at secret police headquarters within a week's time. Their anonymity, Dzerzhinsky promised, would be completely guaranteed and their information greatly appreciated. At the expiration of this week's period of grace, however, Dzerzhinsky warned that "even the most superficial relations and connections with participants in White Guard organizations will invariably entail the most severe punishment—execution, confiscation of property, and confinement of all adult members of families in a [concentration] camp." The VCheka, Dzerzhinsky said, would show no clemency to persons involved in White Guard plots and organizations.[58]

The VCheka was proud of its success in uncovering White Guard conspiracies in the Soviet rear. Hardly a day passed without the discovery of another "counterrevolutionary plot"— more than four hundred in 1918 and the first half of 1919.[59] The enemies of the October Revolution, from monarchists, Mensheviks, Socialist Revolutionaries, and Constitutional Democrats to "professional agents of foreign intelligence," hatched one anti-Soviet plot after another; and everywhere—in Moscow, Petrograd, Kiev, Kharkov, Riazan, Saratov, Chernigov, Smolensk, and Astrakhan—the Chekists worked day and night to smash them. The Soviet press frequently published accounts of the latest conspiracy destroyed by the VCheka, the very names of these groups testifying to their White Guard sympathies: The Organization for the Struggle Against Bolshevism, The White Cross, The Union for the Defense of the Motherland and Freedom, The All-Russian Monarchist Union, The Universal Union of Christian Youth, The Union for the Salvation of the Motherland and the Revolution.[60]

In late September, the VCheka announced that it had foiled yet another dangerous and ramified underground counterrevolutionary organization poised to strike at the very heart of the Soviet Republic. "Lurking like bloody spiders," the conspirators had "spun their net everywhere, from the Red Army to the universities and schools." But once again the traitors and spies had failed to carry out their nefarious designs. "The hand of the revolutionary proletariat seized them by the scruff of the neck and hurled them into the abyss from which there is no return."[61]

The plotters called themselves the National Center and planned to launch an uprising in the capital to coincide with Denikin's march on Moscow and Yudenich's on Petrograd. According to Dzerzhinsky:

> The goal [of the National Center] was to seize Moscow and disorganize our center. At their last meetings they had already made final plans for their offensive. Even the hour had been determined: 6 o'clock in the evening. They hoped to seize Moscow if only for a few hours and take over the radio and telegraph. They intended to notify the fronts of the collapse of the Soviet government, thereby provoking a panic and demoralizing the army. For the implementation of this plan they amassed their own officers here, and three of our military schools were in their hands. They planned to begin their advance in Vishniaki, Volokolamsk, and Kuntsevo, diverting our forces there, and then raise a revolt in the city itself.

Dzerzhinsky estimated that the total strength of the National Center amounted to about eight hundred officers—but apparently no troops—nearly seven hundred of whom had been arrested. Retribution was swift. Within a few days of the breakup of the conspiracy, sixty-six of its leading members were shot.[62]

The destruction of such plots as the National Center has always been among the most celebrated achievements of the VCheka in its struggle against the forces of counterrevolution. Rarely mentioned, however, are those occasions when the VCheka's blows fell on the workers themselves.

The working masses may have been, as Latsis said, "bone of our bone and flesh of our flesh," but there were times when their lack of political sophistication and years of servility would cause them to fall "under the influence of White Guard agitation and give support to the counterrevolutionaries," even to the point of rising up against Soviet power. The VCheka professed to treat these misguided souls not as class enemies but rather as natural allies who had been led astray. In place of their customarily severe methods of repression, the Chekists were said to use persuasion to disabuse the workers of any anti-Soviet sentiments they might acquire.[63]

There was no evidence of leniency on the part of the Chekists when late in 1919 the discontented workers of the Putilov Works in Petrograd held a mass meeting to protest the economic hardship and political repression brought on by the Soviet regime. The workers expressed their views in a resolution that stated:

> We, the workmen of the shipyards of the Putilov Works, declare to all the workers of Russia and of the whole world that the Soviet government has deceived the Russian proletariat, depriving it even of the political liberty it enjoyed under the Tsar's government, and has established an unheard-of Terror, the very thought of which freezes the blood in one's veins. By ruining industry the Bolsheviks have deprived the workers of the possibility of earning their bread, instead of which the starving population gets the knout. Refusing to acknowledge the Bolsheviks as the representatives of Russia, we, the workmen of the Putilov Works, have resolved to support General Yudenich, who is advancing to free us from Bolshevik slavery.

By this declaration the Putilov workers placed themselves on the other side of the barricades, and the Petrograd Cheka mobilized its "best forces" to suppress the counterrevolutionary outbreak. In their work the Petrograd Chekists had the assistance of Yakov Peters, who was sent from Moscow to help his comrades restore revolutionary discipline in the shipyards. At the conclusion of the Cheka's investigation, 189 workers were reported shot.[64]

Looking back on the results of the year's struggle on the internal front, Latsis thought that the VCheka's reputation for pitiless repression had been greatly exaggerated by the hysterical bourgeois press. Arrest and execution figures for 1919, though incomplete, demonstrated that the punitive organ of Soviet power had, in fact, been exceedingly magnanimous in its treatment of class enemies. Citing figures that did not take into account the Ukraine, where some of the bitterest fighting of the year took place, Latsis claimed that the Chekas had arrested 80,662 persons in 1919 for such offenses as counterrevolution (21,032), malfeasance (19,673), and speculation (8,367). A large number of prisoners (26,727) had also been released in 1919 because when "an entire institution, regiment, or military school" was implicated in an anti-Soviet plot, the Chekists would typically arrest everyone and rely on further investigation to sort out the innocent from the guilty. As further and conclusive evidence of Chekist liberality, Latsis noted that only 3,456 persons had been executed in the territory under review in 1919.[65]

At year's end Lenin, too, expressed his continued confidence in the VCheka. The secret police, he told delegates to the Seventh Congress of Soviets in December 1919, was "magnificently organized," and those who wished to curb or abolish it had learned nothing during the past two years of mortal struggle. "Yes," said Lenin, "the terror and the Cheka are indispensable."[66]

The Year 1920

With the White armies everywhere in retreat, the splendid prospect of Bolshevik victory in the Civil War appeared in January 1920. During the preceding three months, the Red Army had dealt devastating blows to several of the Soviet's most formidable armed opponents. In the north, not even British tanks could save General Yudenich and his Northwestern Army from defeat on the outskirts of Petrograd. In the south, General Denikin failed in his drive to take Moscow. Denikin's offensive came to a halt in mid-October near Orel, about 250 miles from the capital, and by December his forces were in full retreat toward the Black Sea. Finally, in Siberia, General Kolchak's army had been driven from its base in Omsk and the self-proclaimed "Supreme Ruler of All the Russias" was himself a prisoner of the Bolsheviks.

Lenin's public utterances during the early part of 1920 reflected these spectacular military successes. Now more confident than ever of victory on the battlefield, Lenin turned his attention to the demands of rebuilding Russia's ruined industry and agriculture and issued a call for victory on a new front, "the front of the bloodless war against hunger and cold, against typhus and destruction, against ignorance and economic chaos."[67] Heralding this shift in fronts, Lenin and Dzerzhinsky signed a decree in mid-January abolishing the death penalty. The capture of such strategic cities as Rostov, Novocherkassk, and Krasnoiarsk had created "new conditions" for the struggle against counterrevolution:

> The annihilation of the organized forces of counterrevolution has undermined the hopes and calculations of various counterrevolutionary groups inside Soviet Russia who wished to overthrow the

power of the workers and peasants by means of plots, uprisings, and terrorist acts. As a measure of self-defense against the counterrevolutionary assaults launched against her by the Entente, the Workers' and Peasants' Government was compelled to resort to the most decisive measures for the suppression of espionage and the disorganizing and rebellious acts of agents of the Entente and the Tsarist generals who serve it.

The destruction of internal and external counterrevolution and the destruction of the major secret organizations of the counterrevolutionaries and bandits, coupled with the improved position of Soviet power that has been achieved thereby, offers us the possibility of renouncing the use of the supreme measure of punishment (i.e., shooting) against enemies of Soviet power.

From the date of publication of this order, the death penalty was no longer to be applied "by sentence of the VCheka and its local agencies."[68]

Not until the end of May 1920, a few weeks after the outbreak of the Russo-Polish War, were the VCheka and its local organs once again authorized to impose the death sentence on persons threatening the military security of the Soviet Republic.[69] But even during the months between January and May, the "supreme measure of punishment" was abolished only on paper, and executions continued all over the country. Indeed, according to the testimony of eyewitnesses, the initial announcement of the abolition of the death penalty in January was less a cause for rejoicing among the condemned than the signal for a new wave of summary executions. Countless Cheka prisoners fell victim to a sudden orgy of slaughter aimed at finishing off as many occupants of Cheka dungeons as possible before the ink had dried on Dzerzhinsky's order. An inmate of a Moscow prison recalled that

the 160 persons who still remained in the Cheka building and in the local cellars and dungeons and concentration camps were all taken out and shot. They were exclusively persons whom the Cheka feared might prove troublesome if left alone. . . . All throughout the 13th and 14th [of January] people were shot. On the morning of the 13th the Moscow Cheka forwarded to our prison hospital a man so badly wounded in the jaw and tongue that it was only by signs that he could explain to us that he had been duly "executed," but not killed outright, and then remitted to the surgical ward. . . . Clearly he was finding it difficult to credit his good fortune. And though to this day I do not know his name, nor what the affair in which he had become involved, I do know that on the next night he was taken away (his bandages still upon him) and shot a second time.[70]

That a bloodbath did in fact take place in Moscow and other Soviet cities at this time is confirmed by Victor Serge, then an official of the Comintern with many contacts among the top Bolshevik leaders. In his memoirs Serge wrote:

> For several days the prisons, crammed with suspects, had been living in tense expectation. They knew immediately of the tremendous good news, the end of the Terror; the decree had still not appeared in the newspapers. On the 18th or 19th [of January] some of the comrades at Smolny told me in hushed voices of the tragedy of the preceding night—no one mentioned it openly. While the newspapers were printing the decree, the Petrograd Cheka was liquidating its stock! Cartload after cartload of suspects had been driven outside the city during the night, and then shot, heap upon heap. How many? In Petrograd between 150 and 200; in Moscow, it was said, between 200 and 300. In the dawn of the days that followed, the families of the massacred victims came to search that ghastly, freshly dug ground, looking for any relics, such as buttons or scraps of stocking, that could be gathered there.[71]

Within a fortnight the Soviet government took the additional step of providing the Chekists with a convenient legal basis for circumventing the spirit and the letter of the decree abolishing the death penalty. On January 28, the Presidium of the Central Executive Committee issued a supplementary decree ("not to be published") which exempted the front zones from its provisions.[72] The VCheka leadership was quick to grasp the terroristic possibilities created by this decision and shortly thereafter issued the following secret order: "In view of the abolition of the death penalty, it is suggested that persons whose crimes would otherwise have rendered them liable to the supreme penalty now be dispatched to the zone of military operations where the decree concerning capital punishment does not apply."[73] How many luckless Cheka prisoners were executed in accordance with this order is impossible to determine.

After two years of struggle on the internal front, it had also become obvious that Soviet prisons were overflowing with thousands of persons who did not really belong there, including large numbers of highly trained specialists whose skills could be put to far more productive use on the bloodless front of labor and reconstruction. The findings of a special Revision Commission of the Soviet government, published in April 1920, support the supposition that many prisoners were victims of indiscriminate and unjustified arrests made by overzealous Chekists. The Revision Commission, composed of representatives of the Workers' and Peasants' Inspection, the VCheka and the Moscow Cheka, and the Union of Youth, investigated the conditions in thirty-eight prisons and concentration camps in the Moscow area and recommended the release of many of the inmates. In all, the cases of 7,312 prisoners were examined, of whom 43 percent had been sentenced by the VCheka and the Moscow Cheka. (The rest of the prisoners had been sentenced by various civilian and military courts and tribunals.)

It was the opinion of the Revision Commission that nearly half (or 3,074) of these prisoners could be released without danger to the Soviet Republic and utilized on the labor front according to their specialties. Thus, of the 263 prisoners in the Andronevsky Forced Labor Camp, more than half could be liberated. The prisoners in this camp were for the most part hostages, deserters, and prisoners of war sentenced to long terms of imprisonment "or without any term at all (50 percent)." Sixty percent of the prisoners in the Vladykinsky Forced Labor Camp might also be released. Sanitary conditions in this camp were extremely poor. Filth and rubbish were everywhere. In the preceding three months alone, seventy-nine prisoners had died of typhus, and more than a hundred had escaped as a result of careless supervision. The Ivanovsky Special Camp had an inmate population of 457, mostly hostages and counterrevolutionaries, about 70 percent of whom had been imprisoned by order of the VCheka. Regarding this camp, the report stated:

> Administrative accountancy not in order. Food of prisoners bad; issues below starvation norm. Even the food for the sick is insufficient. Sanitary conditions completely unsatisfactory. . . . An enormous number of cases of illness among the prisoners was noted (mostly caused by malnutrition). During three months there were 507 cases of sickness, of which eight ended fatally. Fewer than one-third of the prisoners are occupied with work, the remainder live idly.

The Revision Commission recommended that more than half the prisoners in the Ivanovsky Special Camp be released. Then, of course, there was the dreaded Butyrki Prison, in which Dzerzhinsky had spent some difficult months under the Tsarist regime in 1916–17. Now, some three years after his own release, Dzerzhinsky and his fellow Chekists had taken over the Butyrki and filled it with a new generation of political prisoners. Ninety-five percent of the prison's 1,569 inmates were docketed to the VCheka and the Moscow Cheka, but only forty-five prisoners had been sentenced; the rest were still "under investigation." Because the vast majority of cases had not yet been determined, the Revision Commission found it possible to decide on the permissibility of releasing only 20 percent. According to the Commission's report, "these were for the most part persons against whom no charge had been made and who had sat without trial for more than a year, or even two years." But at least from the Butyrki "there were no escapes."[74]

In his account of the VCheka's struggle on the internal front, Martyn Latsis wrote:

> The October Revolution turned the old world upside down. The former slave—the worker and the peasant—whose labor maintained the old order, became the master, and the former master, his subordinate.
>
> And so the former landlord found himself without his land, the former factory owner without his profits, the banker without his interest, and the Tsarist bureaucrat without his power and position.

As might have been expected, the formerly privileged elements of Russian society did not resign themselves to the new order of things, but chose instead the path of counterrevolution. "The junkers and officers, former officials, the landlords, factory owners, merchants, the rich peasants, the priests, and some students as well—all, in a word, who had lived well and were unable to reconcile themselves to the new order of things—took up arms against Soviet power." These rabble were the "outright counterrevolutionaries" *(priamye kontr-revoliutsioneri)* who "know what is happening and why" and "cannot but fight their enemies—the workers and peasants—who have thrust them out of the saddle." The pitiless struggle the VCheka waged against these mortal enemies of Soviet power required, in Latsis's opinion, no further justification.[75]

There was, however, another type of adversary against whom the VCheka had to fight, an adversary whose counterrevolutionary intentions were not so readily apparent, but who nonetheless damaged the cause of the workers and peasants. Latsis had in mind those people who imagined themselves on the side of the toiling masses and may have sincerely hoped for their victory but who were unable in practice to shed their deeply rooted petit-bourgeois attitudes and made common cause, sometimes consciously, sometimes unwittingly, with the enemy. These were "counterrevolutionaries through stupidity" *(kontr-revoliutsioneri po nedomysliiu),* and into this category Latsis placed "all the 'socialist' parties," in particular the Socialist Revolutionaries and the Mensheviks. They were people who

> have no faith in the struggle of the working class and therefore want to bargain with the class enemy—the bourgeoisie. They forget that civil war is war to the death, a war in which prisoners are not taken and agreements not reached, but the enemy is killed off. Just as there can be no friendship between the wolf and the lamb, neither can there be any reconciliation between the bourgeoisie and the workers.

The Mensheviks, for example, with their advocacy of freedom of speech and press for all socialist parties, were following a dangerous middle course between "our trenches and the trenches of the enemy." Although the Mensheviks were not exactly "overt counterrevolutionaries," their activities were "more than a mere hindrance" to the Bolsheviks. "That is why," said Latsis, "we put them out of the way, so they won't get under our feet and don't interfere as we finish off the counterrevolution. We have found a cozy secluded place for them, in the Butyrki, and there they will stay until the struggle between labor and capital has come to an end."[76]

Concentration camps were also rather widely used to "isolate" the socialist traitors. According to Latsis, "all Right and Left Socialist Revolutionaries and part of the active Mensheviks and Anarchists" were put behind barbed wire. Nor was proof of guilt or of active involvement in armed opposition to Soviet power a necessary precondition for so isolating an individual from society: "Common sense prompts one to protect oneself from stabs in the back. And this it is impossible to do if one searches for material evidence in every case. . . . Taking extra precautions never hurts." Dissident socialists had to be swept out of the way because "any obstacle in our path which weakens us in this last and decisive struggle can tilt the victory to the side of the counterrevolutionaries."[77]

The VCheka's top secret Circular Letter No. 5, dated June 1, 1920, gave detailed instructions for the suppression of several of the Bolsheviks' leading socialist rivals. Intended for the guidance of the "dear comrades" in the provinces, the circular began by noting a most distressing fact: after two years of civil strife and hardship "the physically exhausted workers and peasants, not receiving a rapid improvement in their material condition, are beginning to express their dissatisfaction even to the point of taking part in strikes and uprisings." Unless the Chekas roused themselves to "new efforts and intense work," the Socialist Revolutionaries and the Mensheviks might become the chief beneficiaries of this growing unrest. Faced now with a war against Poland, and fully aware that "hunger, cold, and ruin" would present the Soviet Republic with "still another difficult winter," the VCheka ordered its local branches to smash the "counterrevolutionary fortress" once and for all. Such lawless tactics as the arrest of suspicious persons on spurious charges were viewed by the VCheka as the most efficacious means of silencing those socialist parties that continued to challenge the policies of the Bolshevik dictatorship.

The first group singled out for repression was the Right Socialist Revolutionary Party. The Right Socialist Revolutionaries, unlike their brethren on the Left, never supported the Bolshevik Party and repudiated their seizure of power from the beginning. The fact that the Right Socialist Revolutionaries had rallied to the support of the Red Army during the current Russo-Polish War did not, in the opinion of the VCheka, signify a change of heart on their part; their opposition to Bolshevik rule was believed to be as strong as ever. The Right Socialist Revolutionaries were rendering support to the Red Army only to avoid discrediting themselves in the eyes of the masses and to establish a stronger foothold for the conduct of anti-Bolshevik agitation among the troops. Steps had to be taken at once to stop them from further strengthening their position. Local Chekas were ordered to take "decisive measures to isolate organizationally" the leaders of the Right Socialist Revolutionary Party and deprive them of information regarding defects in the political, economic, and cultural life of the provinces that could be exploited to the disadvantage of the Soviet authorities. Suspicious persons traveling between the capital and the provinces were to be intercepted and a careful watch kept on non-Bolshevik workers in administrative, economic, and cultural institutions who might have access to damaging information about Soviet internal conditions.

The circular went on to note that the Left Socialist Revolutionaries, who had joined in a short-lived coalition with the Bolsheviks in 1918, had recently split into two factions, one led by I. N. Steinberg, the former Commissar of Justice, and the other by the irrepressible Maria Spiridonova. Steinberg and his faction were said to have given up armed struggle against the Bolsheviks and for the time being presented no real threat. The Chekists were instructed, nonetheless, to keep the Steinberg faction under close surveillance in order to paralyze any attempt on its part to launch another "savage attack" against the Bolsheviks. Spiridonova and her supporters, who still enjoyed considerable popularity among the "petit-bourgeois peasants," were a more serious problem, and "an energetic struggle" had to be waged against them. The provincial Chekas were reminded in this connection that "all arrested Left Socialist Revolutionaries must be sent to Moscow immediately upon completion of the preliminary investigation. Here we can elicit from them the maximum use, and, as has already been done more than once, recruit from their ranks new and valuable workers for the provincial Chekas."

In dealing with the Mensheviks, the Bolsheviks' closest Marxist relatives, the Chekas were advised to "involve the local Menshevik organizations in the upcoming October festivities, thereby demoralizing their party discipline and organizational unity." The Chekists were to direct special attention to the activities of Mensheviks working in professional unions, cooperatives, and other establishments where their party's strength was concentrated, and diligently gather incriminating evidence that could be used to indict them "not as Mensheviks but as speculators and strike instigators, etc." The arrest of members of "anti-Soviet political parties" such as the Mensheviks and Socialist Revolutionaries on trumped-up charges offered the most expedient approach to neutralizing organized opposition to Bolshevik rule. The VCheka urged its provincial organs to "use martial law and indict their members . . . as speculators, counterrevolutionaries, public officials delinquent in the performance of their duties, demoralizing the rear, and harming the front, and as collaborators of the Entente and its agents."

Finally, the VCheka's circular letter turned to the Zionists, who unfortunately were not being pursued with sufficient vigor by the local Chekas. The Zionists, it was pointed out, were a "nationalist organization" that harmed the Soviet cause by undermining "the work of the cultural organs of the Soviet authorities and, in particular, the work of Jewish Communists who are spreading the ideas of communism among the Jewish masses." The Zionists desired to establish a Jewish state in Palestine, and their cause embraced "all Jewish intellectuals." If the Zionist dream were to be translated into reality, the Soviets might be deprived of "an enormous cadre of workers necessary for the reconstruction of our economy: engineers, doctors, pharmacists, architects, and other 'specialists' who, in our poverty, must be valued for the time being." The VCheka admitted that this was "an unprincipled reason" for striking out at Zionist organizations, "but if we want to achieve our communist principles, we must take this practical consideration into account." The circular recommended that an "ideological struggle" be waged against the Zionists by Jewish Communists and that various steps be taken to disrupt their organizational life. Thus, the Zionists were to be denied permission to hold public meetings, and any unauthorized assemblies were to be broken up by force; their correspondence was to be intercepted; and "gradually, under various pretenses," Zionist quarters were to be taken over by the state. "In general," the circular concluded, "this destructive work should be conducted in such a manner that the activities of this organization, which has not been officially outlawed, will to all intents and purposes be blocked and paralyzed."[78]

The quest for victory on the bloodless front led the VCheka to sanction and encourage the use by its local organs of some of the most detested methods of the Tsarist Okhrana. Provocation and entrapment, far from disappearing in the new Soviet state, were practiced on a wider scale than ever before. Secret informers and provocateurs swarmed like flies in government institutions, factories, military units, and apartment houses, wherever enemies of the people might be uncovered. A better way to make good the boast that no aspect of Soviet life escaped the scrutiny of the secret police had yet to be invented.

Another secret report, this one prepared by the Odessa Provincial Extraordinary Commission, described in some detail the manner in which informers and provocateurs were employed to apprehend delinquent government officials, penetrate anti-Soviet political parties, and keep tabs on the mood and attitudes of the population in general. In this document, entitled "The Results and Practice of the Annual Activities of the Odessa Provincial Cheka," covering the year 1920, the authors began by noting that the VCheka attached the utmost importance to the proper functioning of intelligence work and had provided the Odessa Cheka with detailed instructions for the creation of an intelligence apparatus—instructions that were said to have borrowed extensively from the "enormous experience" of the Tsarist intelligence services.

The Odessa Cheka conducted two basic kinds of intelligence operations. "External intelligence" was intended to keep the movements and activities of suspected persons under close surveillance and was the responsibility of a staff of Cheka "inspectors" and the network of agents they recruited and trained. "Internal intelligence" was far more demanding since it involved the actual penetration by Cheka agents of Soviet institutions and non-Communist political parties. In their efforts to unmask Soviet officials suspected of malfeasance, Cheka agents are shown to have relied on provocation:

> Internal intelligence work in Soviet institutions is conducted in accordance with a plan aimed at embracing all persons involved in various kinds of official misconduct. In a given case the agent gradually tracks down all the culprits, one after the other, beginning with the ringleaders, and ending with the small fry, thus constructing a full picture of the crime. Very often the agent must take part in the crime and

sometimes even hold a leading position in the criminal conspiracy. In his work the agent must establish close contact with criminals and win their confidence so as to work side by side with them as an accomplice in the crime. Only such an approach makes it possible for an intelligence agent to fulfill the tasks entrusted to him.

Recruitment problems initially plagued the Odessa Cheka just as they had so many other secret police agencies. It had been especially difficult to recruit secret informers from the ranks of the local proletariat, who were still infected with petit-bourgeois attitudes and therefore failed to understand the Cheka's vital revolutionary mission. Those "efficient and sensible Communists" who did work in the intelligence apparatus had to meet high standards of political reliability and knowledge. They had to be dedicated, tested revolutionaries familiar with the program of the Communist Party as well as with the programs of the anti-Bolshevik groups they were to infiltrate. According to the document:

> Just as external surveillance requires that the agent turn his careful attention to the study of makeup and disguises, agents engaged in gathering inside information must develop a knack for gaining people's confidence and must familiarize themselves with the ruses of the criminal and the subterfuges of the speculator. When infiltrating political parties, the agent must possess a knowledge of the programs of all parties and of human psychology.

In addition, agents had to be capable of "taking into account all the nuances and statements made by speakers belonging to anti-Soviet parties" and carefully observe the reactions of those exposed to their words. So skillful were certain Cheka agents that they not only managed to infiltrate anti-Soviet organizations but even succeeded in "recruiting new and dedicated members to their cause." And, "at the opportune moment, when due to the confidence enjoyed by the [the undercover agent] in the organization, all threads were gathered in the hands of the Cheka, those destined to be moved from their private residences to new lodgings in prison were arrested."

The Odessa Chekists strove to put together a complete picture of all political groups that stood in "active or passive opposition to the Communist Party and Soviet power." This was accomplished by placing secret informers in the factories, government offices, and military units where their influence was believed to be most pronounced. On the basis of the informers' reports, the Cheka not only identified and compiled dossiers on the most active members of these groups, which made their subsequent arrest a simple matter, but also determined the attitudes of those workers and soldiers who had been exposed to anti-Soviet views. Intelligence work conducted along the lines described in their annual report were said to have "yielded sufficiently noteworthy results" for the Odessa Chekists in 1920.[79]

From one end of European Russia to the other, the Chekists were particularly active throughout 1920 in regions liberated from the White armies, where they conducted a thorough purge of all remaining "counterrevolutionaries." In April 1920, about two months after the collapse of the anti-Bolshevik regime in the northern provinces of Russia, Mikhail Kedrov was sent on another mission to clean up the provinces of Arkhangelsk, Vologodsk, and Severo-Dvinsk. Kedrov and his entourage immediately set about purging the population centers in the northern region of "White Guards," "Anglo-American agents," and other anti-Soviet elements. Fragmentary reports of Kedrov's northern exploits appeared from time to time in the local press. Between April 18 and April 20, for example, Kedrov mobilized more than 3,500 persons, including all local Communists as well as reliable Red Army units, for a thorough search of the town of Arkhangel. The search was part of a continuing struggle against counterrevolution and produced significant, though unspecified, results. At about the same time a Russian émigré newspaper reported that Kedrov had arrested some 1,200 officers, loaded them on to barges, and ordered his men to open fire with machine guns. "Fully half of them were killed."[80]

Meanwhile, in the south of Russia where the last major battles of the Civil War were fought, the Chekists were busy stamping out the remnants of armed resistance to Bolshevik rule. One of the objectives of Cheka operations in the Black Sea coastal zone was the destruction of the numerous anti-Soviet guerrilla bands that roamed the Kuban region and the foothills of the northern Caucasus. These insurgent bands were known as the "Greens," from the forests they used as their refuge, and at one point were reliably said to number about 15,000. The Green movement was composed chiefly of peasants and of deserters from both the Red and White armies. In the Maikiop district, for example, a sizable force consisting of the remnants of the armies of Generals Ulagai and Fostikov attacked transport moving between Armavir and Tuapse and always killed the commissars and Communists captured during its raids. In the area around Piatigorsk and Terek, several thousand Cossacks were wreaking havoc in the villages, stealing stock and arms and killing Soviet officials. Other bands were reported to have brought all traffic along the Vladikavkaz-Grozny railway to a halt.[81]

Putting an end to the menacing Green bands was a task made to order for the local Chekists. In the fall of 1920, the Plenipotentiary Representative of the VCheka for the Northern Caucasus, Lander, issued an order to the local population calling upon it to assist the Soviet authorities in the struggle against the insurgents or face "cruel punishment" at the hands of the Cheka. Since the defeat of Denikin, Lander's order began, the Soviets had been generous to the Don, Kuban, and Terek Cossacks, forgiving them their past sins; but the activities of the Green bands had increased markedly in recent months, and certain villages were known to be providing the bandits with food and recruits. Lander ordered the inhabitants of the Kuban region to provide information on the whereabouts of the bands, to take an active part in the campaign against them, and to immediately inform the authorities of any suspicious persons in their villages. For failure to comply with the Cheka demands, and for continuing to give assistance to the insurgents, the guilty could expect to suffer the most severe punishment. Lander threatened to burn to the ground the villages that sheltered the bandits and execute their entire adult populations. Local residents were also advised that they would pay with their lives for "mass uprisings on the part of any town or village." Lander assured the inhabitants of the Kuban that these were not just empty warnings. "Soviet power has sufficient means," he said, "to carry out these threats."[82]

It was in the Crimea, after the expulsion of General Wrangel and his forces, that the Cheka's campaign of terror in southern

Russia reached its peak. Statements like the following, which appeared in the local press in December 1920, set the tone for the bloody purge inaugurated by the Soviet authorities:

> We need pitiless, unceasing struggle against the snakes who are hiding in secret. We must annihilate them, sweep them out with an iron broom from everywhere. The great fighter for the great future, the worker-titan, bearing peace to the whole world through a sea of precious blood shed in the struggle for a bright future, knows neither pity nor neglect. . . .
>
> Too many White Guards remain in liberated Crimea. Now they have become quiet, hiding in corners. They await the moment to throw themselves on us again. No. We pass over to the attack.
>
> With the punishing merciless sword of Red Terror we shall go over all the Crimea and clear it of all the hangmen, enslavers, and tormentors of the working class. We shall take away from them forever the possibility of attacking us.[83]

Though official figures were never published, witnesses believed that the victims of the Crimean terror ran into the thousands.

The mass arrests conducted throughout the Soviet Republic in 1920 caused responsible officials to complain of their difficulties in maintaining the hopelessly overcrowded prisons. Thus, the Commissar of Justice, in his report *Prison Affairs in 1920,* estimated that the prison population numbered around 60,000; almost one-third were prisoners of the Chekas, while the rest were docketed to the revolutionary tribunals and other Soviet judicial organs. (Less than half of all prisoners had been sentenced; 52 percent were still under investigation.) Prison conditions during this time of famine, epidemics, and extreme hardship were universally grim. In some prisons, three inmates shared each available space meant for one. The daily ration of 1,922 calories for each inmate, which had been established by the Commissariat of Food Supply, was not only completely inadequate for the proper nourishment of working prisoners, but remained an ideal to be striven for rather than a reality. "There is no possibility," the Commissar of Justice said, "of completely implementing [this ration] during the present food-supply crisis." Nevertheless, the Commissar of Justice managed to arrive at an optimistic overall assessment of prison conditions in 1920: "There remain almost no places where prisoners are starving in the literal sense of the word. . . . The material conditions of prison life, however slowly, are improving.''[84]

The VCheka leadership, apparently having concluded that the publication of even incomplete statistics on executions carried out under its aegis only damaged the prestige of the Soviet government, offered no information on the scope of secret police repression during the first year of the bloodless front. Some idea of the extent of sanguinary events may, however, be gauged from a confidential document entitled ''A Report of the Central Administration of the Extraordinary Commissions attached to the Council of People's Commissars of the Ukraine for 1920.'' According to this report, which was prepared for the edification of delegates to the Fifth All-Ukrainian Congress of Soviets in February 1921 and covered an area that witnessed some of the bitterest fighting of the year, the Chekists executed 3,879 persons. The Crimean port of Odessa accounted for 1,418 of the victims, far more than any of the other major population centers of the region.[85] So ended the first year on the bloodless front.

The Year 1921

''The external fronts are no more,'' declared Felix Dzerzhinsky in VCheka Order No. 10, dated January 8, 1921.[86] General Wrangel, the last of the White Army commanders, had been driven into the sea, the Entente powers had withdrawn their troops from the territory of European Russia, and an armistice had been signed with Poland. After three years of bitter fighting, the Soviet Republic was secure from the immediate danger of being overthrown militarily. The purpose of VCheka Order No. 10 was to revise the punitive policies of the nationwide network of Cheka organs in the light of the more favorable conditions.

The chairman of the VCheka began by reminding his provincial comrades that the Civil War had left ''a grievous legacy.'' All over the country, prisons were ''overflowing mostly with workers and peasants and not with the bourgeoisie,'' a situation that had to be corrected at once. Those prisoners who posed no real threat to the Soviet authorities were to be released, and, henceforth, only persons dangerous to the security of the Soviet Republic were to occupy prison cells. Order No. 10 specified in this regard: "In the future, bandits and persistent recidivists must be given short shrift, but the confinement in prison of multitudes of workers and peasants, sent there for minor theft or speculation, is intolerable." It would be wiser, Dzerzhinsky suggested, if the Chekas sent weak-willed workers and peasants, whose minor offenses against the revolutionary order stemmed from "the social conditions attending the transition from capitalism to socialism," back to their places of work, where they could improve through honest labor under the watchful eyes of "responsible comrades." From then on the slogan of the Chekas had to be: "Prison for the bourgeoisie, but comradely influence over the workers and peasants."

To empty the prisons of minor offenders was easily accomplished, but to keep them from overflowing again was more difficult and would require some new methods of operation. Dzerzhinsky pointed out: "Soviet power is too strong, and too poor, to build new camps for offenders against whom there is no evidence and whose imprisonment now serves no useful purpose." The time had come to put aside such proven methods as mass arrests and repressions. These devices were well suited for the height of the Civil War when White armies were approaching Petrograd and Moscow, but now, at a time when the internal and external situations had improved so markedly, their continued use "would only furnish grist for the counterrevolutionary mills and increase mass discontent." The greatest threat to the safety of the Soviet Republic at present emanated from political and economic spies working for the Entente, bourgeois specialists firmly entrenched in Soviet institutions who used their positions to sabotage the nation's economic reconstruction, and underground Right Socialist Revolutionary organizations that were committing terrorist acts and fomenting uprisings in the famine-stricken villages. The best way to deal with the situation was to register and maintain surveillance over all those "suspicious elements" still capable of taking part in "active struggle against the Soviet Republic."

Dzerzhinsky also directed the local Chekas to inspect area prisons with an eye to reviewing the cases of convicted workers and peasants. Henceforth, Dzerzhinsky continued, "not one worker or peasant is to be arrested without substantial evidence of the gravity of his crime."

Members of the former privileged classes were to receive different treatment: "With respect to the bourgeoisie, repression is to be intensified." The Civil War had been won, but Dzerzhinsky called for more repression against the class still considered "hostile." Bourgeois prisoners were to be released on bail "only as a last resort" when it had been demonstrated that they were irreplaceable specialists whose skills were needed; and while in prison they were to be isolated from the workers and peasants. (This was perhaps intended as a precaution to prevent the minds of those proletarians residing in Soviet prisons from being contaminated by too close proximity to the "class enemy".) To make the isolation of bourgeois prisoners even more complete, VCheka Order No. 10 further directed that "special concentration camps be established for the bourgeoisie."

The new, more flexible approach to dealing with the occupants of Cheka cells spelled out in VCheka Order No. 10 was offered as a demonstration that the secret police was not a rigid thing: "It changes its attitude toward anti-Soviet elements and [its] actions according to the time, place, and circumstances."[87] Certainly, the circumstances in which the Soviet government found itself in January 1921 were more auspicious than at any time since Lenin's seizure of power. But even then, when economic reconstruction had displaced the struggle for physical and political survival as the main preoccupation of the Soviet government, the sword of the revolution was not to be sheathed. Undoubtedly reflecting the views of his colleagues in the Lubianka, Martyn Latsis was quick to point out that the VCheka was still as vital to the security of the Soviet Republic as ever. The enemies of Soviet power, though beaten, had not been completely destroyed and it was certain that, "if not today, then tomorrow," they would strike again. "Therefore," Latsis said, "we must be ready." Just when the concessions that the government was granting to foreign capitalists to rebuild the nation's shattered economy were threatening to become "oases of counterrevolutionary thought and action," nothing could be more fraught with danger and folly, in Latsis's opinion, than dismantling those organs that had already proved their worth in the struggle against the forces of reaction.[88]

Not only was the VCheka retained, but, Dzerzhinsky's Order No. 10 notwithstanding, Soviet forced-labor camps and prisons were still overflowing at the end of 1921. And, as before, most of the prisoners were ordinary workers and peasants, the bulk of them arrested by Cheka organs. The People's Commissariat of Internal Affairs, which was responsible for the administration of the network of Soviet forced-labor camps, reported that the number of such camps had increased from 107 in January to 120 in December 1921 and that almost 80 percent of the prisoners, who altogether numbered 40,913 at the end of 1921, were illiterate or had only a minimum of schooling—hardly the characteristics associated with the formerly privileged classes. The Chekas had sentenced nearly half these prisoners, far more than had any of the other punitive organs of the Soviet government.[89] The 267 prisons administered by the Commissariat of Justice were also reported to be filled to overflowing at the end of 1921, with more than 73,000 prisoners occupying facilities with a capacity for no more than 60,000. (The total prison population of the Soviet Republic was in fact much larger than this figure would indicate because the figure did not include the many additional prisons and improvised detention facilities maintained by the VCheka, the militia, and other Soviet punitive organs in areas wracked by peasant and worker disturbances.) Interestingly, the farther removed they were from the center, the greater was the role of the Chekas in filling Soviet prisons. In Moscow, only 4.4 percent of prisoners were docketed to the secret police; in the industrial provinces the percentage was 12.3; and in Siberia it jumped to 48.3.[90]

Soviet prisons and forced-labor camps remained full in 1921 because victory on the military fronts did not bring peace to the internal front. As William Henry Chamberlin succinctly stated in his history of the Russian Revolution:

> The spectre that haunted the Kremlin at . . . the beginning of 1921 was not that of forcible overthrow by foreign armies or by organized Russian Whites. It was rather that of sheer collapse from within, as a result of the profound mood of disillusionment and dissatisfaction among the masses. . . . The country as a whole was cold, hungry,

disease-ridden, exhausted and embittered; and this was true as regards the majority of the industrial workers and a good many of the rank-and-file Communists.[91]

A wave of peasant revolts swept across the Soviet Republic in 1921. These disturbances, together with the havoc caused by thousands of marauding bandits, assured that the VCheka and its local organs were in no danger of becoming superfluous institutions. As Dzerzhinsky said in the summer of 1921: "Right now an enormous amount of work has been entrusted to the VCheka . . . . We have to work without any kind of interruption."[92]

The Bolshevik leaders were sensitive to the dangers confronting the Soviet Republic as a result of years of war and devastation. They quickly took steps to prevent a resurgence of counterrevolutionary activity among the bourgeoisie and the discontented workers and peasants. On March 17, 1921, former Chekists who could be spared from their present duties for the defense of Soviet power against "technical betrayal and underground counterrevolutionary work, etc." were recalled to duty. A few days later the Central Committee of the Party warned local officials that counterrevolutionary elements could be expected to continue to use all their rich experience and all the means at their disposal to disrupt and undermine Soviet power. For this reason it was imperative that the VCheka and its local organs, "our fighting apparatus for the struggle against counterrevolution on the internal front," be given all necessary material and moral support.[93]

One of the VCheka's main concerns at this time was the suppression of "political banditry." Thousands of armed and organized bandits were roaming the Soviet countryside, pillaging towns and villages, killing innocent people. Latsis pointed to the former Tsarist-capitalist system as the source of the bandit plague. According to Latsis, it was only by turning to a life of crime that many impoverished workers and peasants had been able to escape pitiless exploitation at the hands of landlords and factory owners. With the collapse of the old regime, the bandits had been able to rob and kill with impunity in the absence of effective countermeasures, because the Soviet authorities were concentrating their best forces on the military struggle. In some areas the bandits were so bold as to occupy whole towns, which they would lay waste before returning to their forest hideouts. At a time when the proletariat was waging its "last and decisive battle" against the older order, the bandits impeded the quest for victory and did considerable damage to the Soviet cause. When they managed to apprehend these "degenerates," the Chekists dealt most unceremoniously with them. Said Latsis: "We remove them from society forever, that is, we shoot them."[94]

Banditry reached epidemic proportions in the immediate aftermath of the Civil War. The Soviet leaders knew that not all these countless outlaws were longstanding members of a criminal underclass spawned by the bourgeoisie. Many were disgruntled former Red Army soldiers. Lenin told delegates to the Tenth Congress of the Communist Party, meeting in March 1921, that an unforeseen consequence of the recent demobilization of the Red Army had been to further aggravate the bandit problem:

> The war had habituated us—hundreds of thousands of men—the whole country—to wartime tasks, and when a great part of the army, having solved [its] military tasks, finds very much worse conditions and incredible hardships in the countryside, without any opportunity . . . to apply its labor, the result is something midway between war and peace. We find that it is a situation in which we cannot very well speak of peace. . . . The demobilization . . . brings about a continuation of the war, but in a new form. We find ourselves involved in a new kind of war, a new form of war, which is summed up in the word "banditism"—when tens and hundreds of thousands of demobilized soldiers, who are accustomed to the toils of war and regard it almost as their only trade, return, impoverished and ruined, and are unable to find work.[95]

One measure to prevent the scourge of banditry from becoming worse had already been taken. On January 18, 1921, Lenin signed a secret order canceling demobilization decrees in various areas in light of the "fresh intrigues of the Entente" and "the ever-increasing risings among the peasantry." This unpopular decision was expected to provoke dissatisfaction among the troops, and military commanders were urged to explain to their men that the measure was only temporary. Lenin added that "every endeavour must be made to pacify [the troops] by making all possible kinds of promises (such as offers of remunerative positions, increased rations, etc.), but in cases where it is absolutely necessary to uphold law and order, the malcontents [should] be shot without hesitation.''[96]

A few days after this order was issued, a new government organization dedicated to the suppression of banditry made its appearance on the Soviet scene. The Central Joint Commission for the Struggle against Banditry was created on January 26 to coordinate a nationwide campaign against the bandits. The Joint Commission was composed of representatives of the Red Army, the Central Committee of the Communist Party, the Council of Labor and Defense, and the VCheka; its first meeting was held under the chairmanship of Felix Dzerzhinsky. The Commission met at least once a week for eighteen months to review the latest reports on the depredations of the bandits coming in from all parts of the Soviet Republic and to recommend military and political measures for their eradication.[97]

In its full extent, the bandit plague embraced both the central and outlying provinces of the country. In the Ukraine it was reported that banditry in the early months of 1921 had taken ''the shape of a fierce struggle against Soviet power'' and had resulted in substantial damage to the economic life of the region. The bandits were concentrating their attacks on tax-collecting and food-requisitioning personnel, grain-collecting stations, and rail transport. By the end of the year, according to figures that were admitted to be far from complete, 3,785 persons had been killed by bandits in the Ukraine, 1,475 abducted, and 745 wounded. Moreover, there had been almost 1,400 attacks on populated areas, 259 attacks on Soviet governmental agencies, and 145 attacks on tax-collecting organs.[98] Nationwide, in April 1921, it was estimated that 165 large marauding bands numbering 51,000 men were plundering the Soviet countryside. The situation was so grave that thirty-six provinces remained under martial law until the end of 1922.[99]

From the northern forests of Karelia to the steppes of the Ukraine and the sands of Central Asia, the VCheka was in the forefront of the struggle to suppress banditry. One of the Chekists' favored tactics was to ''destroy the ground on which [the bandits] lean and tear the bonds which join them to their sympathizers among the population.'' The families of those known to be involved in banditry were exiled and their property confiscated. On the Volga, according to the Soviet newspaper *Bednota,* the repressive measures applied by the Chekists and other punitive organs "in the most pitiless manner" soon produced visible results:

> Bandits are being disarmed daily in Saratov and exiled to Krasnodar. Besides, the repressive measures have also cured the population of their sympathies with banditism and willynilly they are obeying us and not only giving away the bandits but searching for and handing over their hidden arms to us.
>
> Seven hostages were shot in Ter Province and after that the population themselves offered to go and bring us all the bandits from the woods. In twenty-four hours we had caught sixty with their leader. By such drastic methods we shall very soon make an end of the bandits in the Northern Caucasus.[100]

Elsewhere Cheka troops fought pitched battles against the bandits. In 1921, the Ukrainian Cheka reported that fifty-two "large and medium-size bands" had been liquidated, including the bands of such anti-Soviet partisans as Makhno, Avidenko, Bogatyrenko, Donchenko, Kravchenko, and Sazonov. Among the Chekist combat trophies were thousands of rifles, machine guns, and horses. An even larger quantity of weapons and ammunition was confiscated from the population at large. Within just a few months of its creation in February 1921, the troops of the Don Division of the VCheka alone killed more than 1,250 bandits. Many Chekists also lost their lives in these clashes, but their sacrifices were not in vain. By the end of 1922, the largest bandit gangs had been destroyed.[101]

The author of a recent Soviet historical monograph cautioned his readers against lumping all counterrevolutionary outbreaks of the post–Civil War period under the heading "political banditry." To do so, he pointed out, would be to lose sight of the social and political significance of the large-scale anti-Soviet uprisings that took place in late 1920 and early 1921. These revolts, which overflowed the villages and engulfed whole districts and even provinces, could not be considered just another manifestation of "kulak" hostility toward the revolution. "Their peculiarity," wrote the Soviet historian, "was that at this time, as a result of the increasing dissatisfaction of the peasant masses, the middle and poor peasantry participated in the revolts."[102]

The anti-Soviet uprisings of 1920–21 not only had the support of a broad spectrum of the peasant population, but also took place on an unprecedented territorial and human scale. Major revolts broke out in the Ukraine, western Siberia, the Volga region, and the central provinces of the Soviet Republic. The insurgents numbered in the tens of thousands. Thus, Antonov, the rebel leader of the peasant partisans of Tambov Province, had almost 50,000 men in his ranks at the beginning of 1921, while the forces of the western Siberian rebels in Tiumen Province numbered almost 60,000.[103]

A confidential publication of the Soviet Military Academy gives a candid description of the conditions that precipitated this wave of "counterrevolutionary uprisings." In the December 1921 issue of the journal *Red Army,* an article ("not to be made public") described how a combination of bitterly resented government policies and inept Soviet officials frequently drove entire villages to open rebellion:

> The aim of the peasantry during the revolution and civil war was dictated by its economic interests and did not go beyond the individual achievement of more favorable conditions for small-scale farming. . . . The forced requisition of grain and mobilization of labor stood in opposition to the basic tendencies of individual peasant farming. . . . As a result of our mobilization, which was poorly planned with respect to registration procedures, we were unable to enlist in the army all those subject to conscription, while at the same time preventing these people from engaging in productive labor. Having been called [for military service] and not having appeared, such citizens considered themselves lawbreakers and felt quite uneasy and insecure since at any time they could be arrested and subjected to legal punishment. They had to hide themselves in the forests and could work their fields only in snatches and on the sly while the mobilization apparatus remained unaware of their existence. . . . Bureaucracy and illegal acts on the part of various representatives of the government in their dealings with the peasants played a significant role in creating dissatisfaction among the masses. . . . Clumsiness, waste, and a criminal attitude toward public property on the part of several economic agencies also played a major role in creating disaffection among the board masses of the people. For example, what kind of morally corrupt impression does the spoilage of all sorts of agricultural produce and raw materials gathered by means of requisitioning make on the peasants, when

literally thousands of pounds of bread, meat, and eggs, etc., spoil before their very eyes and whole trainloads of potatoes freeze? And what kind of unjust and sometimes cruel deeds are committed by such "representatives" in the villages during the collection of grain? The irresponsible and provocative acts of such government officials sometimes provoke entire villages to rise up against us. . . . Officials sent from the center to work in outlying areas and lacking a knowledge of local customs and ways of life have as a result made a number of unpardonable mistakes, displaying colonizing tendencies and provoking widespread dissatisfaction among the people and even revolts (in Bashkiria, Turkestan, the northern Caucasus).[104]

Lenin knew that his agrarian policy and its accompanying "grain crusades" had by early 1921 driven the country to the edge of disaster. On March 8, he informed the Tenth Congress of the Communist Party that relations between the working class and the peasant majority were "not what we had believed them to be." The strained relations between the cities and the villages were now "a far greater danger than all the Denikins, Kolchaks, and Yudeniches put together," and to cope with the problem "much greater unity and concentration of forces on the part of the proletariat" were required. Lenin predicted matter-of-factly that "the peasant will have to go hungry for a while in order to save the towns and factories from famine. That is something quite understandable on a countrywide scale, but we do not expect the poverty-stricken farmer to understand it. And we know that we shall not be able to do without coercion, about which the impoverished peasants are very touchy."[105]

The chief instrument of coercion was the VCheka. It brutally crushed the peasant revolts that swept across the Soviet heartland, arresting, deporting, and executing the rebels and burning their villages to the ground. Thus in the black-soil province of Tambov, where the rebel movement reached such proportions that the Soviet government eventually had to send 30,000 infantry and 8,000 cavalry to restore order, it was decided, in the words of the Bolshevik plenipotentiary on the scene, "to redouble the Red Terror in relation to the bandits, their families, and those who conceal them." The ghastly forms assumed by the Red Terror in one particular district suspected of haboring and sympathizing with the peasant insurgents were described by the same

Bolshevik official: "Parevsk, a stubbornly bandit [district], was broken by the firm application of the system of hostages, by the public shooting of members of the bands and of hostages in groups until they surrendered their arms."[106] Many Chekists, we are told, received the Order of the Red Banner for bravery and heroism in Tambov in the spring and summer of 1921.[107]

Popular resistance to the Bolsheviks reached a symbolic climax in March, when the sailors of Kronstadt, a strategic island fortress and naval base in the Gulf of Finland about twenty miles west of Petrograd, raised the banner of revolt under the slogan "Soviets without Communists." Kronstadt had been a Bolshevik stronghold in 1917 and the garrison played an active and important role in the revolution. During the Civil War, too, the sailors of Kronstadt "remained the torchbearers of revolutionary militancy," fighting and dying on every critical front.[108] The anger and disillusionment that brought these same sailors—once described by Trotsky as the pride of the revolution—to rise up against the regime they helped to create was expressed in an article entitled "What We Are Fighting For," published in the rebels' short-lived newspaper:

> After carrying out the October Revolution, the working class had hoped to achieve its emancipation. But the result was an even greater enslavement of the human personality. The power of the police and the gendarme monarchy passed into the hands of the Communist usurpers, who, instead of giving the people freedom, instilled in them the constant fear of falling into the torture chambers of the Cheka, which in their horrors far exceed the gendarme administration of the tsarist regime. The bayonets, bullets, and gruff commands of the Cheka *oprichniki*—these are what the workingman of Soviet Russia has won after so much struggle and suffering. The glorious emblem of the workers' state—the sickle and the hammer—has in fact been replaced by the Communist authorities with the bayonet and barred window, for the sake of maintaining the calm and carefree life of the new bureaucracy of Communist commissars and functionaries.
>
>   . . . . To the protests of the peasants, expressed in spontaneous uprisings, and those of the workers, whose living conditions have driven them out on strike, they [the Communists] answer with mass executions and bloodletting, in which they have not been surpassed even by the tsarist generals. . . . The picture has been drawn more and more sharply, and now it is clear that the Russian Communist

Party is not the defender of the toilers that it pretends to be. The interests of the working people are alien to it. Having gained power, it is afraid only of losing it, and therefore deems every means permissible: slander, violence, deceit, murder, vengeance upon the families of the rebels.

The Kronstadters denounced the Communist dictatorship, "with its Cheka . . . whose hangman's noose encircles the necks of the laboring masses and threatens to strangle them to death," and demanded the restoration of political freedom, the release of imprisoned socialists, and re-elections to the soviets.[109]

On March 16, some 50,000 Red Army troops and cadets under the command of General Tukhachevsky, began to cross the open ice and attack the island fortress, which was defended by 15,000 well-entrenched soldiers and sailors. After two days of bitter and costly fighting, Kronstadt was once again in Communist hands.

There is no documentary evidence that Cheka troops played a major role in the assault on the Kronstadt rebels. According to a Soviet historian of the VCheka, the revolt actually caught the Chekists off guard:

Many Chekists, accustomed to confronting the enemy face to face, did not notice the new methods of struggle that the counterrevolutionaries were turning against Soviet power. It was precisely this fact that explains why the Petrograd Chekists overlooked preparations for the Kronstadt uprising. Hearing about the possibility of an uprising . . . , they took no measures to isolate the leaders of the plot.[110]

But after the rebel guns of Kronstadt had been silenced, the Chekists began to work overtime carrying out cruel reprisals. Soon the jails and dungeons of Petrograd were filled with Kronstadters. "Months later," wrote a well-placed witness of those days, "they were still being shot in small batches, a senseless and criminal agony. . . . This protracted massacre was either supervised or permitted by Dzerzhinsky."[111] Others were condemned to slow and agonizing deaths at forced labor. According to a victim of early Soviet repression, about 2,000 Kronstadt sailors passed through the gates of the VCheka's Kholmogory concentration camp in the spring of 1921.[112]

The transition from war to peace was not accompanied by any weakening of the Bolsheviks' single-party dictatorship. Indeed,

Lenin's attachment to one-party rule was as strong in 1921 as it had been during the most desperate moments of the Civil War when he declared: "When we are reproached with having established a dictatorship of one party . . ., we say, 'Yes, it is a dictatorship of one party! This is what we stand for and we shall not shift from this position'"[113] Lenin's proletarian dictatorship always presumed the dictatorship of his own Party, and, more than any other institution, the VCheka was responsible for the campaign of intimidation and violence that eventually destroyed the last vestiges of organized opposition to Bolshevik rule.

Bolshevik suppression of independent political activity took on special urgency in 1921. With discontent igniting the flames of revolt throughout the country, it was absolutely necessary to prevent the Mensheviks and Socialist Revolutionaries, still the Bolsheviks' foremost socialist rivals, from making political capital of the unrest. It was only a matter of time before the VCheka found evidence linking the wave of anti-Soviet uprisings to the machinations of these and other political opponents of the Kremlin. According to a VCheka statement published in July 1921:

> The anti-Soviet movement of the past few months has shown that we are faced with the old, amicable chorus of counterrevolution, from the extreme monarchists to the Mensheviks, inclusive. Its eventual goal is the restoration of bourgeois landlord power; its methods of struggle are bandit uprisings, terror, and destruction. The lessons of the late White Guards and the agents of the imperialist plunderers must not be lost upon the Russian workers. As long as Soviet Russia remains the isolated center of the Communist revolution and finds itself in a capitalist encirclement, she will still need an iron hand to suppress the White Guard adventurers. The fighting organ of the proletarian dictatorship must be on guard.[114]

Throughout the year the VCheka and its local organs made mass arrests of the regime's various political opponents. This was completely in keeping with Lenin's publicly expressed belief that recent events had demonstrated that "the place for Mensheviks and Socialist-Revolutionaries . . . is not at a non-Party conference but in prison."[115] Thus, on March 11, the Ukrainian Chekists launched a mass operation against the Mensheviks, who had taken the "disgraceful counterrevolutionary line" that the

Kronstadt uprising was "not at all directed against Soviet power"
as such, but was simply "the result of spontaneous mass dissatisfaction with the policy of the Bolsheviks." The Ukrainian
Chekists arrested all known Menshevik activists in Kiev,
Poltava, Ekaterinoslav, Taganrog, Odessa, and other towns. It
was reported that "as a result of the mass arrests conducted by
the All-Ukrainian Cheka, the Mensheviks . . . were completely
deprived of the possibility of carrying on organizational and mass
work." At the same time it was decided to "liquidate" the
remnants of the Left Socialist Revolutionaries in the Ukraine. Although these socialists had not openly called for a revolt against
the Bolsheviks, they had conducted "malicious agitation and
published underground the most provocative proclamations."
The entire Central Committee of the Left Socialist Revolutionaries was arrested together with a substantial number of rank-
and-file members of the party. (The right wing of the Socialist
Revolutionaries suffered the same fate in Kharkov, Kiev, and
Odessa.) By the end of 1921, these and other "petit-bourgeois
anti-Soviet parties" had "almost ceased to exist" in the Ukraine.
They were all reported to be in an advanced stage of "ideological
and organizational collapse from which it will not be in their
power to recover soon or even raise their heads."[116]

For over four years the VCheka served, in the words of one of
its leaders, as "the fighting organ of the Communist Party, paving
the road to the kingdom of Communism."[117] It was a road paved
with the blood and bones of thousands of people. In a eulogy to
his fallen comrades, Latsis declared that work in the Chekas was
both difficult and dangerous. It was difficult because "there are
no normal working hours in the Cheka. Quite often one must
work several days at a time without sleep." Nor did the Chekas
"know holidays, since the counterrevolutionaries do not know
them either and usually use those occasions when we are not
awake or when we celebrate for their plots." And the work was
dangerous because "no fighting organization ever surrenders
without a fight and no bandit ever missed an opportunity to shoot
a guard of the revolutionary order." On the basis of incomplete
reports, Latsis estimated that more than seven thousand Chekists
had been killed in the line of duty during the Civil War. "There
was not one area of work in the rear," he said, "that did not re-

quire many sacrifices, and there was not one area where the work was not carried out with zeal." This was the special strength of the comrades who worked in the Extraordinary Commissions: they were "fanatics for their cause."[118]

Casualties on the side of the "enemies of the people" can only be estimated. During the early days of the Red Terror, the Soviet authorities noted approvingly that their calls for bloodshed had met "a ready response" throughout the country. Reports of mass arrests and executions were said to be pouring in from all corners of the Soviet Republic. Nor was any overt act of opposition to Soviet rule a necessary precondition for arrest and execution. It was common practice to execute people simply for belonging to the wrong social class. "We do not have a list of persons shot," it was observed in the pages of *Izvestiia,* "with an indication of their social status so as to enable us to compile precise statistics, but, according to individual, casual, and far from complete lists, persons shot are, for the most part, former officers, members of various counterrevolutionary organizations, former police officials and dignitaries of Tsarist Russia."[119]

The obvious class basis of the Red Terror, at least during its initial phase, should not obscure the fact that many (if not most) victims of early Soviet repression were in no way connected with the formerly privileged classes of society. They were men and women loosely categorized as "counterrevolutionary elements" whose only sin was real or imagined resistance to the policies of a minority party determined to impose its exclusive sway over the entire country. Peasants who revolted against the confiscation of their crops were branded kulaks while workers who refused to labor for starvation wages became White Guard sympathizers. Despite the issuance of occasional amnesties, Soviet prisons and concentration camps at the end of the Civil War were still full of proletarians and tillers of the soil. That people with calloused hands so frequently found themselves in the clutches of the secret police is not surprising. These people constituted the overwhelming majority of the population, and it was their mounting resistance to Bolshevik policies that put them on a collision course with the Chekists, who were sworn to preserve revolutionary order on the internal front at all costs.

In a publication of 1921 the chief chronicler of Chekist exploits,

Martyn Latsis, stated that a total of 12,733 persons had been executed by the VCheka and its local agencies throughout all of
Russia in the entire period since the Bolshevik seizure of
power.[120] This figure must be rejected as a gross underestimate.
A year earlier Latsis had written that during the first year and a
half of Bolshevik rule the secret police had already shot 8,389
people, and this in just twenty provinces of central Russia (about
one-third of the territory under Bolshevik control).[121] If over
8,000 people were executed during the first eighteen months of a
protracted struggle that was at its most savage in regions (the
Urals and the Ukraine) not included in these figures, than the
total number executed throughout the length and breadth of the
country from 1918 to 1921 must have been much higher than
anything the VCheka was willing to admit publicly. On the basis
of his own extensive reserach, Robert Conquest, a scholar whose
books on Soviet history have earned him an international reputation, estimated that "a minimum of 200,000 official executions"
took place in Lenin's Russia. Conquest did not include those shot
during the suppression of the many rebellions that swept the Soviet Republic during these years and those who perished in Soviet
prisons and concentration camps from maltreatment, hunger, and
disease. "Together," Conquest has written, "these are conserva-
tively estimated to have accounted for at least twice as many lives
as the executions proper. If we put forward a total of 500,000 victims for the period we shall certainly be erring on the side of
underestimation."[122] Of greater historical significance than these
blood statistics, which in any case were multiplied many times
over during the Stalin era, is the inescapable fact that the supreme
Bolshevik leadership deemed an officially sanctioned campaign
of mass terror necessary for the preservation and consolidation of
Communist rule in Russia.

5

The Secret Police and Its Critics

Almost from the day of its inception, the status and powers of the secret police in the evolving Soviet governmental structure were the subject of sharp controversy. As we have seen, it was relatively easy during the first few weeks of the VCheka's existence for Dzerzhinsky—always, of course, with Lenin's cooperation and support—to rebuff challenges to his organization's seemingly arbitrary actions when the opposition came from I. N. Steinberg, the Left Socialist Revolutionary Commissar of Justice in Lenin's short-lived coalition government. But criticism of the secret police did not cease with the resignation of the Left Socialist Revolutionaries from the Council of People's Commissars in March 1918.

"All Power to the Chekas"

As the VCheka established a formidable countrywide reputation for ruthlessness and unbridled power, especially in the months following the inauguration of the Red Terror, it became the object of renewed attack. And this time its critics could not so easily be dismissed, because they were not spokesmen for rival political parties but rather leading Soviet functionaries and high-ranking Communists. These were people who, from their vantage points in the Party and state apparatus, were in a position to know better than others the full extent of the VCheka's excesses.

Severe condemnation of Cheka methods and prerogatives was

voiced in July 1918 when local representatives of the Commissariat of Justice met in Moscow. It was evident from the testimony of several angry delegates that the local Chekas were demonstrating complete contempt for the rights and privileges of other Soviet organs charged with the maintenance of revolutionary order. Thus, the Commissar of Justice from Orlov Province told his colleagues:

> In the localities the question of the activities of the Extraordinary Commissions is a very acute one. The Commissions do everything they please. Before my departure, the presidium of the executive committee instructed me to find out what the jurisdiction of the Cheka is. The chairman of the Orlov Provincial Cheka said: ''I am subordinate to no one; my powers are such that I can shoot anybody.''[1]

The remarks of the Commissar of Justice from Kursk Province suggested that the situation was not much different there:

> The Commissariat of Justice has nothing in common with the Extraordinary Commission . . . . The work of the Extraordinary Commission amounts to filling the jails and keeping people there indefinitely, while the Commissariat of Justice has a decree limiting the period of detention to forty-eight hours. The Cheka completely ignores this decree saying that it does not apply to it. Those who suffer finally come to us—to the Commissariat of Justice—but not only can we not interfere, we don't even know what to say.[2]

The Commissar of Justice from Saratov Province noted that the Chekas in his area had assumed a host of ordinary police and judicial functions, including the arrest and punishment of drunkards. By their actions, it seemed to this speaker, the local Extraordinary Commissions were striving to take over the rightful functions of the Soviet organs of justice. Unless some outside controls were established over the Chekas there was a danger, he concluded, that ultimately they would become ''a state within a state.''[3]

Before they adjourned their conference, the provincial Commissars of Justice passed a resolution aimed at correcting what they viewed as the most serious irregularities in the operations of the local Chekas. They proposed that the activities of the local Chekas be placed under ''the direct control'' of the provincial soviet executive committees and that ''the most serious attention'' be directed "to the composition of the staffs of the Extraordinary Commissions," an obvious reference to the damage being done to the Soviet cause by the corrupt elements who had gained employment in the secret police.[4]

The first All-Russia Congress of Representatives of Provincial Soviets, which met early in August 1918, echoed the concerns about the Chekas expressed by their co-workers in the Commissariat of Justice. These officials also resented the apparent immunity of the secret police from any visible outside control and deemed it essential that the Chekas be subordinated to the local organs of administration in whose name the Bolsheviks had seized power under the slogan "All Power to the Soviets." The resolution of this meeting included the following pronouncement:

> In view of the fact that the fundamental aim of local government is to establish administrative unity . . . [and] that the past practice of the Chekas, which led a separate and independent existence, has resulted in constant friction and opposition among the different parts of the local administrative machinery . . . , the First All-Russia Congress of Representatives of Provincial Soviets . . . considers it absolutely essential to include . . . the provincial and district Chekas in the administrative departments of the corresponding local soviets."[5]

The VCheka leadership soon made clear its intention to permit no other institution to define its area of competence or to subordinate local Chekas to itself. A VCheka order dated August 29, 1918, and signed by Felix Dzerzhinsky, amounted to a virtual declaration of independence for the VCheka and its local branches:

> The Liaison Department [of the VCheka] has received a mass of information regarding friction arising between various local agencies, including the soviets and the local Extraordinary Commissions.
>
> The Liaison Department finds it necessary to point out to all the Extraordinary Commissions the necessity of maintaining the closest contact with all local agencies of the Soviet authorities in their area of activity, at the same time pointing out to the latter that the Chekas are *unquestionably autonomous* [my emphasis] in their work and must implicitly fulfill all decisions originating with the VCheka as the superior agency to which they are subordinate . . . In no case may a soviet, or any of its departments, either nullify or suspend an order of the Extraordinary Commission which has been issued by the All-Russian Extraordinary Commission.[6]

Another bold statement of secret police autonomy was contained in VCheka Order No. 47, issued in late Spetember, which also addressed itself to the friction that had recently arisen between the Chekas and the local soviets.[7] In many places the soviets were persisting in their attempts to subordinate secret police organs to themselves. This the VCheka considered totally unacceptable and proclaimed:

> In its activities the VCheka is completely independent, carrying out searches, arrests, and executions, afterward submitting an account to the Council of People's Commissars and the All-Russian Central Executive Committee . . . . The Commissariats of Justice and Internal Affairs cannot interfere in the activites of the Extraordinary Commissions.

Local Chekas were obliged to make reports on their operations to the corresponding provincial and district soviet executive committees only after those operations had been carried out.

The basic issue in the altercation between the Chekists and the soviets was succintly described by Dukhovsky, a high-ranking official of the Commissariat of Internal Affairs, the parent body responsible for directing the work of the local soviets. Dukhovsky characterized the strained relations as one of the most intense issues of the day. "Immense disorganization in the field of administration in the provinces" had resulted, he said, from "the struggle for power" between the Chekas and the soviets. This was not simply an interdepartmental feud. What was at stake was a matter of fundamental importance for the future of the revolution: "The question can be put quite bluntly: to whom does power in the provinces belong? To the soviets in the person of their executive committees, or to the Chekas?" Dukhovsky added that the soviet executive committees, unlike the Chekas, were elected by the people and were composed mostly of Communists. They were therefore the institutions best suited to breathe life into the proletarian dictatorship and wage the struggle against counterrevolution. At the present time, however, the soviets could not perform this task and it appeared, as a result, that the revolution had entered a new and alarming phase, in which the rallying cry of the October Revolution, "All Power to the Soviets," was in danger of being replaced by the slogan "All Power to the Chekas."[8]

Latsis (*seated, center*) and members of the All-Ukrainian Cheka, 1919

Dzerzhinsky (*center*) and members of the Collegium of the GPU, 1922

Dzerzhinsky and Joseph Stalin, 1924

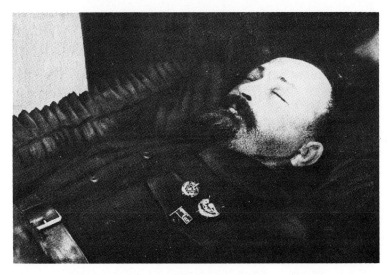

Dzerzhinsky in his coffin in the Hall of Unions, July 21, 1926

Chekist leaders at Dzerzhinsky's grave, July 22, 1926

Tenth anniversary celebration of the VCheka/GPU/OGPU, Bolshoi Theater, December 1927

Yakov Peters, deputy chairman of the VCheka, claimed in an interview published in *Izvestiia* not to be surprised by the demands that the Chekas be subordinated to the soviets. The Cheka leader characterized those individuals who favored putting an end to the independent existence of the secret police as "naive" in their outlook. They were deluded in thinking that the forces of reaction had already been decisively beaten and no longer posed a serious threat to the revolutionary order. Peters insisted that the difficult class struggle the Chekas were waging in a "planned and deliberate manner" was far from being won, since the counterrevolutionary elements had not been completely routed. In many cities and towns the kulaks and their bourgeois allies were merely laying low, gathering strength and waiting for the most opportune moment to strike again. This was why, he said, "we must maintain the strong centralized power of the Extraordinary Commissions for the prompt suppression of counterrevolutionary assaults and the strengthening of Soviet authority." As for the notion that subordinating the Chekas to the local soviets would somehow eliminate the abuses attributed to overzealous Cheka commissars, he noted: "In practice, the Cheka would argue just the reverse: from a whole series of examples it is evident that precisely where these institutions exist on an independent basis, abuses are much less frequent." Most of the illegal acts and excesses attributed to the Chekists, he added, were in reality the work of swindlers and blackmailers posing as Chekists. Actual instances of criminal misconduct by Cheka agents were relatively rare, "no more or less than trifles," and unavoidable during a time of "moral and economic ruin." As a final shot at the VCheka's critics, Peters observed that "all this hubbub and weeping against the energetic and firm measures of the Chekas do not deserve the attention they are getting; they could come only from comrades who are occupied in journalists' offices and not in the active struggle with the enemies of the proletariat."[9]

One of those Communists "occupied in journalists' offices" who emerged in the latter part of 1918 as an uncompromising critic of the VCheka was Mikhail Stepanovich Olminsky (1863–1933). A veteran Bolshevik and publicist who had devoted more than thirty years to the cause of socialism, Olminsky expressed the revulsion felt by an influential segment of rank-and-file Party members toward the secret police and its methods. (A few days after the publication of Peters's interview, Olminsky reminded the deputy chairman of the VCheka that newspaper work did not imply inactivity in the struggle against the enemies of the proletariat. After all, had not the great leader of the Soviet state, Comrade Lenin, spent most of his life writing in workers' newspapers?)[10] Olminsky and his like-minded Communist brethren did not attack the VCheka simply to protect or enhance their own institutional prerogatives. After a year of Soviet power, these charter members of the "vanguard of proletariat" had not forgotten the idealistic goals of the revolution and were genuinely repulsed by the arbitrary practices and unchecked powers of the VCheka and its local organs. Olminsky, a member of the editorial board of *Pravda,* became a spokesman for those who wished to see the VCheka's independent authority to carry out arrests and executions sharply curtailed. His signed articles in the Soviet press combined shocking revelations of Chekists excesses with calls for fundamental reform of the entire secret police apparatus.

Commenting in *Pravda* on the VCheka's self-proclaimed right, as put forth in its Order No. 47, to conduct searches, arrests, and executions on its own authority with merely the proviso that it "afterward" render an account to the Council of People's Commissars, Olminsky noted: "Regarding accounts of searches and arrests made 'afterward,' it is still possible to eliminate irregularities engendered by a lack of restraints. The same cannot be said, however, regarding executions." It appeared to him that nobody except perhaps the highest government officials enjoyed any guarantees of personal security from the secret police. Everyone else, including members of local Party organizations, might suddenly find themselves under arrest or sentenced to death "by any district Cheka with an account rendered 'afterward' . . . " It was clear to Olminsky that determining the proper scope of the VCheka's powers was a matter of the utmost urgency.[11]

On another occasion this outspoken journalist wrote that he had received many complaints concerning the senseless terror that continued to reign in the provinces. The tragic episodes described in the letters led Olminsky to conclude that what was taking place in the countryside was "not a 'Red Terror' but rather a criminal terror." One of these barely literate letters had evidently come from a simple peasant, who begged to remain anonymous. He wrote:

> There was a meeting of all peasants at the district office. The peasants came to talk and wanted to re-elect the Cheka. The Cheka heard that they wanted to re-elect them. The Chekist Iosif came out and said that if they continued with such talk he would arrest them . . . and called his men to arms. The Chekists readied their rifles. The people began to run away. Iosif ran after the peasant Vladislav who had also fled. Iosif overtook him and shot him from behind with his revolver. Pay special attention to this and write in the newspaper: that here is a fellow who can kill whomever he wants. This must not be. Well, who was he before? All the people know that he was not chosen by them and we do not know who put him here in such a post. He is sixteen years old, still a pup, and already he has the right to kill people. Yes, and all the peasants know too, that they [the Chekists] behave like hooligans, beating and stealing. And now Soviet power has taken them in. But, most likely, the Soviet power does not know about such things . . . . Everyone knew who Vladislav was. He was the first organizer of the district. I am afraid for my freedom to sign my name.

Did the author of these lines really have anything to fear, Olminsky asked his readers. A brief press announcement published a few days earlier suggested an answer: "By decree of the Samara Provincial Cheka, Mikhail Lukachev was shot for making a false denunciation." Olminsky admitted to knowing nothing of the sort of people who worked in the Samara Cheka, but he was well acquainted with what was going on in other places and wondered: "For exactly what kind of 'false denunciation' was Lukachev shot? And who attested to the falseness of his accusations? And why was it necessary to close so quickly and forever the lips of this informer?" While officials in Moscow debated whether to deprive the VCheka of the right to impose and carry out its own sentences, in the provinces the Chekists were continuing to "execute and execute for no apparent reason, as if they were competing in the invention of grounds for shooting people: this one for playing cards, that one for making 'false denunciations'—what other grounds can be devised for executions?"[12]

It was not only Cheka commissars in distant provincial towns who exhibited a marked tendency toward the most scandalous forms of misconduct. In Petrograd, the first capital of the Workers' and Peasants' Government, a young heroine of the revolution named Larisa Reisner experienced Chekist arrogance and brutality firsthand. Her "cheerful story" of a day in the Petrograd Cheka is a striking example of how Chekists met the public and of the contempt in which the secret police was held even by members of the new ruling class, who, one might suppose, would appreciate the "energetic and firm measures" employed by the Chekas in defense of Soviet power.

Reisner had been sent to the headquarters of the Petrograd Cheka by her employer, the Maritime Collegium of the Port of Petrograd, to secure the release of seven sailors who had been arrested "without sufficient grounds" and already held in custody for three months. Her initial impressions of Cheka headquarters at 2 Gorokhovaia Street were hardly favorable: "The premises of the Petrograd Cheka are labyrinthine and filthy, like a snail's shell, and especially downstairs in the waiting room for petitioners there is preserved that vile odor of moist felt boots mingled with the burned wax seals and still something else indescribable, which is exhaled to glorify the Russian office." The official at the entrance desk glanced furtively at her fur coat and her face, but otherwise took no notice of her. "He was like an inaccessible cliff," the young woman said. "I was depressed by the grandeur of his wooden moustaches and his wooden face, by the something like fear that this man exuded." No sooner had she begun to state her business than the Chekist abruptly cut her off: "It's a holiday," he announced without looking up from the papers that were occupying his attention.

"I know it's a holiday, but I have urgent business, and if by some chance a member of the Commission is available, perhaps you would permit me to speak to him or at least announce that I have come on the instructions of R." (one of the members of the Revolutionary-Military Council of the Republic).

"It's a holiday," the official repeated, still without looking up from his desk.

"You said that already," Reisner replied, her patience wearing thin. She produced some documents having to do with the subject of her visit and asked that the Chekist on duty give her a receipt for their transmission. He examined these documents, noting that they did not bear the required serial number.

"Your paper has no number, and I won't give you a receipt for it."

"Permit me, but there is a date and signature."

"I won't give it . . . ."

"Perhaps then you could give me the telephone number of some member of the Cheka [Collegium] and I could call him."

"I'm not your information bureau."

This exchange brought Larisa Reisner's temper to a boil, and she began to upbraid the official. This was no way to run a place, she said, but a "most outrageous and foolish mockery." Her unexpected outburst finally caused the Chekist to interrupt his work. Looking Reisner straight in the eyes for the first time, he threatened:

"Just say a little more and I'll put you in a cell. It's evident that you're anxious to spend the night in the cooler."

Reisner, an undaunted veteran of four difficult months on the front lines, dared the official to make good his threat. Without uttering another word, he rose quietly from his seat, smiled ominously, and ushered the young woman into the building's inner sanctum. They climbed staircases and walked for what seemed to be a long time down narrow corridors before coming to a stop in front of a door marked "Commandant," where she found herself in a large, smoke-filled room surrounded by ten heavily armed men dressed in riding breeches and high boots. Reisner described what happened next:

> The Commandant of these warlike comrades, whom the soldiers at the front call "trash" or "staff macaroon," did not desire to hear me out. The official from the front desk wholly monopolized his attention and had already contrived the matter to the effect that I was dissatisfied with the existing order of things, meaning that I would like to see the restoration of the old order, which was near and dear to me . . . .
> This outrageous lie, thrown directly in my face without any shame or fear, deprived me of my last resources of self-control. I told the Commandant that I considered these formalistic cavilings to be shameful and malfesance. A holiday! And this said in a time of revolution, when every day is precious and irrecoverable. In an institution having the power of life and death over hundreds of people there is not even a

regular duty officer. And if I were bringing a pardon and vindication for someone sentenced to death? You would have shot him by this evening, and postponed consideration of the paper until a working day. Shame, shame, and shame! I blush for you and for your torture chamber.

Reisner stormed out of the Commandant's office, and it seemed for a moment that her stinging denunciation had caught the Chekists off guard because none of them moved to block her departure. But no sooner had she taken a few steps down the corridor than the whole gang came charging after her; she was immediately surrounded, seized, and thrust into a cell.

Larisa Reisner was lucky. After an hour a member of the Cheka Collegium accidentally was made aware of her arrest, and she was released. "Then began the apologies, the dressings down, and the promises, in the midst of which the Commandant, who had put me in a cell on bread and water, bustled about and sought for the guilty persons more energetically than all the rest."

About a week later Reisner returned to the building, once again to seek the release of the seven sailors:

> The same official was sitting in his previous place, and every minute women with red blotches on their cheeks, disfigured with tears and helpless rage, came away from him. In their hands could be seen damaged packages, hurled back almost in their faces, crusts of bread and underclothing, scraped together so carefully and despairingly [for imprisoned husbands, relatives and friends].
>
> How he talked to them, this hollow man! There was a whole system by which he contrived to give no one definite information, and untiringly and coolly refused everyone and everything. "A meeting in prison?" Impossible! "To send underclothing?" Impossible! "Alive or shot?" Impossible! "When will the trial be?" Impossible!
>
> My official recognized me from some distance and became noticeably animated.
>
> "Ah, you have come again! It is in vain, madame. I am not going to let you pass anywhere."
>
> And he did not let me pass.

Here Larisa Reisner's "cheerful story" ended, except for one question: "What is the moral of this story? Oh, no moral. It is more correct to say that the moral is still in the future."[13]

Not even such an illustrious Chekist as Martyn Latsis could escape ridicule in the pages of *Pravda*. Latsis had earlier published a celebrated formula for determining the fate of Cheka prisoners based exclusively on the accused's class origin, education, and occupation. Actual evidence of opposition to the revolution in word or deed he deemed unnecessary for sentencing a prisoner to death. Now a writer in the Party's own newspaper observed: "We have many very respected comrades of bourgeois origins. I can just imagine Karl Marx or Comrade Lenin in the hands of such a ferocious investigator. 'Your name?' 'Karl Marx.' 'Your class origins?' 'Bourgeois.' 'Education?' 'University.' 'Profession?' 'Lawyer and writer.' 'What else is there to discuss, to search for signs of guilt or evidence of opposition to the Soviets with weapons or words? To the wall with him, and that is that.' " The writer of these lines took comfort from the fact that he was not of bourgeois origin, had not received a higher education, and did not have a job that would arouse the suspicion of Comrade Latsis and his collaborators.[14]

The public debate on the role and powers of the secret police in the Soviet state had been going on for several months. Nothing could better reflect the wall of fear and distrust that had arisen between the VCheka and a broad statum of the Communist Party than the scathing charges and countercharges that appeared in the pages of the Soviet press. Finally, a group of leading Chekists protested that the opprobrium that was almost daily heaped upon their organization was beginning to have an adverse effect on Cheka morale. Yakov Peters and other members of the Communist Party collective of the VCheka had always taken it for granted that the secret police would be "an eyesore in the view of the philistines and bourgeoisie." The "warm response" of the Soviet proletariat, however, had been most gratifying. Without the cooperation and active participation of the toiling masses who, the Chekists said, provided much valuable information about "the secret and criminal activities of the counterrevolutionaries" and led them to the hiding places where the bourgeoisie concealed their wealth and weapons, "the Extraordinary Commissions would not have been able to play the role that belonged to them in the proletarian revolution." Recently, however, the secret police had become the target of undeserved ridicule and condemnation and its workers the victims of "lying abuse and filth malignantly poured on their heads" by a certain unnamed segment of the Party. Those who reproached the Chekas for the Red Terror failed to understand that the secret police did not put into effect its own policies and tactics, but only "the policies and will of the proletariat, of its agencies of power, its vanguard, the Communist Party." Errors were sometimes made, it was true, but these were mainly the results of excessive zeal on the part of small-town provincial Chekas. The thankless task of the Chekists had become even more burdensome now that Party members were themselves "flinging mud" at these staunch defenders of the revolution. Was it possible, the Chekists asked, that the Communist Party had turned against the VCheka? The Chekists were sure that "the Communist Party as a whole could not hurl such reproaches." The crusade against the Chekas was really the work of only "a definite stratum of the Party." Whenever it wished, the Communist Party could reorganize the secret police or even abolish it, and of course the Chekists would abide by its decision. But in the meantime "as long as the Chekas exist, as long as they function within the limits set by the Party, as long as individual workers of the Cheka are compelled by Party discipline to remain at their posts, just so long do they have the right to demand that undeserved filth not be hurled at them."[15]

On December 12, 1918, Dzerzhinsky appeared before the Central Committee of the Communist Party to protest what he considered to be the unfounded and malicious articles aimed at the VCheka by the Soviet press. Such articles, he claimed, would only obstruct the VCheka's vigorous struggle against counter-revolutionary elements. On the basis of Dzerzhinsky's appeal, the Central Committee decided that "there is no place in the pages of the Party and Soviet press for malicious criticism of Soviet institutions of the kind that have appeared in several articles dealing with the activities of the VCheka whose work proceeds under especially severe conditions."[16] Still the debate continued into the new year, its tone becoming more and more acrimonious.

The Chekists versus the Tribunalists

Toward the end of October 1918, the campaign against the VCheka entered its most acute phase when a new and resolute adversary entered the fray. At this time spokesmen for the revolutionary tribunals opened up an unprecedented barrage of protest against the secret police network and its alleged abuses of power. The uncompromising demands of these more juridical-minded Bolsheviks for the limitation of the hitherto unfettered powers assumed by the Chekists constituted the most serious intragovernmental challenge yet faced by the VCheka leadership. The bitter dispute that raged between the Chekists and the tribunalists in the winter of 1918–19 finally compelled the Communist Party to proclaim publicly its true conception of the VCheka as the punitive arm of its own dictatorship, subject only to the commands of the Party summit.

A network of revolutionary tribunals was first created by the "Decree on the Courts" promulgated in late November 1917, about a month after the Bolshevik seizure of power. In it the tribunals were charged with the task of safeguarding the revolutionary order by judging persons accused of counterrevolution, sabotage, speculation, and malfeasance. In keeping with Lenin's view that the masses (under proper Bolshevik supervision) should be drawn into the administration of Soviet justice, it was stipulated that the tribunals be staffed by a chairman and six temporary co-judges appointed by local soviet authorities with no mention of legal training as a qualification for these positions.[17]

This very brief formulation on the revolutionary tribunals was considerably broadened during Steinberg's short tenure as Commissar of Justice in Lenin's coalition government. In December 1917, he signed a decree that gave the tribunals jurisdiction in cases of persons who took part in anti-Soviet uprisings, engaged in sabotage against the government, willfully interfered in the production of essential goods, or abused their official positions. The penalities that could be imposed on those convicted by the tribunals included imprisonment, fines, confiscation of property, imposition of compulsory public work, designation of the offender as an "enemy of the people," and exile.[18] The conspicuous absence of the death penalty from the list was not accidental; it was another reflection of Steinberg's determination to prevent execution from becoming an accepted norm of Soviet penal policy.

As soon as the coalition with the Left Socialist Revolutionaries came to an end, Lenin, who was firmly convinced of the necessity of shedding blood in a revolution, wrote to the newly appointed Bolshevik Commissar of Justice that the time had come to turn the tribunals into "a really revolutionary court that is rapid and mercilessly severe in dealing with counterrevolutionaries, hooligans, idlers, and disorganizers."[19] Lenin wanted the tribunals to have the right to inflict the death penalty; without it he believed they would be unable to fulfill their revolutionary mission. In accordance with Lenin's wishes, a new decree was issued in June 1918 that repealed all previous acts and affirmed that henceforth the revolutionary tribunals were "not bound by any limitations" in sentencing to punishment.[20]

The truth was that the Bolshevik leadership never intended the revolutionary tribunals to be courts in the usual sense of the word. They were meant to be instruments of the class struggle, for the suppression of the counterrevolutionary tendencies of the bourgeoisie. Rendering justice was secondary to enforcing this dictatorship. In the words of a high-ranking official of the Commissariat of Justice: "We always looked upon the revolutionary tribunals as . . . on a court of class dictatorship, as on a court of political struggle and not as a court in the proper sense of the word . . . . The principle of suppression prevailed over that of justice."[21]

At least at the outset, however, the revolutionary tribunals were not nearly as terrible as these words suggest. In the first place, the early decrees on the tribunals provided for certain minimal procedural guarantees. The tribunals were to be "open, public courts, with both prosecution and defense participating in the trial," and the proceedings were to take place in the presence of the accused.[22] Moreover, the tribunals proved in practice to be far from stern in punishing persons convicted of endangering the revolutionary order. Thus, despite Lenin's proddings, the death penalty was rarely applied by the tribunals during the first frenzied months of the Red Terror. According to a survey conducted by the Statistical Department of the Commissariat of Justice and based on responses from thirty provincial-level tribunals, 8,393 people were tried during the period from December 1917 to December 1918. Over 70 percent were accused of speculation and involvement in counterrevolutionary activities; the remainder were charged with such crimes as malfeasance, inciting pogroms, and espionage. The sentences imposed upon these individuals were indicative of the generally humane approach adopted by the tribunalists in dealing with the assorted enemies of the revolution whose fates were in their hands: 3,910 were acquitted or released; 1,716 were sentenced to prison; 1,483 were fined; 1,155 were subjected to relatively minor punishments such as public censure and the deprivation of "political rights"; 95 had their property confiscated; 20 were sent into exile; and 14 were executed. Of the fourteen persons executed during this formative period, twelve were convicted of counterrevolutionary activity, but this represented less than 2 percent of those actually charged with this most serious political offense. Most counterrevolutionaries were either sentenced to prison or were fined; some received even lighter sentences. In Moscow, it was not until the end of 1918 that the revolutionary tribunal finally applied the death penalty as "a measure of judicial repression." Interestingly enough, the prisoner in this case was not an unrepentant counterrevolutionary of the bourgeois stripe but rather one of Dzerzhinsky's own hand-picked subordinates, the Chekist Kosyrev.[23]

Despite the close parallels between the jurisdiction of the revolutionary tribunals and that of the secret police, their official relationship remained obscure and poorly defined in early government decrees. This was a condition that could not but contribute to friction between the two punitive organs. Motives are almost always mixed, however, and it appears that more was involved in the protracted struggle between the tribunalists and the Chekists than a bureaucratic feud. Also at issue were the conflicting inclinations of the protagonists. The tribunalists, who never completely abandoned the notion that they presided over an orderly judicial apparatus with prescribed procedures and definite powers and jurisdiction, opposed the Chekists' proudly proclaimed penchant for unyielding repression, terrorism, and summary procedures. The troubled relationship between the tribunals and the Chekas was described by a leading Soviet jurist of the day as "extraordinarily delicate . . . because this area in itself represents, I should say, the life pulse of our political life." The tribunals and the Chekas, he explained, stood for opposing tendencies within the revolution, and the outcome of their dispute would have far-reaching consequences. "On the one hand, there is the tendency, arising from theory, which places the interests of the whole above all else." It was the secret police that embodied this tendency with its accompanying emphasis on "overall security to the detriment of the interests of the individual." The other tendency, represented by the tribunals, stood for the preservation of "a whole series of legal guarantees, the possibility of saving oneself, and demands an explanation of why they [the Chekists] want to shoot people out of hand and so forth."[24]

Taking up the cudgels on behalf of the tribunals was Nikolai Vasilevich Krylenko (1885–1938), who was appointed chairman of the Supreme Revolutionary Tribunal in the latter part of 1918. (In later years, before he was himself denounced as a traitor and spy, Krylenko achieved a measure of renown as the Chief Prosecutor of the USSR and the star performer of the earliest Moscow show trials). In Krylenko's opinion, the VCheka was "undoubtedly a temporary" organ needed to suppress the resistance of the former ruling class during the most critical period of the revolution.[25] Any sign that the VCheka was interfering with the work of the tribunals or was attempting to establish itself as a permanent feature of Soviet rule was enough to arouse his Communist ardor. The enormous growth of the VCheka's powers during the first few months of Soviet rule Krylenko attributed to the failure of the former Commissar of Justice, I. N. Steinberg, to commit the tribunals to a policy of sufficiently harsh repression against internal foes. As Krylenko put it: "The whole period before . . . the month of June 1918 [when the tribunals were freed from all restrictions in imposing punishments] is nothing other than a period in which, under the influence of the requirements of life and the class struggle, the sword of repression passed from the hand of the People's Commissariat of Justice to the hand of the VCheka."[26] Krylenko desired nothing more than to see the "sword of repression" placed back in the hands of the revolutionary tribunals.

In a series of post–Civil War lectures on the development of the Soviet legal and judicial system, Krylenko surveyed the vast powers that the VCheka had assumed during its first year of operations. "Until November 1918," he said, the VCheka

existed without any statutes and norms whatsoever. In this period it underwent an enormous evolution and was transformed from one of the commissions of the Council of People's Commissars into a whole People's Commissariat, having branches in all provincial and district centers, terribly severe in its repression, with everything that went on inside completely hidden from all eyes. Aside from the right to conduct arrests, it assumed the right to decide questions of life and death, allowing of no appeal; these decisions were made by three- and five-man boards of the Chekas without any sort of norms defining either jurisdiction or the method of deciding cases.

The young Soviet state was of course fighting for its life in the latter part of 1918. That a ''series of excesses and abnormalities'' might arise in the work of the VCheka, an organ called upon to defend the proletarian dictatorship during this time of great peril, was ''fully understandable.'' No less understandable, however, was the ''justified reaction'' provoked by these excesses in other quarters.[27]

By the time the first Congress of Chairmen of Revolutionary Tribunals met in Moscow in late October 1918, enough angry resentment toward the secret police had accumulated in tribunalist ranks to evoke Krylenko's ''justified reaction.'' One of the most urgent problems discussed by the delegates was Chekist intrusion into the work of the revolutionary tribunals. While not wishing either to deny the important contributions the Extraordinary Commissions had made to the proletarian revolution or to reject the ''possibility'' that at some future time the necessity for ''immediate and merciless repression'' might once again require the displacement of the ''usual forms of struggle with counter-revolution by means of the judicial process,'' the tribunalists nevertheless felt compelled to point out and seek remedies for the ''dark side'' which had appeared in the activities of the Chekas. The source of the trouble was said to be twofold: the lack of publicity concerning the procedures of the secret police and the absence of legal definitions of the rights and powers of the Chekas.

These major shortcomings had already created an intolerable situation. The Chekists were accused of trying to take over the activities of the judicial institutions by such means as unilaterally and arbitrarily insisting on examining cases that were already under the jurisdiction of the tribunals, reviewing sentences that had been passed by the tribunals, and ''liquidating'' cases that had not yet been completed by the tribunals and the courts. The situation had reached the point at which the tribunalists could protest that they, like the officials of the Commissariat of Justice several months earlier, were completely unable to carry out their functions. As a result, for example, of the Chekists' practices of releasing or rearresting persons who had already been either arrested or released by the tribunals and of transferring arrested persons from one place of detention to another without informing the tribunals, the latter could confess that they did "not know the whereabouts or fate of those persons whose cases are under their jurisdiction, nor in general what their fate will be."[28]

This was an unacceptable state of affairs, and the tribunalists intended to tolerate it no longer. The Congress passed a resolution calling upon the Soviet government to issue a "precise statute on the rights and plenary powers of the Chekas," which would include a strict determination of the conditions under which "extrajudicial liquidation" would be regarded as not only permissible, but obligatory, and bestow upon the tribunals "the right of judicial control" over all secret police agencies "to the same extent applicable to other governmental institutions."

Other, even more far-reaching and specific reforms in the operating procedures of the secret police in the form of "urgent and essential instructions" were addressed to the VCheka:

1. All the Chekas are forbidden to conduct parallel investigations in cases already transferred by the Cheka [to a tribunal] or arising independently of it and being conducted by the tribunals or other courts.

2. All the Chekas are forbidden to register as being under their jurisdiction, without the consent of the revolutionary tribunal, any person or persons already under the jurisdiction of revolutionary tribunals or other courts . . . .

3. The transfer of arrested persons already under the jurisdiction of the tribunals or other courts without permission of the tribunals . . . from one place of detention to another, their release on bail or under other conditions, the repeated arrests of persons released by decisions of investigating agencies or courts are forbidden to the Chekas.

4. The Chekas are forbidden to inflict administrative punishments in cases being transferred by them for court examination or under the jurisdiction of the courts.

5. The Chekas are forbidden to confine persons in prison for any period whatever unless such a confinement was provided for in manda-

tory orders of the Cheka or of the appropriate authorities and unless the individual was arrested for the violation of such an order.

Finally, the Chekists were warned that the tribunals would bring to trial any secret police official charged with malfeasance "to the same extent as agents of other government institutions and that the Chekas enjoy no privileges whatever in this regard."[29] Never before had the Chekists been openly threatened with punitive action for their transgressions by another judicial organ of the Soviet government.

Of course, the resolutions and "instructions" of the tribunalists did not have the force of law, but, as a sign of growing dissension within those agencies charged with preserving the security of the Bolshevik regime on the internal front, their implications for the most effective performance of this duty could not be ignored. It was probably not coincidental, therefore, that just as the first Congress of Chairmen of Revolutionary Tribunals was about to adjourn, a "Statute on the All-Russian and Local Extraordinary Commissions" was promulgated by the Soviet government.[30] This enactment, a product of a special interdepartmental commission composed of representatives of the commissariats of Justice and Internal Affairs and the VCheka, clarified somewhat the scope of VCheka activity, but only vaguely defined its relations with other Soviet agencies active in the administrative and judicial areas. And regarding the most contentious issue of all—the powers of the secret police—the law was silent. The statute described the VCheka as "the central organ that unites the work of the local Extraordinary Commissions and systematically implements the direct struggle with counterrevolution, speculation, and malfeasance on all the territory of the Russian Socialist Federated Soviet Republic." The VCheka was further defined as "an organ of the Council of People's Commissars" and was obliged to work "in close contact with the People's Commissariats of Internal Affairs and Justice." This "close contact" was to be achieved by placing representatives of the two commissariats in the VCheka, while the chairman of the VCheka himself was to sit on the Collegium of the Commissariat of Internal Affairs. As for the local Chekas, they were said to be organs of struggle against counterrevolution organized by the local soviets with "rights identical to those of other departments" of the soviets. Members of the local Chekas could be appointed and removed by local soviet executive committees, but their chairmen had to be approved by the VCheka. Moreover, the VCheka was authorized to issue instructions to the local Chekas and exercise a veto power over their decisions.

This law was certainly not the "precise statute" that had been demanded by Krylenko and his tribunalist colleagues. It said not a word about the VCheka's powers of arrest, its investigative procedures, or its right to pass and carry out sentences independently nor did it provide any redress of grievances for the tribunalists. The "close contact" between the VCheka and commissariats of Internal Affairs and Justice never materialized, because the law was silent regarding the specific rights and duties of the representatives who were to serve in the VCheka. According to Krylenko, after futile attempts to influence the internal operations of the VCheka, the representatives walked out, with the result that the rival agencies existed in a state of "open struggle" having, in effect, broken off "diplomatic relations."[31]

Comparing the law to the concrete proposals that had been put forward by the tribunalists, Krylenko said: "It must be recorded that, unfortunately, a great deal that was clear to our tribunals was not quite clear to our responsible leaders of overall policy." When Krylenko went to see Yakov Sverdlov, chairman of the All-Russian Central Executive Committee and one of the men involved in drafting this decree, he told him: " 'This is not a law, but God knows what. Why don't you want to say openly what is the matter?' Sverdlov replied: 'What for? It is clear to everyone.' "[32] What was clear to everyone was that the Bolshevik leadership was unwilling to impose restrictions on the secret police that would inhibit its ruthless supression of any manifestations of anti-Soviet activity.

Lenin himself came forward a few days after the statute was published to reassure the Chekists of his continued support. He told a rally of Chekists on November 7, 1918:

> It is not at all surprising to hear the Cheka's activities frequently attacked by friends as well as enemies. We have taken on a hard job. When we took over the government of the country, we naturally made many mistakes, and it is only natural that the mistakes of the Extraor-

dinary Commissions strike the eye the most. The narrow-minded intellectual fastens on these mistakes without trying to get to the root of
the matter. What does surprise me in all these outcries about the
Cheka's mistakes is the manifest inability to put the question on a
broad footing. People harp on individual mistakes the Chekas make,
and raise a hue and cry about them.

   We, however, say that we learn from our mistakes . . . . When I
consider its activities and see how they are attacked, I say this is all
narrow-minded and futile talk.

It was Lenin's opinion that the "forcible suppression of the exploiters" was necessary for the emancipation of the working
class, and in this respect he considered the service of the VCheka
"invaluable," for it was "directly exercising the dictatorship of
the proletariat."[33]

The VCheka Attempts Reform

In public utterances, the VCheka high command routinely denied
the substance of their critics' charges while impugning their motives and dedication to the cause of the revolution. Protests
against the VCheka's campaign against the enemies of Soviet
power, went the usual refrain, played into the hands of the
counterrevolutionaries and could only come from naive, spineless comrades blind to the requirements of putting into effect the
dictatorship of the proletariat. Behind the scenes and without
much publicity, however, the Chekists were simultaneously taking steps to put their own house in order and ameliorate their
strained relations with the judicial agencies of the Soviet state.
Numerous VCheka orders and instructions of the period indicate,
for example, that the masters of the Lubianka were aware that
criminals and other social misfits had gained employment in the
secret police. It was in the fall of 1918 that the *VCheka Weekly*
began to take note of the presence in the local Chekas of large
numbers of persons with energy above the average but morals
below it. Calls for a purge of all "undesirable elements" and the
introduction of careful bookkeeping procedures to keep track of
confiscated goods reflected the VCheka's apparently sincere
desire to reduce the incidence of flagrant abuses in Chekist ranks.
Other documents show that the VCheka was also prepared to

make some concessions to the tribunals, its chief competitors for supremacy in the struggle against counterrevolution and crime in the Soviet heartland.

In VCheka Order No. 46, dated September 19, 1918, Felix Dzerzhinsky reaffirmed the right of local Chekas to conclude all cases initiated by them. At the same time, in the interests of establishing a more mutually acceptable division of labor between the secret police and the judicial agencies of the Soviet government, Order No. 46 held out the possibility of transferring certain categories of cases to the jurisdiciton of the courts and tribunals. Thus, local Chekas were advised to handle only those cases of malfeasance that were of "special importance," all other cases being turned over to the courts. The Chekists were also directed to turn arrested speculators over to the courts for trial and relinquish confiscated goods to the appropriate Soviet agency.[34]

Various provisions of the secret "Instructions to the Extraordinary Commissions in the Localities," adopted by the Second All-Russian Conference of Chekas in December 1918, made some noteworthy concessions to the institutional integrity of the revolutionary tribunals. Responding to the demand of the tribunalists that the Chekas cease their bold intrusions into the operations of these organs of revolutionary justice, the instructions placed several restrictions upon local secret police agencies:

Article 39: It is forbidden to initiate at any stage and by any procedure whatsoever paralleling investigations of cases already transferred to the revolutionary tribunals or to other judicial agencies.

Article 40: It is forbidden, without the knowledge and consent of the appropriate judicial agency, to hold a prisoner under guard who is docketed to a tribunal or other judicial agency unless, of course, the Cheka has another case against him, separate from that which is being conducted by the judicial institutions.

Article 41: It is forbidden independently and without the knowledge of the tribunals and the courts to transport prisoners docketed to judicial agencies from one place of detention to another, to set them free under bond or on any other basis whatsoever, to rearrest persons released by decisions of investigative or judicial authorities unless the Cheka has grounds for a new case against a given person or group of persons distinct from the case that is under the jurisdiction of the judicial agencies. But also, in the latter case, the transfer, release, or arrest can take place only in the event that it meets with no objection or protest from the judicial agency.

Article 42: It is forbidden to impose simultaneous administrative punishment in cases forwarded for court investigation or being considered by judicial agencies.

Article 43: The Chekas are forbidden to imprison persons for any period of time whatever if such imprisonment has not been provided for by an obligatory decision of the Cheka or an investigative authority.[35]

At long last it appeared that the VCheka was willing to recognize the right of the courts and tribunals to function alongside the Chekas without having to endure the most disruptive forms of Cheka interference.

Another source of resentment and confusion throughout the Soviet bureaucracy was the Chekists' tendency to make indiscriminate arrests of valuable non-Bolshevik government employees who for one reason or another aroused their suspicion. A case in point was the arrest in Samara of more that two hundred persons employed by the Administration of Irrigation Work. These specialists were en route to Turkestan when they were denounced by a "provocateur" and jailed by the Samara Cheka in the fall of 1918. Only the timely intervention of Lenin and Dzerzhinsky, who ordered the specialists released, saved the Turkestan expedition from "complete destruction." According to a government official connected with the case, "there was a complete absence of any kind of facts pointing to the existence of a counterrevolutionary organization among the employees of the Administration [of Irrigation Work]." It was reported that members of the group were arrested because the Samara Chekists considered the study of the English and Kazak languages by some of the personnel to be "a counterrevolutionary occupation." Indeed, the Chekists viewed the very presence of the expedition in Samara as sufficient proof of its intention of joining the enemy.[36]

It was to reduce the incidence of such scandalous episodes, which frequently resulted in the disruption of the institutions concerned, that a decree was issued on December 14, 1918, requiring the VCheka and its local organs to inform departments affected by "arrests of responsible workers . . . and also all specialists, engineers, and technicians employed in industrial enterprises and on the railroads'' beforehand whenever possible and ''without fail no later than forty-eight hours after the arrest if advance notification is not possible.'' In order to prevent the detention of valuable workers without good reason, the law also stipulated that representatives of the People's Commissariats and provincial and city committees of the Communist Party were to participate in the investigation of persons arrested by the Chekas. These same organizations were also given the right to request the release of ''all those persons arrested by orders of the Cheka for whom there is submitted a written guarantee signed by two members of the collegium of the commissariat or two members of a city or provincial committee of the Communist Party.'' If the VCheka refused to accept the guarantees submitted by these agencies, the case would be transferred to a ''higher instance'' for a final decision.[37]

A few days later the chairman of the VCheka signed an order calling upon his ''dear comrades'' in the provinces to avoid making unnecessary or inexpedient arrests. There was no need, he said, ''to arrest people on the basis of hearsay, mere suspicion, or for petty crimes.'' It was especially important that the Chekists not arrest bourgeois specialists whose talents could be useful to the Soviet government unless their direct participation in White Guard organizations, speculation, or espionage had been definitely proven. The basic question to be answered in any given case was: would the bourgeois specialist under suspicion be of more use in jail or working for the Soviets? In general, Dzerzhinsky instructed his subordinates to resort to arrests only when there was direct evidence of a serious crime and when there was reason to believe that the guilty party would otherwise try to escape punishment.[38]

VCheka Order No. 113, ''On Changing and Improving Methods of Work,'' issued on December 19, 1918, contained yet another tacit admission that the punishing fist of the proletarian dictatorship was trouncing more than just class enemies and counterrevolutionary elements. In many places, it was said, the local Chekas had not adequately grasped the political decisions of the Soviet authorities, and as a result some Chekas were actually adopting policies and methods that were in conflict with the guidelines laid down by the center. Not only were the Chekists arresting "at every turn" valuable bourgeois specialists, thereby discrediting the Cheka as an organ of state power, but in areas conquered by the Bolsheviks the Chekists were also conducting a mindless reign of terror that was alienating the "peaceful inhabitants." The local Chekas were instructed to cease terrorizing law-abiding citizens who showed no interest in politics. It was especially important not to provoke the hatred of the workers and poor peasants in the course of suppressing the bourgeoisie and the kulaks. Only "clear enemies" and "hangers-on" were to be purged in these newly acquired territories.[39]

The Lubianka's self-rectification campaign of the fall and winter of 1918 did not silence the influential critics of the VCheka, who continued to demand a drastic curtailment of its powers. In late January 1919, the Chekists and some of their most outspoken opponents confronted each other at a district meeting of the Moscow Communist Party attended by close to three hundred persons. The ensuing debate was reported in considerable detail in *Izvestiia* and was aptly characterized as "a hot exchange of opinions." The VCheka was represented on this occasion by Latsis and Peters. Ranged against them were a high-ranking Soviet official named Khmelnitsky; Diakonov, president of the Moscow Revolutionary Tribunal; and the VCheka's arch-rival, Krylenko.

Peters began by taking a familiar line in defense of the VCheka. As long as counterrevolutionary activity had not yet been eliminated from the territory of Soviet Russia, he argued, it was "impossible to liquidate the Chekas," which constituted the Party's most dependable bulwark against the twin dangers of counterrevolution and banditry. As for the claims of cruelty and destructiveness attributed to the Chekists, Peters believed that these were greatly exaggerated. "We are reproached for cruelty," he said, "but nobody has been able to verify that we have shot more than five hundred persons at a time when our comrades, out there where counterrevolution is triumphant, are being shot in masses." (Peters did not specify the basis for this figure, but its falsity was confirmed a year later by Latsis's admission that well over six thousand persons had been executed by the VCheka and its local agencies in 1918.)

The Soviet official Khmelnitsky began his speech by declaring:

"The Moor has served his purpose." The Chekas, he said, should now be replaced by agencies more in accord with current needs. At a minimum, the Chekas should be deprived of the right to impose sentences by administrative procedures. Khmelnitsky added that as a result of "enormous abuses" the Chekas had aroused considerable distrust, which had infected not only the Party rank and file, but also the All-Russian Central Executive Committee and even the Council of People's Commissars. In opposing the lawless practices of the Chekas, Khmelnitsky insisted that he had no desire to disarm the revolution, but was seeking only to make sure that the instruments of Soviet defense were properly deployed against the enemy.

The President of the Moscow Revolutionary Tribunal, Diakonov, took a more legalistic approach in his criticism of the secret police, making a basic objection: "There was no decree upon the basis of which the Chekas came into existence. [The ensuing] lack of control over the Chekas creates a favorable soil for provocation, and for various [other] kinds of abuses that have become systematic." To this charge Latsis was quick to reply that his organization had, in fact, been "founded on the basis of specific decrees of the supreme Soviet power" and that the work of the Chekas was subject to "precise directives from the Council of People's Commissars and the All-Russian Central Executive Committee."

The next speaker was the VCheka's most persistent and outspoken antagonist, Nikolai Krylenko. He attacked the secret police in the most uncompromising terms, demanding that it be deprived of most of its powers and wholly absorbed into the judicial system. According to the newspaper account, Krylenko "began with a statement of facts showing that criminal elements very frequently infiltrated the Chekas and occupy responsible posts."

> The lack of control [over the Chekas] creates an atmosphere fully favorable to abuses and provocation. The Chekas consider themselves to be organs completely detached from the general system of Soviet institutions. That which is decided in the closed offices of a Cheka inspires a lack of trust. Only the publicity of a court and the possibility of controlling investigations can achieve the desired results. A com-

plete reform, converting the Chekas into investigative departments of the revolutionary tribunals, will give order and unity to the judicial system. The reform of the Chekas is inevitable, for on this depends the future development of the revolution.

Peters responded with an appeal for the sympathy of his audience. For him personally, he admitted, "it was a heavy burden to play the role of revolutionary hangman." He asked that his listeners not forget that he too had once been opposed to violence and coercion, but "as a Communist in a period of exacerbated civil war," he did not "hesitate to assume this thankless role since the fate of the revolution depended on it." Peters then turned to the VCheka's most unrelenting critic, denouncing Krylenko as a product of the bourgeoisie whose attitudes and behavior were excessively influenced by his nonproletarian origins. Krylenko seemed to be more interested in protecting the interests of lawyers who were unable to break their ties with the old legal system than in safeguarding the revolutionary order. Nor was there any truth to the allegation that the secret police operated without any external control. "Not one important question is decided by me," Peters said, "without the agreement of authoritative persons or institutions."

At the conclusion of this verbal melee a vote was taken on the two resolutions that had been put on the floor—Krylenko's that the existence of a countrywide system of revolutionary tribunals had made the Chekas superfluous; and Peter's, reaffirming the necessity for the existence of the secret police as an independent institution, while at the same time proposing that the Chekas and the judicial agencies of the Soviet government work "in full contact." When the votes were counted, the decision was 214 to 57 in favor of the Chekist position. Krylenko was quick to point out to the readers of *Izvestiia* that this vote was not an accurate reflection of Communist Party sentiment. Employees of the VCheka, the Moscow Cheka, and other local Cheka agencies, he charged, had packed the meeting. In fact, Krylenko was able to derive a certain satisfaction from this episode: if the secret police had to defend itself in this manner, he was sure that "one must conclude that its goose is cooked."[40]

The Debate Ends

After several months of acrid debate in the press, in countless meetings, and in the upper echelons of the government bureaucracy, the moment finally arrived when the Bolshevik leadership was compelled to issue its own authoritative verdict on the role of the secret police in the Soviet state. It was published on February 8, 1919, in the form of an appeal, "To the Communist Workers of All the Chekas," and was signed in the name of the Central Committee of the Russian Communist Party. Although his signature was not appended to it, the Central Committee's appeal unquestionably reflected Lenin's will. Throughout his years at the helm of the Soviet state, no important decision affecting the powers and status of the secret police was made without Lenin's direct participation, approval, or at least tacit consent. Lenin's power was such that he could have acted unilaterally to end the debate on the Chekas, but this was not his usual way. Lenin always tried to avoid making and announcing important decisions in his own name out of concern that the prestige of the Communist Party would be diminished as a result. Ordinarily he spoke instead through the supreme organs of Party and state authority—the Central Committee, the Council of People's Commissars, and the Central Executive Committee of the Soviets. This was such an occasion.

In essence, the Central Committee affirmed what few involved in the debate over the secret police had ever seriously doubted, namely, that "the Chekas were created, exist, and work only as direct agencies of the Party, under its directives and under its control." Established at a time of crisis, when the enemies of the revolution "were strangling the power of the workers and peasants" and the judicial organs of the young Soviet Republic were inadequate for the energetic, decisive, and merciless struggle that had to be waged against the enemies of the proletariat, the Chekas were meant to be instruments of "summary justice," and the necessity for them, according to the Central Committee, "was recognized by our entire Party from top to bottom." True, the Chekas were guilty of certain "deficiencies and errors"; sometimes criminal elements did in fact manage to infiltrate their ranks. But what Soviet institution did not suffer from the same affliction? The Central Committee had nothing but praise for those honorable Chekists who had "demonstrated in full measure that decisiveness, devotion to the proletarian revolution, and consciousness of duty to the Party which the Party counted on in creating the VCheka." In making their manifold contributions to the safeguarding of the revolution, the Chekists had "fulfilled . . . solely the will of the Party and the proletariat as they tirelessly hunted down the enemies of the working class." Having thus established a close link between the secret police and the Communist Party, and Central Committee served notice that the public debate on the Chekas must end. Henceforth, criticism of the VCheka would be tantamount to criticism of the Party itself. Finally, the Central Committee promised the critics of the secret police a reform in the shape of "a new regulation governing the work of the Chekas." In the meantime, the Central Committee summoned the Chekists to "further energetic and disciplined work in accordance with the directives and instructions of the Party."[41]

Dzerzhinsky himself unveiled the promised reforms at a meeting of the All-Russian Central Executive Committee held on February 17, 1919.[42] After reviewing some of the more illustrious pages in the short but eventful history of the secret police, Dzerzhinsky observed that a pronounced change for the better had occurred on the internal front. At the present moment, he said, the revolution was safe from the large-scale counterrevolutionary assaults that had posed such serious threats during the past year or so. Although the counterrevolutionary forces had not yet been completely routed, the struggle had nonetheless entered a new phase that required new methods of combat. The fight was no longer primarily against open enemies in open battle, but rather against individual treacheries. According to Dzerzhinsky, traitors and saboteurs had managed to worm their way into almost all Soviet institutions, hindering in every possible way their most efficient operation and waiting for the day when they could join forces with other counterrevolutionary elements to snatch victory from the hands of the proletariat. In the light of this development the main thrust of VCheka operations had to be aimed at cleaning out the Soviet state apparatus itself, at combating "that internal sabotage which exists in our institutions, that negligence, that sluggishness, that bureaucratic red tape, which upsets and frustrates all our projects and efforts."

Dzerzhinsky was of the opinion that under these new conditions, the laws of war that had earlier permitted the secret police to mete out summary justice no longer applied. But at the same time he hastened to remind the Central Executive Committee: "We must say to our enemies that if they dare to rise up against us with arms in hand, then all the plenary powers that the Chekas had before they will be given again, and more." Dzerzhinsky then proceeded to outline a series of proposals intended to reflect the new internal situation and eliminate the "dissonance" that had developed between the Chekas and the revolutionary tribunals. He called for the reorganization of the tribunals with an eye toward eliminating "all unnecessary formalities" in their procedures and the "parallelism" between them and the secret police.

Dzerzhinsky's proposals were adopted by the All-Russian Central Executive Committee in the form of a law, "On the All-Russian Extraordinary Commission," intended to supplement the earlier enactment of November 2, 1918.[43] This latest attempt to heal the breach between the VCheka and the revolutionary tribunals appeared to represent a striking victory for those Bolsheviks who had always opposed the Lubianka's unfettered powers of arrest and administrative punishment. Article One of the new law declared that the right to pass sentence on all cases initiated by the Chekas henceforth belonged exclusively to the tribunals. Other provisions authorized the tribunalists to "verify" the investigative activities of the Chekas and visit the prisons maintained by the Chekas in order to make certain there was a legal basis for the detention of prisoners. Any operational significance these provisions may have had, however, was nullified by other parts of the law of February 17, which simultaneously recognized the right of the Chekas (1) to hold a prisoner in custody for an indefinite time by initiating a special petition to the appropriate soviet; (2) to sentence people to concentration camps for unlimited periods; (3) to shoot people involved in armed counterrevolutionary attacks and banditry anywhere in the territory of the Soviet Republic; and (4) to execute persons for an even wider range of crimes in areas under martial law. These provisions gave the Chekists plenty of leeway for disposing of prisoners on their own or refusing to turn them over to the tribunals.

The enactment of February 17 also overhauled the structure and operations of the tribunals in order to eliminate what Dzerzhinsky had described as "all unnecessary formalities." The tribunals were henceforth to consist of three judges to be chosen for one-month terms by the executive committees of the local soviets. The accused were to be brought to trial no later than forty-eight hours after the conclusion of the tribunals' investigation, and the tribunals' decisions could not be appealed. Moreover, the tribunals themselves were given the exclusive right to determine which witnesses, if any, could be called and whether the presence of counsel or prosecutors was to be permitted. The only personal guarantees for those brought to trial were that the sessions of the tribunals had to be held in public and with the presence of the accused. This enactment marked the beginning of a new era of harsh repression. The humane tendencies that had earlier characterized the decisions of the tribunals gave way to a much more frequent application of the most severe forms of punishment.[44] Overall, the decree of February 17 did little more than establish an uneasy truce between the tribunalists and the Chekists. Those provisions of the law that appeared to represent a victory for the more juridical-minded Bolsheviks remained, in Krylenko's words, "only on paper." Neither side, he said, had "sacrificed an iota of its principles."[45]

With Lenin's support the Chekists had successfully defended their extraordinary powers. The Chekists argued that counterrevolution remained a single entity regardless of the particular forms it might assume and therefore had to be opposed by a single all-powerful institution enjoying the complete confidence of the Communist Party leadership. Any other arrangement, it was said, would inevitably lead to those twin evils of "parallelism" and "competition" that were so "very harmful" in the struggle against the forces of reaction.[46] And until the end of the Civil War the VCheka continued to function as a combined police, judicial, and punitive apparatus with virtually unlimited powers of life and death over millions of Soviet citizens. At a time when security took precedence over all other considerations, no laws or legal procedures could be permitted to interfere with the VCheka's task of defending the Bolshevik dictatorship by means of ruthless terror.

6

The Offspring of the VCheka

"Our enemies—where are they now?" asked Dzerzhinsky on the fifth anniversary of the founding of the Soviet secret police. "They have long since been cast into the realm of shadows." Just as the Red Army had defeated the armies of the White Guard generals on the external front, so had the VCheka delivered crushing blows to the counterrevolutionaries on the internal front. But even now, in the absence of armed plotters bent on overthrowing Soviet power, vigilance was still necessary. The workers still had enemies whose treachery threatened the nation's economic reconstruction. Suppressing these foes of the proletarian dictatorship was the task of "the offspring of the VCheka."[1]

The GPU and the OGPU

The very appellation of the All-Russian Extraordinary Commission was meant to connote its provisional nature. During the Civil War the secret police was viewed by some leading Bolsheviks as an institution that would surely pass into oblivion once the bitter struggle for survival had been won. Zinoviev, the head of the Party organization in Petrograd, prophesied in 1918 that the time was not far off when Cheka headquarters on Gorokhovaia Street would be converted into a kindergarten.[2] Latsis himself wrote that the VCheka, "as a provisional and extraordinary organ, is not a part of our constitutional system. The time of civil war, the time of extraordinary conditions of existence for Soviet power, will pass and the Extraordinary Commissions will become superfluous: sooner or later, looking over the success of their efforts, they will cease their work and be removed from the Soviet apparatus of power."[3]

The VCheka was indeed "abolished" by a decree of the Central Executive Committee on February 6, 1922.[4] But hardly a Chekist stirred from the Lubianka, for in its place the Soviet government simultaneously conceived its "offspring"—the State Political Administration *(Gosudarstvennoe politicheskoe upravlenie)* or GPU. Like its predecessor, the GPU was broadly charged with the suppression of counterrevolution, banditry, espionage, and smuggling, the defense of Soviet frontiers, railroads, and waterways, and the implementation of special orders of the Council of People's Commissars and the Central Executive Committee. The continuity between the old and the new Soviet secret police was also evident in that the GPU retained "special troop units" as well as the familiar special departments and transport departments to combat counterrevolution in the armed forces and on the railways.

There were, however, some major differences between the VCheka and its successor agency. Most important, the GPU lacked organizational autonomy. It was designated a branch of the Commissariat of Internal Affairs and was to function under "the personal chairmanship of the People's Commissar of Internal Affairs and his deputy." (It will be recalled that Felix Dzerzhinsky had occupied the post of Commissar of Internal Affairs since March 30, 1919.) Definite procedural requirements were also imposed upon the secret police. Recognizing that the GPU would have to apply "preventive measures" against persons who violated the revolutionary order, the GPU was authorized to conduct searches, seizures, and arrests. But only when offenders were caught red-handed could GPU agents apply these measures without a special decision of the central GPU or one of its local officials. In all other cases, arrests, searches, and seizures required a "special decision of the GPU or its local organs over the signature of their chairmen and according to orders that are to be issued . . . by the GPU and confirmed by the People's Commissariat of Justice." Furthermore, persons arrested by the GPU had to be charged within two weeks and released within two months or their cases transferred to the jurisdiction of the courts unless permission was received from the Presidium of the All-Russian Central Executive Committee to extend the duration of a prisoner's detention.

Finally, the decree curtailed the jurisdiction of the secret police:

> All general crimes including speculation, malfeasance, and other offenses that, until the publication of this decree, were dealt with by the All-Russian Extraordinary Commission and its organs, shall be transferred within two weeks to the revolutionary tribunals or the people's courts. Henceforth, all cases of crimes directed against the Soviet order or representing violations of the laws of the RSFSR shall be subject to settlement exclusively by judicial procedures conducted by the revolutionary tribunals or the people's courts.

Thus, the scope of GPU activity was limited to combating overt threats to the political security of the Soviet Republic.

That major changes in the secret police were in the offing became evident six full weeks before the decree abolishing the VCheka was made public. In a major speech to the Ninth All-Russian Congress of Soviets on December 23, 1921, Lenin let it be known that he was in favor of a thorough "reform" of the secret police. During the first years of Soviet rule, he said, the VCheka served well as an "effective weapon against the numerous plots and attacks on Soviet power made by people who were infinitely stronger than us." To its credit, the VCheka had responded to these threats with "merciless, swift, and instant repression." Lenin continued in praise of the VCheka:

> Gentlemen Russian and foreign capitalists! We know that you will never come to love this institution. No wonder! It was able to repulse your intrigues and plots better than anyone else, at a time when you throttled us, invaded us from all sides, when you organized internal plots and committed every possible crime in order to frustrate our peaceful work. Our only response is through an institution aware of the plotters' every move and able to retaliate immediately instead of engaging in persuasion. As long as there are exploiters in the world, who have no desire to hand over their landowner and capitalist rights to the workers on a platform, the power of the working people cannot survive without such an institution.

At the same time, Lenin noted that "a man's merits may become his faults." Such was now the case with the VCheka. Its vast powers and arbitrary practices were suited to a period of emergency but were out of tune with the development of trade and industry and the establishment of "greater revolutionary legality," the chief tasks confronting the Soviet Republic during the recently inaugurated New Economic Policy (NEP). As the Soviet leader put it: "The closer we approach conditions of unshakable and lasting power and the more trade develops, the more imperative it is to put forward the firm slogan of greater revolutionary legality, and the narrower becomes the sphere of the institution which matches the plotters blow for blow." His assessment of existing requirements led him to conclude: "We say categorically that it is essential to reform the Cheka, define its functions and powers, and limit its work to political problems."[5]

Lenin's speech had been preceded by weeks of behind-the-scene discussions between the Communist Party leadership and the VCheka. Late in November 1921, Lenin received a report from Politburo member Lev Kamenev, who had been conducting talks with the secret police chiefs about a new VCheka statute. Kamenev laid before Lenin the proposals thad had been drawn up in agreement with the Collegium of the VCheka and appended this note:

> Have a look at this. This is the maximum Dzerzhinsky will agree to.
> . . . I insist on this maximum: (1) Unburden the Cheka, leaving
> political crimes, espionage, banditism [sic] and the protection of rail-
> ways and warehouses in its charge. Not more. The rest—to the
> People's Commissariat for Justice. (2) The Cheka's investigation ap-
> paratus to be merged with the People's Commissariat for Justice,
> handing it over to the revolutionary tribunals.

The Collegium of the VCheka objected to the idea of transferring cases initiated by it to "the various organs of inquiry and investigation" and also considered it "premature to separate from each other (to transfer to various organs) political cases and cases involving large-scale stealing of public property and official misconduct."[6] Lenin nevertheless sided with Kamenev on the matter and wrote back to him on November 29: "My view is closer to yours than to Dzerzhinsky's. I advise you not to give in and to take it to the Politburo. Then we shall secure the maximum of maximums."[7]

A couple of days later, on December 1, Lenin introduced to the Politburo a proposal to reform the VCheka. It called for a restriction of the VCheka's jurisdiction, limitations on its powers of arrest, an increased role for civil organs of justice, and a change in name. The Poliburo adopted Lenin's proposals and set up a commission consisting of Dzerzhinsky, Kamenev, and Kursky, the Commissar of Justice, to work out the details.[8] Thus, by the time Lenin made his speech to the Congress of Soviets, the reorganization of the secret police was already well under way. It only remained for the Politburo to approve the final provisions of the decree abolishing the VCheka at its meeting of January 23, 1922, and for the Central Executive Committee to make it public on February 6.

The reorganization of the secret police was prompted by the exigencies of Soviet domestic and foreign policy. After years of internal strife and international ostracism, the Soviet leaders were trying to heal wounds at home and to attract foreign support for the difficult task of reconstruction. The formal abolition of the VCheka, one of the most dreaded and despised instrumentalities of Soviet rule, was a step in this direction. Yet at no time did Lenin contemplate the total renunciation of a weapon that had become indispensable again during the retreat signaled by the adoption of the New Economic Policy. The danger of panic, he believed, was "enormous" because "if everybody started rushing back now, it would spell immediate and inevitable disaster." Hence, " a hundred times more discipline" was required and "the slightest breach of discipline must be punished severely, sternly, ruthlessly. . . . " The situation was analagous to that of an army in retreat: "When a real army is in retreat, machineguns are kept ready, and when an orderly retreat degenerates into a disorderly one, the command to fire is given, and quite rightly too."[9]

It will be recalled that the decree of February 6, 1922, did not bestow any extrajudicial powers upon the GPU. This omission evidently so impaired the ability of the secret police to ensure "an orderly retreat" that by midsummer the Soviet government deemed it necessary to issue a corrective. An enactment of

August 10 authorized provincial and higher-level GPU organs to exile for up to three years by "administrative procedure" persons carrying on "counterrevolutionary agitation" in instances where it was not feasible to arrest them.[10] Two months later, on October 16, 1922, the Central Committee issued another decree, which authorized the GPU to "inflict punishment, including execution by shooting, without trial upon all persons guilty of banditism [sic] and armed robbery caught at the scene of the crime."[11] (This law also created the Special Commission of the People's Commissariat of Internal Affairs, which was authorized "to exile and to confine . . . in forced labor camps at the place of exile . . . active members of anti-Soviet political parties" and other persons twice convicted of certain crimes mentioned in the criminal code.) Within a few months the GPU thus managed to gain many of the extraordinary powers formerly possessed by the VCheka.

In conjunction with the formation of the Union of Soviet Socialist Republics, the secret police underwent another reorganization and change in name. The first constitution of the USSR, adopted in July 1923 and ratified in January 1924, established the Unified State Political Administration *(Obedinennoe gosudarstvennoe politicheskoe upravlenie)*, or OGPU. Gone now was the pretense that the secret police was only an "extraordinary" and temporary organ of suppression created to defend the revolutionary order during its desperate struggle for survival. Article 61 of the Constitution of the USSR affirmed that the OGPU was a permanent part of the Soviet system and described it as an organ "uniting the revolutionary efforts of the Union Republics in the struggle against political and economic counterrevolution, espionage, and banditism [sic]." Other provisions of the Constitution made the OGPU responsible for the activity of all local secret police branches and the special departments of the fronts and armies, the protection of the boundaries of the USSR, and the "direction of operative work on an All-Union scale." No longer even nominally subordinate to the Commissariat of Internal Affairs, the OGPU was given the status of a unified commissariat with "representatives attached to the Council of People's Commissars of the Union Republics." At the center, the chairman of the OGPU was made a member of the Council of People's Commissars of the USSR and given a "consulting voice" in its deliberations. The grants of extrajudicial power contained in the decrees of August and October 1922 were not affected by this latest reorganization of the secret police.[12]

The organizational structure of the GPU/OGPU is difficult to determine in the absence of authentic in-house directives of the sort that have been cited in these pages to illuminate the inner workings of the VCheka and its local organs. A lid of secrecy was clamped on the secret police beginning in the early 1920s. Only on ceremonial occasions were such luminaries as Latsis and Peters permitted to publish their reminiscences, and these tended to be both more hagiographic and less informative than their earlier writings had been. Even present-day Soviet sources are generally silent on most aspects of this period of the Lubianka's history. Fortunately, however, a handful of well-informed defectors from the Soviet Union in the late 1920s provided valuable information on the GPU/OGPU.

Georges Agabekov was such a defector, one of over sixty Soviet officials to seek refuge in the West between 1928 and 1930. As a veteran Chekist, Agabekov had extensive knowledge of the structure as well as of the domestic and foreign activities of the GPU/OGPU. Agabekov joined the Cheka of Ekaterinoslav in 1920 and for the next ten years held various posts in the secret police, eventually attaining the position of director of OGPU operations in the Near and Middle East. Judging from Agabekov's description, the Soviet secret police in the 1920s had many of the same concerns and organizational features as the VCheka. Felix Dzerzhinsky remained the chairman of the GPU/OGPU and the Lubianka was still its nerve center.

Like its predecessor, the OGPU was directed by a collegium consisting of the chairman, two deputy chairmen, and the chiefs of the various departments. The division into departments was as follows: *The Secret Division* was responsible for activities aimed against underground opposition movements and political parties, deviations within the ranks of the Communist Party itself, and organized religion. *The Intelligence Division* was charged with counteracting foreign espionage within the USSR and with the surveillance of foreign embassies and consulates and the foreign diplomatic corps in Moscow. *The Foreign Division* conducted Soviet espionage abroad. "Residents" of the foreign division of the OGPU were assigned under various covers to Soviet embassies all over the world. In addition to their espionage function, OGPU agents abroad spied on Russian émigré colonies and reported on the conduct of Soviet diplomatic and commercial representatives. *The Economic Administration* was expected to keep a "sleepless watch on all the commercial and industrial establishments of the USSR, nosing out infractions of economic laws and regulations, ascertaining the cause of deviations from the prescribed plans, [and] countering economic sabotage." *The Information Division,* through its vast network of informers, kept abreast of the mood and opinion of all segments of the population. It also acted as an arm of the regime's censorship. *The Special Division* maintained surveillance over the morale and political reliability of Red Army and Navy personnel. *The Operative Division* performed searches, arrests, and executions, and also maintained close surveillance over persons under suspicion by other departments of the OGPU apparatus. OGPU organs were established at the union republic and provincial levels as well as in cities and towns of sufficient importance to warrant the presence of secret police officials. The entire apparatus was, of course, under the direct control of the OGPU in Moscow.[13]

Other sources indicate that the transition from the VCheka to the GPU/OGPU was accompanied by a significant reduction in the size of the staff built up by the secret police during the Civil War period. According to figures compiled by the Commission for the Reduction of Personnel in Institutions of the RSFSR, the VCheka employed 143,000 persons in December 1921. By May 1922, however, the figure had dropped to 105,000.[14] The less reliable elements hastily recruited between 1918 and 1921 had been weeded out. As Dzerzhinsky put it in a statement published in 1922: "The GPU has trimmed its apparatus but has strengthened its quality."[15]

Detachments of the Special Troops of the OGPU were deployed throughout the USSR and in all important administrative, industrial, and strategic centers, where they carried on in the tradition of the armed forces of the VCheka, combating banditry and crushing attempts at massed resistance to the Soviet authorities. (The Kremlin, the Lubianka, and other important government buildings as well as munitions factories were also guarded by detachments of the Special Troops.) The Special Troops were recruited through the same conscription procedures as Red Army soldiers except that only the most reliable young conscripts were retained for service in the OGPU. After several months' training in the OGPU's own schools, the recruits were ready for duty on the internal front.[16]

The vital nature of the Special Troops' assignment made the political education of its personnel a priority item. Dzerzhinsky told the delegates to the Second Congress of Representatives of the Special Troops in mid-April 1923: "The internal troops of the GPU must be a school for future workers in the organs of the GPU and a breeding ground for the principled, cohesive, and skilled strength needed for the struggle against counterrevolution and attempts to undermine our Soviet economy."[17] According to information supplied to the congress, the political complexion of the Special Troops was 36 percent Communists, 14 percent candidate members of the Communist Party, 19 percent members of the League of Communist Youth, and 31 percent non-Party. Considering that the Special Troops constituted "the mainstay of Soviet authority," the congress resolved that in the future the armed forces of the secret police should have a higher percentage of Communist Party members in its ranks. "This can best be achieved," it was said, "by replacing the older men with young people, preferably from the League of Communist Youth." Moreover, careful attention had to be paid to the continual political indoctrination of the troops. Regular attendance at Party schools was to be supplemented by examinations in political knowledge at least twice a year.[18]

Since late 1920, when the defense of Soviet borders had been entrusted to the Special Department of the VCheka for Border Security, the armed forces of the secret police had provided the manpower necessary for ensuring the integrity of the Soviet Republic's extensive land and sea frontiers. On September 27, 1922, in a move aimed at creating a more specialized force for border security, the Council of Labor and Defense ordered the creation of a Detached Border Corps of the GPU *(Otdelnyi pogranichnyi korpus voisk GPU)* to handle all aspects of Soviet border security. The strength of the force was set at 50,000 men, with one-sixth of the units designated as cavalry.[19]

From Poland to the desolate expanses of Mongolia and China,

detachments of GPU/OGPU border guards patrolled the Soviet Union's frontiers. The exploits of the border guards during the first decade of Soviet rule are celebrated in a rich collection of documents drawn from the Soviet archives and first published in 1973. These secret police records illuminate the ceaseless struggle waged by the OGPU border guards against smuggling, espionage, and banditry on the periphery of the USSR. The documents reveal such accomplishments as the following:

Between 1922 and 1925, OGPU border guards on the Western frontier captured a total of 11,641 border violators. Of these, 675 were described as "spies and terrorists" and 2,604 as "smugglers." The plenipotentiary representative of the OGPU for the Western Region reported that the value of the smuggled goods confiscated by the border guards under his command between January 1924 and December 1925 totaled almost 1.9 million roubles.[20]

In the period from 1926–28, the OGPU border guards of Central Asia are said to have "arrested and destroyed more than 5,000 enemies." This number included such elements as rebellious Basmachi, saboteurs, and smugglers.[21]

On January 26, 1926, an eleven-man detachment of OGPU border guards patrolling a section of the Russo-Turkish frontier engaged a band of sixty smugglers, thirty of whom were armed. After the battle twenty-one smugglers were dead and almost 13,000 roubles' worth of goods was confiscated. The OGPU registered 101 similar clashes in 1927, most of them (81) on the Turkish, Persian, and Afghan frontiers, where smuggling reached awesome proportions.[22]

The plenipotentiary representative of the OGPU in the Far East found ample justification for praising the performance of the border guard detachment that patrolled the area of Nikolsko-Ussuriisk. Between 1922/23 and the end of 1927 this detachment fought battles against forty-nine armed bandit gangs. These engagements, which often found the border guards greatly outnumbered, resulted in 269 bandits killed and 58 wounded. No less heroic were the deeds of the OGPU border guard detachment stationed at Vladivostok, which clashed with twenty-eight bandit gangs during the same period, killing 158 and wounding 10. Casualties among both border guard detachments totaled 21 killed and 20 wounded.[23]

In 1927, the OGPU reported a total of 228 shooting incidents involving the armed forces of neighboring states. The bulk of these episodes (125) occurred along the tense Russo-Polish and Russo-Rumanian frontiers. Altogether in 1927, the OGPU border guards killed 403 border violators and wounded 170 more. Casualties on the Soviet side were 58 border guards killed and 55 wounded.[24]

The Secret Police Abroad

Late in 1920 the Estonian police arrested a former military man who had recently found new employment as a Soviet secret agent. This hapless Soviet spy, whose code name was Comrade Gregory, was apprehended in possession of his "very secret" instructions together with an elaborate code for transmitting important information to Moscow. According to his instructions, Comrade Gregory was to devote special attention to the activities of all anti-Soviet organizations based in Estonia. The Lubianka was interested in such things as the names and past histories of the leaders of these organizations as well as lists of their employees and agents. The departure of these agents from Estonia into Soviet Russia, the guises they used in making the journey across the frontier, the assignments given to individual agents, and their contacts on both sides of the Russo-Estonian border were also to be part of Comrade Gregory's reports. To acquire this information, Comrade Gregory was advised "either to bribe or to become fast friends with both those holding responsible posts and the lower officials of such [White Guard] organizations." Through these strategically placed contacts the Soviet agent was to gain access to the most important papers of the organizations in question and make copies of them.

To facilitate Comrade Gregory's work, he was supplied with an initial sum of 15,000 roubles for expenses. Moscow cautioned its agent that "on no account" was he to squander the money "except perhaps in cases where the results will be the obtaining of very desirable military or diplomatic information." Some of the money, it was suggested, might be used to buy the services of collaborators. But Comrade Gregory was cautioned not to promise large sums for services rendered; instead he was told "always try and bargain with your man."

Naturally, it was important that Comrade Gregory take every precaution to avoid arousing the suspicions of the local police. In this connection he was advised to be careful how he acted in private life: "For instance, refuse absolutely to make acquaintances or be in contact with left[wing] elements, but act on the contrary as far as right[wing] groups are concerned." He was to keep no compromising documents in his own house. It was particularly important that the code used for the transmission of secret information to Moscow be committed to memory and the text destroyed as soon as possible. Unfortunately for Comrade Gregory his career as a Soviet spy was involuntarily terminated before he had a chance to carry out this part of his instructions.[25]

The arrest of Comrade Gregory approximately coincided with the establishment, on December 20, 1920, of the Foreign Department *(Inostrannyi otdel)* of the VCheka. One of its first chiefs was the veteran Bolshevik Mikhail Abramovich Trilisser.[26] But the discovery of the secrets, both diplomatic and military, of other governments was an activity in which the Soviet secret police had been engaged since the early days of the Civil War, when underground Cheka agents conducted extensive espionage and counterintelligence operations behind enemy lines.

In the Ukrainian port of Odessa, for example, an underground Cheka was created in the spring of 1918 immediately following the occupation of that city by Austro-German forces. The main tasks of this underground Cheka were to expose and liquidate provocateurs and spies in the Bolshevik Party and conduct military reconnaissance work.[27] The structure of the underground Cheka of Odessa reflected these two overriding concerns. The political section, originally composed of three groups of five men each, was responsible for all measures connected with the internal security of the Odessa branch of the Bolshevik Party. The men and women of the political section are credited with unmasking and killing numerous spies and double agents who managed to penetrate the Bolshevik underground. Indeed, according to the memoirs of one of these Chekists, the Bolshevik revolutionary underground in Odessa owed its very existence during this dangerous period of foreign occupation and White Guard supremacy to the vigilance and determined action of the political section. The military section, which consisted at the outset of two groups of five men each, conducted surveillance and reconnaissance of the city's port facilities and railroad terminals, and reported on the movements of the armed forces of the White Guards and the foreign occupiers (first Austro-Germans and later French, Greeks, and Rumanians). The information gathered by the military section is said to have been of great value to the Red Army and the Red partisans operating in the Ukraine. Agents of the Odessa underground Cheka were also instrumental in establishing similar counterintelligence and espionage organizations in other enemy-occupied Ukrainian cities.

The work of the underground Cheka of Odessa was made especially hazardous by the presence in the city at one time or another of no fewer than eighteen different anti-Soviet counterintelligence organizations. The secret war fought between the Bolsheviks and the agents of German, French, Greek, Rumanian, and White Guard counterintelligence claimed many lives before the city was finally occupied by Soviet forces.

There seems never to have been any doubt in the minds of the underground Chekists of Odessa that once their city was liberated they would form the nucleus of a regular Cheka organization. And they were not disappointed. When Red troops occupied Odessa in mid-April 1919, the Soviets found a ready-made Cheka organization of "several tens" of reliable and experienced agents who had already demonstrated a mastery of "underground revolutionary techniques, initiative, courage, and dedication to the October Revolution." The underground Cheka needed only to be reorganized and reinforced to meet its new responsibilities in the open struggle against class enemies and White Guards. In time, some Chekists who had served their apprenticeship in the underground Cheka of Odessa were transferred to branches of the secret police throughout the Ukraine and the entire Soviet Republic.

By the end of 1920, all large-scale, organized armed resistance to Bolshevik rule had been crushed by the Red Army and the VCheka. True, the Japanese still occupied parts of the Far East, and uprisings and rebellions were endemic in parts of European Russia, but the Communists were nevertheless the undisputed victors of the Civil War and the masters of most of the former Russian Empire. Lenin and Dzerzhinsky did not, however, regard the defeat of General Wrangel as the last chapter in the struggle against counterrevolution. In the first place, the proletarian revolutions that Lenin had earlier so confidently prophesied for western Europe either failed to materialize or were nipped in the bud, and the Soviet Republic, surrounded by hostile powers, became a pariah in the family of nations. Moreover, at least a million Russian refugees, including some 150,000 followers of General Wrangel, had fled their native land and were now scattered in enclaves from Belgrade to New York. For the most part, these émigrés had taken little with them but a consuming hatred of communism and a dream of one day returning to a Russia free of the Bolshevik yoke.

In particular, the politically active émigrés and the paramilitary forces that some of them maintained in their adopted homelands were a continuing source of concern to the Soviet government. These Russian émigré organizations, sometimes with the support of the host governments, trained, equipped, and transported over the Soviet border individuals and groups determined to continue the struggle against the Bolsheviks. Once inside Soviet Russia, these daring souls attempted to disrupt and disorganize the Soviet authorities by disseminating anti-Bolshevik literature, formenting uprisings and strikes, and, if need be, committing sabotage and terrorist acts in the tradition of an earlier generation of revolutionaries. As "Comrade Gregory's" instructions made plain, one of the most important tasks assigned to Soviet agents abroad was the penetration of the anti-Bolshevik émigré organizations. This undertaking was considered a defensive one, since its aim was to protect the Soviet government from the intrigues and subversive activities of political opponents who were determined to continue the struggle from afar.

As early as December 1, 1920, Lenin had directed the chairman of the VCheka to devise a plan for neutralizing these most irreconcilable foes and to prevent the formation of combat units capable of striking inside Soviet Russia. Within a few days, Dzerzhinsky had prepared a "very secret" directive that outlined a multifaceted approach for dealing with the threat posed by the émigrés. Dzerzhinsky proposed that the number of hostages from among the relatives of prominent Russian émigrés be increased and special detachments formed to carry out "acts of terrorism" against enemies of the Soviet Republic living on foreign soil. Dzerzhinsky also recommended the creation of secret police front organizations capable of infiltrating the most virulently anti-Bolshevik émigré groups and luring their agents back to Russia and their doom.[28] The most widely celebrated, though by no means the only, deception operation of the kind Dzerzhinsky had in mind went by the name of the "Trust." Masterminded by some of the Lubianka's most fertile minds, the "Trust" not only succeeded over a period of several years in neutralizing the leading anti-Communist émigré organizations in western Europe, but also led to the capture and death of Boris Savinkov and Sydney Reilly, two of the most daring anti-Bolshevik conspirators of the time.[29]

Another approach to counteracting the émigré threat was the subject of a secret circular issued over the signature of Joseph Unshlikht, deputy chairman of the GPU, which was sent to certain Soviet officials abroad early in 1923. This document instructed Soviet agents to increase their activity in émigré circles for the purpose of furthering the voluntary and legal return of refugees to Russia. The most experienced agents were to infiltrate émigré organizations and keep a careful watch on those persons indicating a desire to return to their homeland. Refugees with experience and skills needed by the Soviets were to be given special consideration. Once it had been determined that their political views would permit their residing on Soviet territory, they were to be given visas and a promise of amnesty on one condition: "they make a statement in writing to the effect that in future they will refrain from participation in any anti-Bolshevik movement." Even refugees whose political loyalty remained suspect were to be afforded every opportunity to return to Russia. In the case of these unrepentant émigrés, all evidence against them was to be communicated to the GPU, which promised to see that they were arrested the moment they crossed the border.[30]

During the early and mid-1920s—at the same time that such Lubianka-inspired operations as the "Trust" were disrupting the activities of anti-Bolshevik émigré organizations—the GPU/OGPU was also building an offensive espionage apparatus whose mission was to steal the political, military, and scientific secrets of other governments. The nucleus of the apparatus was recruited from the ranks of comrades who had acquired a high degree of proficiency in the conspiratorial arts during years in the revolutionary underground. To evade the watchful eye of the Okhrana, the Bolsheviks and their fellow revolutionaries early began to practice a variety of clandestine-action techniques. They learned, for example, how to forge passports, invent ciphers, conceal their true identities and affiliations, establish and maintain covert channels of communication, and in general take all the precautions of the underground conspirator.[31] Men and women familiar from their prerevolutionary days with the requirements of covert operations provided the Soviet Republic with an indispensable reservoir of trusted intelligence-gathering and espionage experience. Lenin himself expressed confidence at the end of 1920 in his government's "splendidly organized" intelligence service even though, much to his regret, it did not yet extend to the United States of America.[32]

In another area, however, the human resources of the early Soviet espionage apparatus were very inadequate: it lacked a corps of competent, well-trained resident agents with extensive, firsthand knowledge of conditions outside Russia. To make good this deficiency, the Soviet secret police looked to the Communist parties of Germany, Poland, Austria, and Hungary as a recruiting ground for spies. Although the recruitment of members of indigenous Communist parties for hazardous espionage work was greatly facilitated by the close institutional ties existing between the Soviet secret police and the Communist International (Comintern), it remained a practice that was fraught with danger.[33] The experience and training of these agents was inadequate, and, no matter how good their intentions, there was a heightened risk that they might be exposed together with the operations of an entire network. Nevertheless, these amateur spies played an important role in the early Soviet espionage apparatus at a time when professional Soviet-trained agents were still in short supply.[34]

By the end of 1924 substantial progress had already been made in the construction of an extensive and productive Soviet espionage apparatus. In a report to the Council of People's Commissars late in 1924, Dzerzhinsky described what in his opinion was one of the most important accomplishments of the VCheka/GPU/OGPU during the preceding few years: the creation of "a network of information [and] intelligence agencies in all the large centers of Europe and North America. Responsible workers of the OGPU are detailed to all the diplomatic and trade missions of the Union of Soviet Socialist Republics abroad." Dzerzhinsky added that the Foreign Department of the OGPU, with a staff of 1,300, had "repeatedly rendered service to the Commissariat of Foreign Affairs and the Staff of the Red Army by supplying secret information both of a political and military nature."[35]

As Dzerzhinsky's report indicated, Soviet foreign intelligence networks established in the 1920s were operated almost exclusively out of diplomatic and trade missions. At a time when the Soviets were just beginning to establish diplomatic ties with their European neighbors, the secret police seized every opportunity to dispatch its agents to foreign countries disguised as diplomats, attachés, and other official government representatives. It was with this purpose in mind that Dzerzhinsky late in 1922 informed the Soviet ambassador in Germany that as of January 1, 1923, "special sections" of the GPU would be organized abroad. The sections, which were to be established in several Soviet diplomatic missions including the Berlin embassy, were to be under the exclusive control of the Foreign Department in Moscow, "from which each will receive instructions, credits, and all necessary information and to which they will forward all their correspondence." Dzerzhinsky added that it was very important that GPU agents operating out of Soviet embassies and legations occupy "official posts" as covers for their espionage activities, and he expected the representatives of the Russian Socialist Federated Soviet Republic abroad to "endeavor to regulate this matter without delay."[36] Thus was established the practice, which has remained a basic ingredient of Soviet espionage ever since, of systematically abusing diplomatic immunity for espionage purposes.

In addition to its espionage and intelligence operations abroad, the GPU maintained a close surveillance over foreign nationals residing in the Soviet Union, in particular members of foreign missions and their Russian employees. In a series of letters written in mid-1924 to Maxim Litvinov, the Assistant Commissar of Foreign Affairs, the British chargé d'affaires in Moscow strongly protested what he described as "the atmosphere of terrorism" with which the GPU had deliberately surrounded his mission and other foreign missions. The British diplomat wrote in May 1924:

> The atmosphere [of terror] seems to get thicker every day, and I am compelled to ask you to take serious measures in order to dispel it. It is today impossible to invite personal friends [to the British mission] without receiving the reply that, since acquaintance with foreigners entails acquaintance with the GPU, they are unable to accept. Unfortunately, numerous incidents show that these apprehensions cannot be dismissed as unfounded.[37]

The British mission had become the object of "the disgusting attentions" of the secret police almost from the moment of its arrival in the Soviet capital in 1921. The VCheka and its successor agencies had persistently sought to isolate the diplomatic community with what the British chargé d'affaires described as "something in the nature of a Chinese Wall intended to prevent contact between the missions and any but selected [Soviet] citizens." Moreover, there was evidence that the Lubianka attempted to force Russian nationals employed by the foreign missions to serve as spies. While the British chargé d'affaires expressed doubt that the elaborate machinery at the disposal of the GPU had produced much in the way of results during the preceding three years, the British diplomats for their part could at least claim to have acquired a considerable insight into the *modus operandi* of the secret police:

> The methods employed by the secret police include the intimidation of young girls and of domestic servants, male and female; the dragging off of old women to the Lubianka and the refusal to release them until they give undertakings to spy upon the mission; the condemnation to death for espionage for the benefit of the mission of an individual who was practically unknown to it.[38]

A case in point was the experience of a young Russian maid-servant employed by the British mission. In the early part of 1922 she was called to the Commissariat of Foreign Affairs, where she was interviewed by an official of the secret police who tried to recruit her to spy on her employers. When the girl stubbornly refused to accept his offer, the official passed from friendly persuasion to threats and informed her that continued refusal to cooperate would result in her disappearance into a prison cell. Completely intimidated, she finally agreed to work for the GPU. About a year later, the same GPU agent approached an old lady in the used-furniture business and tried to persuade her to spy on the British chargé d'affaires, with whom she had become acquainted. When she balked, the GPU's representative had her removed to the Lubianka, where she was told that she would not leave the place alive unless she consented to act as a spy. When the old woman asked what would be expected of her, she was told that instructions would be given her shortly and that they would require her to steal papers from the British mission.

The British mission was not the only diplomatic establishment in Moscow to discover firsthand that even the most innocent contacts with Russians might expose the latter to grave danger. Early in 1924, for example, a former White officer who had subsequently served in the Red Army was sentenced to death as a spy in the pay of the Norwegian legation. Although the man in question had received money and occasional food parcels from relatives in Norway through the head of that legation, he had never rendered any services in return and had in fact paid duty on the parcels that came through customs. Indeed, the Soviet government later admitted privately to the Norwegians that, whatever other offenses he might have committed, the accused was quite innocent on this count since there was never any question that the Norwegian legation was involved in espionage. Thus was a man condemned to death for doing what his government officially declared he had not done.[39]

Another series of episodes demonstrated that the mere act of visiting a foreign mission for the most legitimate purposes could entail severe punishment. A Russian woman was arrested after inquiring at the British mission about the possibility of emigrating to Canada. After three harrowing weeks in prison, she was released through the intervention of the mission and the Commissariat of Foreign Affairs. "It is owing to the multiplicity of events of the kind," the British chargé d'affaires wrote in a confidential report to the Foreign Office in September 1925, "that the impression has become indelibly fixed in the minds of all Russians that acquaintance with foreigners is fraught with danger, and that it is as much as their personal safety is worth to visit foreign missions.''[40] It was not at all uncommon for applicants for British visas simply to refuse to go to the mission to supply the vice-consul with the information required before applications could be forwarded to London. Even high-ranking technical specialists being sent to England by the Soviet government were afraid of appearing on the premises. The daily presence of persons loitering outside the British mission, whose appearance and conduct left little room for doubt as to their occupation, increased the pervasive atmosphere of fear that surrounded the diplomatic missions.

The Foreign Department, it should be noted, was not the only branch of the Soviet secret police to engage in espionage. With their proximity to neighboring states, the OGPU border guards were an ideal vehicle for directing frontier intelligence and counterespionage. A "very secret" circular dated August 22, 1927, from the chief of the Pskov Provincial OGPU to the commanders of the 9th, 10th, and 11th Frontier Detachments of the OGPU stationed on the Russo-Latvian frontier, drew attention to "the need for acquiring information on well-arranged lines among the enemy's frontier defense forces and the frontier population on enemy territory within a radius of 12½ kilometers." Such information, it was believed, would yield valuable data for the struggle against espionage, counterrevolution, and smuggling. The chief of the Pskov Provincial OGPU therefore ordered his commanders to establish at once a "transfrontier system of espionage" and "a strong network of agents in those places where it can be anticipated that the frontier will be crossed."

The agents in this transfrontier espionage network were to be recruited from among the local inhabitants residing in the enemy's frontier zone. Their task would be to acquire detailed information regarding the numbers, characteristics, and armaments of enemy frontier guards; particulars of persons crossing into the Soviet Union and of persons known to have been arrested and/or released after crossing from the USSR; the names of enemy intelligence agents; and general information about military preparations and movements in the enemy's frontier zone. The circular added: "All possible methods must be employed to recruit transfrontier agents, chief of which is to utilize relations living on [Soviet] territory." On no account, however, was the principle of "quantity" to be followed in recruitment work. Agents were to be carefully chosen on the basis of their reliability and potential usefulness. (Agents could be paid, but only for services rendered and never in advance.)

Absolute secrecy was to shroud the work and identities of all OGPU transfrontier agents. Under no circumstances were agents to be known to one another, nor were they to be allowed to recruit on their own, even in districts where conditions made it impossible for the OGPU to recruit directly. Otherwise a "chain" might develop, and agents would learn too much about the workings of the espionage network as a whole. Departures from this iron rule of secrecy, it was pointed out, could have disastrous consequences for the entire network and might even lead to diplomatic complications should a recruit be apprehended on foreign soil or turn out to be a double agent. Finally, the agents were to understand that they would be granted refuge in the USSR only if they had failed to execute an assignment so vitally important that their instructions had required them to attempt it "without weighing the consequences of failure."[41]

The Secret Police and the New Economic Policy

The New Economic Policy (or NEP), with its legalization of private trade and ownership of small industries and enterprises, which Lenin introduced in March 1921, added another dimension to the work of the Soviet secret police. The NEP represented a retreat from the overhasty drive toward communism of the first years of Bolshevik rule and was intended to help rebuild Russia's shattered economy by means of a partial return to private enterprise. To a considerable extent the plan worked. During the NEP years the Bolsheviks consolidated their grip on power, and the Soviet economy showed signs of recovery from the devastation of war, revolution, and civil war. But there was a dark side to the NEP experiment—an alarming increase in the incidence of "economic counterrevolution," a broad category of crime that included such offenses as bribery, speculation, and malfeasance.

The causes of the upsurge in economic crime that accompanied the NEP were at least twofold. In the first place, the complex and unwieldy system of trusts brought into existence to manage each segment of Soviet industry (they eventually numbered 486) provided a home for many an unreliable "bourgeois specialist." In the opinion of a prominent Bolshevik economist, the defects of the Soviet economic apparatus constituted a dangerous form of economic counterrevolution and resulted directly from "the fact that the entire apparatus is really in the hands of bourgeois and petit-bourgeois elements, which are our class enemies, usually definitely hostile and at best fundamentally indifferent to our work." According to the same official, data collected during an investigation of Soviet economic organs painted "a picture of unbelievable chaos. . . . Everywhere a complete absence of bookkeeping and, consequently, of a plan of work." After reviewing the defects of several important economic agencies the writer concluded: "Involuntarily the thought occurs that bureaucratism and red tape, for which our institutions are becoming so notorious, are deliberately developed in order to give the 'appearance' of activity and not reveal that the whole apparatus is working to absolutely no purpose." Until an adequate number of "Red" specialists could be trained the only solution was to force the bourgeois specialists to work honestly. This in turn required the strictest kind of control with severe penalties for every infraction. [42]

The NEP also spawned a new commercial class of small urban capitalists, or NEPmen, as they were called, who were encouraged by the government to buy and sell on the free market. The bourgeois habits rekindled by the NEP soon led to widespread graft and corruption involving both NEPmen and Soviet economic officials who accepted bribes in return for raw materials liberated from Soviet institutions on forged requisitions. One dismayed eyewitness recounted the wheeling and dealing NEPmen:

Business livens up society, after a fashion, but it is the most corrupt kind of business imaginable. Retail trade . . . has passed into the hands of private enterprise, which has triumphed over the co-operative and State trading systems. Where does this capital, non-existent five years ago, all come from? From robbery, fraudulent speculation, and superbly skillful racketeering. Twisters start up a fake co-operative; they bribe officials to give them credits, raw materials, and orders. . . . Once launched, they carry on, determined to become the universal middlemen between socialized industry and the consumer. They double the price of everything. Soviet trade, as a consequence of our industrial weakness, has become the hunting ground for a flock of vultures in whom the shape of tomorrow's toughest and smartest capitalists can be clearly discerned. . . . NEP has become one big confidence trick.[43]

Stern measures were recommended for dealing with these abuses. Lenin demanded that the death sentence and other "no-joke" penalties be imposed on those who went "beyond the framework of state capitalism in our meaning of the concept."[44]

Soviet criminal statistics of the period document the wave of economic crime that accompanied the NEP. According to data compiled by the Commissariat of Justice of the RSFSR, 29 percent of those sentenced in the forty-eight provinces of the Republic during the first half of 1923 were charged with bribery; during the same period in 1924 the figure had jumped to more than 40 percent. And in Petrograd, from April to September 1923, nearly 37 percent of all persons brought to trial for various crimes were government employees. Overall, bribery increased 50 percent between 1922 and 1924, while embezzlement increased fivefold between 1922 and 1926. Those found guilty of "economic counterrevolution" during the NEP years were for the most part representatives of "the new bourgeoisie and its agents in the Soviet apparatus." Of the more than 32,000 persons convicted of malfeasance in 1926, for example, 72.4 percent were white collar workers.[45]

To keep the commercial instincts awakened by the NEP within reasonable bounds and to combat the corruption that was rife in the economic agencies of the Soviet government, the iron broom of the GPU/OGPU began a vigorous campaign to sweep "the scum of the NEP" from the proletarian landscape. It was in connection with this campaign that on October 22, 1923, Dzerzhinsky requested the Central Committee of the Communist Party to authorize the OGPU to expel profiteers and currency speculators from Moscow and other cities. Said Dzerzhinsky on this occasion:

Not the least of the factors inflating the prices of manufactured goods are the malicious profiteers who, by their intrigues, entangle our system of trusts and cooperatives and their employees. Moscow in particular, where the largest trusts and banks are located, attracts these elements, and from here they penetrate all corners of the USSR. They take over the markets and the illegal currency exchanges. The chief methods of their operations are graft and corruption. If you ask them what they live on, they won't tell you, but live they do and stylishly. These are parasites, corrupters, leeches, malicious speculators. They are the ones who are corrupting our economic administrators.[46]

Dzerzhinsky was certain that the OGPU could rid Moscow and other Soviet cities of these criminal elements and make a real contribution to the well-being of the entire Soviet economy in the process. The Central Committee agreed with Dzerzhinsky and approved his program for purging the urban centers of the USSR of profiteers, currency speculators, and other "parasitic elements."

Two months later, on December 25, 1923, *Izvestiia* published a proclamation signed by Dzerzhinsky, addressed "To All Citizens of Moscow," informing them that the OGPU had recently arrested and expelled from the city a sizable number of "socially dangerous elements" who "instead of participating in normal trade exchange and production took to the exploitation of the New Economic Policy." A total of 916 persons was arrested, of whom 522 were shipped out of Moscow to unspecified destinations. The arrested included alcohol dealers (110), "adventurers" and card swindlers (156), currency speculators (120), persons without definite occupations (453), cocaine dealers (24), and bordello owners (53). Dzerzhinsky warned that persons who came to Moscow with the intention of leading a "parasitic life" could expect unceremonious arrest and expulsion by the OGPU to "the distant parts of the Republic." On the other hand, Dzerzhinsky promised individuals engaged in legal commercial activities immunity from persecution or expulsion.[47]

This was, however, only the beginning of the OGPU's campaign. In a report to the Council of People's Commissars delivered in March 1924, Dzerzhinsky provided evidence that all over the country the secret police was conducting mass arrests of persons engaged in speculation—a most pernicious form of economic counterrevolution. During the two-week period from February 15 to March 1, 1924, the OGPU had taken 2,372 speculators into custody in Moscow alone and exiled 1,900 of them to northern Russia and Siberia. The figures for other Soviet cities were also impressive:

City	Arrested	Exiled	To Be Tried
Leningrad	1,187	1,145	45
Kharkov	730	651	79
Kiev	514	503	11
Rostov	358	320	38
Odessa	306	293	13
Kursk	240	232	8
Voronezh	217	192	25
Tambov	164	157	7
Kazan	109	100	9

Dzerzhinsky hastened to add that these figures were incomplete since not all local branches of the OGPU had been heard from. Nevertheless, the chairman of the OGPU felt certain that the arrest of more than six thousand speculators in a two-week period constituted proof that his agency's campaign against economic counterrevolution was being waged in earnest and on a considerable scale. Certainly the secret police could not be accused of patronizing the excesses of the NEPmen and their accomplices.[48]

Elsewhere on the economic front, the secret police was utilized to overcome a variety of problems that resulted from the inadequacy of existing repressive measures. In September 1922, the Council of Labor and Defense created the Commission for the Struggle with Bribery and appointed Dzerzhinsky its head. Between October 10, 1922, and January 1, 1923, more than 1,700 bribe-takers were reported to have been apprehended in just twenty provinces. When, in March 1924, the Soviet government was suddenly faced with a critical shortage of copper for coins, Dzerzhinsky ordered the OGPU into action; soon a sufficient supply of copper found its way to the mint. Commenting on this particular operation, a Soviet writer noted that it had "considerable economic and political significance since the strengthening of the Soviet monetary system depended on the issuance of new money." The OGPU was also active in the struggle against counterfeiters. Between September 15, 1923, and June 1, 1925, the

Economic Administration of the OGPU is reported to have un-covered a total of 256 counterfeiting rings and to have "repressed" 1,743 counterfeiters.[49]

On February 2, 1924, just two weeks after Lenin's death, Dzerzhinsky was appointed chairman of the Supreme Council of the National Economy (VSNKh), the state organ responsible for supervising all Soviet industry. The tireless Dzerzhinsky served concurrently as chairman of the OGPU and, working by day in his office at the Supreme Council of the National Economy and late into the night at the Lubianka, he was able to give his per-sonal attention to both demanding posts. (By this time the Soviet leaders had come to recognize that Dzerzhinsky's efficiency and drive were as applicable to the economy as to the secret police.) Dzerzhinsky did not achieve any economic miracles, but by force of example and the most drastic disciplinary measures he fought graft and corruption wherever he found it.[50]

As chief of Soviet industry, Dzerzhinsky continued to rely on the OGPU, drawing it more deeply than ever into the economic life of the nation. Not only did he bring with him to the Supreme Council of the National Economy such trusted Chekist comrades-in-arms as Katznelson, the head of the Economic Administration of the OGPU, Mantsev, Redens, and Blagonravov, but he assigned the secret police the task of enforcing the government's economic policies as well. Thus, in October 1925, Dzerzhinsky called for an end to the rise of retail prices caused in large part by widespread speculation. The "bacchanalia" of rising prices was having a devastating impact on the entire economy. If it continued, he said, the government's policy of market regulation, its price policy, and the stability of the currency would be endangered. As an example of the penetration of Soviet economic organs by speculators Dzerzhinsky pointed to the findings of a recent inspection of the Commissariat of Domestic Trade of the RSFSR that revealed that during just one quarter some 550 car-loads of manufactured goods had been illegally sold in Moscow to speculators for the sum of 22 million roubles. This glaring abuse had been only one of many committed in recent months. Manu-factured goods of all kinds, instead of reaching the consumers by the most direct route, passed from speculator to speculator, contributing to a general merchandise famine, driving up prices, and enriching the speculators. Dzerzhinsky insisted that all organs of the Supreme Council of the National Economy take steps to reduce the retail prices of products of Soviet industry. The motto of this campaign was to be: "Down with speculators and speculation, down with the middlemen between state and industry and the masses of consumers, the workers and peasants."

Dzerzhinsky ordered all trading organs of the Supreme Council of the National Economy, all producing trusts and syndicates, and all government sales offices to purge their transactions and their staffs of speculators, turning those guilty of speculation over to the courts to be "speedily and mercilessly punished." The OGPU was meanwhile ordered: to assist the organs of the Supreme Council of the National Economy, giving them unlimited support in the enforcement of these measures; to intensify surveillance of Soviet trade organizations; and to give Dzerzhinsky weekly personal reports through the chief of the Economic Administration of the OGPU. The direct supervision and management of the entire campaign Dzerzhinsky entrusted to his Chekist colleague, Mantsev.[51]

The Secret Police and the Political Opposition

The economic concessions made by the NEP—the legalization of private trade and enterprise and the cessation of forced requisitions and class warfare in the villages—were not accompanied by any loosening up in the political sphere. There could be no question of allowing the more relaxed conditions on the economic front to be exploited by dissidents either inside or outside the Communist Party. In mid-February 1922, Lenin called for an "intensification of reprisals against the political enemies of Soviet power and the agents of the bourgeoisie (*specifically* the Mensheviks and S. R.s)." Lenin wanted these reprisals mounted by the "compulsory staging of a number of *model* (as regards speed and force of repression, and *explanation* of their significance to the masses of people through the courts and the press) trials in Moscow, Petrograd, Kharkov and several other key centers."[52] And in a letter written to the Commissar of Justice, D. I. Kursky, on May 17, 1922, in connection with a new criminal code that was then in preparation Lenin said: "The paragraph on terror must be formulated as widely as possible, since only revolutionary consciousness of justice can determine the conditions of its application."[53] Thus did Lenin, during the twilight months of his rule, reaffirm the primacy of terror and dictatorship in the land of the victorious proletariat.

The launching of a new and more vigorous campaign against the Bolsheviks' socialist rivals—the Mensheviks, the Socialist Revolutionaries, and the Anarchists—was given official sanction by the Twelfth Communist Party Conference, which met August 4–12, 1922. The records of the Conference show that the delegates were confident that the overall position of the Soviet government had been strengthened during the first year of the NEP due to the appearance of numerous splits and divisions within the "anti-Soviet camp" both at home and abroad. Nevertheless, there were indications that danger still lurked on the internal front. "Anti-Soviet parties and tendencies" had established close ties with "European capitalist reaction" and were changing their tactics in order to take advantage of the legal opportunities provided by the more relaxed climate of the NEP in pursuit of their counterrevolutionary goals. These anti-Soviet groups were, in the opinion of the delegates, seeking nothing less than the gradual transformation of the RSFSR into a "bourgeois democracy." Their nefarious intentions were reflected in efforts to "transform rural cooperatives into instruments of kulak counterrevolution, university chairs into a platform for undisguised bourgeois propaganda, and the legal publishing firms into a means of agitating against the Workers' and Peasants' Government." The resolutions of the Conference called upon the Party to deal decisively with these new manifestations of anti-Soviet activity by a combination of "repression" and intensified propaganda to counter the influence of the various anti-Soviet parties and tendencies.[54]

Naturally, the GPU, as the political watchdog of the Soviet government, would play a major role in this campaign. Felix Dzerzhinsky quickly devised a battle plan aimed at delivering "knockout blows" to the opposition political parties, the Mensheviks in particular. In order to deprive the Mensheviks as well as other anti-Bolshevik spokesmen of the means of communicating their views to the Russian people, a strict censorship was to be enforced in the publication of newspapers, magazines, and books. In addition, the Soviet bureaucracy, from top to bottom, was to be purged of all persons whose loyalty was suspect. Finally, the more dangerous elements were to be physically removed by means of arrest and exile. Dzerzhinsky was confident that this multipronged approach offered the most efficacious means of crushing internal resistance to Bolshevik rule once and for all.[55]

The legal basis for a GPU-enforced censorship of "all matter intended for publication or dissemination, both in manuscript and in print," was provided in an enactment dated June 6, 1922. This law created the Main Administration for Affairs of Literature and Publishing and authorized it to prohibit the publication and distribution of printed matter containing agitation against the Soviet power; disclosing the military secrets of the Soviet Republic; exciting public opinion through the communication of false reports; exciting nationalistic and religious fanaticism; or having a pornographic nature. The GPU was designated to enforce censorship and was charged with

> combating the dissemination of matter prohibited by the Main Administration for Affairs of Literature and Publishing; the surveillance of typographies . . . ; combating surreptitious publications and their distribution; combating the importation from abroad for distribution in the territory of the Russian Socialist Federated Soviet Republic of literature which it is forbidden to circulate; . . . and the confiscation of books prohibited by the Main Administration for Affairs of Literature and Publishing.[56]

It has already been noted that the GPU was authorized to exile and deport persons for periods of up to three years without public trial. Further instructions for the application of administrative exile were contained in a decree signed by Dzerzhinsky on January 3, 1923.[57] According to the provisions of this decree, administrative exile was a form of punishment applicable to "persons whose presence in a certain place appears, from their activity, their past, or their connection with criminal circles, dangerous from the point of view of safeguarding the revolutionary order." Individuals falling under any of these categories were subject to three different types of administrative exile: exile from a given locality, accompanied by a ban on the right of residence in certain specified places in the Republic; exile from a given locality to a definite region of the Republic; exile outside the territory of the Republic, that is, abroad. The final decision regarding the type of administrative exile to be applied in a particular case rested with the Special Commission of the Commissariat of Internal Affairs, a body chaired by the Commissar of Internal Affairs and composed of another representative of that agency and a representative of the Commissariat of Justice. The Special Commission acted on the basis of recommendations received from GPU organs not below the provincial level with the "knowledge and consent" of the corresponding soviet executive committee. The only apparent safeguard against the totally unwarranted imposition of a sentence of administrative exile was the requirement that the dossier of each person submitted to the Special Commission contain the following information: "(*a*) Name; (*b*) Age; (*c*) Class origin; (*d*) Occupation at present and before the revolution; (*e*) Family situation; (*f*) Exact reasons for exile, with a detailed statement of the necessity for it."

In late August 1922, the GPU announced in *Pravda* that an unspecified number of opposition political party members and representatives of the "bourgeois intelligentsia" had already been exiled by administrative decree from Petrograd, Moscow, Kiev, and other Soviet cities. The exiled included professors, doctors, agronomists, and writers. Some were said to have been shipped to the northern provinces of Russia, while others were deported abroad. The removal of these "counterrevolutionaries" had been dictated by their stubborn refusal to abandon their "senseless hope for the restoration of the old order." The GPU desired that their fate serve as a "first warning" to the remainder of this potentially harmful stratum of the population.[58]

Secret reports on the internal situation presented by Felix Dzerzhinsky to the Council of People's Commissars in late 1922 and early 1923 indicated that the GPU was making good Lenin's dictum that the proper place for the Bolsheviks' rivals and critics was prison. Dzerzhinsky told the leaders of the Soviet government on November 14, 1922, that the secret police had been extremely active in recent weeks coping with a marked increase in the number of political offenses. This Dzerzhinsky attributed, in a manner that echoed the sentiments of the delegates to the

Twelfth Party Conference, to the close ties existing between the regime's domestic opponents and the centers of "world reaction" abroad. No sooner did the Soviet government experience a worsening in its international position than the Menshevik, Socialist Revolutionary, and monarchist "marionettes" began to move as if guided by some invisible but experienced hand. These counterrevolutionary elements were once again trying to undermine the Soviet government by sowing provocative rumors calculated to produce unrest and disaffection among the working masses.

Dzerzhinsky proceeded to document the growth of counterrevolutionary activity in Soviet Russia during the latter half of October as measured by GPU arrest figures. In the Tiumen region of western Siberia, an area that had experienced widespread unrest, the GPU arrested 2,037 "counterrevolutionaries" during the last two weeks of October in comparison with a paltry 563 arrests during the whole of September. In the Petrograd area during the same two-week period, 5,921 political offenders had been arrested. Dzerzhinsky also disclosed that the GPU had unearthed a plot to blow up the building in which the Fourth Congress of the Third International was to meet. A total of 137 conspirators had been arrested in connection with this plot, of whom 40 were shot. Meanwhile, in Moscow Province another 4,485 persons had been arrested for "counterrevolutionary agitation," "pogrom agitation," and "participation in organizations inimical to the Soviet government." Dzerzhinsky added:

> I have to point out that in the provinces of both Petrograd and Moscow the number of political arrests made in the first and second half of September is less than half the number arrested in the first and second half of October. It is possible that this increase in political offenders is partly due to unemployment. The main reason, however, is due to increased activity in Socialist Revolutionary and Menshevik circles.

Dzerzhinsky assured the Council of People's Commissars that the GPU's energetic pursuit of all enemies of Soviet power would make it impossible for the Mensheviks, the Socialist Revolutionaries, and their ilk to re-establish an internal front against the Soviet government. "Each counterrevolutionary attempt," he promised, "will be smothered in its initial stages."[59]

About two months later, on January 10, 1923, Dzerzhinsky informed the Council of People's Commissars that after a long investigation the GPU had succeeded in uncovering and smashing an extensive counterrevolutionary organization based in Siberia. The objective of the Socialist Revolutionary plotters, who, according to the chairman of the GPU, headed this particular underground association, was to establish a Siberian Peasants' Republic apart from the RSFSR. To this end, peasant uprisings had been planned for February in the provinces of Tobolsk, Tomsk, Omsk, and Semipalatinsk. (Simultaneously with the armed uprisings, the plotters had intended to provoke a railway strike in order to impede the movement of Red Army troops from the local garrisons.) With its headquarters in Omsk and with cells scattered throughout Siberia in Ekaterinburg, Tomsk, Pavlodar, Krasnoyarsk, Novonikolaievsk, Irkutsk, and other towns, the organization's total membership, Dzerzhinsky estimated, was at least five thousand persons, of whom some five hundred of the most important leaders had recently been arrested.[60]

The punishments inflicted on the thousands of persons arrested during this wave of secret police repression ranged from imprisonment and exile to execution. Although comprehensive data on the number of persons shot by the secret police during the NEP years are not available, enough scattered evidence does exist to confirm that GPU/OGPU executions continued unabated throughout the Soviet Union, though not on the scale of the Red Terror of the Civil War years. The historian Sergey Melgounov, citing what he described as official GPU figures, wrote that the secret police executed 262 persons during January and February 1922, 348 in April, and 758 in May.[61] According to figures supplied by Dzerzhinsky himself, 895 "bandits" were executed by the OGPU in 1924, and 2,237 more were killed in armed clashes with the secret police that year.[62] A sudden flurry of executions took place in the White Russian Soviet Republic in the fall of 1925. These shootings, which were never made public, occurred just prior to the announcement of an amnesty to celebrate the eighth anniversary of the revolution. In a secret order reminiscent of an earlier day, local OGPU agencies were instructed to empty their cells. All persons accused of armed opposition to the Soviet authorities or of participation in counterrevolutionary activity were to be shot. As a result of this order, 167 persons were executed in various parts of the White Russian Republic during the week of September 19–26: 121 persons (mostly peasants) for armed rebellion, 35 for robbery and murder, and 11 for espionage.[63] It is likely that similar orders went out to secret police agencies in other parts of the USSR as well.

The majority of political prisoners (as distinguished from armed insurgents) arrested during the NEP were not shot. Some, like the writer Mikhail Osorgin, were deported. It was in the summer of 1922 while vacationing in the countryside that Osorgin learned that his Moscow apartment had been "visited" by GPU agents. A short time later, when the GPU men drove out to his country home, Osorgin avoided arrest by hiding in the woods for three days. Finally, having assured himself that at worst he risked only deportation abroad, Osorgin decided to turn himself in. His examination at GPU headquarters took only half an hour since an accusation and a sentence had been drawn up in advance. The formal charge against him was "that during five years he refused to become reconciled with the Soviet power and harmed it during the most difficult period of its existence." His sentence was relatively mild—deportation abroad for a period of three years. Osorgin was made to understand, however, that his banishment was in reality permanent. Before his release he was required to sign this statement: "In case of attempting to escape on the way or [of] returning from abroad without the permission of the Soviet power, I shall be liable to suffer the extreme penalty (to be shot)." Faced with an injunction to leave the Soviet Republic within five days, Osorgin managed to gather together some necessary belongings and books and purchased a one-way ticket to Germany.[64]

Not so fortunate in escaping the grip of the GPU were the thousands of political prisoners who were sentenced to exile or concentration camps in the most remote and desolate corners of the country. Arrest could come at any time of the day or night and without warning, at home, at work, or on the streets. A prisoner's fate was, as a rule, decided only after a period of "preliminary deprivation of freedom," which lasted anywhere from a few days to several months and even years. In cases of administrative exile, sentences were passed in camera, with no opportunity to produce witnesses on one's behalf, let alone have the services of counsel. A sample of the charges on which political prisoners were convicted, when they were informed of formal charges, included the following: "Keeping and spreading counterrevolutionary literature and undermining the Soviet government by agitating and spreading counterrevolutionary literature." "Counterrevolutionary activity." "Opposition to the Soviet authorities." "Case not proved and therefore quashed. But, because of anti-Soviet activity, exiled for two years. . . . " "Participation in an organization aiming to give aid to the international bourgeoisie." "Three years in prison as an Anarchist."[65]

Hunger strikes and letters of protest to the Soviet authorities were common during this period, but rarely did they have any effect on the harsh and often extralegal persecution to which political prisoners were subjected. In an "Open Letter to the People's Commissar of Justice of the Russian Socialist Federated Soviet Republic, Citizen Kursky," dated June 24, 1922, four members of the Socialist Revolutionary Party, who had already spent from eight to fourteen months each in prison, protested against the sentences of administrative exile imposed upon them by the GPU in violation of existing statutes. The letter contained this recounting of an exchange between the prisoners and a GPU official who tried to convince them of the futility of protesting their sentences:

> I am surprised at your not proceeding into exile," [the GPU official] said to us on May 11, [1922] in the office of [the Taganka Prison]. "We shall not hand your cases over to the courts anyway, and you will remain in prison, perhaps for three years longer. The Presidium of the Central Executive Committee permits us to keep you in prison until the conclusion of the investigation, and we can drag out the investigation as long as we please." In reply to our remark that [administrative] exile violates the laws of the Soviet Republic [note: the first decree on administrative exile was not issued until August 10, 1922], the official said: "Once the Presidium of the Central Executive Committee approves it—and this it will do—it is lawful. The Presidium can do anything. If it orders the GPU to shoot half of Moscow's population, we shall execute it."[66]

A feature of the early Soviet exile system that was especially resented by the political prisoners was the GPU's practice, borrowed from Tsarist days, of sending exiles to their destinations by *étape,* that is, by slow stages in prison convoys, from one provincial prison to another, rather than by the most direct, speedy route. The long, agonizing journey into exile exposed the prisoners to all the ravages of harsh climates, aggravated by lack of proper food, clothing, medical attention, and shelter, as well as by brutal treatment from local jailers. When a place of exile was some distance from the nearest railroad, as was frequently the case, the last stage of the journey had to be completed on foot or by whatever other means of conveyance was available. A young woman wrote of her own journey into exile to the uninhabited parts of the Narym territory of northern Siberia: "It took us only a month by rowboat to get there, a distance of nine hundred *versts,* along the Parabel and Kenghe rivers, besides some 'hiking' across marshland."[67] It was no wonder that people often arrived in exile physically broken and ill equipped to withstand the rigorous conditions awaiting them.

Banished to desolate places with names like Temira, Irghis, Akhmolinsk, Ust-Syssolsk, and Sol-Vitchegodsk, the exile's worst psychic enemies were loneliness and depression. Cut off from the civilized world, the exiles suffered great mental anguish. One prisoner, from his place of exile in Ust-Kulom, which in the local dialect meant "The Gates of Death," wrote that the village "deserves that name. A hole, a gap in human culture. The village is not marked on any map. . . . No possibility of obtaining even baked bread. . . . There are five exiles in Ust-Kulom."[68] Olga Romanova, the eighteen-year-old exile whose journey to Narym was mentioned above, spent many hours wandering aimlessly in the wilderness surrounding her cabin. Her thoughts during these excursions were despondent:

I questioned myself: "Where am I? Why am I here? Whence these century-old cedars?" That would last but a moment. Then I would shake it all off and recover my consciousness and realize fully what, where, and why. Then a burning yearning would creep again into my heart, a yearning for freedom, for life, for people. I would want to cry out: "I desire liberty, freedom!" But to whom could I cry out? Not to the aged cedars. They will understand nothing, . . . To the birds, mice and beavers who every now and then raised their heads from under the tree trunks? They too will understand and say nothing. . . . So I would remain sitting in a petrified condition, my hands clenched in despair till my fingers cracked.[69]

Nor was the approach of the last days of one's term of exile a cause for rejoicing. It was common practice for the GPU to rearrest a person on some pretext and banish him anew to an even more remote corner of the country. As one of the exiles put it: "Today you may be sent out to Orenburg for two years, and in six months you may find yourself in Akhtibinsk, in another month in Tcherges, then in Tchelgara, and then you may unexpectedly get another sentence of three years to some most desolate spot in Kirgisia. And so endlessly."[70]

There was little to allay the mental anguish of the political prisoners banished by GPU/OGPU fiat to the most uninhabitable parts of the Soviet Union. But at least the exiles were spared the harsh regime endured by those held under guard in the concentration camps administered by the secret police. Concentration camps, it will be recalled, first appeared during the early days of the Civil War, when they were used to isolate proven and suspected opponents of the Bolshevik regime. The end of armed hostilities did not, however, bring their dismantlement. Quite the contrary, the number of concentration camps increased significantly during the NEP period, from 132 in 1921 to 355 in October 1923. (There were in addition more than three hundred corrective labor camps, prisons, and agricultural colonies in operation at the same time.)[71]

Most of the concentration camps and other "places of deprivation of freedom," as they were euphemistically known, were administered by the Main Administration of Places of Confinement (abbreviated GUMZ), attached to the Commissariat of Internal Affairs. But the GPU/OGPU continued to administer its own separate network of camps and prisons whence prisoners were dispatched by administrative decree. The Northern Camps of Special Designation (*Severnye lageria osobogo naznacheniia*), or SLON, were the best known and most notorious. Located in the Russian far north at Kholmogory, Archangelsk, Kem, Pertominsk, and other settlements around the White Sea coast, they were established at the end of the Civil War in 1921. Among the first to enter SLON were officers of the defeated Wrangel army, Tambov peasants, Kronstadt sailors, and a variety of ordinary criminals. Later, in connection with the wave of repression directed against the Bolsheviks' socialist rivals, Mensheviks, Socialist Revolutionaries, and Anarchists began to arrive at the SLON camps in ever-increasing numbers. There to greet them were GPU officials like Bachulis, the sadistic commandant of the Kholmogory concentration camp. It was said of Bachulis that he divided the prisoners into groups of ten and, in the event of an escape attempt or other infraction of discipline committed by any one, he would have the remaining nine shot. According to a former inmate, from May to November 1921 about three thousand prisoners passed through the Kholmogory camp. Cold, hunger, and disease took their toll of the prisoners, 442 dying during the six-month period.[72]

By the summer of 1923 the original SLON facilities on the mainland were already outgrown and the camp administrators were ordered to move the prisoners offshore to the Solovetsky Islands. Located some forty miles from the mainland settlement of Kem, the Solovetsky Islands were first settled in the late fifteenth century by a group of monks seeking complete seclusion from the world. As the religious community took root, a monastery was constructed on the central Solovetsk Island and numerous churches and cloisters on neighboring islands. But the monks were not the only ones to appreciate the isolation afforded by the ice floes that cut the islands off from the mainland for the better part of the year. Since the days of Ivan the Terrible, the rulers of Russia had used the Solovetsky Islands as a place of banishment and the Bolsheviks did not break from this tradition. On July 1, 1923, the first batch of 150 political prisoners made the steamboat journey to Solovetsk. By the end of the year, according to the well-informed Menshevik journal *Sotsialisticheskii vestnik,* there was a total of 252 socialists on the Solovetsky Islands.[73]

There may have been a shortage of many things in Soviet Russia during the NEP era, but counterrevolutionaries were not one of them. In a speech to a gathering of secret police officials in Moscow, Dzerzhinsky labeled the counterrevolutionaries and their allies—priests, sectarians, and kulaks—"our worst enemies." Even if temporarily inactive ("because we have seized them by the throat"), they still might take advantage of an opportune moment to stab the Soviets in the back. "The sooner we get rid of them," Dzerzhinsky said, "the sooner we will reach socialism." To achieve this end, he called for "a struggle the final

result of which must be that not one counterrevolutionary sur-
vives." This was to be the watchword of all honorable Chekists,
who were to remember it every minute and be guided by it in their
daily work.[74]

Every strike or uprising in any part of Russia and every new
wave of GPU repression resulted in a further influx of prisoners
to the distant Northern Camps of Special Designation. From a
total of about four thousand inmates in 1923, the convict population swelled to more than half a million by the end of the
decade.[75] And what an assortment of citizens of the workers' and
peasants' state were cast upon the sacred shores of the
Solovetsky Islands, the most desolate of the GPU's network of
concentration camps. According to a former prisoner:

> There was hardly a nationality of Russia, a creed, a profession, a class,
> or a trend of thought that was not represented at Solovki. Socialists,
> Anarchists; so-called "counterrevolutionaries," that is, former
> members of the "white" movement and rightist enemies of the regime;
> common criminals and prostitutes; former tradesmen and Soviet
> merchants who had trusted the NEP; people sentenced as "spies"
> (actual spies were shot without ado); clergymen of all denominations,
> especially the Greek-Orthodox; workers guilty of striking and peasants
> accused of rioting; Soviet officials who had served their country body
> and soul and had been charged with wrecking; delinquent GPU agents;
> at the end of the 'twenties Trotskyites and members of other opposi-
> tion groups within the ruling party—all were present at Solovki.[76]

The inmates of the Northern Camps fell into three broad categories: common criminals, counterrevolutionaries, and political
offenders. Among the counterrevolutionaries (or "K-R's") were
persons who had served in the anti-Bolshevik armies of Denikin,
Kolchak, Wrangel, and Yudenich, former Tsarist officials,
kulaks, and priests. In addition, large numbers of NEPmen and
their families were arrested by the secret police and banished to
the far north, where they were joined by thousands of people who
had worked as hired employees in the private enterprises legalized by the Soviet government during the NEP years. The
political offenders were a minority of the camps' inmates and
consisted of the various socialist rivals of the ruling Communist
Party swept up in the net of the secret police. Out of deference to
their common revolutionary heritage, the Bolsheviks at first

spared their imprisoned socialist opponents the compulsory labor regimen imposed on the criminals and "K-R's." The protests and hunger strikes of the politicals were of no avail once the Soviets began to phase out this policy of preferential treatment in the mid-1920s.

Life in the Northern Camps was grim. Prisoners' quarters consisted mainly of buildings that had been constructed before the revolution. Poorly heated and overcrowded beyond belief, they afforded the inmates only the most rudimentary protection against the arctic climate. No special clothing was issued to the prisoners during their period of incarceration. They wore what they came with or whatever was left by prisoners who died. The typical ration consisted of fish, soup, and bread (about 1½ pounds a day). Ordinary sanitation was nonexistent. Certain prisoners were detailed to haul away refuse, but this method of disposal was so inadequate that the prisoners lived in appalling filth. Prisoners were also required to perform heavy physical labor. Some cut timber and peat while others were assigned to roadbuilding and mining. Sickness and exhaustion meanwhile claimed the lives of thousands of prisoners in the Northern Camps who were unable to endure these difficult conditions.[77]

Death at the Fighting Post

Lenin made the secret police responsible for extirpating the virus of counterrevolution in every area of Soviet life, and it was only a matter of time before the Lubianka's formidable presence was felt in the ranks of the Communist Party itself. No sooner had the last major battle of the Civil War been won than Lenin turned his attention to the health of the Party. His diagnosis was an alarming one. The Party, he wrote in January 1921, was ailing: "We must have the courage to face the bitter truth. The Party is sick. The Party is down with the fever. The whole point is whether the malaise has affected only the 'feverish upper ranks,' and perhaps only those in Moscow, or the whole organism." The fever in the Party was caused by the spirit of internal dissension, and Lenin intended to exorcise it once and for all. He told the delegates to the Tenth Congress of the Russian Communist Party, meeting in March 1921 under the shadow of the Kronstadt uprising, that the

Soviet government was "passing through a period of grave danger" and that the threat of "petit-bourgeois counterrevolution" was greater than ever before. It was "no trifling matter to form an opposition in such a Party at such a moment," he said.[78]

Lenin was referring to the protests of a group calling itself the Workers' Opposition. Led by the veteran Bolshevik Alexander Shliapnikov, a former metalworker and the first Commissar of Labor in Lenin's government, the Workers' Opposition was a small but vocal minority on the periphery of the Communist Party, which decried the excessive bureaucratization of the revolution and the abandonment of the ideals of 1917. Shliapnikov and his small band of followers called for the creation of an independent All-Russian Congress of Producers to administer the nation's economy as a step toward the creation of a genuine workers' democracy. Lenin condemned the "anarcho-syndicalist deviation" of the Workers' Opposition and implied that it was linked to the counterrevolutionary tendencies at work in the country. The atmosphere of controversy generated by the Workers' Opposition was "becoming extremely dangerous" and constituted "a direct threat to the dictatorship of the proletariat." Therefore Lenin demanded an immediate end to all opposition within the Party:

> I think we have had enough of this discussion! All the arguments about freedom of speech and freedom to criticize . . . which run through all the speeches of the Workers' Opposition . . . have no particular meaning at all. . . . We have spent quite a lot of time in discussion, and I must say that the point is now being driven farther home with "rifles" than with the opposition's theses. Comrades, this is no time to have an opposition. Either you're on this side, or on the other, but then your weapon must be a gun, and not an opposition. . . . I think the Party Congress will have to draw the conclusion that the opposition's time has run out and that the lid's on it. We want no more oppositions![79]

The Congress dutifully proceeded to outlaw organized opposition within the Party and, in a secret resolution, authorized the expulsion of Party members who persisted in this noxious form of anti-Party activity.

From the first signs of organized dissension in the ranks of the Party, Dzerzhinsky unhesitatingly threw his influence and that of the secret police to the side of the Leninist (and later Stalinist) majority. With independent political activity outside the Communist Party virtually extinguished, the destiny of the country hinged on the outcome of factional disputes within the ruling Communist Party itself. The fact that Dzerzhinsky began to thrust the GPU/OGPU into these disputes, tilting the scales in favor of one side and against another, was therefore a portentous development that "radically changed the character of the ruling Party and the [secret police] as well.[80]

Dzerzhinsky does not appear to have been motivated in these matters by a desire to curry favor with the Party leadership or to improve his own position, which was already firmly established, in the ruling circle. He acted, rather, in accordance with his own deeply held belief in the necessity of "Party unity," which for him was the supreme arbiter in all such disputes. As Dzerzhinsky once said:

> No Party democracy whatever can be allowed to bring about an insurrection, if one can express oneself thus, against a decision of the Party congress. No democracy, no rules, no member of the Party, no Party organization, is given such a guarantee or can be given one. The Party rules and our Party democracy are based exclusively on the unity of the Party. . . . And the unity of the Party must be preserved; it must be sacred for all of us, not just in a formal sense . . . but in its essence.[81]

To preserve "Party unity" Dzerzhinsky was willing to take action even against "people with Party cards." From then on, not even members of the proletarian vanguard were immune from secret police surveillance, arrest, and repression.

In the summer of 1921, at Lenin's urging, the first major purge of the Communist Party was launched. Nearly 170,000 members, or almost one-quarter of the total membership, were expelled. This action was necessary, Lenin said, to rid the Party of the "influence of the petit-bourgeois and petit-bourgeois–anarchist elements," as well as "of rascals, of bureaucratic, dishonest or wavering Communists, and of Mensheviks who have repainted their 'facade' but who have remained Mensheviks at heart."[82]

Evidence soon began to accumulate at GPU headquarters that the expulsion of thousands of "wavering" and otherwise suspect

Communists was not having the desired effect of silencing them. A secret GPU circular of November 1922 noted that there had been a recent increase in the incidence of anti-Soviet activity on the part of persons newly purged from the Party. Not only did these former members continue their criticism of the Party leadership and its policies, but they also claimed to be the "real Communists" in contrast to those who merely possessed Party membership cards. The circular added:

> It is to be observed that those expelled from the RCP [Russian Communist Party] who had formerly belonged to other parties have reverted again to the platforms of these parties, act upon their orders, and advance such slogans as "freedom of speech and press," "free soviets," and "full political rights and freedoms," of which all anti-Soviet parties take full advantage.

Because these dissidents had considerable experience as agitators and organizers, they were capable of sowing the seeds of dissension among both young Party members and the responsible though less sophisticated Party workers in the rural areas. For this reason the GPU considered such persons dangerous anti-Soviet elements against whom "all the methods of struggle used against other anti-Soviet parties" could be applied. Specifically, the GPU deemed it necessary to

> 1. register quickly all former members of the RCP who have spoken out at assemblies, meetings, congresses, and conferences with various kinds of agitation and are spreading false rumors, etc. . . . ;
> 2. place the most active [former Party members] immediately under secret surveillance and determine their actions and connections with other parties, etc.;
> 3. determine which of the expelled members of the RCP have not been removed from responsible posts (especially in rural and village soviets, departments of district Party organizations, factories and plants), establish how they are conducting themselves, and, in cases where they manifest any acts of an anti-Soviet character, approach the appropriate Party committee with a request for the removal of such persons.

The GPU instructed its local branches to carry out this assignment in "strict secrecy" since many former Party members had once held "responsible posts" and "at the present time have not lost their contacts."[83]

The secret police went beyond secret surveillance in its dealings with another opposition movement known as the Workers' Group. The Workers' Group, which according to the GPU numbered about two hundred in the summer of 1923, was led by Gabriel Miasnikov. Miasnikov and his small band of followers denounced the oligarchic tendencies in the Communist Party and attacked the New Economic Policy as a return to capitalism. On September 25, 1923, Dzerzhinsky informed the Central Committee of the Communist Party that the GPU had recently searched the premises of members of the Workers' Group and had found proclamations and documents calling upon the workers to launch a general strike. The Central Committee branded the Workers' Group "anti-Communist and anti-Soviet" and authorized the secret police to take action against it. Seventeen members of the Worker's Group were taken into custody; Miasnikov was arrested by Dzerzhinsky personally. The Workers' Group was the last intra-Party opposition to be smashed by the GPU while Lenin was still alive. It was also the last rank-and-file opposition to be destroyed with the blessing of all the top Soviet leaders, who soon began to fight among themselves over Lenin's mantle.[84]

In the struggle for power after Lenin's death on January 21, 1924, Dzerzhinsky invariably stood by Stalin. The chief victim of their combined animosity, Leon Trotsky, claimed in his memoirs that the Dzerzhinsky-Stalin alliance was cemented in February 1924, when, at Stalin's request, Dzerzhinsky was appointed chairman of the Supreme Economic Council of the Republic. According to Trotsky, Dzerzhinsky had long yearned to play a greater part in the construction of Russia's socialist economy and grew increasingly dissatisfied when he "realized that Lenin did not think him capable of directing economic work. It was this that threw Dzerzhinsky into Stalin's arms."[85] Dzerzhinsky's elevation to candidate membership in the Politburo of the Communist Party in June 1924 undoubtedly established an even closer tie between Stalin and the secret police chief. (Under Lenin, Dzerzhinsky's highest position in the Party had been as a member of the Central Committee.) It is unlikely, however, that Dzerzhinsky sided with Stalin only to achieve greater personal power or advancement. The two men were old friends and had worked amicably together on the front lines of the Civil War. As early as December 1917, when Dzerzhinsky was contending with the criticism of I. N.

Steinberg, the non-Bolshevik Commissar of Justice in Lenin's coalition government, Stalin seemed aware of the power inherent in the punitive arm of the proletarian dictatorship and defended the VCheka's position. Indeed, Stalin never ceased to show a substantial interest in the secret police. (It has been suggested that Stalin's liaison man at secret police headquarters was I. K. Ksenofontov [1884–1926], a member of the VCheka Collegium.)[86] Stalin's shadow presence in the Lubianka was not unwelcome to Dzerzhinsky. Not only did their views on important economic and political issues coincide, but, as Wolin and Slusser have suggested, "Dzerzhinsky, true to his conception of the relations between the secret police and the Party leadership, would have been ready in any case to work loyally with and for Stalin in his capacity as one of the top Party leaders."[87]

Years of physical and nervous strain had meanwhile begun to undermine Dzerzhinsky's fragile health, which, in any case, had never fully recovered from the privations of years spent in Tsarist prisons. In 1922 his physician had warned him that he would not last more than two or three years unless he reduced his frenetic pace. At the end of 1924, he suffered a severe attack of angina pectoris, but he rejected his doctors' advice to limit his working day to four hours. Only in the summer of 1925 was Dzerzhinsky persuaded to take a month's vacation at the southern resort town of Kislovodsk. Upon his return to Moscow, he continued to put in the same exhausting sixteen- to eighteen-hour days as before, dividing his time between his offices at the Supreme Council of the National Economy and at the Lubianka.

In July 1926, shortly after returning from a long inspection tour of metallurgical enterprises in the Don Basin, Dzerzhinsky was again stricken with chest pains. This time he did not consult his doctors at all, fearing that any treatment they might prescribe would interfere with a major speech he was preparing for delivery to a joint session of the Central Committee and the Central Control Commission of the Communist Party. The meeting, scheduled for July 20, had been convened to discipline Trotsky, Zinoviev, Kamenev, and other leading members of the United Opposition. Dzerzhinsky was to defend the economic policies of the Stalinist majority in the Politburo, and he worked late into the night on the eve of the meeting, preparing his speech.

Dzerzhinsky was in an angry mood when he rose to address the leadership of the Communist Party at noon on July 20, 1926. To the Party hierarchs who had gathered in the ornate Grand Palace of the Kremlin, he denounced the waste and bureaucracy in Soviet industry, which, he said, "simply strikes me with horror." In Dzerzhinsky's opinion, it was the incompetence and "anti-Soviet" policies of such prominent members of the opposition as Kamenev, the Commissar of Trade, and Piatakov, his own deputy at the Supreme Council of the National Economy, whom he now branded "the biggest disorganizer in industry," that were largely responsible for the poor state of the Soviet economy. The meeting was soon in an uproar as Trotsky, Kamenev, and Piatakov vainly attempted to respond to Dzerzhinsky's charges. Dzerzhinsky replied to an interjection from the floor by Trotsky by saying: "This is what I think. This is not the first day that you witness how the minority hopes to disturb the equilibrium of the majority, and I shall not pay attention to such remarks, for the more attention we pay to them, the more possibilities we give to the opposition to disorganize our businesslike work." And when Kamenev tried to defend his record by pointing out that he had only been appointed Commissar of Trade a few months earlier, Dzerzhinsky scornfully answered: "You may be commissar for forty-four years and will not be any good because you are dabbling in politics instead of doing work."

In a passage that was deleted from the press account of his speech, Dzerzhinsky accused the United Opposition of the ultimate crime—bringing about a split in the Party's ranks. He was particularly incensed about a recent secret meeting of members of the opposition held outside Moscow. Dzerzhinsky regretted that he had not known of this "lamentable and quite inadmissible action" in advance. Otherwise, he said, he would "not have hesitated to take two companies of GPU troops with machine guns and settle matters" once and for all.

Even as he spoke, Dzerzhinsky was gripped by excruciating pain. He grew pale, and his forehead was soon bathed in perspiration. But mustering his strength, he continued his impassioned speech, determined to speak his mind. In emotional words that could have been his epitaph, he said: "You know very well wherein my strength lies. I never spare myself, . . . never. And that is why all of you here love me, because you trust me. I am never insincere; if I see something is going wrong, I come down on it with all my strength."[88]

When Dzerzhinsky finally left the rostrum, it was not to summon a doctor. He returned to his seat and tried to listen to the other speakers but soon had to be helped from the hall. For the next three hours, until the stormy session ended, he remained in an anteroom, resting on a divan. Feeling somewhat better after an injection of camphor, Dzerzhinsky, accompanied by two Chekist aides, slowly made his way back to his Kremlin apartment. There, within minutes of his arrival, he collapsed. A Kremlin physician came on the run, but it was too late. The proletarian Jacobin was dead. He was not yet fifty years of age.[89]

For two days Dzerzhinsky's body lay in state in the Hall of Trade Unions. Late in the afternoon of July 22 his coffin, escorted by a battalion of OGPU troops, was borne to Red Square where Communist Party and OGPU dignitaries perorated to a large but seemingly indifferent crowd. Stalin spoke these words over the body of his fallen comrade:

> The old Leninist Guard has lost another of its finest leaders and fighters. The Party has sustained another irreparable loss.
>
> Standing now by Dzerzhinsky's bier and looking back at his whole life's path—prison, penal servitude, exile, the Extraordinary Commission for Combating Counterrevolution, the reconstruction of the ruined transport system, the building of our young socialist industry—one feels that the characteristic of this seething life was a fiery ardour.
>
> The October Revolution placed him at a difficult post—the post of leader of the Extraordinary Commission for Combating Counterrevolution. No name was more hated by the bourgeoisie than that of Dzerzhinsky, who repelled the blows of the enemies of the proletarian revolution with an iron hand. "The terror of the bourgeoisie"—that's what they called Dzerzhinsky.
>
> When the "era of peace" began, Dzerzhinsky applied his burning energy to repairing the devastated railroads, and then, as Chairman of the Supreme Council of the National Economy, he worked to build our industry. Never resting, never shunning the most difficult tasks, giving all of his powers and all of his energy to the work entrusted to him by the Party, he burned himself out for the proletariat.
>
> Farewell, hero of October! Farewell, loyal son of the Party!
> Farewell, builder of the unity and might of our Party![90]

Then, to the strains of the "Internationale," the coffin was lowered into a grave beneath the Kremlin wall just a few steps from Lenin's mausoleum.

The gap in Communist ranks left by the death of Felix Dzerzhinsky was second only to that created by the loss of Lenin. A man of exceptional energy, Dzerzhinsky devoted his life to the cause of the revolution. As one of his colleagues once said, "Dzerzhinsky did not serve the revolution, he lived for it."[91] (In a questionnaire he filled out as a delegate to the Tenth Communist Party Congress in 1921, Dzerzhinsky had described his specialty as "revolutionary—that's all.")[92] Dzerzhinsky's bequest to the Soviet state was a coercive apparatus of unprecedented scope and power dedicated to the relentless pursuit of all enemies of the dictatorship. As chairman of the VCheka/GPU/OGPU from 1917 to 1926, Dzerzhinsky provided an important element of continuity in the top leadership of the secret police. There can be no doubt that his forceful personality and outlook left a deep impact on the organization he guided through its formative years. From the moment Lenin called it into being, the Soviet secret police was intended to serve but one master, the supreme Party leadership. Echoing this cardinal Chekist principle, Dzerzhinsky is reported to have said: "As long as the Cheka is an organ of the Central Committee it is a revolutionary organ; without the Central Committee the Cheka will become an organ of counter-revoltuion."[93] Nevertheless, the relation between the Lubianka and the Kremlin that was established during Dzerzhinsky's years at the helm "carried in itself the seeds of an unparalleled strengthening and coarsening of the dictatorship."[94] For it was under Dzerzhinsky's direction that the secret police departed from the Leninist conception of it as an instrument of the whole Party leadership and was gradually transformed into a weapon of one of its warring factions. This ominous transformation, which had originated in Dzerzhinsky's efforts to preserve "the unity of the Party," culminated in the decimation of that Party and the pitiless destruction of millions of ordinary Soviet citizens.

The Sword of the Revolution

The denizens of the Lubianka were out in force on the morning of December 18, 1927. This cold wintry day marked the tenth anniversary of the founding of the secret police, and the Soviet government intended it to be a memorable occasion. After a spectacular parade of the OGPU's mounted and armored might on Red Square, a mass rally to honor the Chekists was held in the Bolshoi Theater. Among the thousands who filled the splendid hall, its stage decorated with the emblem of the secret police and a portrait of "the first Chekist," Felix Dzerzhinksy, were important Communist Party and government officials and delegations of workers from all parts of the country. The audience cheered and applauded as a succession of distinguished speakers extolled the virtues and achievements of the secret police. The Commissar of War praised the heroism of those Chekists who had fallen in battle and the sterling qualities of the many devoted men and women who were following in Dzerzhinsky's footsteps. Politburo member Nicholai Bukharin spoke on behalf of the Communist Party leadership and received "stormy applause" when he declared that the greatest accomplishment of the secret police, working hand in hand with the Party over the previous decade, was the transformation it had wrought in the attitudes and behavior of the Russian masses. The Russian man, whose mysticism and backward Slavic soul were proverbial, had been jolted out of his quiescence and was finally overcoming his clumsiness, ignorance, and sloth. The horizons of the Russian masses had been greatly enlarged and superior Bolshevik qualities instilled by the combined efforts of the Party and its faithful servant, the VCheka/GPU/OGPU.

Representatives of the Soviet proletariat then offered tokens of gratitude to their OGPU guardians. The workers of the Dynamo Factory had hammered and shaped a great sword, so unwieldy that it required several men to carry it onto the stage. A spokesman for the workers asked that it not be sheathed until "all that remains of the bourgeoisie is a memory." Until that time, the Chekists would be able to count on the continued support of the Soviet proletariat, which looked upon the OGPU as "the blood of the blood and the bone of the bone of the working class."

The audience applauded again when Dzerzhinsky's designated successor as chairman of the OGPU, Viacheslav Menzhinsky, made a brief apperance on the podium to acknowledge the approbation that had been showered upon the organization he now headed.[1] Menzhinsky was a sick man, and his remarks were of necessity short and to the point. The greatest merit of a Chekist, Menzhinsky reminded his listeners, had always been an ability to keep silent and he wished to depart from this tradition only to give an assurance to the Soviet people: "We shall fulfill the task that has been set for us here—the struggle against domestic and international counterrevolution."

For days thereafter the Soviet press paid homage to the beloved OGPU. Pictures of the usually unobstrusive secret police leaders were displayed in the pages of *Pravda* and *Izvestiia,* to which the regional press added photos of local Chekist plenipotentiaries. Whole columns were filled with messages of praise and support from Party, state, and workers' organizations from all corners of the Soviet Union. Latsis, Peters, and other illustrious figures from the secret police pantheon contributed reminiscences of the VCheka's glorious deeds during the Civil War and its aftermath. The underlying theme of the writings was the fear the secret police inspired not only among class enemies of the proletariat but also among the Soviet and Communist Party workers themselves. Latsis wrote: "If there is anything to be regretted now, it is not that we were too cruel, but that we were too lenient to our foes." Another writer added that just as the "heroic and selfless work" of the VCheka in the rear had made possible the victory of the Red Army during the Civil War, so now during the period of "peaceful construction" the OGPU was directing its blows against new foes whose "disorganizing tactics" were aimed at disrupting the construction of socialism:

> Kulaks and NEPmen, embezzlers and pillagers of public funds, spies and bandits—the punishing fist of the OGPU reaches them all and lays all by the heels. And when world imperialism, organizing new attacks against the Soviet Union, sends one terrorist band after another against our country, it meets the granite wall of the OGPU, against which all its plans and designs are smashed to bits.

It was not only internal class enemies and foreign agents who felt the punishing blows of the OGPU. In a thinly veiled reference to the Lubianka's participation in Stalin's routing of Trotsky, Zinoviev, and other members of the United Opposition, one commentator noted that the OGPU was

> one of our most vital *political* [my emphasis] organizations, and that is why it is absurd to accuse it of interfering in our intra-Party struggle. In revolution one distinguishes a friend from a foe not by documents [that is, by possession of a Party membership card], but by deeds. Those who increase the innumerable mass of anti-Soviet elements, no matter in what disguise they act, are enemies of the proletarian dictatorship, and anyone who assumes such a role must not complain if the blows of the battle hammer of this dictatorship fall on his head.[2]

Finally, for their display of exceptional energy during the most difficult of times, for their devotion to the struggle against counterrevolution, and for their untiring pursuit of the enemies of the Soviet state, thirty-five prominent OGPU officials were awarded the highest combat decoration of the Soviet Union, the Order of the Red Banner. No other gesture could better underscore the regime's continued reliance on its loyal guardian and faithful servant, the secret police.

The desperate and chaotic conditions produced by revolution and civil war had originally provided the impetus for the rapid expansion of secret police operations in Lenin's Russia. The VCheka had proved to be among the few effective instruments of control available to the beleaguered Bolsheviks, and because there was so much that required controlling, the scope of its activities had been continually enlarged. "A socialist revolution," Lenin once said, "is inconceivable without internal war which is even more devastating than external war, and . . . implies a state of extreme indefiniteness, lack of equilibrium and chaos."[3] The secret police, which grew out of the turmoil of internal war, was his chief weapon in the struggle against disintegration from within.

We have seen that the secret police was made responsible for much more than the destruction of a seemingly endless line of counterrevolutionary plots and conspiracies. The secret police functioned as the enforcement arm of the proletarian dictatorship and, at the behest of the revolution's supreme leaders, penetrated all critical areas of the country's political, economic, and social life. Heavily armed secret police detachments maintained "revolutionary order" throughout the length and breadth of the Soviet Republic. The Chekists suppressed hundreds of peasant uprisings, patrolled and sealed the borders, guarded the Soviet transport system, helped establish Soviet power in newly conquered areas, served as the regime's political watchdog and physical inquisitor in both the military and civilian officialdom, and intervened in the administration of the nation's economy. But this by no means exhausts the list of all the areas of Soviet life in which the Chekists were involved. As Latsis once remarked, Lenin developed a habit of "giving Comrade Dzerzhinsky missions which were in no way inherent in this organ." Thus the Vcheka guarded and supported "serious inventors" whose work Lenin considered it necessary to keep secret. Even the government's collection of rare musical instruments owed its existence to the VCheka, which foiled a plot to smuggle these priceless objects out of the country.[4] The Soviet leaders readily acknowledged the important contribution made by the secret police to the consolidation of Bolshevik rule. Lenin himself declared that without such an institution as the VCheka his regime could not survive.[5]

The secret police developed into a pillar of the Soviet state with Lenin's support and approval. Until illness forced him to relinquish the reins of power at the end of 1922, Lenin directed and controlled the activities of the VCheka and the GPU. It was Lenin who bestowed terroristic powers on the secret police and exhorted its cadres to suppress mercilessly all "enemies of the people." And it was Lenin who assured, through the many orders and decrees that bore his signature, that no vital aspect of Soviet life escaped the Lubianka's powerful web of scrutiny and control.[6] Although the special role played by the secret police in establishing Stalin's personal dictatorship lies outside the scope of this study, it should be noted that without the apparatus of repression created by Lenin, the General Secretary would have been deprived of a key weapon in his drive for absolute power.

Lenin's relationship with Felix Dzerzhinsky, the man he entrusted with the sword of the revolution, was for the most part a close and cordial one.[7] Lenin valued and respected Dzerzhinsky's organizational talents and revolutionary fervor. (When, in January 1920, after the defeat of Kolchak and Denikin, the Soviet government awarded the chairman of the VCheka the coveted Order of the Red Banner, it was in recognition of his "outstanding organizational ability, indefatigable energy," and for "constantly placing the interests of the working class above all other considerations and feelings.")[8] Dzerzhinsky was a frequent participant in the deliberations of the supreme policy-making bodies of the Soviet government, and Lenin often visited secret police headquarters on Bolshaia Lubianka Street. "Felix Dzerzhinsky usually met Lenin in the lobby," we are told, "and together they walked to the office of the Chairman of the VCheka. There Vladimir Ilich looked over the depositions of prisoners and material evidence and participated in the discussion of cases."[9]

Dzerzhinsky's reputation as a tough and tireless administrator who could be counted on to get the job done was well earned. During his years as a leader of the Soviet state he gladly accepted some of the most difficult and thankless tasks, and to each he brought the same self-discipline and tenacity. Even a partial listing of the many responsible posts held by Dzerzhinsky during the early Soviet period—chairman of the VCheka and the GPU, People's Commissar of Internal Affairs and Ways of Communication, chairman of the Committee on Compulsory Labor, chief of the Rear of the Southwestern Front, chairman of the Commission to Improve the Life of Children, chairman of the Commission to Fight Bribery—testifies to Lenin's confidence in the boundless energy and determination of the proletarian Jacobin.

Victory on the external and internal fronts of the Civil War did not signal the dissolution of the Soviet secret police. The GPU and the OGPU, the offspring of the VCheka, continued to serve as the watchdogs of the regime. "We are stronger than ever," wrote the Chekist Peters at the end of 1922, but, he cautioned, "we must not forget that under the conditions of the NEP our worst enemies still surround us." The vanquished bourgeoisie, Peters said, was not like a corpse that could be safely buried in the earth. Its remains were decomposing in the midst of Soviet society, and the stench posed a threat to all healthy elements. Hence it was necessary for the Chekists to remain vigilant and at their posts to guard against the revival of the old social order.[10] During the NEP years the secret police was principally occupied with the struggle against "economic counterrevolution" and foreign espionage and counterespionage, but it also uprooted the last vestiges of independent political activity inside the Soviet Union and, in the name of Party unity, stifled dissent within the ruling Communist Party itself. By the end of its first decade, the secret police had become an integral part of the Soviet system whose fear-inspiring presence was felt from the uppermost reaches of the Party hierarchy to the most distant and remote village crossroads.

Why, then, as once prophesied, was the Petrograd Cheka never converted into a kindergarten, and why does the Lubianka remain to this day the center of a pervasive apparatus of coercion and repression? The answer to these questions goes to the very heart of the Soviet political system. Lenin was no more prepared to dismantle the secret police when it had fulfilled its original mandate to defend the revolution against its internal foes than his successors have been in subsequent decades. Even in the absence of certifiable class enemies and counterrevolutionaries, a strong secret police had to be kept in readiness as a constant threat and reminder that the Soviet government, whose policies were neither determined by public wants nor legitimized by public consent, was prepared to enforce those policies at any cost. The mere existence of the secret police, with its formidable reputation for ruthlessness, served Lenin, as it has served his successors, as an indispensable tool for producing compliance. And because Soviet leaders have never been willing to make any concessions that would limit their control over society, the secret police continues to occupy a powerful and privileged position in the Soviet state.

The tenth anniversary of the creation of the secret police found the generation of Chekists trained by Dzerzhinsky at the height of their glory and prestige. During the formative years of Bolshevik rule, when violence and terror were extolled by men of theory and freely indulged in by men of action, they had imprisoned and executed thousands upon thousands to preserve the Bolshevik monopoly of power. For this they earned the sincere gratitude of the Party's leaders. Ten years later, however, many of these Chekists perished ignominiously at the hands of another and even more pitiless generation of executioners. It was the ultimate fate of Martyn Latsis, Yakov Peters, and hundreds of other veterans of the VCheka to disappear forever into the dungeons of the Lubianka during Stalin's great purge, victims of the terror machine which they had forged under the tutelage of Lenin and Dzerzhinsky.

Notes

Chapter 1. From the Butyrki to the Lubianka

1. In the words of a leading secret police official: "For the struggle against the external enemy there was established the Red Guard, which later grew into the Red Army. It was also necessary to create an organ to fight against the internal enemy, defend the rear of the Red Army, and ensure the peaceful work of establishing the Soviet form of government. Such an organ was created in the form of the All-Russian Extraordinary Commission to Fight Counterrevolution and Sabotage. Its work was subsequently enlarged to include official malfeasance, speculation, and banditry'' (Martyn Latsis, *Chrezvychainye komissii po bor'be s kontr-revoliutsiei* [Moscow, 1921], p.7).

2. Lev Kamenev, quoted in *Izvestiia,* no. 287 (Dec. 19, 1922), p. 3.

3. V. I. Lenin, *Collected Works* (Moscow, 1960–1970), V, 19.

4. *Ibid.,* IX, 56.

5. *Ibid.,* XIII, 476–78.

6. *Ibid.,* XXV, 389.

7. *Ibid.,* XXVIII, 236.

8. *Ibid.,* XXV, 413.

9. *Ibid.,* p. 410.

10. *Ibid.,* p. 414.

11. *Ibid.,* XXVIII, 465.

12. *Ibid.,* XXV, 456.

13. *Ibid.,* p. 464.

14. *Ibid.,* p. 462.

15. *Ibid.,* p. 463.

16. *Ibid.*

17. *Ibid.,* XXVI, 498.

18. Ernest V. Hollis, Jr., "Police Systems of Imperial and Soviet

Russia," (draft of a Ph.D. dissertation, Archive of Russian and East European History and Culture, Columbia University, 1957), p. 410.

19. Lenin, *Collected Works,* XXVII, 245.

20. "There can be little doubt," wrote the distinguished historian of the Russian Revolution, William Henry Chamberlin, "that if all the hatreds which the activities of the Soviet government generated in various classes of the Russian people had ever found concentrated expression at one time under a single leadership the Bolsheviki would have been swept out of existence" (Chamberlin, *The Russian Revolution* [New York, 1965], II, 454.

21. Martyn Latsis, *Dva goda bor'by na vnutrennem fronte: Populiarnyi obzor dvukhgodichnoi deiatel'nosti chrezvychainykh komissii po bor'be s kontr-revoliutsiei, spekuliatsiei i prestupleniiami po dolzhnosti* (Moscow, 1920), p. 9.

22. Martyn Latsis, "Tov. Dzerzhinskii i VChK," *Proletarskaia revoliutsiia,* IX (Sept. 1926), 81.

23. V. Mitskevich-Kapsukas, "Iz vospominanii F. E. Dzerzhinskogo," *Proletarskaia revoliutsiia,* IX (Sept. 1926), 55.

24. *Ibid.*

25. V. Speranskii, "Felix Dzerzhinskii," *Living Age,* Sept. 11, 1926, p. 574.

26. F. E. Dzerzhinskii, *Prison Diary and Letters,* trans. John Gibbons (Moscow, 1959), p. 140.

27. Mitskevich-Kapsukas, "Iz vospominanii F. E. Dzerzhinskogo," p. 58.

28. F. E. Dzerzhinskii, *Izbrannye proizvedeniia* (2d ed.; Moscow, 1967), I, 1.

29. Quoted in Sofia Dzerzhinskaia, *V gody velikikh boev* (Moscow, 1964), p. 28.

30. Quoted in Iuz. Krasnyi, "F. E. Dzerzhinskii: Materialy o zhizni i podpol'noi deiatel'nosti," *Proletarskaia revoliutsiia,* IX (Sept. 1926), 17–18.

31. Dzerzhinskii, *Prison Diary and Letters,* p. 132.

32. Quoted in Krasnyi, "F. E. Dzerzhinskii: Materialy o zhizni i podpol'noi deiatel'nosti," p. 21.

33. Central Party Archives of the Institute of Marxism-Leninism, collection 76, shelf 1, unit 762, sheet 2, quoted in A. F. Khatskevich, *Soldat velikikh boev: Zhizn' i deiatel'nost' F. E. Dzerzhinskogo* (Minsk, 1961), p. 98.

34. M. N. Gernet, *Istoriia tsarskoi tiurmy,* V (Moscow, 1963), 304.

35. Dzerzhinskii, *Prison Diary and Letters,* p. 219.

36. Quoted in Gernet, *Istoriia tsarskoi tiurmy,* p. 316.

37. Dzerzhinskii, *Prison Diary and Letters,* p. 86.

38. Konstantin Shteppa, "Feliks Dzerzhinskii: Creator of the Cheka and Founder of 'Chekism,' " in *The Soviet Secret Police,* ed. Simon Wolin and Robert M. Slusser (New York, 1957), p. 68.

39. Dzerzhinskii, *Prison Diary and Letters,* p. 20.

40. *Ibid.*, p. 134.

41. *Ibid.*, p. 21.

42. *Ibid.*, p. 136.

43. *Ibid.*, p. 21. Dzerzhinsky claimed that he was first elected to the Central Committee of the Russian Social-Democratic Workers' Party in April 1906. It was at this meeting that Dzerzhinsky met Lenin and became, in the words of one of his Soviet biographers, "not only a true disciple, but a famous associate, friend, and comrade-in-arms of Vladimir Il'ich" (Khatskevich, *Soldat velikikh boev,* p. 69).

44. Dzerzhinskii, *Prison Diary and Letters,* pp. 227–78.

45. *Ibid.*, p. 288.

46. The fall of the Russian monarchy, one of the major political turning points of the twentieth century, was not the result of planned actions by any particular organized group or party. The Revolution was, in the words of one historian, "a series of spontaneous, unrehearsed, and jumbled events which no one controlled . . . . Its essence was a lack of order" (Warren Bartlett Walsh, *Russia and the Soviet Union: A Modern History* [Ann Arbor, 1958], p. 372).

47. N. Zubov, *F. E. Dzerzhinskii: Biografiia* (2d ed.; Moscow, 1965), pp. 124–25. Only a few weeks before his sudden and dramatic return to freedom, Tsarist officials had extended Dzerzhinsky's term yet another three years, from 1919 to 1922.

48. Lenin, *Collected Works,* XXVI, 27.

49. G. N. Golikova et al., eds., *Oktiabr'skoe vooruzhennoe vosstanie v Petrograde* (Moscow, 1957), p. 228.

50. Leon Trotsky, *Lenin: Notes for a Biographer,* trans. Tamara Deutscher (New York, 1971), p. 124.

51. P. G. Sofinov, *Ocherki istorii vserossiiskoi chrezvychainoi komissii, 1917–1922 gg.* (Moscow, 1960), p. 11 (hereafter cited as *Ocherki istorii VChK*). To carry out its various assignments, the Military-Revolutionary Committee was divided into several departments and commissions: defense, liaison, supply, and propaganda. Other departments included the commandant's office, the department of provisions, the department of the press, and the investigating commission that was charged with the struggle against counterrevolution.

52. Quoted in G. A. Belov et al., eds., *Iz istorii vserossiiskoi chrezvychainoi komissi, 1917–1922 gg.: Sbornik dokumentov* (Moscow, 1958), p. 22 (hereafter cited as *Iz istorii VChK*).

53. John Reed, *Ten Days That Shook the World* (New York, 1960), pp. 75–76. See also P. D. Malkov, *Reminiscences of a Kremlin Commandant,* trans. V. Dutt (Moscow, n.d.), pp. 48–121.

54. *Izvestiia,* no. 244 (Dec. 6, 1917), quoted in D. L. Golinkov, *Krakh vrazheskogo podpol'ia: Iz istorii bor'by s kontrrevoliutsiei v sovetskoi Rossii v 1917–1924 gg.* (Moscow, 1971), p. 19. Bonch-Bruevich's Commission operated until the departure of the Soviet government to Moscow early in March 1918, when its affairs were taken over by the Commissariat of Justice and the VCheka.

55. Central State Archives of the October Revolution, collection 1236, shelf 1, file3, sheet 4, quoted in Belov et al., *Iz istorii VChK,* p. 21.

56. Central State Archives of the October Revolution, collection 1236, shelf 1, file 4, sheet 57, cited in Khatskevich, *Soldat velikikh boev,* p. 176.

57. Dzerzhinskii, *Izbrannye proizvedeniia,* I, 256.

58. Central State Archives of the October Revolution, collection 1236, shelf 2, file 14, sheets 124–27, quoted in Khatskevich, *Soldat velikikh boev,* p. 183.

59. Latsis, *Dva goda bor'by na vnutrennem fronte,* p. 11. This is how John Reed described the situation confronting the Bolsheviks during their first days in power: "Trotsky went to the Ministry of Foreign Affairs; the functionaries refused to recognize him, locked themselves in, and when the doors were forced, resigned. He demanded the keys of the archives; only when he brought workmen to force the locks were they given up. Then it was discovered that Neratov, former assistant Foreign Minister, had disappeared with the Secret Treaties. . . .

"Shliapnikov tried to take possession of the Ministry of Labor. It was bitterly cold, and there was no one to light the fires. Of all the hundreds of employees, not one would show him where the office of the Minister was. . . .

"Alexandra Kollontai, appointed the . . . . Commissar of Public Welfare—the department of charities and public institutions—was welcomed with a strike of all but forty of the functionaries in the Ministry. Immediately the poor of the great cities, the inmates of institutions, were plunged in miserable want: delegations of starving cripples, of orphans with blue, pinched faces, besieged the building. With tears streaming down her face, Kollontai arrested the strikers until they should deliver the keys of the office and the safe. . . .

"In the Ministry of Agriculture, the Ministry of Supplies, the Ministry of Finance, similar incidents occurred. And the employees, summoned to return or forfeit their positions and their pensions, either stayed away or returned to sabotage" (Reed, *Ten Days,* pp. 347–48).

60. Central Party Archives of the Institute of Marxism-Leninism, collection 19, shelf 1, sheet 4, quoted in Belov et al., *Iz istorii VChK,* p. 72.

61. Lenin, *Collected Works,* XXVI, 374–76.

62. Vladimir Bonch-Bruevich, "Kak organizovalas VChK," in *Vospominaniia o Lenine* (Moscow, 1965), p. 137.

63. Quoted in Zubov, *F. E. Dzerzhinskii,* p. 161.

64. Only two days earlier, on December 18, the Military-Revolutionary Committee had decreed its own demise in a proclamation that stated: "The Military-Revolutionary Committee, having fulfilled its fighting tasks in the days of the Petrograd revolution, and considering that its subsequent tasks must be turned over to the Department for the Struggle with Counterrevolution attached to the Central Executive Committee of the Soviet of Workers', Soldiers', and Peasants' Deputies [a reference to a commission set up earlier at Dzerzhinsky's initiative and still in opera-

tion], decrees that all departments of the Military-Revolutionary Committee be abolished and all matters turned over to the appropriate departments of the Central Executive Committee, the Council of People's Commissars, and the Petrograd or regional Soviets of Workers' and Peasants' Deputies.'' The Military-Revolutionary Committee was to be abolished within seven days (Central State Archives of the October Revolution, collection 1236, shelf 1, file 3, sheet 53, quoted in Belov et al., *Iz istorii VChK*, pp. 71–72).

65. Dzerzhinskii, *Izbrannye proizvedeniia*, I, 270.

66. Latsis, "Tov. Dzerzhinskii i VChK," p. 82.

67. Central Party Archives of the Institute of Marxism-Leninism, collection 19, shelf 1, unit 21, sheet 2, quoted in Belov et al. *Iz istorii VChK*, pp. 78–79. No formal legislation establishing the All-Russian Extraordinary Commission was ever published. Not even the contents of this so-called "founding decree" was made public in its entirety until it appeared in *Pravda* on December 18, 1927, in connection with the tenth anniversary of the Soviet secret police. As explained by the Chekist official Martyn Latsis, Protocol No. 21 creating the VCheka "was hurriedly written by V. I. Lenin himself" and was "more a rough draft than a decree on the organization of the VCheka. But in those days there was no time to polish things. It was necessary to act. The main thrust had been given; the direction more or less pointed out—let the leaders work out the matter, guided by their revolutionary consciousness of the right" ("Tov. Dzerzhinskii i VChK," p. 83).

68. A. V. Tishkov, *Pervyi chekist* (Moscow, 1968), p. 5.

69. Central Party Archives of the Institute of Marxism-Leninism, collection 19, shelf 1, unit 21, sheet 2, quoted in Belov et al., *Iz istorii VChK*, p. 79.

70. Yakov Peters, "Vospominaniia o rabote v VChK v pervyi god revoliutsii," *Proletarskaia revoliutsiia*, no. 10 (1924), p. 10.

71. Tishkov, *Pervyi chekist*, p. 6.

72. *Izvestiia*, no. 248 (Dec. 10, 1917), quoted in Belov et al., *Iz istorii VChK*, p. 84.

73. *Izvestiia*, no. 252 (Dec. 15, 1917), quoted in E. N. Gorodetskii, *Rozhdenie sovetskogo gosudarstva, 1917–1918 gg.* (Moscow, 1965), p. 292.

74. I. N. Steinberg, *In the Workshop of the Revolution* (New York, 1953), p. 64.

75. Wolin and Slusser, *The Soviet Secret Police*, p. 4.

76. *Sobranie uzakonenii i rasporiazhenii rabochego i krest'ianskogo pravitel'stva*, 1917, no. 9, article 146.

77. *Leninskii sbornik*, XXI, 111, quoted in Belov et al., *Iz istorii VChK*, p. 84.

78. *Leninskii sbornik*, XXI, 114, quoted in *ibid.*, p. 86.

79. *Ibid.*

80. Gorodetskii, *Rozhdenie sovetskogo gosudarstva, 1917–1918 gg.*, p. 297.

81. In his memoirs Steinberg told of a remarkably candid exchange

with Lenin: "We were discussing a harsh police measure with far-reaching terroristic potentialities. Lenin resented my opposition to it in the name of revolutionary justice. So I called out in exasperation, 'Then why do we bother with a Commissariat of Justice? Let's call it frankly the Commissariat for Social Extermination and be done with it!' Lenin's face suddenly brightened and he replied, 'Well put, . . . that's exactly what it should be . . . but we can't say that' " (Steinberg, *In the Workshop of the Revolution*, p. 145).

82. *Ibid.*, p. 221.

83. Central Party Archives of the Institute of Marxism-Leninism, collection 19, shelf 1, unit 42, sheets 1, 2, quoted in Belov et al., *Iz istorii VChK*, p. 89.

84. *Ibid.* The Bolshevik members, chosen from a list of twelve names submitted by Dzerzhinsky, were Dzerzhinsky, Ksenofontov, Peters, Fomin, Shchukin, and Menzhinsky. The Central Committee of the Left Socialist Revolutionaries nominated five candidates of whom four were approved by the Council of People's Commissars: Emel'ianov, Volkov, Aleksandrovich, and Sidrov (Teodor Gladkov and Mikhail Smirnov, *Menzhinskii* [Moscow, 1969], p. 187).

85. Latsis, *Dva goda bor'by na vnutrennem fronte*, p. 14.

86. Reed, *Ten Days*, p. 252.

87. D. L. Golinkov, "Pervoe delo VChK," in *Istoriia SSSR*, no. 4 (April 1965), pp. 120–23.

88. Gorodetskii, *Rozhdenie sovetskogo gosudarstva, 1917–1918 gg.*, p. 300.

89. Golinkov, *Krakh vrazheskogo podpol'ia*, pp. 69–70. Two more "bandits" were executed on February 28.

90. Latsis, "Tov. Dzerzhinskii i VChK," p. 85.

91. Latsis, *Chrezvychainye komissii*, p. 9. Among the first *political opponents* executed by the VCheka were several leaders of an anti-Bolshevik organization known as The Union for the Defense of the Motherland and Freedom. Was there any legal basis, Latsis asked rhetorically, for imposing the death penalty on political opponents? "Yes and no," was his reply. In May 1918, he said, the Council of People's Commissars had adopted a decree, never made public, "declaring parties acting against Soviet power to be enemies of the people." In general, Latsis added, Dzerzhinsky was guided in these matters by Party directives, which he "applied each time according to the demands of the moment" ("Tov. Dzerzhinskii i VChK," p. 89).

92. Latsis, "Tov. Dzerzhinskii i VChK," p. 88.

93. Trotsky, *Lenin: Notes for a Biographer*, p. 126.

94. F. Nezhdanov, "Tiur'ma vserossiiskoi chrezvychainoi komissii," in V. Chernov, ed., *Che-Ka: Materialy po deiatel'nosti chrezvychainykh komissii* (Berlin, 1922), pp. 152–54.

95. Dzerzhinskii, *Prison Diary and Letters*, pp. 290–92.

96. Public Record Office, London, Foreign Office 371/8179/2770, Secret Intelligence Service Report, Nov. 18, 1922.

97. L. L. Sabaneev, MS, ch. 31, "Dzerzhinskii," p. 3, Archive of
Russian and East European History and Culture, Columbia University.
98. Louise Bryant, *Mirrors of Moscow* (New York, 1923), pp. 45–46.
99. Dzerzhinskii, *Prison Diary and Letters,* pp. 293–94.
100. *Izvestiia,* no. 64 (April 3, 1918), p. 1.
101. Peters, "Vospominaniia o rabote v VChK," p. 8.
102. *Izvestiia,* no. 68 (April 7, 1918), p. 1.
103. *Izvestiia,* no. 70 (April 10, 1918), p. 1.

Chapter 2. The Chekas Work Better Every Day

1. Yakov Peters, "Vospominaniia o rabote v VChK v pervyi god revoliutsii," *Proletarskaia revoliutsiia,* no. 10 (1924), p. 11.
2. The Commissariat of Finance summarized the expenditures of the
VCheka during the eighteen-month period from July 1918 to December
1919 as follows:

Item	July-Dec. 1918	Jan.-June 1919	July-Dec. 1919
Maintenance of central VCheka	2,956,500	7,335,000	6,884,000
Maintenance of local Chekas	37,403,437	56,366,750	258,498,995
Rent, repair, and maintenance of premises		2,119,225	4,206,000
Maintenance of arrested persons		4,102,740	1,854,000
Troops of Internal Defense		250,000,000	1,781,989,840
Various management costs		8,334,500	10,646,000
Special expenditures for the struggle against counterrevolution and speculation	12,432,000	20,000,000	30,000,000
Special Department of the VCheka			107,100,000
Totals	52,791,937	348,258,215	2,201,178,835

According to the same source, the VCheka was originally self-support-
ing, its income derived from confiscations and fines. But an audit of the
VCheka treasury in mid-1918 disclosed evidence of serious irregularities
in bookkeeping procedures. To remedy this problem, VCheka accounting procedures were changed to conform to the general rules applicable
to other Soviet institutions and its expenditures were included in the
budget of the People's Commissariat of Internal Affairs. In 1919,
however, the VCheka regained its fiscal autonomy (*Rospis' obshche-*

gosudarstvennikh dokhodov i raskhodov Rossiiskoi Sotsialisticheskoi Federativnoi Sovetskoi Respubliki na iul'-dekabr' 1919 goda [Petrograd, 1921], p. 26; and *Rospis' obshchegosudarstvennikh dokhodov i raskhodov Rossiiskoi Sotsialisticheskoi Federativnoi Sovetskoi Respubliki na ianvar'-iun' 1919 goda: Korrekutra* [Moscow, n.d.], p. 22 and pp. 206–7).

3. *Izvestiia*, no. 54 (March 22, 1918), quoted in G. A. Belov et al., eds., *Iz istorii vserossiiskoi chrezvychainoi komissii, 1917–1922 gg.: Sbornik dokumentov* (Moscow, 1958), p. 103 (hereafter cited as *Iz istorii VChK*).

4. P. G. Sofinov, *Ocherki istorii vserossiiskoi chrezvychainoi komissii, 1917–1922 gg.* (Moscow, 1960), p. 40 (hereafter cited as *Ocherki istorii VChK*).

5. *Izvestiia*, no. 86 (April 30, 1918), p. 6.

6. *Izvestiia*, no. 108 (May 30, 1918), p. 8.

7. *Izvestiia*, no. 122 (June 16, 1918), p. 6.

8. *Izvestiia*, no. 126 (June 21, 1918), p. 4.

9. "Polozhenie o chrezvychainykh komissiakh na mestakh," June 11, 1918, Hoover Institution Archives, Boris I. Nicolaevsky Collection, box 89, folder 4.

10. A law of September 14, 1918, required provincial Chekas to add two auxiliary departments. The economic departments were charged with "the work of conducting the business affairs of the Cheka, safeguarding and distributing confiscated and requisitioned goods, registering and utilizing means of conveyance, keeping the accounts of the Commission, paying salaries, etc." The commandant's office dealt "with the registration and maintenance of prisoners, the distribution of permits for meetings, management of an information desk, etc." (*Sobranie uzakonenii RSFSR*, no. 66, article 728, quoted in Belov et al., *Iz istorii VChK*, pp. 192–95).

In December 1918, the VCheka issued another secret directive regarding the personnel allowance of provincial and district Chekas. According to this document, the full complement of a provincial Cheka, excluding its armed detachment, was ninety-seven persons; the maximum size of a district Cheka was set at twenty-four persons ("Instruktsiia chrezvychainykh komissiiam na mestakh," Dec. 1, 1918, Hoover Institution Archives, Boris I. Nicolaevsky Collection, box 89, folder 5).

A useful though highly selective account of the activities of a provincial Cheka during the Civil War based on Soviet archival sources may be found in V. P. Rachkov, *V bor'be s kontrrevoliutsiei* (Iaroslavl', 1968). This book relates some of the accomplishments of the Iaroslav Provincial Cheka, one of many local secret police organs that played an important role in the consolidation of Soviet power in the provinces. A detailed history of the secret police in the steppes of Central Asia, again reflecting the official Soviet point of view, may be found in R. Aripov and N. Mil'shtein, *Iz istorii organov gosbezopasnosti Uzbekistana: Dokumental'nye ocherki istorii, 1917–1930 gg.* (Tashkent, 1967).

11. "Rukovodstvo dlia instruktorov i agitatorov," n.d., Hoover Institution Archives, Boris I. Nicolaevsky Collection, box 89, folder 7.

12. Ukrainian State Archives of the October Revolution, collection 2, shelf 1, file 13, sheet 19, quoted in P. P. Bachinskii, P. I. Pavliuk, and B. S. Shul'zhenko, eds., *Na zashchite revoliutsii: Iz istorii vseukrainskoi chrezvychainoi komissii, 1917–1922 gg.: Sbornik dokumentov i materialov* (Kiev, 1971), p. 48.

13. Ukrainian State Archives of the October Revolution, collection 2, shelf 1, file 272, sheet 3, quoted in *ibid.*, p. 39.

14. Ukrainian State Archives of the October Revolution, collection 2, shelf 1, file 272, sheets 14–15, quoted in *ibid.*, pp. 39–40.

15. *Ezhenedel'nik chrezvychainykh komissii po bor'be s kontr-revoliutsii i spekuliatsiei*, no. 3 (Oct. 6, 1918), pp. 23–24 (hereafter cited as *Ezhenedel'nik VCheka*).

16. I. N. Steinberg, *In the Workshop of the Revolution* (New York, 1953), p. 154.

17. *Sobranie uzakonenii RSFSR*, 1919, no. 1, article 14, quoted in Belov et al., *Iz istorii VChK*, pp. 243–44.

18. F. E. Dzerzhinskii, *Izbrannye proizvedeniia*, (2d ed.; Moscow, 1967), I, 270–72.

19. *Vlast' sovetov*, 1919, no. 5, pp. 15–16.

20. In March 1919, for example, the Saratov Provincial Committee of the Bolshevik Party called for the re-establishment of district Chekas in connection with an outbreak of "kulak uprisings and the counterrevolutionary agitation of the Mensheviks and Socialist Revolutionaries" (*ibid.*).

21. *Sbornik dekretov i postanovlenii po soiuz kommun severnoi oblasti* (Petrograd, 1919), p. 127.

22. The National Archives, Washington, D.C.: Records of the Department of State Relating to Internal Affairs of Russia and the Soviet Union, 1910–1929, Record Group 59, Micorfilm Publication 316, roll 43, frames 0158–0161 (hereafter cited as RG. 59).

23. "Chekist o Ch. K.," in *Na chuzhoi storone: Istoriko-literaturnye sborniki*, IX (1925), 113–16.

24. The Moscow Cheka was made responsiblie for "all matters dealing with the struggle against counterrevolution, speculation, and malfeasance in the city of Moscow" and was given "all rights conferred upon provincial Extraordinary Commissions." Separate branch offices of the Moscow Cheka were established in various parts of the city, but they were soon abolished, supposedly in the interests of a greater centralization of control over secret police operations in the Soviet capital (*Izvestiia*, no. 1 [Jan. 1, 1919], and no. 22 [Feb. 31, 1919], quoted in Belov et al., *Iz istorii VChK*, pp. 238–40 and 247).

25. *Vlast' sovetov*, 1919, no. 10, p. 26. Lenin himself was a victim of an armed robbery just a short distance from the Kremlin. The bandits fled from the scene of their crime in the automobile that was carrying Lenin to the sanitorium where his wife was convalescing from a serious illness. The Bolshevik leader is said to have escaped with his life only because the bandits did not recognize him. The thieves were soon caught and exe-

cuted by the VCheka (P. Malkov, *Reminiscences of a Kremlin Commandant*, trans. V. Dutt [Moscow, n.d.], pp. 189–92).

26. L. Kamenev and N. Angarskii, eds., *Krasnaia Moskva, 1917–1920 gg.* (Moscow, 1920), columns 629, 633.

27. *Vlast' sovetov*, 1919, no. 10, p. 26.

28. *Ibid.*

29. Kamenev and Angarskii, *Krasnaia Moskva*, columns 630–33.

30. Marguerite E. Harrison, *Marooned in Moscow* (New York, 1921), p. 154.

31. Kamenev and Angarskii, *Krasnaia Moskva*, column 633. Arrest figures for various offenses from December 1, 1918, to November 1, 1920, were summarized as follows: for speculation, 26,692; for malfeasance (extortion, sabotage, desertion, bribery, embezzlement, etc.), 5,249; for counterrevolutionary activity, 5,140; for banditry and other crimes, 2,644.

32. Martyn Latsis, *Chrezvychainye komissii po bor'be s kontr-revoliutsiei* (Moscow, 1921), p. 27.

33. See the organizational chart accompanying U.S. Congress, Senate, Committee on the Judiciary, *Soviet Intelligence and Security Services, Vol. II—Covering 1971 and 1972: A Selected Bibliography of Soviet Publications, with Some Additional Titles from Other Sources*, 94th Cong., 1st sess., 1975.

34. Central Party Archives of the Institute of Marxism-Leninism, collection 76, shelf 1, unit 4518, quoted in Belov et al., *Iz istorii VChK*, p. 400.

35. "Polozhenie o chrezvychainykh komissiakh na mestakh," articles 3, 9–11, and 20.

36. V. I. Lenin, *Collected Works* (Moscow, 1960–70), XXX, 483.

37. Latsis, *Chrezvychainye komissii*, p. 13. Latsis admitted that some people looked upon the Chekists as upon the gendarmes of Tsarist times. His response to them was: "Yes, [we] are Okhraniks, but Okhraniks of Soviet power, and to be an Okhranik of Soviet power is an honor. Without them many of us would long since have ceased to exist" (*Izvestiia*, no. 21 [Jan. 30, 1919], pp. 1–2).

38. Central State Archives of the October Revolution, collection 1235, shelf 93, file 201, sheet 3, quoted in Belov et al., *Iz istorii VChK*, pp. 112–13.

39. Central Party Archives of the Institute of Marxism-Leninism, collection 17, shelf 2, sheets 11–12, quoted in *ibid.*, pp. 116–17.

40. Central State Archives of the October Revolution, Collection of Documents on the History of the VCheka, file 1, quoted in *ibid.*, pp. 347–49. By the beginning of 1920, according to a recent Soviet study, "the leading workers of the Chekas were all Communists," as were nearly 50 percent of the rank and file (Sofinov, *Ocherki istorii VChK*, p. 244).

41. Archives of the Communist Party of the Ukraine, collection 1, shelf 5, file 196, sheet 8, quoted in Bachinskii, Pavliuk, and Shul'zhenko, *Na zashchite revoliutsii*, p. 154.

42. Archives of the Communist Party of the Ukraine, collection 1, shelf 4, file 37, sheet 13, quoted in *ibid., p.* 66.

43. Archives of the Communist Party of the Ukraine, collection 29, shelf 1, file 11, sheet 22, quoted in *ibid.,* pp. 169–71.

44. Peters, "Vospominaniia o rabote v VChK," pp. 10–11.

45. Quoted in N. Zubov, *F. E. Dzerzhinskii: Biografiia* (2d ed.; Moscow, 1965), p. 239.

46. *Ezhenedel'nik VCheka, no.* 6 (Oct. 27, 1918), pp. 21–22.

47. Quoted in Sergey Petrovich Melgounov, *The Red Terror in Russia* (London, 1926), p. 249.

48. Herbert Dinerstein, "Some Information on the Soviet Political Police," U.S. Air Force Project Rand Research Memorandum, RM-403, June 5, 1950, p. 6. Surveying the long history of Russia's despotic regimes, Dinerstein added (pp. 4–5): "In an autocratic regime, there is always the possibility of a coup by disgruntled members of the nobility or of the upper officialdom. If the political police has been in close contact with these potentially seditious groups, and is bound to them by ties of family, familiarity, and shared experiences, they may become partners in plans to overthrow the government. There is always the danger that a praetorian guard . . . may be converted from the staff on which an arbitrary dictatorship leans to a stake which pierces its hand. Therefore, the most autocratic regimes in Russian history which have incurred the displeasure of a great number of elements in the country have made the greatest efforts to keep the political police separate from the population."

49. "Chekist o Ch. K.," p. 132.

50. Dinerstein, "Some Information on the Soviet Political Police," p. 6. For information on the role played by Latvians, another non-Russian element well represented in the secret police, see Ia. P. Krastynia, ed., *Istoriia latyshskikh strelkov, 1915–1920* (Riga, 1972), pp. 245–71.

51. Dinerstein, "Some Information on the Soviet Political Police," p. 4.

52. Zubov, *F. E. Dzerzhinskii,* p. 231.

53. Central Party Archives of the Institute of Marxism-Leninism, collection 76, shelf 1, file 1242, sheet 1, quoted in A. F. Khatskevich, *Pol'skie internatsionalisty v bor'be vlast' sovetov v Belorussii* (Minsk, 1967), p. 138.

54. F. E. Dzerzhinskii, *Prison Diary and Letters,* trans. John Gibbons (Moscow, 1959), p. 297.

55. Latsis, *Chrezvychainye komissii,* p. 11. Without such high personal qualities, Latsis said, persons working in the Extraordinary Commissions would degenerate into "weak neurasthenics and crooks."

56. Archives of the Communist Party of the Ukraine, collection 2, shelf 1, file 1, sheet 20, quoted in Bachinskii, Pavliuk, and Shul'zhenko, *Na zashchite revoliutsii,* pp. 132–33.

57. *Izvestiia ekaterinoslavskogo gubernskogo revoliutsionnogo komiteta,* no. 43 (March 6, 1920), quoted in *ibid.,* pp. 145–46.

58. *Pravda,* no. 269 (Dec. 11, 1918), p. 1.

59. See Melgounov, *The Red Terror in Russia,* pp. 245–66. Brian Chapman, in his incisive work, has suggested that a common feature of such police establishments is to lure into their ranks "the most dangerous and amoral elements of society—the brutal paranoiacs, the dimwitted sadists, the revengeful social misfits—and because characters of this type perform more efficiently, because more wholeheartedly, the most violent tasks of police work, they become the sergeants and captains of the police system" (*Police State* [New York, 1970], pp. 102–3).

60. Steinberg, *In the Workshop of the Revolution,* p. 222.

61. *Izvestiia VUTsIK,* no. 58 (June 5, 1919), quoted in Bachinskii, Pavliuk, and Shul'zhenko, *Na zashchite revoliutsii,* pp. 95–96. The official added that such types did not usually go undetected for long: "Soviet power applies to them the most severe punishment as soon as their crimes are discovered."

62. Central State Archives of the October Revolution, collection 130, shelf 3, file 170, sheet 42, quoted in Belov et al., *Iz istorii VChK,* p. 295.

63. *Ezhenedel'nik VCheka,* no. 1 (Sept. 22, 1918), p. 10. A few weeks later the *VCheka Weekly* noted that "evidence is coming in from all sides that in provincial and especially in district Extraordinary Commissions persons who are not only unworthy but even outright criminals are trying to worm their way in . . . . And naturally, the worse their morals, the worse the results of their work.

"In this connection, we want to turn the attention of the comrades to the realization that such types occupying responsible positions undermine faith in Soviet power and socialism. The people begin to look upon us as they did upon the Okhrana, as 'all-mighty,' 'all-powerful,' and so on. This view of the Socialist government is intolerable and must be fought against with all our strength." A self-purge of Cheka ranks, the statement concluded, was "the best method of fighting against such bad elements" (*Ezhenedel'nik VCheka,* no. 4 [Oct. 13, 1918], p. 6).

64. Latsis, *Chrezvychainye komissii,* p. 11.

65. *Izvestiia,* no. 185 (Aug. 28, 1918), quoted in Belov et al., *Iz istorii VChK,* pp. 174–75.

66. *Ezhenedel'nik VCheka,* no. 1 (Sept. 22, 1918), p. 9.

67. *Izvestiia,* no. 185 (Aug. 28, 1918), quoted in Belov et al., *Iz istorii VChK,* pp. 174–75.

68. The *VCheka Weekly* took note of several conferences of regional, provincial, and specialized Cheka agencies. See no. 2, (Sept. 29, 1918), p. 31; no. 3 (Oct. 6, 1918), pp. 23–24; and no. 5 (Oct. 20, 1918), pp. 1–4.

69. "Polozhenie o chrezvychainykh komissiakh na mestakh," article 32.

70. *Izvestiia,* no. 184 (Aug. 21, 1919), p. 3; and V. N. Plastinin, *Kommunist Kedrov* (Omsk, 1969), pp. 89–91.

71. Lenin, *Collected Works,* XXX, 234.

72. Quoted in Melgounov, *The Red Terror in Russia,* p. 245.

73. Quoted in S. Dzerzhinskaia, *V gody velikikh boev* (Moscow, 1964), p. 306.

74. Maxim Gorky, *Untimely Thoughts: Essays on Revolution, Culture, and the Bolsheviks, 1917–1918,* trans. Herman Ermolaev (New York, 1968), p. 211.

75. *Izvestiia,* no. 189 (Aug. 27, 1919), quoted in Belov et al., *Iz istorii VChK,* pp. 314–17.

76. *Pravda,* no. 281 (Dec. 25, 1918), p. 4; and no. 282 (Dec. 26, 1918), p. 4.

77. *Pravda,* no. 34 (Feb. 14, 1919), p. 4; no. 35 (Feb. 15, 1919), p. 4; no. 37 (Feb. 18, 1919), p. 4; and N. V. Krylenko, *Za piat' let: 1918–1922 gg.* (Moscow, 1923), pp. 511–25.

78. *Izvestiia,* no. 26 (Feb. 6, 1920), pp. 1–2.

79. "Chekist o Ch. K.," pp. 122–41. The minutes of a meeting of the collegium of the All-Ukrainiam Cheka, one of many such documents that fell into the hands of anti-Bolshevik forces, reveals the ease and simplicity with which life-and-death decisions were made by leading Cheka commissars:

Protocol No. 12

Meeting of the Commission of May 19, 1919

Present: Chairman — Degtiarenko
          Secretary — Shub
          Members — Latsis, Iakovlev, Shvartsman,
                    Savchuk, Ugarov, Grinshtein.

Order of the day—Reports of cases:

Heard	Resolved
1. Request of Comrade Popov-Naide for an allowance.	1. To pay expenses for medical treatment
2. Concerning Tsezarsky and Salonino.	2. The earlier decision of the Commission is affirmed
3. Request of Comrade Grinshtein for an allowance for his dead brother.	3. Approved in the amount of 2½ thousand
4. Request of the cellist Sukholinsky for pay for two nights.	4. Approved in the amount of 400 roubles
5. a. Case of Vishnevsky, N. I.	5. To be released and the case closed
b. Pisarev (Special Commission)	″
c. De-Bank, Konstantin	″
d. Burdynsky, M. I.	″
e. Bontsionovsky	″
f. Kolber	″
g. Amgivan	″
h. Bondarsky	″
i. Andre	″

Heard   Resolved

6. Cases of the Special Commission:

	Heard	Resolved
1.	Kozakov, Afanas Semenovich	1. To be shot
2.	Danilov, Kozma Grigorevich	2. "
3.	Tobolin, Aleksandr Aleksandrovich	3. "
4.	Golovushkin, Dmitry Ivanovich	4. To be released
5.	Dembitsky, Iosif Mikhailovich	5. To be shot
6.	Shchegolev, Sergei	6. To be shot and cash confiscated
7.	Sergeev, Nikolai Semenovich	7. To be released
8.	.. . . , Nikolai Stepanovich	8. To be shot and cash confiscated
9.	Buravkin, Aleksei Iakovlevich	9. "
10.	Pavlovich, Iosif Iakovlevich	10. "
11.	Poto, Aleksandr Lvovich	11. To be released
12.	Simiko, Andre Petrovich	12. To be shot and cash confiscated
13.	Bobyr, Aleksandr Pavlovich	13. "
14.	Shipner, Dmitry Alekseevich	14. To be released
15.	Mossakovsky, Ivan Fedorovich	15. To be shot and cash confiscated
16.	Raich, Nikolai Nikolaevich	16. "
17.	Pristuma, Georgy Ignatevich	17. "
18.	Arkashevsky, Petr Iakovlevich	18. "
19.	Vaninkov, Nikolai Petrovich	19. "
20.	Rudakov, Petr Georgievich	20. "
21.	Bashin, Ivan Alekseevich	21. "
22.	Ryzhkovsky, Vikenty Romanovich	22. "
23.	Bekh, Nikolai Stepanovich	23. "
24.	Bubnov, Georgii . . .	24. "
25.	Ivanov, Vladimir Fedorovich	25. "
26.	Malshin, Nikolai Vasilevich	26. "
27.	Molagovsky, Petr Mikhailovich	27. "
28.	Molodovsky, Grigory Georgievich	28. "
29.	Bocharov, Evgeny Afanasevich	29. "

Heard	Resolved
30.Pakhalovich, Feofan Klimo-vich	30.To be released
31.Dumitrishko, Sofia Mikhai-lovna	31.To be shot and cash confis-cated
7. Concerning the Special Com-mission	7. Form the Commission from members of the Secret and Jurid-ical Departments.
8. Request of Comrade Lashkevich	8. To be complied with.
	Signed: Chairman Degtiarenko
	Secretary Shub

This characteristically brief session of the All-Ukrainian Cheka thus judged forty people and sentenced twenty-six of them to death (for what crimes shall never be known) while still finding time to hear appeals for special favors from fellow Chekists. All over Soviet territory, the Chekists regularly passed sentence in the absence of the accused, often not even bothering to record the alleged offense for which the accused suffered "the supreme penalty." (This document is reproduced in *Na chuzhoi storone: Istoriko-literaturnye sborniki,* IV [1924], 205–207.)

80. Quoted in *ibid.,* V (1924), 172–75.

81. *Izvestiia,* no. 275 (Dec. 7, 1919), p. 1.

82. Latsis, *Chrezvychainye komissii,* pp. 10, 12.

Chapter 3. In Defense of the Revolution

1. G. Moroz, "V.Ch.K. i oktiabr'skaia revoliutsiia," in *Vlast' sovetov,* no. 11 (1919), p. 6.

2. Martyn Latsis, *Dva goda bor'by na vnutrennem fronte: Populiarnyi obzor dvukhgodichnoi deiatel'nosti chrezvychainykh komissii po bor'be s kontr-revoliutsiei, spekuliatsiei i prestupleniiami po dolzhnosti* (Moscow, 1920), p. 10.

3. Quoted in N. Zubov, *F. E. Dzerzhinksii: Biografiia* (2d ed.; Moscow, 1965), pp. 163–64.

4. A. V. Tishkov, *Pervyi chekist* (Moscow, 1968), p. 26.

5. P. G. Sofinov, *Ocherki istorii vserossiiskoi chrezvychainoi komissii, 1917–1922 gg.* (Moscow, 1960), p. 39 (hereafter cited as *Ocherki istorii VChK*).

6. Central State Archives of the Soviet Army, collection 38650, shelf 524, file 4, sheets 28–30, quoted in Tishkov, *Pervyi chekist,* p. 27. Konstantin Maksimovich Valobuev (1879–1942), a former Tsarist colonel, was appointed Chief of Staff of the Special Corps of VCheka Troops in October 1918. Although a member of the Bolshevik Party for less than a year at the time of his appointment, Valobuev was entrusted

with broad powers in the general training and supervision of the VCheka's armed forces.

7. *Ezhenedel'nik chrezvychainykh komissii po bor'be s kontr-revoliutsii i spekuliatsiei*, no. 2 (Sept. 29, 1918), pp. 13–15 (hereafter cited as *Ezhenedel'nik VCheka*).

8. VCheka Order No. 72, in *Ezhenedel'nik VCheka*, no. 3 (Oct. 6, 1918), pp. 10–12.

9. V. I. Lenin, *Collected Works* (Moscow, 1960–70), XXXII, 342–43.

10. Latsis, *Dva goda bor' by na vnutrennem fronte*, p. 75. Latsis added that 1,150 "Soviet workers" were killed in the line of duty on the internal front during the same period. But the peasant insurgents suffered even more, which is what one would expect considering that the well-armed Chekists fought poorly organized and ill-equipped peasants usually armed only with pitchforks, clubs, axes, and an occasional rifle or pistol. A total of 3,057 insurgents was killed in battle with the Chekists, and another 3,082 were later shot for their participation in these anti-Soviet uprisings. An additional 455 persons were also executed by the local Chekas for their role in inciting the revolts.

11. *Ibid.*, p. 70. Latsis conceded that "at the first rebuff the kulaks and the leaders scatter and the blows fall upon the poor peasants." For this reason the Chekas usually released "the majority of insurgents" while continuing to ferret out the ringleaders, who were severely punished whenever caught.

12. Quoted in Tishkov, *Pervyi chekist*, p. 30.

13. VCheka Order No. 94, Dec. 4, 1918, Central State Archives of the October Revolution, Collection of Documents on the History of the VCheka, file 1, quoted in G. A. Belov et al., eds., *Iz istorii vserossiiskoi chrezvychainoi komissii 1917–1922 gg.: Sbornik dokumentov* (Moscow, 1958), pp. 233–34 (hereafter cited as *Iz istorii VChK*).

14. *Ezhenedel'nik VCheka*, no. 2 (Sept. 29, 1918), p. 10.

15. "Postanovlenie soveta oboronyi o voiskakh vspomogatel'nogo naznacheniia," in *Dekrety sovetskoi vlasti* (Moscow, 1957–75), V, 508–10.

16. "Polozhenie o voiskakh VOKhR," Central State Archives of the Soviet Army, collection 42, shelf 1, unit 6, sheets 14–16, cited in K. I. Pozniakov, *Krasnyi tyl—frontu* (Kharkov, 1968), p. 32.

17. Tishkov, *Pervyi chekist*, p. 36.

18. *Ibid.*, pp. 34–35.

19. Quoted in Sofinov, *Ocherki istorii VChK*, p. 155.

20. Tishkov, *Pervyi chekist*, pp. 32–33.

21. Quoted in Sofinov, *Ocherki istorii VChK*, pp. 204–5.

22. Quoted in Tishkov, *Pervyi chekist*, p. 82.

23. *Izvestiia VUTsIK*, no. 129 (May 26, 1920), quoted in P. P. Bachinskii, P. I. Pavliuk, and B. S. Shul'zhenko, eds., *Na zashchite revoliutsii: Iz istorii vseukrainskoi chrezvychainoi komissii, 1917–1922 gg.: Sbornik dokumentov i materialov* (Kiev, 1971), pp. 164–66.

24. Tishkov, *Pervyi chekist*, pp. 83–84.

25. Central State Archives of the October Revolution, collection 642,

shelf 1, file 32, sheet 171, quoted in Bachinskii, Pavliuk, and Shul'zhenko, *Na zashchite revoliutsii,* p. 172.

26. Central State Archives of the October Revolution, collection 2, shelf 1, unit 578, sheet 1, cited in Pozniakov, *Krasnyi tyl—frontu,* p. 38.

27. Central State Archives of the October Revolution, collection 2, shelf 1, unit 471, sheet 1, cited in *ibid.,* p. 165; *Izvestiia,* no. 290 (Dec. 18, 1927), p. 3.

28. Central State Archives of the Soviet Army, collection 42, shelf 1, file 1902, sheets 1, 4, and 5, quoted in Tishkov, *Pervyi chekist,* p. 85.

29. A. F. Khatskevich, *Soldat velikikh boev: Zhizn' i deiatel'nost' F. E. Dzerzhinskogo* (Minsk, 1961), pp. 270–71.

30. "Postanovlenie soveta truda i oborony o vnutrennei okhrane respubliki," in *Vlast' sovetov,* no. 8 (1920), pp. 21–22.

31. The National Archives, Washington, D.C.: Record Group 165, Records of the War Department General Staff, Military Intelligence Division, M.I.D. Report from Riga, Latvia, no. 01821, Aug. 5, 1921 (2037-1088/4) (hereafter cited as RG. 165).

32. "Postanovlenie soveta truda i oborony o reorganizatsii voisk vnutrennei sluzhby respubliki," Jan. 19, 1921, quoted in S. K. Tsvigun et al., eds., *V. I. Lenin i VChK: Sbornik dokumentov, 1917–1922 gg.* (Moscow, 1975), pp. 426–28. The 137,106 Troops of the VCheka were reported to be deployed on the following basis:

Troops of the VCheka	*Men*	*Horses*
Moscow	25,057	5,205
Ukraine:		
Kharkov Military District	17,115	3,348
Kiev Military District	9,003	1,528
Donets Coal Mine Region	12,638	2,910
Ural Military District	11,044	2,510
Turkestan	8,816	1,924
Siberia	8,225	1,202
Orel Military District	7,099	1,440
Trans-Volga Military District	6,923	1,498
Northwest Frontier Military District	6,695	1,940
Kirghis Republic	5,981	2,052
North Caucasus	5,934	1,284
Volga Military District	4,945	1,070
Western Frontier Military District	4,695	918
Transcaucasus Military District	3,256	856

The figures are from the National Archives, RG 165, M.I.D. Report from Riga, Latvia, no. 02021, Sept. 23, 1921 (20037-1088/5).

33. Martyn Latsis, *Chrezvychainye komissii po bor'be s kontr-revoliutsii* (Moscow, 1921), p. 26.

34. *Leninskii sbornik,* XXXIV, 33, quoted in Belov et al., *Iz istorii VChK,* p. 158.

35. Latsis, *Chrezvychainye komissii,* p. 30.

36. M. I. Sboichakov, S. I. Tsybov, and M. F. Chistiakov, *Mikhail Sergeevich Kedrov* (Moscow, 1969), p. 94.

37. *Ezhenedel'nik VCheka*, no. 4 (Oct. 13, 1918), pp. 28–30.

38. Central State Archives of the October Revolution, collection 1235, shelf 94, file 176, sheets 283–89, quoted in Belov et al., *Iz istorii VChK*, p. 229.

39. Sofinov, *Ocherki istorii VChK*, p. 126.

40. *Ibid.*, pp. 127–29.

41. Central Party Archives of the Institute of Marxism-Leninism, collection 17, shelf 2, unit 7, sheet 1, quoted in Belov et al., *Iz istorii VChK*, p. 236. The first chief of the Special Department of the VCheka was the same M. S. Kedrov who earlier headed the Military Department of the VCheka. On August 19, 1919, Dzerzhinsky himself took direct command of the Special Department, a reflection of its considerable importance in the secret police system.

42. *Sobranie uzakonenii RSFSR*, 1919, no. 6, article 58, quoted in *ibid.*, pp. 259–61.

43. *Sobranie uzakonenii RSFSR*, 1919, no. 20, article 247, quoted in *ibid.*, p. 259.

44. Latsis, *Chrezvychainye komissii*, p. 30.

45. *Vlast' sovetov*, no. 11 (1919), p. 6.

46. I. Ustikov and K. Kapitonov, "Polevka na boevom postu (Iz istorii organov voennoi kontrrazvedki)," in *Voenno-Istoricheskii Zhurnal*, no. 1 (1969), p. 100.

47. Latsis, *Dva goda bor'by na vnutrennem fronte*, pp. 45–46.

48. *Izvestiia*, no. 39 (Feb. 21, 1920), quoted in Belov et al., *Iz istorii VChK*, p. 373.

49. *Sobranie uzakonenii RSFSR*, 1919, no. 38, article 375, quoted in *Dekrety sovetskoi vlasti*, V, 416–18.

50. *Izvestiia*, no. 252 (Nov. 11, 1919), p. 1.

51. *Izvestiia*, no. 290 (Dec. 18, 1927), p. 3.

52. E. V. Dumbadze, *Na sluzhbe Cheka i Kominterna* (Paris, 1930), p. 28.

53. Ustikov and Kapitonov, "Polevka na boevom postu," p. 100.

54. "Postanovlenie soveta oborony o primenenii repressii k litsam, sabotiruiushchim raschistku zheleznodorozhnykh putei ot snega," Feb. 15, 1919, quoted in *Dekrety sovetskoi vlasti*, IV, 626–27. A month later the Council of Workers' and Peasants' Defense noted that many district and provincial soviet executive committees were still not displaying sufficient engery in the clearing of snowdrifts from the railroad tracks and that the Chekas, "notwithstanding this criminal lack of administrative ability," were not arrresting any of these officials. "Henceforth," the Council decreed, "the chairmen of the Extraordinary Commissions will themselves be subject to immediate arrest if in the future they fail to arrest persons responsible for [not] fulfilling the decrees of the Council of Workers' and Peasants' Defense for the struggle against snowdrifts" ("Postanovlenie soveta oborony," March 17, 1919, quoted in *ibid.*, pp. 510–11).

55. VCheka Order No. 4, June 25, 1919, quoted in Latsis, *Chrezvychainye komissii,* p. 58.

56. "Postanovlenie soveta oborony ob iz'iatii shinelei u naseleniia," Sept. 24, 1919, quoted in *Dekrety sovetskoi vlasti,* VI, 136–39; "Instruktsiia sovet oborony po iz'iatiiu shinelei u grazhdanskogo naseleniia," Oct. 1, 1919, quoted in Tsvigun et al., *V. I. Lenin i VChK,* pp. 269–70.

57. *Izvestiia,* no. 127 (June 13, 1920), quoted in Belov et al., *Iz istorii VChK,* p. 397.

58. "Postanovlenie soveta truda i oborony ob obrazovanii vremennoi komissii pri STO po bor'be s toplivnym krizisom," Feb. 11, 1921, quoted in Tsvigun et al., *V. I. Lenin i VChK,* pp. 435–36.

59. Latsis, *Dva goda bor'by na vnutrennem fronte,* pp. 72–75.

60. *Ezhenedel'nik VCheka,* no. 1 (Sept. 22, 1918), p. 27.

61. "Dekret SNK RSFSR ob uchrezhdenii pogranichnoi okhrany," May 28, 1918, quoted in P. I. Zyrianov et al., eds., *Pogranichnye voiska SSSR, 1918–1928: Sbornik dokumentov i materialov* (Moscow, 1973), pp. 75–76.

62. *Ezhenedel'nik VCheka,* no. 1 (Sept. 22, 1918), p. 26; no. 4 (Oct. 13, 1918), p. 14.

63. *Izvestiia,* no. 126 (June 21, 1918), quoted in Belov et al., *Iz istorii VChK,* p. 135.

64. Sofinov, *Ocherki istorii VChK,* pp. 114–15.

65. *Ezhenedel'nik VCheka,* no. 5 (Oct. 20, 1918), p. 26.

66. *Ezhenedel'nik VCheka,* no. 2 (Sept. 29, 1918), pp. 10–11.

67. "Instruktsiia chrezvychainym komissiiam na mestakh," Hoover Institution Archives, Boris I. Nicolaevsky Collection, box 89, folder 4.

68. A series of decrees issued between June 1918 and July 1919 gave the military authorities complete control over all border-guard operations for the duration of the Civil War. See the relevant documents in Zyrianov et al, *Pogranichnye voiska SSSR,* pp. 86–87, 100–101, 144–45, and 152–53.

69. "Instruktsii ob okhrane gosudarstvennoi granitsy," July 17, 1920, quoted in *ibid.,* p. 163.

70. "Postanovleniia soveta truda i oborony o reorganizatsii okhrany granits RSFSR," Nov. 24, 1920, quoted in *ibid.,* pp. 164–66.

71. The National Archives, RG 165, M.I.D. Report from Riga, Latvia, no. 02021, Sept. 23, 1921 (20037-10084/5). These 94,288 troops were reported to be deployed as follows:

Troops	Men	Horses
Northwest frontier	21,454	6,535
Western frontier	14,787	4,737
Ukrainian frontier	23,599	7,819
Turkestan frontier	14,142	6,711
Siberian frontier	15,472	5,142
Caucasus frontier	3,994	1,509
Northern border	840	220

72. Quoted in Zyrianov et al., *Pogranichnye voiska SSSR,* p. 174.

73. T. K. Gladkov and M. A. Smirnov, *Menzhinskii* (Moscow, 1969), p. 260.

74. From just one stretch of the western frontier infested with well-armed and organized bands, the border region of the Ukrainian province of Podolsk, came this summary report covering the period between August 15 and December 31, 1921: twenty-one bands numbering about 1,600 men were said to be operating in the border zone. The bands had carried out 107 raids, most of them on villages and Soviet enterprises and institutions, in the course of which 220 civilians and Red Army men had been killed. Cheka operations against the bands had meanwhile produced these results: 12 bands destroyed, 257 bandits killed, and 214 captured together with 83 horses, 60 rifles, and 8 machine guns (Zyrianov et al., *Pogranichnye voiska SSSR*, p. 496).

75. Lenin, *Collected Works*, XXVII, 267.

76. *Ezhenedel'nik VCheka*, no. 1 (Sept. 22, 1918), p. 26.

77. "Polozhenie o chrezvychainykh komissiiakh na mestakh," June 11, 1918, Hoover Institution Archives, Boris I. Nicolaevsky Collection, box 89, folder 4.

78. *Izvestiia*, no. 110 (June 1, 1918), p. 5.

79. *Izvestiia*, no. 124 (June 19, 1918), p. 5.

80. *Ezhenedel'nik VCheka*, no. 6 (Oct. 27, 1918), p. 8.

81. *Izvestiia*, no. 169 (Aug. 9, 1918), p. 4.

82. *Ezhenedel'nik VCheka*, no. 6 (Oct. 27, 1918), p. 8.

83. "Postanovlenie soveta raboche-krest'ianskoi oborony," Nov. 12, 1919, quoted in *Dekrety sovetskoi vlasti*, VI, 268–70.

84. VCheka Order No. 203, Nov. 21, 1919, quoted in Latsis, *Chrezvychainye komissii*, pp. 59–60.

85. "Postanovlenie soveta raboche-krest'ianskoi oborony," Feb. 20, 1920, quoted in *Dekrety sovetskoi vlasti*, VII, 260–61, 522–23.

86. *Sobranie uzakonenii RSFSR*, 1921, no. 49, article 258, quoted in Tsvigun et al., *V. I. Lenin i VChK*, pp. 462–63.

87. *Izvestiia*, no. 169 (Aug. 9, 1918), p. 4.

88. Central State Archives of the October Revolution, collection 1235, shelf 94, file 176, sheets 283–89, quoted in Belov et al., *Iz istorii VChK*, pp. 226–27.

89. *Izvestiia*, no. 48 (March 2, 1919), quoted in *Dekrety sovetskoi vlasti*, IV, 454–55.

90. "Postanovlenie soveta raboche-krest'ianskoi oborony," Jan. 16, 1920, quoted in *ibid.*, VII, 102–4.

91. Latsis, *Chrezvychainye komissii*, p. 27. According to U.S. intelligence estimates, nearly 17,000 Chekists were on duty guarding the Soviet transportation network in the summer of 1921 (The National Archives, RG 165, M.I.D. Report from Riga, Latvia, no. 02021, Sept. 23, 1921).

92. *Gudok*, no. 471 (Dec. 6, 1921), quoted in F. E. Dzerzhinksii, *Izbrannye proizvedeniia*, I (2d ed.; Moscow, 1967), 308–9.

93. Khatskevich, *Soldat velikikh boev*, pp. 292–93.

94. Latsis, *Dva goda bor'by na vnutrennem fronte,* pp. 66–68.

95. Sofinov, *Ocherki istorii VChK,* p. 20.

96. *Ezhenedel'nik VCheka,* no. 2 (Sept. 29, 1918), p. 26.

97. *Ibid.* Latsis summarized the VCheka's accomplishments in the struggle against speculation during 1918 and the first seven months of 1919 as follows: number of fines, 4,705 in 1918, 1,174 in 1919, for a total of 5,882 [*sic*]; fines (in roubles), 28,757,772 in 1918, 46,135,019 in 1919, totaling 74,892,791; number of confiscations, 1,003 in 1918, 1,054 in 1919, totaling 2,057; sum of confiscated money (in roubles), 33,910,040 in 1918, 8,483,190 in 1919, totaling 42,313,230 [*sic*]. Not only was Latsis's arithmetic incorrect, but he also offered conflicting figures on the number of persons shot for speculation in the period under review. At one point he noted that about one hundred people were shot (plus another 819 "for embezzlement connected with speculation") while a few pages later he put the figure of executions for speculation at 71 (Latsis, *Dva goda bor'by na vnutrennem fronte,* pp. 68, 75, 76).

98. L. Kamenev and N. Angarskii, eds., *Krasnaia Moskva, 1917–1920 gg.* (Moscow, Dec. 1920), column 326.

99. *Ezhenedel'nik VCheka,* no. 5 (Oct. 20, 1918), p. 27.

100. *Ezhenedel'nik VCheka,* no. 1 (Sept. 22, 1918), p. 20.

101. "Otchet tsentral'nogo upravleniia chrezvychainykh komissii pri sovnarkome Ukrainy za 1920 god," quoted in Bachinskii, Pavliuk, and Shul'zhenko, *Na zashchite revoliutsii,* pp. 254–56.

102. *Izvestiia,* no. 213 (Oct. 1, 1919), p. 1.

103. "Dekret SNK," Oct. 21, 1919, quoted in *Dekrety sovetskoi vlasti,* VI, 217–18.

104. Quoted in Sofinov, *Ocherki istorii VChK,* p. 191.

105. "Dekret SNK," Oct. 21, 1919, quoted in *Dekrety sovetskoi vlasti,* VI, 217–18.

106. *Izvestiia,* no. 280 (Dec. 12, 1920), p. 2.

107. Lenin, *Collected Works,* XLII, 166–74.

108. *Istoricheskii arkhiv,* no. 5 (1957), pp. 182—83, quoted in Belov et al., *Iz istorii VChK,* pp. 360–65.

109. Simon Liberman, *Building Lenin's Russia* (Chicago, 1945), pp. 36–42.

110. James Bunyan, ed., *The Origin of Forced Labor in the Soviet State, 1917–1921: Documents and Materials* (Baltimore, 1967), p. 114.

111. "Postanovlenie SNK," Feb. 3, 1919, quoted in *Dekrety sovetskoi vlasti,* VII, 173–75.

112. Bunyan, *The Origin of Forced Labor in the Soviet State,* p. 114.

113. *Izvestiia,* no. 76 (April 7, 1920), p. 2.

114. *Izvestiia glavnogo komiteta po vseobshchei trudovoi povinnosti,* no. 3, p. 61, cited in Bunyan, *The Origin of Forced Labor in the Soviet State,* p. 157.

115. One of the most serious problems facing the Soviets on the internal front during the early part of 1921 was a critical shortage of fuel for the railroads, as a result of which the cities were receiving inadequate

supplies and the factories were chronically short of raw materials. "Resolving the fuel problem," writes a Soviet author, "meant to breathe new life into rail and water transport, set industry on its feet, and provide the proletarian centers with bread." Dzerzhinsky traveled to the Don Coal Basin region in January 1921 to take personal charge of operations designed to increase coal output. The source of the fuel crisis, he wrote, was "economic dislocation (poverty) and a lack of inflexible will power among the workers and Party to overcome it." The task of the Chekists, "people of action and indefatigable will," was "to exert all. . . strength in the struggle with this devastation." With Dzerzhinsky and his men applying the whip to fortify labor discipline and increase productivity, "the output of coal in the Don Basin began to gradually rise, and the fuel crisis was slowly but surely overcome" (Sofinov, *Ocherki istorii VChK,* p. 213; Belov et al., *Iz istorii VChK,* pp. 426–28; and Khatskevich, *Soldat velikikh boev,* p. 324).

116. F. E. Dzerzhinskii, *Prison Diary and Letters,* trans. John Gibbons (Moscow, 1959), p. 144.

117. *Ibid.,* p. 177.

118. For a full picture of the *bezprizornye* and the ghastly conditions under which they were forced to live, based primarily on official Soviet sources, see Vladimir Zenzinov, *Bezprizornye* (Paris, 1929).

119. Quoted in A. Lunacharskii, "Dzerzhinskii v Narkomprose," in *Felix Dzerzhinskii, 1926–1931: Sbornik statei,* ed. R. Abikh (Moscow, 1931), pp. 182–83.

120. Sofinov, *Ocherki istorii VChK,* p. 217; A. D. Kalinina, *Desiat' let raboty po bor'be s detskoi bezprizornost'iu* (Moscow, 1928), p. 58.

121. Central State Archives of the October Revolution, Collection of Documents on the History of VCheka, file 1, quoted in Belov et al., *Iz istorii VChK,* pp. 423–25.

122. S. Dzerzhinskaia, *V gody velikikh boev* (Moscow, 1964), p. 351.

123. Quoted in *ibid.,* pp. 346–47.

124. *Izvestiia,* no. 71 (March 31, 1923), quoted in Dzerzhinskii, *Izbrannye proizvedeniia,* I, 394–96.

125. Zenzinov, *Bezprizornye,* pp. 181–189.

126. Quoted in Tishkov, *Pervyi chekist,* p. 107.

127. William Reswick, *I Dreamt Revolution* (Chicago, 1952), p. 107. See also an article by the same author, "An Experiment in Freedom," in *The Nation,* CXXI (Nov. 11, 1925), 535.

128. Quoted in Dzerzhinskaia, *V gody velikikh boev,* p. 349.

129. Herbert Dinerstein, "Some Information on the Soviet Political Police," U.S. Air Force Project Rand Research Memorandum, RM-403, June 5, 1950, pp. 37–39.

130. Latsis, *Chrezvychainye komissii,* p. 25.

131. Ernest V. Hollis, Jr., "Police Systems of Imperial and Soviet Russia," (draft of a Ph.D. dissertation, Archive of Russian and East European History and Culture, Columbia University, 1957), p. 422.

132. Latsis, *Chrezvychainye komissii,* p. 26.

Chapter 4. Enemies of the People

1. F. E. Dzerzhinskii, *Izbrannye proizvedeniia* (2d ed.; Moscow, 1967), I, 274.
2. P. D. Malkov, *Reminiscences of a Kremlin Commandant,* trans. V. Dutt (Moscow, n.d.), p. 177; Louis Fischer, *The Life of Lenin* (New York, 1964), p. 282.
3. Fanny Kaplan was immediately arrested and taken to the Lubianka. On September 3, 1918, she was executed on orders of the VCheka (see Malkov, *Reminiscences of a Kremlin Commandant,* pp. 180–81).
4. *Izvestiia,* no. 189 (Sept. 3, 1918), p. 1.
5. *Ezhenedel'nik chrezvychainykh komissii po bor'be s kontr-revoliutsiei i spekuliatsiei,* no. 1 (Sept. 22, 1918), p. 11 (hereafter cited as *Ezhenedel'nik VCheka*).
6. *Sobranie uzakonenii RSFSR,* 1918, no. 65, article 710, quoted in G. A. Belov et al., eds., *Iz istorii vserossiiskoi chrezvychainoi komissii, 1917–1922 gg.: Sbornik dokumentov* (Moscow, 1958), pp. 182–83 (hereafer cited as *Iz istorii VChK*).
7. Leon Trotsky, *Terrorism and Communism* (Ann Arbor, 1961), p. 58.
8. Quoted in Leon Trotsky, *Lenin: Notes for a Biographer,* trans. Tamara Deutscher (New York, 1971), p. 120.
9. *Ibid.,* p. 123.
10. *Ibid.,* p. 124.
11. V. I. Lenin, *Collected Works* (Moscow, 1960–70), XXVI, 404–15.
12. *Ibid.,* p. 459.
13. *Ibid.,* XXXV, 336. About one month later the All-Russian Central Executive Committee adopted a resoluton stating that "Soviet power must secure its rear by putting the bourgeoisie under surveillance and putting into practice mass terror against it" (*Izvestiia,* no. 160 [July 30, 1918], quoted in *Dekrety sovetskoi vlasti* [Moscow, 1957–75], III, 107).
14. *Izvestiia,* no. 32 (Feb. 23, 1918), quoted in Belov et al., *Iz istorii VChK,* pp. 95–96.
15. *Novaia zhizn',* June 8, 1918.
16. *Izvestiia,* no. 181 (Aug. 23, 1918), pp. 1–2.
17. Martyn Latsis, *Chrezvychainye komissii po bor'be s kontr-revoliutsiei* (Moscow, 1921), p. 10.
18. *Izvestiia,* no. 189 (Sept. 3, 1918), p. 4.
19. *Ezhenedel'nik VCheka,* no. 1 (Sept. 22, 1918), p. 6. Echoes of Cheka violence appeared, page after page, in each of the six extant issues of the *VCheka Weekly* as well as in the daily Soviet press. Announcements of executions helped create a pervasive atmosphere of fear and intimidation and served as a warning to all citizens that "the hand that did not tremble" was making good its threat to destory all enemies of the revolution. See *Ezhenedel'nik VCheka,* nos. 1–6 (Sept. 22–Oct. 27, 1918), and almost any issue of *Pravda* and *Izvestiia* during the same period.

20. Victor Serge, *Year One of the Russian Revolution,* trans. Peter Sedgwick (New York, 1972), p. 310.

21. *Krasnyi Terror,* no. 1 (Nov. 1, 1918), quoted in Sergey Petrovich Melgounov, *The Red Terror in Russia* (London, 1926), pp. 39–40. Lenin later rebuked Latsis for the "absurd lengths" to which he had gone in this statement, but nevertheless characterized him as "one of our finest, tried and tested Communists" (Lenin, *Collected Works,* XXVIII, 389).

22. *Novaia Zhizn',* June 8, 1918.

23. "Konstruktsiia otdelov chrezvychainykh komissii," Hoover Institution Archives, Boris I. Nicolaevsky Collection, box 89, folder 4.

24. Ernest V. Hollis, Jr., "Police Systems of Imperial and Soviet Russia," (draft of a Ph.D. dissertation, Archive of Russian and East European History and Culture, Columbia University, 1957), p. 657.

25. A copy of this report was made available to U.S. diplomatic officials in London in November 1920 by the Russian National Committee. A translation is in the National Archives, Washington, D.C.: Records of the Department of State Relating to Internal Affairs of Russia and the Soviet Union 1910–1929, Record Group 59, Microfilm Publication 316, roll 36, frames 0239–0272 (hereafter cited as RG. 59).

26. *Ezhenedel'nik VCheka,* no. 3 (Oct. 6, 1918), pp.6–8. The publication of this article and the accompanying editorial comment led to a stern rebuke from the Party leadership. On October 25, 1918, the Central Committee of the Bolshevik Party resolved "to censure the Nolinsk officials for their article and the editorial staff for its publication." The Central Committee also ordered the discontinuation of the *VCheka Weekly* (Central Party Archives of the Institute of Marxism-Leninism, collection 17, shelf 2, sheet 1, quoted in S. K. Tsvigun et al., eds., *V. I. Lenin i VChK: Sbornik dokumentov, 1917–1922 gg.* [Moscow, 1975], p. 112).

27. The National Archives, Washington, D.C.: RG 59, roll 36, frames 0248–0250.

28. E. V. Dumbadze, *Na Sluzhbe Cheka i Kominterna* (Paris, 1930), p. 89.

29. "The Red Terror in Kiev," *Current History Magazine,* Dec. 1919, p. 491.

30. Melgounov, *The Red Terror in Russia,* p. 177.

31. Lenin, *Collected Works,* XXVIII, 97.

32. *Ibid.,* p. 191.

33. Martyn Latsis, *Dva goda bor'by na vnutrennem fronte: Populiarnyi obzor dvukhgodichnoi deiatel'nosti chrezvychainykh komissii po bor'be s kontr-revoliutsiei, spekuliatsiei i prestupleniiami po dolzhnosti* (Moscow, 1920), p. 75.

34. Latsis, *Chrezvychainye komissii,* p. 10.

35. Central State Archives of the October Revolution, collection 1235, shelf 21, file 8, sheets 109–11, quoted in Belov et al., *Iz istorii VChK,* pp. 251–57.

36. *Sobranie uzakonenii RSFSR,* 1919, no. 12, article 130, quoted in *ibid.,* p. 259.

37. *Gazeta rabochego i krest'ianskogo pravitel'stva,* Jan. 1918, no. 16, quoted in David J. Dallin and Boris I. Nicolaevsky, *Forced Labor in Soviet Russia* (New Haven, 1947), p. 157.

38. Lenin, *Collected Works,* XXXVI, 489.

39. *Sobranie uzakonenii RSFSR,* 1918, no. 65, article 710, quoted in Belov et al., *Iz istorii VChK,* pp. 182–83.

40. *Ezhenedel'nik VCheka,* no. 4 (Oct. 13, 1918), p. 25.

41. See *Vlast' sovetov,* no. 10 (Oct. 1922), p. 25.

42. *Sobranie uzakonenii RSFSR,* 1919, no. 12, article 124, quoted in *Dekrety sovetskoi vlasti,* V, 69–70.

43. *Sobranie uzakonenii RSFSR,* 1919, no. 20, article 235, quoted in *ibid.,* pp. 174–81. Mention should also be made of a later decree dated March 18, 1920, which authorized the VCheka and provincial Chekas to use forced-labor camps as a dumping ground for persons wanted out of the way but whose offenses against the revolutionary order could not be proven in a court or tribunal. This decree gave the secret police the power to sentence to forced-labor camps for up to five years without trial "violators of labor discipline and the revolutionary order and . . . parasitic elements of the population if no evidence sufficient for a criminal prosecution is disclosed against them" (*Sobranie uzakonenii RSFSR,* 1920, no. 22–23, article 115, quoted in *ibid.,* VII, 355.

44. A. V. Tishkov, *Pervyi chekist* (Moscow, 1968), p. 59. Dzerzhinsky officially assumed his duties as Commissar of Internal Affairs on March 30, 1919.

45. *Vlast' sovetov,* no. 10 (Oct. 1922), p. 66; The National Archives, Washington, D.C.: Record Group 165, Records of the War Department General Staff, Military Intelligence Division, file 10058-U-66/1 (hereafter cited as RG. 165).

46. "Instruktsiia iuridicheskomu otdelu," Hoover Institiution Archives, Boris I. Nicolaevsky Collection, box 89, folder 6. Although this top-secret document is undated, it may be assumed from the contents that it was issued some time in 1919.

47. An earlier VCheka secret directive issued on December 1, 1918, specified that six investigators be attached to each provincial Cheka's juridical department, where they would be responsible for "all investigatory work of the Commission." It was further recommended that the juridical departments be divided into specialized investigation units, such as counterrevolution, malfeasance, and speculation. District Chekas were to have three investigators on their staffs ("Instruktsiia chrezvychainym komissiiam na mestakh," Hoover Institution Archives, Boris I. Nicolaevsky Collection, box 89, folder 5). For a firsthand account of the work of a Cheka investigator, see "Chekist o Ch. K.," in *Na chuzhoi storone,* IX (1925), 111–41.

48. "Instruktsiia iuridicheskomu otdelu," Hoover Institution Archives, Boris I. Nicolaevsky Collection, box 89, folder 6.

49. Central Party Archives of the Institiute of Marxism-Leninism, collection 17, shelf 4, file 28, cited in P. G. Sofinov, *Ocherki istorii*

vserossiiskoi chrezvychainoi komissii, 1917–1922 gg. (Moscow, 1960), p. 147 (hereafter cited as *Ocherki istorii VChK*).

50. *Izvestiia*, no. 59 (March 18, 1919), p. 3.

51. *Sobranie uzakonenii RSFSR*, 1918, no. 100, article 1033, quoted in Belov et al., *Iz istorii VChK*, p. 206.

52. VCheka Order No. 208, Dec. 17, 1918, quoted in Latsis, *Chrezvychainye komissii,* pp. 54–55.

53. Latsis, *Dva goda bor'by na vnutrennem fronte,* p. 76.

54. This description of the events in Kharkov is based on the findings of the Denikin Commisssion (The National Archives, RG 59, roll 35, frames 1375–1402).

55. It is likely that similar mass murders took place in Kiev, where the following warning was published by the local Cheka a few days before the city fell to General Denikin's army: "At the present time the entire counterrevolutionary element, from the extreme monarchists to the socialist-traitors, has taken up arms against Soviet power and, with the help of the local counterrevolutionary bourgeoisie and kulaks, is preparing to deliver a fatal blow to it. The Extraordinary Commission has decided to take hostages as a means of thwarting the schemes of the bourgeoisie and to repulse any attacks in the future. The Kiev Provincial Cheka hereby notifies the general public that the slightest action against Soviet power will be punished by the merciless execution of these hostages" (*Izvestiia VUTsIK*, no. 126 [Aug. 26, 1919], quoted in P. P. Bachinskii, P. I. Pavliuk, and B. S. Shul'zhenko, eds., *Na zashchite revoliutsii: Iz istorii vseukrainskoi chrezvychainoi komissii, 1917–1922 gg.: Sbornik dokumentov i materialov* [Kiev, 1971], pp. 125–26).

56. *Sobranie uzakonenii RSFSR*, 1919, no. 27, article 301, quoted in Belov et al., *Iz istorii VChK*, pp. 299–300.

57. VCheka Order No. 174, June 23, 1919, quoted in *ibid.,* pp. 300–301.

58. *Pravda*, no. 151 (July 12, 1919), quoted in *ibid.,* pp. 311–12.

59. Latsis, *Dva goda bor'by na vnutrennem fronte,* pp. 75–76.

60. According to Yakov Peters, the VCheka's success in exposing these plots and conspiracies was due less to any special investigative skills on its part than to the ineptness and cowardice of its adversaries. In an interview with an American journalist, Peters expressed a very low opinion of these foes who lacked the courage and character of real revolutionaries. To avoid punishment, he said, they would willingly give away their companions and even name "father, mother, sister, and brother." Although Peters did not mention it, the VCheka's virtually unlimited power of arrest and its widespread use of torture to extract information may also have had something to do with the cooperativeness of its prisoners (see Albert Rhys Williams, *Journey into Revolution: Petrograd 1917–1918,* ed. Lucita Williams [Chicago, 1969], pp. 54–55).

On the basis of extensive research utilizing all available British and Soviet archival sources, Richard K. Debo concluded that VCheka provocation and entrapment played a large part in one of the most famous of these counterrevolutionary plots, the so-called "Lockhart Plot" of

August 1918. It was Dzerzhinsky, writes Debo, "who ultimately controlled the fate of everyone involved." Dzerzhinsky called the plot into
existence by skillfully exploiting the anti-Bolshevik sympathies of the
British diplomat Bruce Lockhart and finally "ordered the liquidation of
those involved." Debo's careful reconstruction of this chapter in secret
police history may be found in an article appropriately entitled "Lockhart Plot or Dzerzhinskii Plot?" *Journal of Modern History*, XLII, no. 3
(Sept. 1971), 413–39.

61. *Izvestiia*, no. 211, (Sept. 23, 1919), quoted in Belov et al., *Iz istorii
VChK*, pp. 320–21.

62. Dzerzhinskii, *Izbrannye proizvedeniia*, I, 282–83. For further information on the National Center, see Latsis, *Dva goda bor'by na
vnutrennem fronte*, pp. 42–45; D. L. Golinkov, *Krakh vrazheskogo
podpol'ia: Iz istorii bor'by s kontr-revoliutsiei v Sovetskoi Rossii v 1917–
1924 gg.* (Moscow, 1971), pp. 190–204; and Paul Avrich, *Kronstadt 1921*
(Princeton, N.J., 1970), pp. 102–3.

63. Latsis, *Chrezvychainye komissii*, p. 15.

64. Quoted in *Bulletins of the Russian Liberation Committee*, no. 52
(Feb. 21, 1920), pp. 1–2.

65. *Izvestiia*, no. 26 (Feb. 6, 1920), p. 1.

66. Lenin, *Collected Works*, XXX, 233–35.

67. *Ibid.*, p. 347.

68. *Sobranie uzakonenii RSFSR*, 1920, no. 4–5, article 22, quoted in
Belov et al., *Iz istorii VChK*, pp. 356–57. This ostensibly merciful
measure did not rule out a future return to rule by terror. The Soviet
leaders hastened to add that "the resumption by the Entente of attempts
to disrupt the steady position of Soviet power and the peaceful labor of
the workers and peasants by means of armed intervention or material
support to the rebellious Tsarist generals will inevitably force us to resort
again to the methods of terror." The blame for any subsequent recourse
to the weapon of terror would lie "entirely and exclusively upon the
governments and ruling classes of the Entente and the Russian capitalists
who sympathize with them."

69. *Sobranie uzakonenii RSFSR*, 1920, no. 78, article 370, quoted in
Belov et al., *Iz istorii VChK*, pp. 395–96.

70. Quoted in Melgounov, *The Red Terror in Russia*, pp. 58–59.

71. Victor Serge, *Memoirs of a Revolutionary*, trans. Peter Sedwick
(London, 1963), p. 99.

72. "Protocol No. 5 of the Session of the Presidium of the All-Russian
Central Executive Committe," Jan. 28, 1920, quoted in N.V. Krylenko,
Sudoustroistvo RSFSR: Lektsii po teorii i istorii sudoustroistva
(Moscow, 1923), p. 356.

73. Quoted in Melgounov, *The Red Terror in Russia*, p. 60.

74. *Izvestiia raboche-krest'ianskogo inspektsii*, April 1920, quoted in
Interim Report of the Committee to Collect Information on Russia
(London, 1920), pp. 18–23.

75. Latsis, *Dva goda bor'by na vnutrennem fronte*, p. 14.

76. *Ibid.*, pp. 15, 61.

77. *Ibid.*, p. 16. VCheka Order No. 186, issued on December 30, 1920, noted that evidence had accumulated at VCheka headquarters that members of anti-Soviet parties who had been arrested for political reasons were often detained under the most wretched conditions. The VCheka leadership wished it to be understood that these prisoners were being held not as criminals but only temporarily "in the interests of the revolution," and therefore the conditions of their imprisonment should not have a "punitive character" (quoted in Latsis, *Chrezvychainye komissii*, p. 62).

78. The document is quoted in *Sotsialisticheskii vestnik*, no. 5 (April 5, 1921), pp. 12–14. An incomplete version was published in Latsis, *Chrezvychainye komissii*, pp. 56–57.

79. "Itogi i praktika godichnoi deiatel'nosti odesskoi gubcheka," quoted in *Sotsialisticheskii vestnik*, no. 23–24 (Dec. 9, 1922), pp. 18–19.

80. V. Plastinin, *Kommunist Kedrov* (Omsk, 1969), p. 97; *Volya Rossii*, no. 14 (1920), quoted in Melgounov, *The Red Terror in Russia*, pp. 67–68.

81. The National Archives, RG 165, file no. 10058-U-79.

82. N. Voronovich, ed., *Zelenia kniga: Sbornik materialov i dokumentov. Istoriia krest'ianskogo dvizheniia v chernomorskoi gubernii* (Prague, 1921), pp. 152–54.

83. *Krasnyi Krim,* Dec. 4–5, 1920, quoted in William H. Chamberlin, *The Russian Revolution, 1917–1921* (New York, 1965), II, 495.

84. "Tiuremnoe delo v 1920 godu: Otchet narodnogo komissariata iustitsii po tsentral'nomu karatel'nomu otdelu VIII-mu vserossiiskomu s'ezdu sovetov," in *Sbornik materialov tsentral'nogo karatel'nogo otdela,* no. 1 (Moscow, 1920), pp. 113–30.

85. "Otchet tsentral'nogo upravleniia chrezvychainykh komissii pri sovnarkome Ukrainy za 1920 god," cited in Chamberlin, *The Russian Revolution*, II, 75. An incomplete version of the text of this long report may be found in Bachinskii, Pavliuk, and Shul'zhenko, *Na zashchite revoliutsii*, pp. 230–58. The report summarizes Chekist operations against such foes of Soviet power as "Polish counterrevolutionaries," "active Russian counterrevolutionaries," "the Makhno army," "Anarchists," "criminal bandits," "the Ukrainian Party of Left Socialist Revolutionaries," "the Russian Social Democratic Workers Party (Mensheviks)," "Zionists," and "Evangelists."

86. VCheka Order No. 10, Jan. 8, 1921, quoted in Latsis, *Chrezvychainye komissii*, pp. 19–23.

87. *Ibid.*, p. 23.

88. *Ibid.*, pp. 25–26. In a secret letter to the Central Committee of the Communist Party written in mid-January 1921, Dzerzhinsky concluded that the "supreme measure of punishment" was still necessary as well. He urged that the death penalty be retained for such political offenses as terrorist acts and open rebellion. He also thought the death penalty should be applied to bandits and spies, but he especially insisted that it

be retained "for those abuses of office that seriously hinder Soviet power in the reconstruction of the productive forces of the RSFSR." Victory on the economic front was a matter of life and death for the Soviet Republic, and therefore it was necessary to suppress "in the most merciless way" any officials whose crimes obstructed the path of the Russian proletariat (Central Party Archives of the Institute of Marxism-Leninism, collection 2, shelf 1, unit 24495, quoted in Tsvigun et al., *Lenin i VChK*, pp. 424–25).

89. "Obzor deiatel'nosti glavnogo upravleniia prinuditel'nykh rabot za vtoroe polugodie 1921 g.," in *Vlast' sovetov*, no. 1–2 (1922), pp. 41–44. According to these official Soviet figures, which incidentally did *not* include data on forced-labor camps in the Ukraine, the Kirghiz Autonomous Republic, or the Crimea, several sentencing agencies had contributed the following portions of the inmate population: VCheka organs, 44 percent of all prisoners; people's courts, 24.5 percent; revolutionary tribunals, 20.3 percent; other institutions, 11.1 percent. The bulk of the prisoners were charged with criminal offenses (28.5%), anti-social behavior such as drunkenness, prostitution, and idling (18.3%), and counterrevolution (16.9%). See also *Vlast' sovetov*, no. 4–6 (1922), pp. 49–52.

90. "Tiuremnoe delo v 1921 g.: Otchet narkom'iusta, po tsentral'nomu ispravitel'no-trudovomu otdelu, IX-mu vser. s'ezdu sovetov," quoted in *Sotsialisticheskii vestnik*, no. 13–14 (July 20, 1922), p. 8.

91. Chamberlin, *The Russian Revolution*, II, 430–31.

92. Quoted in Sofinov, *Ocherki istorii VChK*, p. 223.

93. "Pis'mo TsK RKP (b) gubernskim komitetam o neobkhodimosti usileniia kontakta s chrezvychainymi komissiiami," April 4, 1921, quoted in Belov et al., *Iz isotrii VChK*, p. 437.

94. Latsis, *Dva goda bor'by na vnutrennem fronte*, pp. 69–70.

95. Lenin, *Collected Works*, XXXII, 172.

96. The National Archives, RG 59, roll 88, frames 0057–0058.

97. I. Ia. Trifonov, *Klassy i klassovaia bor'ba v SSSR v nachale nepa, 1921–1923 gg.: Bor'ba s vooruzhennoi kulatskoi kontrrevoliutsiei* (Leningrad, 1964), pp. 210–15. A communique issued by the Ukrainian Cheka was typical of the reports received by the Joint Commission for the Struggle against Banditry in the spring of 1921. The communique noted the following incidents of bandit violence over a four-day period in a region inundated with outlaws: *April 16, 1921*, Podol'ia Province, Gaisinsky District—A band of ten armed men seized an unspecified amount of grain and killed a Soviet agricultural official in the village of Sokolets. *April 17, 1921*, Poltava Province, Karlovsky Region—A band of fifty mounted men, armed with machine guns, attacked the Lanovsky Sugar Plant killing five guards and one employee, and made off with 306,000 roubles, eighteen horses, and two typewriters. *April 19, 1921*, Kharkov Province, Kupiansk District—A band of two hundred mounted men attacked the railroad station of Topoli and killed twenty-six Red Army men before being driven off by an armored train. ("Operativno-in-

formatsionnaia svodka otdela po bor'be s banditizom VUChK za vtoruiu polovinu aprelia 1921 goda,'' quoted in Bachinskii, Pavliuk, and Shul'zhenko, *Na zashchite revoliutsii,* pp. 286–88.)

98. "Otchet o deiatel'nosti VUChK za 1921 goda,'' quoted in Bachinskii, Pavliuk, and Shul'zhenko, *Na zashchite revoliutsii,* pp. 348–53.

99. Trifonov, *Klassy i klassovaia bor'ba v SSSR v nachale nepa, 1921– 1923 gg.:* pp. 4–5.

100. *Bednota,* no. 1062 (Oct. 29, 1921), p. 1.

101. "Otchet o deiatel'nosti VUChK za 1921 goda,'' in Bachinskii, Pavliuk, and Shul'zhenko, *Na zashchite revoliutsii,* p. 353; Sofinov, *Ocherki istorii VChK,* p. 230. For a detailed region-by-region account of the suppression of banditry during this period, see Trifonov, *Klassy i klassovaia bor'ba v SSSR v nachale nepa, 1921–1923 gg.,* pp. 235–95.

102. Iu. A. Poliakov, *Perekhod k nepu i sovetskoe krest'ianstvo* (Moscow, 1967), p. 204.

103. *Ibid.,* p. 204.

104. "Obshchie prichiny voeniknoveniia banditskikh i krest'ianskikh vosstanii,'' in *Krasnaia Armiia,* Dec. 1921, pp. 30–34, quoted in *Sotsialisticheskii vestnik,* no. 9 (May 2, 1922), pp. 10–11.

105. Lenin, *Collected Works,* XXXII, 188.

106. V. A. Antonov-Ovseenko, "O banditskom dvizhenii v tambovskoi gubernii,'' Trotsky Archives, Harvard University, doc. T686, quoted in Seth Singleton, "The Tambov Revolt (1920–1921),'' *Slavic Review,* XXV (Sept. 1966), 509–10.

107. Sofinov, *Ocherki istorii VChK,* pp. 225–26.

108. Avrich, *Kronstadt 1921,* p. 62.

109. *Izvestiia vremennogo revoliutsionnogo komiteta,* March 8, 1921, quoted in *ibid.,* pp. 241–42.

110. Sofinov, *Ocherki istorii VChK,* pp. 222–23.

111. Serge, *Memoirs of a Revolutionary,* p. 131.

112. S. A. Malsagoff, *An Island in Hell: A Soviet Prison in the Far North* (London, 1926), p. 45.

113. Lenin, *Collected Works,* XXIX, 535.

114. *Izvestiia,* no. 161 (July 24, 1921), quoted in Belov et al., *Iz istorii VChK,* p. 458.

115. Lenin, *Collected Works,* XXXII, 362.

116. "Otchet o deiatel'nosti VUChK za 1921 goda,'' quoted in Bachinskii, Pavliuk, and Shul'zhenko, *Na zashchite revoliutsii,* pp. 343–48.

117. Latsis, *Chrezvychainye komissii,* p. 8.

118. Latsis, *Dva goda bor'by na vnutrennem fronte,* pp. 78, 81.

119. *Izvestiia,* no. 195 (Sept. 10, 1918), p. 1.

120. Latsis, *Chrezvychainye komissii,* p. 9.

121. Latsis, *Dva goda bor'by na vnutrennem fronte,* p. 74.

122. U.S. Congress, Senate, Committee on the Judiciary, "The Human Cost of Communism,'' 92nd Cong., 1st sess., 1971, p. 11. One thing is certain: the VCheka far surpassed the Tsarist government in the magnitude of its repression. For unlike the Bolshevik regime, the Tsarist

government "was neither organized to rule by terror nor willing to do so" (Jacob Walkin, *The Rise of Democracy in Pre-Revolutionary Russia: Political and Social Institutions under the Last Three Czars* [New York, 1962], p. 62).

In *The Gulag Archipelago,* Alexandr Solzhenitsyn cited a work published in 1907 by a group of liberal Russian leaders which "listed by name all those sentenced to death in Tsarist Russia from 1826 to 1906." The list totaled 3,419, including those executed in the aftermath of the first revolution of 1905. Thus, even if one accepts Latsis's figures at face value, the most objective data still clearly indicates that the VCheka executed over three times as many people in 1918, 1919, and 1920 as the Tsarist authorities put to death in a period of eighty years, a turbulent time marked by several attempts on the lives of the Tsars, the assassination of one, several major wars, numerous mass strikes, peasant uprisings, and a revolution. "In all our centuries," wrote Solzhenitsyn, "from the first Ryurik on, had there ever been a period of such cruelties and so much killing as during the post-October Civil War?" (*The Gulag Archipelago, 1918–1956: An Experiment in Literary Investigation, I-II,* trans. Thomas P. Whitney [New York, 1973], pp. 301, 433–35).

Chapter 5. The Secret Police and Its Critics

1. *Materialy narodnogo komissariata iustitsii. Narodnyi sud. Vypusk III. Vtoroi vserossiiskii s'ezd oblastnykh i gubernskikh komissarov iustitsii.* (Moscow, 1918), p. 15.

2. *Ibid.,* p. 16.

3. *Ibid.,* p. 14.

4. *Ibid.,* p. 17.

5. *Vestnik narodnogo komissariata vnutrennikh del,* no. 20 (1918), pp. 11–12, quoted in James Bunyan, ed., *Intervention, Civil War and Communism in Russia, April-December 1918* (Baltimore, 1936), p. 259.

6. *Ezhenedel'nik chrezvychainykh komissii po bor'be s kontr-revoliutsiei i spekuliatsiei,* no. 1 (Sept. 22, 1918), p. 10 (hereafter cited as *Ezhenedel'nik VCheka*).

7. *Ezhenedel'nik VCheka,* no. 2 (Sept. 29, 1918), pp. 11–12.

8. *Pravda,* no. 225 (Oct. 18, 1918), p. 1. Shortly after the appearance of this statement, another official of the Commissariat of Internal Affairs sought to bolster the position taken by spokesmen for the local soviets by presenting the public with the results of a survey his agency had recently conducted. The Commissariat had polled the local soviets requesting their views on relations with the Chekas. Out of 147 replies, it probably came as no surprise that 118 expressed themselves in favor of subordinating the Chekas to themselves (*Izvestiia,* no. 229 [Oct. 20, 1918], pp. 1–2).

9. *Izvestiia,* no. 226 (Oct. 17, 1918), p. 2. Peters's remarks, which we may safely assume reflected the thinking of the rest of the VCheka leadership, drew a quick and pointed response from G. I. Petrovsky, the

Bolshevik Commissar of Internal Affairs. It was the local soviets, Petrovsky argued, that represented the best elements of the toiling people and the Communist Party; the soviets and not the Chekas were therefore the real "agencies of struggle of the masses." From this it followed that the local soviets themselves ought to be the basic units in the struggle against counterrevolution. But in the meantime the Extraordinary Commissions, whose operations were totally independent of local control, had been wreaking havoc upon local administration. Even worse, the Chekas were developing a dangerous kind of internal dynamic of their own. There was evidence, Petrovsky said, that the Chekists were beginning to see what they wanted to see, namely, conspiracies and threats all around. The machinery of the VCheka had been set up to combat counterrevolution, and this it was proceeding to do even when the menace was not really present, in which case it could readily be manufactured: "What are the Chekas going to do in places where there is no counterrevolution—naturally, they are going to try to invent it." Moreover, Petrovsky believed that the unilateral orders issued by the VCheka declaring local secret police organs independent of outside control were illegal, and he demanded that the executive committees of the local soviets be allowed to issue instructions to the Chekas and to participate in the formulation of their tactics and secret operations (*Izvestiia,* no. 230 [October 22, 1918], p. 2).

10. *Pravda,* no. 232 (Oct. 26, 1918), p. 1.

11. *Pravda,* no. 216 (Oct. 8, 1918), p. 1. The Chekist Fomin struck back in the pages of the *VCheka Weekly,* where he described Olminsky as an "impractical man completely unfamiliar with the work of the Chekas," who sat in his office writing articles condemning the secret police for implementing the dictatorship of the proletariat. "In general, in our opinion," Fomin said, "these lines would be unnecessary had your article, Comrade Olminsky, not found such a warm response in the ranks of the petit-bourgeois philistines who spread all kinds of rubbish and cock-and-bull stories about the Cheka" (*Ezhenedel'nik VCheka,* no. 4 [Oct. 13, 1918], pp. 4–5).

12. *Vechernie Izvestiia M. S. R. i Kr. Dep.,* no. 161 (Feb. 3, 1919).

13. *Izvestiia,* no. 277 (Dec. 18, 1918), pp. 1–2.

14. *Pravda,* no. 281 (Dec. 25, 1918), p. 1. A few days later Latsis replied that his words had been taken out of context and distorted. His formula for determining the guilt of the accused, he pointed out, had been written for the guidance of the Chekas on the eastern front at "a moment of the most unrestrained White terror on the part of the enemy, who shot people not only for belonging to or sympathizing with the Bolsheviks, but simply for having calloused hands." At a time of desperate class struggle it was impossible to determine evidence of guilt: "The most valuable information for the investigator consists of facts regarding class membership, class origin, . . . education, and profession" (*Pravda,* no. 285 [Dec. 29, 1918], p. 1).

15. *Izvestiia,* no. 19 [Jan. 28, 1919], p. 3.

16. Central Party Archives of the Institute of Marxism-Leninism, collection 17, shelf 2, unit 7, sheet 1, quoted in A. V. Tishkov, *Pervyi chekist* (Moscow, 1968), p. 55.

17. *Sobranie uzakonenii RSFSR*, 1917, no. 4, article 50, quoted in *Dekrety sovetskoi vlasti* (Moscow, 1957–75), I, 124–26.

18. *Sobranie uzakonenii RSFSR*, 1917, no. 12, article 170, cited in Judah Zelitch, *Soviet Administration of Criminal Law* (Philadelphia, 1931) pp. 35–36.

19. V. I. Lenin, *Collected Works* (Moscow, 1960–70), XXVII, 219.

20. *Sobranie uzakonenii RSFSR*, 1918, no. 44, article 533, quoted in Zelitch, *Soviet Administration of Criminal Law*, pp. 37–38.

21. Quoted in Samuel Kucherov, *The Organs of Soviet Administration of Justice: Their History and Operation* (Leiden, 1970), p. 55.

22. Zelitch, *Soviet Administration of Criminal Law*, p. 35.

23. Iak. Berman, "O revoliutsionnykh tribunalakh," in *Proletarskaia revoliutsiia i pravo*, no. 1 (Jan. 1919), pp. 58–70; and D'iakonov, "Posleoktiabr'skie eskizy," in *Ezhenedel'nik sovetskoi iustitsii*, no. 44–45 (Oct. 1922), p. 11. In the opinion of one prominent Soviet jurist, the tribunals were initially so mild that "their softness with regard to sentences discredited them completely" (*Sovetskoe pravo*, 1922, no. 3, p. 55, quoted in Zelitch, *Soviet Administration of Criminal Law*, p. 36). By way of contrast, in terms of both the dimension of its activity and the severity of its repressive measures, the secret police far exceeded the revolutionary tribunals in 1918. According to figures published by Martyn Latsis, in 1918 the VCheka and its local agencies arrested a total of 47,348 persons. The subsequent fate of most of these prisoners was said to be as follows: 14,829 sent to prison; 14,059 released; 6,407 sentenced to concentration camps; 6,185 shot; 1,800 fate unknown. Some simple arithmetic shows that a prisoner's chances of being executed for his transgressions were much greater if he happened to be at the mercy of the secret police. In 1918, about 13 percent of those arrested by the VCheka and its local agencies were shot while less than one-quarter of 1 percent of those convicted by the revolutionary tribunals met the same fate. It was no wonder that friends and relatives of Cheka prisoners were often prepared to go to almost any length to get the cases of their loved ones transfered to the tribunals (*Izvestiia*, no. 26, [Feb. 6, 1920], p. 1).

24. *Materialy narodnogo komissariata iustitsii: Protokoly III vserossiiskogo s'ezda deiatelei sovetskoi iustitsii, s prilozheniem rezoliutsii s'ezda* (Petrograd, 1921), p. 85.

25. *Izvestiia*, no. 202 (Sept. 18, 1918), p. 2.

26. N. V. Krylenko, *Sudoustroistvo RSFSR: Lektsii po teorii i istorii sudoustroistva* (Moscow, 1923), p. 49.

27. *Ibid.*, p. 97.

28. *Ibid.*, p. 98.

29. *Ibid.*, pp. 99–100.

30. *Sobranie uzakonenii RSFSR*, 1918, no. 80, article 842, quoted in G.

A. Belov et al., eds., *Iz istorii vserossiiskoi chrezvychainoi komissii, 1917–1922 gg.: Sbornik dokumentov* (Moscow, 1958), pp. 203–4 (hereafter cited as *Iz istorii VChK*).

31. Krylenko, *Sudoustroistvo RSFSR*, p. 101.

32. *Ibid.*, p. 100.

33. Lenin, *Collected Works*, XXVIII, 169–70.

34. VCheka Order No. 46, Sept. 19, 1918, quoted in Martyn Latsis, *Chrezvychainye komissii po bor'be s kontr-revoliutsiei* (Moscow, 1921), p. 52.

35. "Instruktsiia chrezvychainym komissiiam na mestakh," Dec. 1, 1918, Hoover Institution Archives, Boris I. Nicolaevsky Collection, box 8, folder 5.

36. *Izvestiia*, no. 277 (Dec. 18, 1918), p. 2.

37. *Sobranie uzakonenii RSFSR*, 1918, no. 94, article 941, quoted in Belov et al., *Iz istorii VChK*, pp. 235–36.

38. VCheka Order No. 208, Dec. 17, 1918, quoted in Latsis, *Chrezvychainye komissii*, pp. 54–55. This and similar appeals for restraint from the Lubianka seem to have had little immediate impact on Cheka practices. More than a year later, the VCheka leadership let it be known that it was still receiving "daily complaints from persons and institutions, both central and local," that secret police organs were not adhering to the provisions of the decree of December 14, 1918. Sudden and unannounced arrests of valuable Soviet workers were continuing to have a devastating effect on the work of various institutions that were unable to find suitable replacements. To correct this "abnormal and harmful" situation, the VCheka again demanded that its local branches implement the decree of December 14, 1918, to the letter and warned all local Cheka chairmen "for the last time": "Nonfulfillment by them of decrees promulgated by Soviet power and orders of the VCheka, and also every deviation from their implicit implementation, will be severely punished" (VCheka Order of February 28, 1920, quoted in Belov et al., *Iz istorii VChK*, pp. 374–75).

39. VCheka Order No. 113, Dec. 19, 1918, quoted in Belov et al., *Iz istorii VChK*, pp. 236–38).

40. *Izvestiia*, no. 17 (Jan. 25, 1919), p. 1, and no. 20 (Jan. 29, 1919), p. 1.

41. *Izvestiia*, no. 29 (Feb. 8, 1919), p. 3. According to Boris Nicolaevsky, "an influential group within the Council of People's Commissars insisted on abolishing the Cheka altogether and transferring its functions to a reorganized People's Commissariat of Justice. Lenin opposed these reforms and decided to make the Cheka directly subordinate to the Party Politburo, with an official representative of the latter placed in the Cheka Collegium with veto power. This decision was never published. . . . The Politburo representative on the Cheka was first Bukharin, then Stalin, and it was in this capacity . . . that Stalin began to acquire his knowledge of the Cheka's machinery" ("Communism's Terror Machine," in *The New Leader*, Feb. 17, 1958, p. 24).

To further consolidate Party control over the secret police, and perhaps also to curb the excesses of secret police organs in the provinces, Lenin had signed a decree on December 3, 1918, requiring that all responsible posts in the provincial Chekas be filled by Communists of at least two years' standing ("Postanovlenie komissii soveta oborony o rabote VChK," Dec. 3, 1918, quoted in *Dekrety sovetskoi vlasti,* IV, 569–71).

42. Central State Archives of the October Revolution, collection 1235, shelf 21, file 8, sheets 109–111, quoted in Belov et al., *Iz istorii VChK,* pp. 251–57.

43. *Sobranie uzakonenii RSFSR,* 1919, no. 12, article 130, quoted in *ibid.,* pp. 258–59.

44. The repressive measures applied by the revolutionary tribunals in the period 1919–22 were reliably summarized as follows:

Punishment	1919 (%)	1920 (%)	1921 (%)	1922 (%)
Executed	14	11	5	1
Imprisoned	50	62	78	32
Forced labor	8	8	6	2
Confiscation of property	8	6	1	49
Other	20	13	10	16

Figures are from A. A. Gertsenzon, *Bor'ba s prestupnost'u v RSFSR po materialam obsledovaniia NK RKI SSSR* (Moscow, 1928), p. 57.

45. Krylenko, *Sudoustroistvo RSFSR,* p. 103.

46. Latsis, *Chrezvychainye komissii,* p. 26. The continued struggle for competence between the tribunalists and the Chekists was reflected in a series of compromise decrees defining and redefining the scope, powers, and relations of the two institutions. None of these laws, however, had any lasting effect on the extralegal character of secret police operations. See E. H. Carr, "The Origin and Status of the Cheka," in *Soviet Studies,* X (July 1958), 8–10.

Chapter 6. The Offspring of the VCheka

1. *Izvestiia,* no. 287 (Dec. 19, 1922), p. 3.

2. *Ezhenedel'nik chrezvychainykh komissii po bor'be s kontr-revoliutsiei i spekuliatsiei,* no. 6 (Oct. 27, 1918), p. 22 (hereafter cited as *Ezhenedel'nik VCheka).*

3. Martyn Latsis, *Chrezvychainye komissii po bor'be s kontr-revoliutsiei* (Moscow, 1921), p. 27.

4. *Sobranie uzakonenii RSFSR,* 1922, no. 16, article 160, quoted in G. A. Belov et al., eds., *Iz istorii vserossiiskoi chrezvychainoi komissii, 1917–1922 gg.: Sbornik dokumentov* (Moscow, 1958), pp. 471–74 (hereafter cited as *Iz istorii VChK).*

5. V. I. Lenin, *Collected Works* (Moscow, 1960–70), XXXIII, 175–77. Lenin's will was embodied in a resolution of the Congress. Having taken note of the "heroic work accomplished by the organs of the All-Russian

Extraordinary Commission in the most critical moments of the Civil War and the enormous services rendered by it to the strengthening and defense of the conquests of the October Revolution from internal and external assaults,'' the delegates resolved that ''the present . . . strength of Soviet power permits the restriction of the scope of activities of the All-Russian Extraordinary Commission and its organs and the entrustment of the struggle against violations of the laws of the Soviet Republic to the judicial organs.

''Consequently, the Congress of Soviets charges the Presidium of the All-Russian Central Executive Committee with promptly reviewing the statute of the All-Russian Extraordinary Commission and its organs for the purpose of its reorganization, limiting its authority and reinforcing the principle of revolutionary legality'' (*Sobranie uzakonenii RSFSR,* 1922, no. 4, article 42, quoted in Belov et al., *Iz istorii VChK,* pp. 470–71).

6. Lenin, *Collected Works,* XLV, 694.

7. *Ibid.,* p. 389.

8. *Ibid.,* pp. 694–95.

9. *Ibid.,* XXXIII, 282. E. H. Carr, in his history of the period, commented on the abolition of the VCheka: ''It is difficult to believe that, at a time when the introduction of NEP, through its toleration of capitalist and petty bourgeois elements, had increased the need for vigilance, the party leaders could seriously have thought of dispensing with so powerful an instrument of security [as the secret police]'' (Edward Hallett Carr, *The Bolshevik Revolution, 1917–1923* [New York, 1951], I, 180).

10. *Izvestiia,* no. 185 (Aug. 18, 1923), p. 3.

11. *Izvestiia,* no. 236 (Oct. 19, 1922), p. 3.

12. D. A. Gaidukov, V. F. Komok, and S. L. Ronin, eds., *Istoriia sovetskoi konstitutsii: Sbornik dokumentov, 1917–1957* (Moscow, 1957), pp. 235–36.

13. Georges Agabekov, *OGPU: The Russian Secret Terror,* trans. Henry W. Bunn (New York, 1931), pp. 255–67.

14. *Ekonomicheskaia zhizn',* no. 101 (May 9, 1922), p. 2. See also Robert M. Slusser, ''The Budget of the OGPU and the Special Troops from 1923–4 to 1928–9,'' *Soviet Studies,* X (April 1959), 375–83. In a report to the Council of People's Commissars delivered on December 9, 1924, Dzerzhinsky said that the OGPU was then served by a staff of 24,700 employees, which, he added, ''taking into consideration the extent of the territory of the USSR is not at all excessive.'' In addition, the Special Troops of the OGPU comprised, in Dzerzhinsky's words, ''the impressive force of approximately 110,000 bayonets [infantry] and 28,000 sabres [cavalry]'' (The National Archives, Washington, D.C.: Records of the Department of State Relating to Internal Affairs of Russia and the Soviet Union, 1910–1929, Record Group 59, Microfilm Publication 316, roll 56, frames 1057–1067 [hereafter cited as RG 59]).

15. F. E. Dzerzhinskii, *Izbrannye proizvedeniia* (2d ed.; Moscow, 1967), I, 370–71.

16. The National Archives, Record Group 165, Records of the War De-

partment General Staff, Military Intelligence Division, G-2 Report no. 7512, June 16, 1930, "Military Establishment [of] the O.G.P.U.," file 2037-1552/15 (hereafter cited as RG 165).

17. P. I. Zyrianov et al., eds., *Pogranichnye voiska SSSR, 1918–1928: Sbornik dokumentov i materialov* (Moscow, 1973), p. 207.

18. The National Archives, RG 59, roll 88, frames 1526–1529.

19. "Postanovlenie soveta truda i oborony o sozdanii otdel'nogo pogranichnogo korpusa," Sept. 27, 1922, quoted in Zyrianov et al., *Pogranichnye voiska SSSR,* pp. 198–99.

20. *Ibid.,* p. 525, 528.

21. *Ibid.,* p. 726.

22. *Ibid.,* p. 250.

23. *Ibid.,* pp. 836–37.

24. *Ibid.,* p. 252.

25. The National Archives, RG 165, Evan E. Young, Commissioner of the United States for the Baltic Provinces of Russia, to the Secretary of State, Dec. 10, 1920, file 10058–948/2.

26. A. V. Tishkov, *Pervyi chekist* (Moscow, 1968), p. 100. The pre-revolutionary career of this important figure of the early Soviet secret police is traced in a Soviet biography, *Dorogoi bor'by* by O. N. Ioganson (Moscow, 1963).

27. Sidorov, "Pidpil'na ChK v Odesi v 1918–1919 r.r. (Iz peredistorii ChK na Ukraini)," in *Letopis revoliutsii,* no. 4 (1928), pp. 123–33.

28. The National Archives, RG 165, Colonel Mathew C. Smith, Chief, Negative Branch, to J. Edgar Hoover, Dec. 23, 1920, file no. 10058-890/3.

29. For further information on the "Trust" see Geoffrey Bailey, *The Conspirators* (New York, 1960); Paul W. Blackstock, *The Secret Road to World War II: Soviet Versus Western Intelligence, 1921–1929* (Chicago, 1969); and S. L. Voitsekhovsky, *Trest: Vospominaniia i dokumenty* (London, Ontario, 1974).

30. The National Archives, RG 59, roll 51, frames 1411–1415.

31. As early as 1899 Lenin had urged his fellow revolutionaries to heed the lessons of "the whole preceeding [Russian] revolutionary movement" and "concentrate all their efforts on organizing the Party, on strengthening its internal discipline, and on developing the technique for illegal work" (*Collected Works,* IV, 181). See also G. M. Deich, "Voprosy konspirativnoi tekhniki 'Iskry' v pis'makh V. I. Lenina 1900–1903 godov," in *Voprosy istorii,* no. 7 (1969), pp. 49–66.

32. Lenin, *Collected Works,* XXXI, 444.

33. Mikhail Trilisser served simultaneously as head of the Foreign Department of the GPU/OGPU and as a member of the International Relations Section of the Comintern; his colleague Joseph Unshlikht, the deputy chairman of the GPU, was deeply involved in the activities of the Comintern's Executive Committee during the early 1920s.

34. A thorough study of early Soviet espionage in western Europe may be found in David J. Dallin, *Soviet Espionage* (New Haven, 1955).

35. The National Archives, RG 59, roll 56, frames 1057–1067. Accord-

ing to a British intelligence report (Public Record Office, London, Foreign Office [hereafter cited as F.O.], 371/9337/2523, Secret Intelligence Service Report, April 10, 1923), the Foreign Department of the GPU maintained eight major espionage centers, each responsible for the work of Soviet agents in several countries: the Berlin center was responsible for Germany, Austria, Hungary, and Czechoslovakia; Stockholm for Sweden, Denmark, and Norway; Paris for France, Switzerland, Belgium, Italy, Great Britain, Spain, Portugal, and Holland; Tashkent for India, Persia, Indochina, and the British and Spanish colonies; Sofia for Rumania, Greece, Turkey, Yugoslavia, and Bulgaria; New York for the United States and Australia; Helsingfors for Finland, Estonia, Latvia, Lithuania, and Poland; and Peking for China, Japan, and Korea.

36. The National Archives, RG 59, roll 89, frames 0758–0759.

37. F.O. 371/10495/2686.

38. *Ibid.*

39. *Ibid.*

40. F.O. 371/11026/2688.

41. The National Archives, RG 59, roll 89, frames 0704–0728.

42. *Pravda,* no. 30 (Feb. 11, 1921), p. 1.

43. Victor Serge, *Memoirs of a Revolutionary, 1901–1941,* trans. Peter Sedgwick (London, 1963), pp. 200–201.

44. Lenin, *Collected Works,* XXXVI, 561.

45. I. Ia. Trifonov, *Klassy i klassovaia bor'ba v SSSR v nachale nepa, 1921–1925 gg.: Podgotovka ekonomicheskogo nastupleniia na novyiu burzhuaziiu* (Leningrad, 1969), pp. 116–67; A. A. Gertsenzon, *Bor'ba s prestupnost'iu v RSFSR* (Moscow, 1928), p. 26, 65.

46. Quoted in Trifonov, *Klassy i klassovaia bor'ba v SSSR v nachale nepa, 1921–1925 gg.,* p. 175.

47. *Izvestiia,* no. 295 (Dec. 25, 1923), p. 2.

48. The National Archives, RG 59, roll 72, frames 1441–1444. Dzerzhinsky also noted in his report that an immense network of speculation had enveloped the majority of Soviet trusts and certain departments of the Supreme Council of the National Economy. In his opinion, only when every Communist in charge of a government department fearlessly disclosed all evidence of activity interfering with the progress of their work to "proletarian justice" would the problem be solved.

49. Tishkov, *Pervyi chekist,* pp. 117–18, 126, and 127.

50. Trotsky wrote of this aspect of Dzerzhinsky's career: "In his economic work, [Dzerzhinsky] accomplished things through sheer temperament—appealing, urging, and lifting people off their feet by his own enthusiasm" (*My Life* [London, 1930], p. 451). For more information on Dzerzhinsky's role as chairman of the Supreme Council of the National Economy see R. W. Davies, "Some Soviet Economic Controllers—II," in *Soviet Studies,* XI, no. 4 (1960), 373–92; and N. Valentinov (Volsky), *The New Economic Policy and the Party Crisis after the Death of Lenin,* ed. J. Bunyan and V. Butenko (Stanford, 1971), pp. 94–141.

51. *Izvestiia*, no. 249 (Oct. 30, 1925), p. 2. See also D. L. Golinkov, *Krakh vrazheskogo podpol'ia: Iz istorii bor'by s kontr-revoliutsiei v sovetskoi Rossii v 1917–1924 gg.* (Moscow, 1971), pp. 340–47.

52. Lenin, *Collected Works*, XXXVI, 560–61. In the summer of 1921 Moscow was the scene of one of the earliest show trials, that of the leading Socialist Revolutionaries. This and other show trials of the Lenin era are described in Alexandr I. Solzhenitsyn, *The Gulag Archipelago, 1918–56: An Experiment in Literary Investigation, I–II,* trans. Thomas P. Whitney (New York, 1973), pp. 334–70.

53. Lenin, *Collected Works*, XXXIII, 358–59. Lenin's draft of the paragraph was: "Propaganda, or agitation, or participation in an organization or cooperation with organizations, having the effect (i.e., the propaganda or agitation) of helping in the slightest way that part of the international bourgeoisie which does not recognize the equal rights of the communist system coming to take the place of capitalism, and which is endeavoring to overthrow it by force, whether by intervention, or blockade, or by espionage, or by financing of the press, or other means— is punishable by death or imprisonment.'' In his study of the formative years of Soviet rule, Leonard Schapiro noted that the law Lenin was trying to shape "was not intended as a temporary measure, but as the foundation of a permanent system of justice to replace the system in use during the civil war. . . . No one knew better than Lenin that the application of the law, which he was proposing . . . would in practice be extended to every criticism of the Soviet system to which the rulers of the country objected'' (Schapiro, *The Origin of the Communist Autocracy* [New York, 1965], p. 189).

54. Golinkov, *Krakh vrazheskogo podpol'ia*, p. 270.

55. Tishkov, *Pervyi chekist*, p. 116.

56. *Izvestiia*, no. 137 (June 23, 1922), p. 5.

57. *Sobranie uzakonenii i rasporiazhenii rabochego i krest'ianskogo pravitel'stva za 1923 god,* no. 8, article 108.

58. *Pravda*, no. 189 (Aug. 31, 1922), quoted in Golinkov, *Krakh vrazheskogo podpol'ia*, p. 302.

59. F.O. 371/8180/2688, Secret Intelligence Service Report no. 1002, Dec. 13, 1922. Figures may be exaggerated.

60. F.O. 371/9336/2523, Secret Intelligence Service Report no. 1076, Feb. 13, 1923. Figures may be exaggerated.

61. Sergey Petrovich Melgounov, *The Red Terror in Russia* (London, 1926), p. 98.

62. Tishkov, *Pervyi chekist*, pp. 119–20. Dzerzhinsky reported that an additional 8,692 bandits were arrested by the OGPU in 1924.

63. The National Archives, RG 59, roll 87, frames 0455–0457.

64. *Letters from Russian Prisons: Consisting of Reprints of Documents by Political Prisoners in Soviet Prisons, Prison Camps and Exile . . . Published by the International Committee for Political Prisoners* (New York, 1925), pp. 55–56.

65. *Ibid.,* p. 264.

66. *Ibid.*, p. 233.

67. *Ibid.*, p. 21.

68. *Ibid.*, p.63.

69. *Ibid.*, p. 24.

70. *Ibid.*, p. 51.

71. Alexandr I. Solzhenitsyn, *The Gulag Archipelago, 1918–1956: An Experiment in Literary Investigation, III–IV*, trans. Thomas P. Whitney (New York, 1975), p. 21.

72. X. X., "Kholmogorskii konstentratsionnyi lager," in V. Chernov, ed., *Che-Ka: Materialy po deiatel'nosti chrezvychainykh komissii* (Berlin, 1922), pp. 242–47.

73. *Sotsialisticheskii vestnik*, no. 9 (79) (April 17, 1924), p. 14.

74. Quoted in N. I. Kiselev, "Lageri smerti: Zapiski byvshago chekista," in *Rul'*, no. 3285 (Sept. 16, 1931), p. 5.

75. *Ibid.*, no. 3283 (Sept. 13, 1931), p. 5.

76. Quoted in David J. Dallin and Boris I. Nicolaevsky, *Forced Labor in Soviet Russia* (New Haven, 1947), p. 174.

77. According to the testimony of N. I. Kiselev, a former Chekist employed in the Northern Camps, almost 33,000 inmates died in the years 1925–26 ("Lageri smerti," in *Rul'*, no. 3283. [Sept. 13, 1931], p. 5).

78. Lenin, *Collected Works*, XXXII, 43, 192.

79. *Ibid.*, pp. 178, 200.

80. Konstantin Shteppa, "Feliks Dzerzhinskii: Creator of the Cheka and Founder of 'Chekism,' " in *The Soviet Secret Police*, ed. Simon Wolin and Robert M. Slusser (New York, 1957), p. 89.

81. Dzerzhinskii, *Izbrannye proizvedennia*, II, 270–71.

82. Lenin, *Collected Works*, XXXIII, 39–41.

83. Quoted in *Sotsialisticheskii vestnik*, no. 8–9 (April 24, 1923), p. 19.

84. Tishkov, *Pervyi chekist*, pp. 121–22. Several months earlier the GPU, at Stalin's urging, had arrested Sultan-Galiev, a prominent Tatar communist, who had challenged the Party's nationality policy by calling for the creation of an autonomous Moslem Communist Party.

85. Trotsky, *My Life*, p. 431.

86. Wolin and Slusser, *The Soviet Secret Police*, pp. 375–76.

87. *Ibid.*, p. 12.

88. *Pravda*, no. 175 (Aug. 1, 1926), quoted in Dzerzhinskii, *Izbrannye proizvedennia*, II, 381–92; The National Archives, RG 59, roll 59, frames 0128–0129.

89. S. Dzerzhinskaia, *V gody velikikh boev* (Moscow, 1964), pp. 400–403.

90. J. V. Stalin, *Works* (Moscow, 1954), VIII, 203–4.

91. N. Bukharin, "Geroicheskaia pesn': Chekist Feliks Dzerzhinskii," in *Feliks Dzerzhinskii, 1926–1931*, ed. R. Abikh (Moscow, 1931), p. 340.

92. Quoted in N. Zubov, *F. E. Dzerzhinskii: Biografiia* (2d ed.; Moscow, 1965), p. 272.

93. V. Menzhinskii, "O Dzerzhinskom," in *Dzerzhinskii v VChK: Vospominaniia*, ed. M. Smirnov (Moscow, 1967), p. 14.

94. Wolin and Slusser, *The Soviet Secret Police*, p. 11.

The Sword of the Revolution

1. Like his predecessor, Viacheslav Rudolfovich Menzhinsky (1874–1934) was of Polish ancestry. He too joined the revolutionary movement as a young man and compiled a long record of faithful service to the Bolshevik cause. Menzhinsky was first posted to the VCheka in December 1917. After a year in Berlin as the general consul of the RSFSR, he resumed his work in the VCheka and was appointed head of the Special Department in 1920. In 1921 he became chief of the VCheka's Secret-Operational Directorate, and in 1923 he was designated the first deputy chairman of the OGPU. Menzhinsky is portrayed in Soviet writings as a conscientious and erudite leader whose special talents lay in the areas of espionage and counterespionage. (He is also said to have had a flair for foreign languages and spoke a dozen fluently.) Trotsky, on the other hand, had a very low opinion of Menzhinsky and dismissed him as "not a man, but the shadow of some unrealized man." Trotsky claimed, probably correctly, that Menzhinsky lacked his predecessor's ability and strength of character. Menzhinsky was certainly instrumental in turning the OGPU into an even more compliant tool of the General Secretary in his quest for victory over the United Opposition. Menzhinsky's tenure as chief of the secret police was punctuated with long periods of illness and incapacitation. Much of the responsibility for running the OGPU therefore rested in the hands of his deputy, Genrikh Yagoda. For more information on the life and career of the second chief of the Soviet secret police, see T. K. Gladkov and M. A. Smirnov, *Menzhinskii* (Moscow, 1969).

2. In the fall of 1927 the OGPU infiltrated the organization of the United Opposition. The evidence gathered by OGPU agents provided Stalin with the ammunition he needed to have Trotsky, Zinoviev, and more than ninety other members of the opposition expelled from the Party. The extravagant festivities surrounding the tenth anniversary of the Soviet secret police were a token of Stalin's satisfaction with the work of the OGPU in routing his rivals and are detailed in *Izvestiia,* nos. 290–91 (Dec. 18–20, 1927), and *Pravda,* nos. 290–91 (Dec. 18–20, 1927). For a detailed discussion of the role of the OGPU in the intra-Party struggle, see Leonard Schapiro, *The Communist Party of the Soviet Union* (New York, 1960), pp. 298–306.

3. V. I. Lenin, *Collected Works* (Moscow, 1960–70), XXVII, 264.

4. N. Zubov, *F. E. Dzerzhinskii: Biografiia* (2d ed.; Moscow, 1965), p. 221.

5. Lenin, *Collected Works, XXXIII,* 176.

6. As a recent Soviet study of Lenin's leadership of the secret police put it: "Constantly exercising political leadership of Chekist organs, V. I. Lenin directed and controlled their work. He always insisted that the methods of struggle adopted by the organs of state security corresponded to the political tasks of the Party and that these methods were altered when changes were required.

"The activities of the VCheka in the center and in the localities always took place with the knowledge of V. I. Lenin. He not only defined its basic direction but in many instances exercised direct control over measures applied by Chekist organs. . . . He also gave concrete orders on the methods to be used in operations aimed at suppressing enemy agents and counterrevolutionary elements in the country'' (S. K. Tsvigun et al., eds., *V. I. Lenin i VChK: Sbornik dokumentov, 1917–1922 gg.* (Moscow, 1975), pp. 5, 7.

Lenin's *Collected Works* contains numerous notes to various secret police officials inquiring about the circumstances surrounding the arrest of this or that individual. Sometimes Lenin scolded overzealous Chekists, as when he heard that a young woman had been arrested in Tsaritsyn for defacing his portrait, and ordered the release of prisoners who had been unjustifiably detained. But such examples of Lenin's personal intervention in the activities of the secret police, which have been offered as demonstrations of the Bolshevik leader's commitment to the principle of ''revolutionary legality,'' only underscore the essential arbitrariness and terroristic tendencies of the VCheka and its local organs.

7. Dzerzhinsky was a loyal Bolshevik, but he was not, as one writer put it, ''a blind follower of the majority.'' On more than one occasion Dzerzhinsky disagreed with Lenin about important policy matters. Thus, he did not support Lenin on the Treaty of Brest-Litovsk and abstained from the crucial vote on the treaty in the Party's Central Committee. Dzerzhinsky also endorsed Trotsky's plan for the militarization of labor during the trade union debate of 1921. In 1922, in an investigation he conducted into Stalin's highhanded policies in Soviet Georgia, Dzerzhinsky again provoked Lenin's ire by supporting Stalin. But from this point on, ''Dzerzhinsky was politically by and large a Stalin man'' (R. W. Davies, ''Some Soviet Economic Controllers—II,'' *Soviet Studies,* XI [April 1960], 377).

8. *Izvestiia,* no. 18 (Jan. 28, 1920), p. 2.

9. A. F. Khatskevich, *Soldat velikikh boev: Zhizn' i deiatel'nost' F. E. Dzerzhinskogo* (3d ed.; Minsk, 1970), p. 284.

10. *Izvestiia,* no. 286 (Dec. 17, 1922), p. 3.

Bibliography

A rich and extensive literature on the secret police has appeared in the Soviet Union since the Twentieth Congress of the CPSU in 1956. Several thousand recent titles, including many collections of documents, biographies, and memoirs, are listed in two extremely valuable U.S. government publications:

U.S. Congress, Senate, Committee on the Judiciary. *Soviet Intelligence and Security Services 1964–1970: A Selected Bibliography of Soviet Publications, with Some Additional Titles from Other Sources.* 92nd Congress, 1st session. Washington, D.C.: Government Printing Office, 1972.

U.S. Congress, Senate, Committee on the Judiciary. *Soviet Intelligence and Security Services.* Volume II. *Covering 1971 and 1972: A Selected Bibliography of Soviet Publications, with Some Additional Titles from Other Sources.* 94th Congress, 1st session. Washington, D.C.: Government Printing Office, 1975.

The following selected bibliography includes those works that have been most helpful in the preparation of this study.

Soviet Publications

Bachinskii, P. P., P. I. Pavliuk, and B. S. Shul'zhenko, eds. *Na zashchite revoliutsii: Iz istorii vseukrainskoi chrezvychainoi komissii, 1917–1922 gg.: Sbornik dokumentov i materialov.* Kiev: Izdatel'stvo politicheskoi literatury Ukrainy, 1971.

318   *Bibliography*

Belov, G. A., A. N. Kurenkov, A. I. Loginova, Ia. A. Pletnev, and V. S.
    Tikunov, eds. *Iz istorii vserossiiskoi chrezvychainoi komissii, 1917–
    1922 gg.: Sbornik dokumentov.* Moscow: Gosudarstvennoe
    izdatel'stvo politicheskoi literatury, 1958.
Bonch-Bruevich, Vladimir. *Vospominaniia o Lenine.* Moscow:
    Izdatel'stvo "Nauka," 1965.
Bulatov, A. I. and A. A. Khalestskaia. "Vydaushchiisia revoliutsioner i
    gosudarstvennyi deiatel' (Obzor dokumentov fonda F. E. Dzerzhin-
    skogo 1897–1926 gg.)." *Voprosii istorii KPSS,* no. (March 1965), pp.
    85–93.
Chugaev, D. A., ed. *Petrogradskii voenno-revoliutsionnyi komitet:
    Dokumenty i materialy.* Vols. I-III. Moscow: Izdatel'stvo
    "Nauka," 1967.
Dekrety sovetskoi vlasti. Vols. I-VII. Moscow: Gosudarstvennoe
    izdatel'stvo politicheskoi literatury, 1957–75.
Dzerzhinskaia, S. *V gody velikikh boev.* Moscow: Izdatel'stvo
    sotsial'no-ekonomicheskoi literatury, 1964.
Dzerzhinskii, F. E. *Izbrannye proizvedeniia.* 2d ed. Moscow:
    Izdatel'stvo politicheskoi literatury, 1967.
——. *Prison Diary and Letters.* Trans. John Gibbons. Moscow: Foreign
    Languages Publishing House, 1959.
*Ezhenedel'nik chrezvychainykh komissii po bor'be s kontr-revoliutsiei i
    spekuliatsiei.* Nos. 1–6. Moscow, 1918.
"Felix Edmundovich Dzerzhinskii po arkhivnym materialam," *Krasnyi
    arkhiv,* XVI (1926), i-xx.
"Felix Edmundovich Dzerzhinskii po pis'mam i dokumentam,"
    Proletarskaia revoliutsiia, no. 7 (1927), pp. 211–46.
Fomin, F. *Zapiski starogo chekista.* Moscow: Gosudarstvennoe
    izdatel'stvo politicheskoi literatury, 1962.
Gladkov, T. K., and M. A. Smirnov. *Menzhinskii.* Moscow: Izdatel'stvo
    TsK VLKSM "Molodaia gvardiia," 1969.
Golinkov, D. L. *Krakh vrazheskogo podpol'ia: Iz istorii bor'by s kontrre-
    voliutsiei v sovetskoi Rossii v 1917–1924 gg.* Moscow: Izdatel'stvo
    politicheskoi literatury, 1971.
Goncharov, A. K., and L. A. Doroshenko. "F. E. Dzerzhinskii o revo-
    liutsionnoi zakonnosti," *Istoricheskii arkhiv,* no. 1 (1958), pp. 95–
    112.
Gusev, K. V. *Krakh partii levykh eserov.* Moscow: Izdatel'stvo
    sotsial'no-ekonomicheskoi literatury, 1963.
Ioganson, O. N. *Dorogoi bor'by.* Moscow: Izdatel'stvo politicheskoi
    literatury, 1963.
Iroshnikov, M. P. *Sozdanie sovetskogo tsentral'nogo gosudarstvennogo*

apparata: Sovet narodnykh komissarov i narodnye komissariaty.
Leningrad: Izdatel'stvo "Nauka," 1966.

Izvestiia. 1917–27.

Kanev, S. N. "Krakh russkogo anarkhizma," *Voprosy istorii,* no. 9
(1968), pp. 50–75.

Khatskevich, A. F. *Soldat velikikh boev: Zhizn' i deiatel'nost' F. E.
Dzerzhinskogo.* 2d rev. ed. Minsk: Izdatel'stvo nauka i tekhnika,
1965.

Komodaite, I. B. "Revoliutsionnaia deiatel'nost' F. E. Dzerzhinskogo v
Litve v 1895–1899 gg.," *Istoricheskie zapiski,* XLV (1954), 220–34.

Kotov, V., and V. Zhuravlev, "Iz istorii vnutrennikh voisk," *Voenno-
Istoricheskii Zhurnal,* no. 11 (1972), pp. 90–95.

Krasnaia Moskva, 1917–1920 gg. Moscow: Gosudarstvennaia ob-
raztsovaia tipografiia, 1920.

Krasnyi, Iuz. "F. E. Dzerzhinskii: Materialy o zhizni i podpol'noi
deiatel'nosti," *Proletarskaia revoliutsiia,* no. 56 (1926), pp. 5–54.

Krylenko, N. V. *Sudoustroistvo RSFSR: Lektsii po teorii i istorii sudoustroistva.* Moscow: Iuridicheskoe izdatel'stvo NKIu, 1923.

———. *Za piat' let: 1918–1922 gg.* Moscow: Gosudarstvennoe
izdatel'stvo, 1923.

Latsis, M. Ia. [Ian Fridrikhovich Sudrabs]. *Chrezvychainye komissii po
bor'be s kontr-revoliutsiei.* Moscow: Gosudarstvennoe izdatel'stvo,
1921.

———. *Dva goda bor'by na vnutrennem fronte: Populiarnyi obzor
dvukhgodichnoi deiatel'nosti chrezvychainykh komissii po bor'be s
kontr-revoliutsiei, spekuliatsiei i prestupleniiami po dolzhnosti.*
Moscow: Gosudarstvennoe izdatel'stvo, 1920.

———. "Tov. Dzerzhinskii i VChK," *Proletarskaia revoliutsiia,* no. 56
(1926), pp. 81–97.

———. "Vozniknovenie narodnogo komissariata vnutrennykh del i orga-
nizatsiia vlasti na mestakh," *Proletarskaia revoliutsiia,* no. 2 (1925),
pp. 136–59; no. 3 (1925), pp. 142–66.

Lenin, V. I. *Collected Works.* Vols. I-XLV. Moscow: Progress
Publishers, 1960–70.

Malkov, P. D. *Reminiscences of a Kremlin Commandant.* Trans. V.
Dutt. Moscow: Progress Publishers, n.d.

Mitskevich-Kapsukas, V. "Iz vospominanii F. E. Dzerzhinskogo,"
Proletarskaia revoliutsiia, no. 56 (1926), pp. 55–64.

Naumov, Ia. N. *Chekistka.* Moscow: Izdatel'stvo politicheskoi
literatury, 1965.

Nikolaev, A. "F. E. Dzerzhinskii na frontakh grazhdanskoi voiny,"
Voenno-Istoricheskii Zhurnal, no. 9 (1967), pp. 64–72.

Ozolin, Ia. "Iz vospominanii o ChK," *Rabochii sud,* no. 24 (1927), pp. 1953–60.

Peters, Ia. "Vospominaniia o rabote v VChK v pervyi god revoliutsii," *Proletarskaia revoliutsiia,* no. 10 (1924), pp. 5–32.

Piontkovskii, S. A. "Voenno-revoliutsionnyi komitet v oktiabr'skie dni," *Proletarskaia revoliutsiia,* no. 10 (1927), pp. 70–102.

Pozniakov, K. I. *Krasnyi tyl–frontu.* Kharkov: Izdatel'stvo khar'kovskogo gosudarstvennogo universiteta im. A. M. Gor'kogo, 1968.

Pravda, 1917–27.

Roshal', Mikhail Grigor'evich. *Zapiski iz proshlogo.* Moscow: Izdatel'stvo "Nauka," 1969.

Rozvadovskaia, M. F., and V. M. Slutskaia, eds. *Rytsar'revoliutsii: Vospominaniia sovremennikov o Felikse Edmundoviche Dzerzhinskom.* Moscow: Izdatel'stvo politicheskoi literatury, 1967.

Sboichakov, M. I., S. I. Tsybov, and N. F. Chistiakov. *Mikhail Sergeevich Kedrov.* Moscow: Voennoe izdatel'stvo ministerstva oborony SSSR, 1969.

Serebrianskii, Z. "Sabotazh i sozdanie novogo gosudarstvennogo apparata," *Proletarskaia revoliutsiia,* no. 10 (1926), pp. 5–17.

Sidorov. "Pidpil'na ChK v Odesi v 1918–1919 r.r. (Iz peredistorii ChK na Ukraini)." *Letopis revoliutsii,* no. 4 (1928), pp. 123–33.

Smirnov, M., ed. *Feliks Edmundovich Dzerzhinskii v VChK.* Moscow: Bibliotechka zhurnala "Pogranichnik," 1967.

Sofinov, P. *Ocherki istorii vserossiiskoi chrezvychainoi komissii, 1917–1922 gg.* Moscow: Gosudarstvennoe izdatel'stvo politicheskoi literatury, 1960.

———. *Stranitsy iz zhizni F. E. Dzerzhinskogo.* Moscow: Gosudarstvennoe izdatel'stvo politicheskoi literatury, 1956.

Solov'ev, O. F. *Velikii oktiabr' i ego protivniki.* Moscow: Izdatel'stvo "Mysl," 1968.

Tatarov, I. "Nachalo revoliutsionnogo puti tov. Dzerzhinskogo," *Proletarskaia revoliutsiia,* no. 10 (1926), 207–24.

Tishkov, A. V. *Dzerzhinskii.* Moscow: Izdatel'stvo "Molodaia gvardia," 1974.

———. *Pervyi chekist.* Moscow: Voennoe izdatel'stvo ministerstva oborony SSSR, 1968.

Tomash. "Vospominaniia o Felikse Dzerzhinskom," *Proletarskaia revoliutsiia,* no. 9 (1926), pp. 65–71.

Trifonov, I. Ia. *Klassy i klassovaia bor'ba v SSSR v nachale nepa, 1921–1923 gg.: Bor'ba s vooruzhennoi kulatskoi kontrrevoliutsiei.* Leningrad: Izdatel'stvo leningradskogo universiteta, 1964.

———. *Klassy i klassovaia bor'ba v SSSR v nachale nepa, 1921–1925 gg.:*

Podgotovka ekonomicheskogo nastupleniia na novyiu burzhuaziiu.
Leningrad: Izdatel'stvo leningradskogo universiteta, 1969.
Tsvigun, S. K., A. A. Solov'ev, G. N. Golikov, M. A. Kozichev, V. F.
Nikitchenko, and A. V. Prokopenko, eds. *V. I. Lenin i VChK:
Sbornik dokumentov, 1917–1922 gg.* Moscow: Izdatel'stvo politicheskoi literatury, 1975.
Ustikov, I., and K. Kapitonov. "Polevka na boevom postu (Iz istorii organov voennoi kontrrazvedki)," *Voenno-Istoricheskii Zhurnal,* no.
1 (1969), pp. 99–102.
Vlast' Sovetov: Organ narodnogo komissariata vnutrennikh del.
Moscow, 1919–22.
Zubov, N. F. E. *Dzerzhinskii: Biografiia.* 2d ed. Moscow: Izdatel'stvo
politicheskoi literatury, 1965.
Zyrianov, P. I., R. A. Bakhromeev, P. V. Volobuev, V. V. Dushen'kin,
and P. A. Zhilin, eds. *Pogranichnye voiska SSSR 1918–1928:
Sbornik dokumentov i materialov.* Moscow: Izdatel'stvo "Nauka,"
1973.

Independent Studies

Armstrong, John A. *Ideology, Politics, and Government in the Soviet
Union.* New York: Frederick A. Praeger, 1967.
Aronson, Gregor. *Na zare krasnogo terrora.* Berlin: Buchdruckerei
Gebr. Hirschbaum, 1929.
Avineri, Shlomo. *The Social and Political Thought of Karl Marx.*
Cambridge: Cambridge University Press, 1968.
Avrich, Paul. *Kronstadt 1921.* Princeton, N.J.: Princeton University
Press, 1970.
Barghoorn, Frederick C. "The Security Police," *Interest Groups in Soviet Politics,* ed. H. Gordon Skilling and Franklyn Griffiths
(Princeton, N.J.: Princeton University Press, 1971).
Batsell, Walter R. *Soviet Rule in Russia.* New York: Macmillan Co.,
1929.
Bernaut, Elsa, and Melville J. Ruggles. *Collective Leadership and the
Political Police in the Soviet Union.* Santa Monica, Calif.: The Rand
Corporation, 1956.
Bramstedt, Ernest K. *Dictatorship and Political Police: The Technique
of Control by Fear.* London: Kegan Paul, Trench, Trubner & Co.,
1945.
Bromage, Bernard. *Man of Terror: Dzherzhynski.* London: Peter Owen,
1956.
Brunovsky, Vladimir. *The Methods of the OGPU.* London: Harpers,
1931.

Bryant, Louise. *Mirrors of Moscow*. New York: Thomas Seltzer, 1923.

Brzezinski, Zbigniew. *The Permanent Purge*. Cambridge, Mass.: Harvard University Press, 1956.

Bulletins of the Russian Liberation Committee. London, 1919–20.

Bunyan, James, ed. *Intervention, Civil War and Communism in Russia, April-December 1918*. Baltimore, Md.: The Johns Hopkins Press, 1936.

———. *The Origin of Forced Labor in the Soviet State, 1917–1921: Documents and Materials*. Baltimore, Md.: The Johns Hopkins Press, 1967.

———, and H. H. Fisher. *The Bolshevik Revolution, 1917–1918: Documents and Materials*. Stanford, Calif.: Stanford University Press, 1934.

Carr, E. H. *A History of Soviet Russia: The Bolshevik Revolution, 1917–1923*. 3 vols. London: Macmillan and Co., 1950–53.

———. "The Origin and Status of the Cheka," *Soviet Studies*, X (July 1958), 1-11.

Carter, Allan J. "The Bolshevist Substitute for a Judicial System," *Illinois Law Review*, XVI (Jan. 1922), 123–35.

Chamberlin, William H. "The Evolution of Soviet Terrorism," *Foreign Affairs*, XIII (Oct. 1934), 113–21.

———. *The Russian Revolution, 1917–1921*. 2 vols. New York: Macmillan Co., 1965.

Chapman, Brian. *Police State*. New York: Frederick A. Praeger, 1970.

"Chekist o Ch.K.," in *Na chuzhoi storone: Istoriko-literaturnye sborniki*, IX (1925), 111–41.

Chernov, V., ed. *Che-Ka: Materialy po deiatel'nosti chrezvychainykh komissii*. Berlin: Izdaniye tsentral'nogo byuro partii sotsialistov-revoliutsionerov, 1922.

Conquest, Robert. *The Great Terror*. New York: Macmillan Co., 1968.

———. *The Soviet Police System*. New York: Frederick A. Praeger, 1968.

Dallin, Alexander, and George W. Breslauer. *Political Terror in Communist Systems*. Stanford, Calif.: Stanford University Press, 1970.

Davies, R. W. "Some Soviet Economic Controllers—II," *Soviet Studies*, XI, no. 4 (1960), 373–92.

Debo, Richard K. "Lockhart Plot or Dzerzhinskii Plot?" *Journal of Modern History*, XLIII, no. 3 (1971), 413–39.

Dobin, S. "Some Questions of Early Soviet Legal History," *Soviet Studies*, VII (April 1956), 366–71.

Dumbadze, Ye. V. *Na sluzhbe Cheka i Kominterna*. Paris: Mishen', 1930.

Fainsod, Merle. *How Russia is Ruled*. Rev. ed. Cambridge, Mass.: Harvard University Press, 1964.

———. *Smolensk under Soviet Rule.* Cambridge, Mass.: Harvard University Press, 1958.

Fischer, Louis. *The Life of Lenin.* New York: Harper & Row, 1964.

Footman, David. *The Civil War in Russia.* New York: Frederick A. Praeger, 1961.

Gorky, Maxim. *Untimely Thoughts: Essays on Revolution, Culture, and the Bolsheviks, 1917–1918.* Trans. Herman Ermolaev. New York: Paul S. Eriksson, 1968.

Gsovski, Vladimir. *Soviet Civil Law.* Ann Arbor: University of Michigan Press, 1948.

Gul', Roman. *Dzerzhinskii, Menzhinskii, Peters, Latsis, Yagoda.* Paris: Imp. de Navarre, 1936.

Hingley, Ronald. *The Russian Secret Police: Muscovite, Imperial Russian, and Soviet Political Security Operations.* New York: Simon and Schuster, 1970.

Interim Report of the Committee to Collect Information on Russia. London: His Majesty's Stationery Office, 1920.

The International Committee for Political Prisoners. *Letters From Russian Prisons: Consisting of Reprints of Documents by Political Prisoners in Soviet Prisons, Prison Camps and Exile. . . .* New York: Albert and Charles Boni, 1925.

Leggett, George H. "Lenin, Terror, and Political Police," *Survey,* XXI, no. 4 (1975), 157–87.

Levytsky, Boris. *The Uses of Terror: The Soviet Secret Police, 1917–1970.* Trans. H. A. Piehler. New York: Coward, McCann & Geoghegan, 1972.

Liberman, Simon. *Building Lenin's Russia.* Chicago: University of Chicago Press, 1945.

Malsagoff, S. A. *An Island Hell: A Soviet Prison in the Far North.* Trans. F. H. Lyons. London: A. M. Philpot, 1926.

Masloff, S. S. *Russia after Four Years of Revolution.* Trans. A. G. Paschkoff. London: P. S. King & Sons, 1923.

Maximoff, P. G. *The Guillotine at Work: Twenty Years of Terror in Russia.* Chicago: Chicago Section of the Alexander Berkman Fund, 1940.

Medvedev, Roy A. *Let History Judge: The Origins and Consequences of Stalinism.* Trans. Colleen Taylor. Ed. David Joravsky. New York: Alfred A. Knopf, 1971.

Melgounov, Sergei. *The Red Terror in Russia.* London: J. M. Dent, 1926.

Moore, Barrington. *Terror and Progress: USSR.* New York: Harper & Row, 1966.

Nicolaevskii, Boris. "Iz istorii mashiny sovetskogo terrora," *Sotsiali- sticheskii vestnik,* no. 8–9 (Aug.-Sept. 1959), pp. 167–72.

Popoff, George. *The Tcheka: The Red Inquisition.* London: A. M. Philpot, 1925.

"The Red Reign of Terror in Kief: A Red Cross Report," *Literary Digest,* Oct. 16, 1920, pp. 61–64.

Schapiro, Leonard. *The Origin of the Communist Autocracy, 1917–1922.* Cambridge, Mass.: Harvard University Press, 1955.

Scott, E. J. "The Cheka," *St. Anthony's Papers,* no. 1. Soviet Affairs no. 1. London: Chatto & Windus, 1956.

Serge, Victor. *Memoirs of a Revolutionary: 1901–1941.* London: Oxford University Press, 1963.

Singleton, Seth. "The Tambov Revolt (1920–1921)," *Slavic Review,* XXV (Sept. 1966), 497–512.

Slusser, Robert M. "The Budget of the OGPU and the Special Troops from 1923–4 to 1928–9," *Soviet Studies,* X (April 1959), 375–83.

Solzhenitsyn, Alexandr I. *The Gulag Archipelago.* 2 vols. New York: Harper & Row, 1974–75.

Sotsialisticheskii vestnik. 1921–25.

Speranskii, Vladimir. "Felix Dzerzhinsky," *Living Age,* Sept. 11, 1926, pp. 572–75.

Steinberg, I. N. *In the Workshop of the Revolution.* New York: Rinehart Co., 1953.

Trotsky, Leon. *Lenin: Notes for a Biographer.* Trans. Tamara Deutscher. New York: G. P. Putnam's Sons, 1971.

———. *My Life.* London: Thornton Butterworth, 1930.

———. *Terrorism and Communism.* Ann Arbor: The University of Michigan Press, 1961.

Ulam, Adam B. *The Bolsheviks.* New York: Macmillan Co., 1965.

Walter, Eugene V. *Terror and Resistance: A Study of Political Violence.* New York: Oxford University Press, 1969.

Wolin, Simon, and Robert M. Slusser, eds. *The Soviet Secret Police.* New York: Frederick A. Praeger, 1957.

Zelitch, Judah. *Soviet Administration of Criminal Law.* Philadelphia: University of Pennsylvania Press, 1931.

Zenzinov, Vladimir. *Bezprizornye.* Paris: Izdatel'stvo "Sovremennyia Zapiski," 1929.

Unpublished Sources

Chisholm, Henry J. "The Function of Terror and Violence in Revolu- tion." Unpublished M. A. thesis, Georgetown University, 1949.

Dinerstein, Herbert. "Some Information on the Soviet Political Police."
   Santa Monica, Calif.: The Rand Corporation, June 5, 1950.
Hollis, Ernest V., Jr. "Police Systems of Imperial and Soviet Russia."
   Draft of a Ph.D. dissertation, Archive of Russian and East European
   History and Culture, Columbia University, 1957.
The Hoover Institution on War, Revolution, and Peace, Stanford
   University. Important documents pertaining to the early Soviet
   secret police are to be found in the Boris Nicolaevsky Collection and
   the Melgunov Collection on the Red Terror.
National Archives of the United States, Washington, D.C. A consider-
   able number of reports and translations of Soviet documents on the
   secret police are contained in State Department, Records Relating to
   Internal Affairs of Russia and the Soviet Union, 1910–29, Record
   Group 59. See also Records of the War Department General and
   Special Staffs, Record Group 165.
Slusser, Robert M. "Chekist Leaders from Dzerzhinsky to Yezhov:
   Variations on a Theme." Paper presented at the 88th meeting of the
   American Historical Association, San Francisco, California, Dec.
   1973.

Index